THE CONCISE CATALOGUE

SCOTTISH NATIONAL GALLERY

MODERN ART

rary

Joan Miró
Maternity 1924
Purchased in 1991 with financial assistance from the National Heritage
Memorial Fund, the National Art Collections Fund (William Leng Bequest)
and members of the public

The Concise Catalogue of the Scottish National Gallery of Modern Art

COMPILED BY PATRICK ELLIOTT

THE TRUSTEES OF THE NATIONAL GALLERIES OF SCOTLAND

EDINBURGH 1993

Designed by Gerald Cinamon, London
Typeset by Kitzinger, London
Photography by Antonia Reeve, Edinburgh
Printed by BAS Printers Ltd, Over Wallop, Hampshire
ISBN 0 903598 39 6

Cover illustrations

Front: *Rocky Mountains and Tired Indians* (detail) by David Hockney
Back: *Untitled (Figure with Raised Arm)* (detail) by Georg Baselitz

CONTENTS

FOREWORD AND ACKNOWLEDGEMENTS

This is the first comprehensive, concise catalogue of the Scottish National Gallery of Modern Art's collection. It replaces the catalogues published in 1977 and 1984, which excluded all the prints, and marks the transfer of the Gallery's hand-written and typed records onto computer disk. It is the latest in a series of permanent collection catalogues, published by the National Galleries of Scotland, which so far includes the *Concise Catalogue of the Scottish National Portrait Gallery* (1990) and the revised edition of *Italian and Spanish Paintings in the National Gallery of Scotland* (1993); the concise catalogue of the National Gallery of Scotland's collection is currently in preparation. The aim of the series is to make the collections of the National Galleries of Scotland known to as wide a public as possible.

We are particularly grateful to Patrick Elliott, Assistant Keeper at the Gallery of Modern Art, who compiled the catalogue, and to the Gallery's curators, past and present, upon whose research his work is based. We should also like to thank Alan Guest and Gordon Cooke for their assistance in cataloguing some of the early twentieth-century British prints. For this catalogue, every work in the collection has been unframed, re-examined and re-measured with the help of the technicians and conservators working in the Conservation Department. The job of transferring the Gallery's old records onto computer disk and entering the updated information was carried out by Sheila Perry and Elisabeth Smith. Philip Long assisted in checking the new records and Janis Adams supervised publication. Many artists kindly responded to queries about their work and experts from public and commercial galleries were unfailingly helpful in providing information.

TIMOTHY CLIFFORD
Director of the National
Galleries of Scotland

RICHARD CALVOCORESSI
Keeper of the Scottish
National Gallery of Modern Art

THE SCOTTISH NATIONAL GALLERY OF MODERN ART:

A BRIEF HISTORY

The Scottish National Gallery of Modern Art was founded in 1959 and opened in 1960. Its collection now numbers some 4,500 items, of which about 800 are paintings, 200 sculptures, and the remainder prints and drawings. The Gallery is one of three sister institutions, all based in Edinburgh, known as the National Galleries of Scotland and funded by central government through the Scottish Office Education Department. The National Gallery of Scotland, sited on the Mound in the centre of Edinburgh, holds a distinguished collection ranging from the early Renaissance to the Post-Impressionists; and the Scottish National Portrait Gallery in Queen Street houses an unrivalled collection of portraits of eminent Scots. The Gallery of Modern Art's collection spans about a century, the earliest prints belonging to Max Klinger's portfolio, *On the Finding of a Glove*, first published in 1881, while the earliest painting is an oil of *c.* 1892, Edouard Vuillard's *La Causette*. Although the break-off date between the National Gallery of Scotland and the Gallery of Modern Art stands at 1900, this date is, of course, treated with some flexibility. Paintings of a Victorian character executed in the early years of the twentieth century might be hung at the Mound, while works of a more modern style, dating from the 1890s – for example Vuillard's early paintings – are shown at the Gallery of Modern Art.

The National Gallery of Scotland opened in 1859, the nucleus of its collection having been transferred from the Royal Institution, and the Scottish National Portrait Gallery in 1889. From 1906 both were managed by a single Board of Trustees. Before 1903 neither Gallery received a purchase grant from the Treasury but in that year the National Gallery was granted £1,000 per annum and the following year the Portrait Gallery £200. In 1953 these sums were increased to £2,500 and £300 respectively. The collecting policy of each gallery ruled against the acquisition of works by living artists, a consideration owing as much to the limitations of space as to a wish not to be put under pressure by academicians and others. However, some exceptions were made, mainly in the acquisition of twentieth-century British prints and also in the occasional purchase or gift of paintings and sculpture: for example, a marble *Young Athlete* by the French sculptor Jean-Baptiste L'Arrivé was bought in 1911, the year in which it was exhibited at the Royal Scottish Academy, but it was a very traditional work which might almost have been made 100 years earlier. Gifts of recent works were occasionally accepted – a landscape by George Leslie Hunter in 1933, three or four years after it was painted, and a Peploe still-life in 1939, four years after the artist's death. More controversial was the acquisition in April 1942 of an allegorical landscape with figures by Oskar Kokoschka, *Zrání (Summer)*, offered by President Beneš on behalf of the Czech government-in-exile. The offer came via the art historian Herbert Read (formerly Professor of Fine Art at Edinburgh University) and although several of the Trustees objected to the work and argued that the rules should not be bent and the offer refused, it was eventually decided to accept the gift to 'mark appreciation of Scottish interest and sympathy with the Czechoslovakian cause'. Thus the first work by a modern master entered the collections – a work which was to have a profound impact on the development of Scottish painting.

The acquisition of the Kokoschka owed much to the persuasive powers of Stanley Cursiter, Director of the National Galleries of Scotland from 1930 to 1948 and, like several of his predecessors, a painter. It was Cursiter who had been responsible for purchasing, in 1930, Bourdelle's monumental *Virgin of Alsace* 1919–21, a sculpture he greatly admired. One of Cursiter's more supportive Trustees at the time of the Bourdelle purchase was the Glasgow-born painter and etcher D. Y. Cameron, who on his death in 1945 bequeathed the bulk of his estate to the National Gallery of Scotland, including works by Epstein and Gill. Staff and Trustees were thus aware that the absence of twentieth-century art in the collection was an unsatisfactory arrangement.

Fig. 1. Alan Reiach, Proposed *Museum of Modern Art*, Queen Street, Edinburgh 1940 (Model made by Stanley Cursiter)

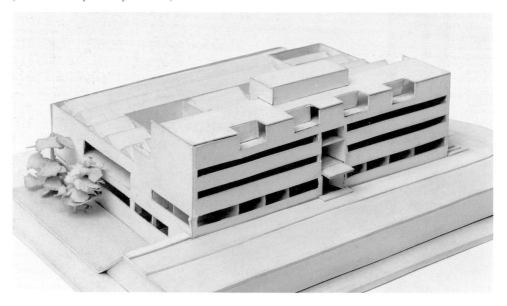

The idea for a separate 'gallery of modern pictures' goes back to 1827 but calls for its establishment became more numerous after 1906 when modern art was effectively excluded from the National Gallery. In its reports issued in 1929–30, the Royal Commission on National Museums and Galleries gave high priority to the setting up of 'a Tate Gallery for Edinburgh' but argued that it would have to be privately financed; this remained a regular recommendation of the Standing Commission that followed. In 1934 an anonymous benefactor came forward but, with no prospect of a site being made available, withdrew his offer. Cursiter's efforts to persuade the government to move the Department of Agriculture out of York Buildings, a Crown property opposite the

Portrait Gallery in Queen Street, were frustrated by bureaucratic indecisiveness. Undeterred, he continued to campaign throughout the 1930s for a new gallery on this site, and in 1940 privately commissioned the architect Alan Reiach (1910–92) to design a three-storey building linked by a pedestrian subway to the Portrait Gallery and with the possibility of using the east end of Queen Street Gardens for showing sculpture outdoors (fig. 1). The proposal was adopted by the Trustees, and supported by the Standing Commission, but the war put paid to further progress. In 1949 the government's agreement in principle to the establishment of a Gallery of Modern Art was reaffirmed and in March 1951 the Secretary of State for Scotland assured Parliament that such a Gallery would be built on the York Buildings site, though no undertaking was given on when the project could be included in the government building programme. By this time Reiach was independently working on a scheme for a new gallery in Princes Street Gardens, directly beneath the Royal Scottish Academy (fig. 2); the estimated cost of this in 1956 was £160,000. David Baxandall (Cursiter's successor but one) and the Earl of Crawford and Balcarres, Chairman of the Trustees, expressed interest but preferred to stick with the York Buildings site.

Fig. 2. Alan Reiach, Proposed *Gallery of Modern Art,*
Princes Street Gardens, Edinburgh 1956

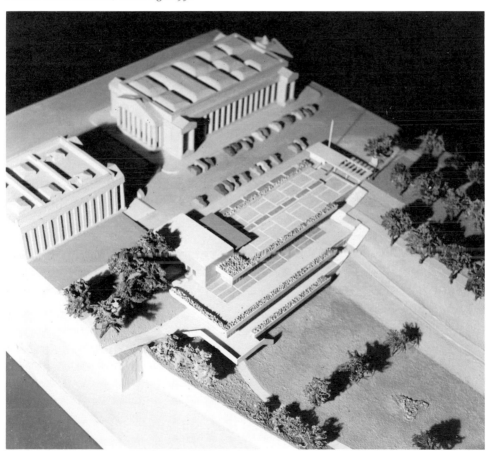

Fig. 3. Inverleith House,
home of the Scottish National Gallery of Modern Art 1960–84

In 1958 another Crown property which had become vacant was offered to the Trustees as temporary accomodation for the Gallery of Modern Art, and accepted. This was Inverleith House (fig. 3), a late eighteenth-century mansion built on a rise in Edinburgh's Royal Botanic Garden, about a mile north of Princes Street. Although comparatively small, it offered neatly proportioned exhibition rooms in an unrivalled setting; the grounds provided a spectacular arena for the siting of sculptures. The National Galleries of Scotland Act of 1959 enabled Parliament to vote the money necessary for the operation of the new gallery and gave the Director and Trustees of the other two National Galleries of Scotland the powers to run it. Baxandall considered the separate annual purchase grant from Treasury of £7,500 hopelessly inadequate for the job of 'illustrating the more important moments in the development of modern painting . . . from fauves and cubists onwards', and realised that the Gallery would have to rely heavily on loans and gifts. On 10 August 1960 Sir Kenneth Clark expressed the honour he felt at being asked to open 'the first National Gallery exclusively devoted to modern art in the British Isles'.

Baxandall and his Assistant Keeper (later Director) Colin Thompson together ran the Gallery – there being provision for warding, but not curatorial, staff – until November 1961, when money was found to appoint a Keeper, Douglas Hall, who presided over the growth of the collection for the next twenty-five years.

At the time of opening, the few twentieth-century paintings and sculptures belonging to the National Gallery of Scotland – a total of thirty-eight works – were transferred. A much larger complement of twentieth-century graphic material was also transferred: some 500 prints and seventy drawings by artists such as Eric Gill, Gwen Raverat and John Copley. These works had come principally from three separate sources. Kenneth Sanderson, a former Chairman of the Scottish Modern Arts Association, bequeathed a collection of mainly British work in 1943; as has already been mentioned, D. Y. Cameron, a former Trustee, bequeathed a substantial number of works in 1945; and in 1949 the Gallery purchased a large collection of graphic work which had been amassed by the printmaker E. S. Lumsden, mainly of British prints of the period 1900–40. The Gallery's first purchase was Sickert's portrait of the writer Israel Zangwill; this was followed by Matthew Smith's *Circus Woman* 1925. Gifts from private individuals of paintings by Dufresne, Wadsworth and Sutherland were made to mark the opening of the Gallery. In 1960 Alexander (later Sir Alexander) Maitland QC, a former Trustee, gave a highly important group of mainly late nineteenth-century paintings to the National Gallery of Scotland, in memory of his wife Rosalind. The collection included works by Courbet, Degas, the Impressionists and Post-Impressionists, and also a few works executed at the turn of the century or later by Picasso, Rouault, Vuillard and Bonnard. The latter paintings were hung at the National Gallery until Maitland's death in 1965, when the Picasso and Rouault, along with Matisse's *The Painting Session* which Maitland had retained, were transferred to the Gallery of Modern Art; it was not until 1984 that the Vuillard and Bonnard paintings were transferred.

The National Gallery of Scotland owned important late nineteenth-century paintings by artists such as Van Gogh and Gauguin, and it was intended that the new Gallery of Modern Art should acquire international works of similar merit, and not simply represent Scottish art. In early policy documents, the Trustees had agreed that rather than spend money quickly in order to build up a collection that would fill the new Gallery, funds would be saved and put towards the acquisition of a smaller number of works of the highest quality. Thus, in its first years, loans from other collections, both public and private, were actively sought, and continue to be so, particularly of works by artists beyond the Gallery's means. A second understanding was that a collection of twentieth-century art begun in 1960 could not hope to be comprehensive. Certain artists and movements would have to be represented – Picasso, Matisse, Cubism, Surrealism – but limitations on funds and space would preclude the building of a fully comprehensive survey collection. In spite of such constraints, in the first decade of the Gallery's existence works by Picasso, Léger, Kirchner, Nolde, Jawlensky and Lipchitz were purchased, as well as post-war paintings by Morandi, de Staël, Dubuffet and Appel. Purchases of work by English and Scottish artists, both pre-and post-war, were no less impressive. But with prices rising steeply, the Trustees took the decision in 1970 to set aside £25,000 per annum from the purchase grant (then standing at £72,000) 'for buying expensive works historically essential for the collection'. A 1905 Fauve painting by Derain was bought from this reserve fund in 1973.

In 1967 the Gallery received a donation of forty-three works from the collection of Mr and Mrs Scott Hay, mainly of modern Scottish paintings. Ten years later nearly 300 works, again principally by Scottish artists, including 168 paintings, drawings and watercolours by William Gillies, were bequeathed by Dr Robert Lillie. The modest size of Inverleith House had always made it a temporary location for the Gallery of Modern Art and with Lillie's bequest only a small proportion of the collection could be displayed, especially if a worthwhile exhibitions programme was to be maintained.

The decision to occupy Inverleith House did not, in the eyes of the Trustees, release the government from its obligation to build the Gallery of Modern Art on the Queen Street site. In 1963 an attempt by the Ministry of Works to persuade the Galleries to surrender its claim to York Buildings in return for a vague promise of a site somewhere in the future development of Edinburgh University was firmly resisted by Baxandall and Lord

Crawford. From 1966 the Trustees regularly publicised the inadequacy of the space at Inverleith House and, with no real prospect of York Buildings being vacated, began to look at various ways of building onto the Gallery. A proposal to extend Inverleith House towards the west gate of the Botanic Garden by means of a series of pavilions linked by glazed corridors following the contours of the land (inspired by the example of the Louisiana Museum in Denmark) was given serious consideration in 1970; but nothing came of it.

Eventually, in 1977, the year of the Lillie Bequest, the Crown Estate Commission purchased John Watson's School with revenue from the North Sea oil industry and offered to lease it to the government for an enlarged Gallery of Modern Art (fig. 4). The

Fig. 4. The Scottish National Gallery of Modern Art
(formerly John Watson's School), with banners by Bruce McLean 1989

offer was accepted. Designed by William Burn in 1825, this handsome, if austere, neo-classical building (to the west of the city centre) was originally an institution which housed, clothed and educated the sons and daughters of professional men who had died leaving insufficient funds to keep them. In 1935 it became a fee-paying school and in 1957 received full secondary status. In 1975, however, partly as a result of the Labour government's policy of phasing out Direct Grant-aided schools, it was forced to close. Work on the conversion (by the PSA and architects Robert Matthew, Johnson Marshall and Partners) did not start until 1981. On 14 August 1984 the Gallery was finally reopened in its new premises by the then Secretary of State for Scotland, George Younger. To mark the occasion, a group of turn-of-the-century paintings by Vuillard (three of which formerly belonged to the Glasgow industrialist Sir John Richmond and had been presented by his niece, Mrs Isabel Traill, in 1979) and two works by Bonnard, all previously hung at the National Gallery, were transferred to the Gallery of Modern Art. The new building provided greatly increased space for displaying the permanent collection and for holding temporary exhibitions, and also extensive grounds suitable for the siting of sculpture and for possible expansion in the future. Part of the building was made available to the Galleries' central service departments (e.g. Conservation) and there was also room for a car park, a café and better storage.

Meanwhile, the Gallery's purchase allocation had grown from £72,000 in 1975 to £624,000 in 1985 (out of a total purchase grant for all three of the National Galleries that year of nearly £1.5 m). Since 1986 the Trustees have centralised the larger part of the grant, but with regular access to central funds the Gallery has continued to acquire pre-eminent examples of twentieth-century art, including the first oil painting by Lucian Freud to enter the collection; a watercolour and a piece of furniture by Charles Rennie Mackintosh (hitherto unrepresented in the National Galleries of Scotland); and sculptures by Barlach and Baselitz that enhance the Gallery's already impressive holding of German art. With the acquisition in the early 1990s of paintings by Magritte, Picabia and Miró, a sculpture by Giacometti and Duchamp's *Boîte-en-valise*, the Gallery now boasts a Dada and Surrealist collection of international stature.

None of this would have been easy, or indeed possible, given the enormous rise in prices for modern and contemporary art in the latter half of the 1980s, without the generous support of private foundations and charities, such as the National Art Collections Fund and the Henry Moore Foundation, or of the publicly funded National Heritage Memorial Fund. All of them have helped the Gallery considerably since 1987 to acquire major international works: for example, Miró's *Maternity*, Vuillard's *Two Seamstresses in the Workroom* (which had been in Scotland since 1893) and Henry Moore's *The Helmet*. We have also benefited from the system by which owners are offered fiscal concessions if they agree to sell a work to a museum, rather than putting it on the open market (the Private Treaty sale). Finally, donations of works of art or of funds play as vital a role in the development of the collection as they did three decades ago, when two anonymous individuals each gave £500 – a small sum today, but at the time it permitted the Gallery to buy outstanding paintings by the Russian artists Natalya Goncharova and Mikhail Larionov. Important donations made in recent years include more than 250 drawings by Joan Eardley, presented in 1987 by the artist's sister, Pat Black; a fine selection of twentieth-century Scottish watercolours and paintings bequeathed by George and Isobel Neillands in 1988; works on paper by Nash, Moore and Sutherland bequeathed by Mr H. J. Paterson, also in 1988; and a splendid collection of English art of the period 1920–50 bequeathed by Elizabeth Watt in 1989. Together these gifts have significantly improved our holding of British art.

RICHARD CALVOCORESSI

EXPLANATORY NOTES

This catalogue includes all works in the collection acquired by May 1993. Works which were acquired before 1959, when the Scottish National Gallery of Modern Art was established, were previously held at the National Gallery of Scotland but were later transferred.

The volume is divided into three sections. The first is a catalogue of the collection; the second is a list of the Gallery's large holding of prints, cards and booklets by Ian Hamilton Finlay; and the third contains a selection of illustrations.

SECTION ONE: A CATALOGUE OF THE COLLECTION

This section is arranged alphabetically by artist. Each artist's work is listed in chronological order. Where an artist has made prints (e.g. etchings, lithographs or screenprints) in addition to paintings, drawings or sculptures, the prints are separated from the other works by a thin line; for the purposes of this catalogue, monoprints and monotypes are treated as drawings rather than as prints. Works which cannot accurately be dated are listed after dated works. The following details may also be noted:

Inventory numbers: All works are catalogued with a GMA (Gallery of Modern Art) prefix.

Titles: Where known, titles are given in the original language, with English translations following in square brackets.

Dates: Where a work is inscribed with a date by the artist, this is indicated by the letter 'd'. Circa dates are denoted by a small 'c'. Dates which include a dash, such as 1950–55, indicate that the work was made over an extended period, while a diagonal stroke, such as 1950/1955, indicates that it was worked on in the years specified, but not in-between. The dates of a small number of editioned prints are preceded by the terms 'exh.' or 'by', indicating that a copy of the print was exhibited in the given year, or is known to have been in existence in that year, but may have been executed earlier. Casting dates for sculptures and printing dates for prints are recorded if they are known to differ widely from the original date of execution.

Medium: The term 'black chalk' has been used to denote charcoal, crayon and pencil, where the exact medium cannot be identified.

Sizes: All sizes are given in centimetres, height preceding width (which in turn precedes depth in the case of sculptures). Two sizes are specified for prints, indicating the size of the printed image or plate and the size of the sheet of paper.

Edition Numbers and States: Where a print or sculpture is inscribed with the edition number, this is recorded; similarly, where marked 'Artist's Proof' (or 'épreuve d'artiste') this is recorded with the notation 'A.P.'. Print states are indicated where known.

Catalogue Raisonné details: Where the Gallery has a number of prints by an artist and a catalogue raisonné of that artist's prints exists, these catalogue details are recorded in square brackets after the title of the work, and the author of the catalogue is indicated at the foot of the entry (see, for example, Austin, Bauer, Bone and Gill).

Asterisks: An asterisk indicates that the work is illustrated.

SECTION TWO: PRINTS, CARDS AND BOOKLETS BY IAN HAMILTON FINLAY

These works are arranged by title in alphabetical order. Finlay's works are normally executed by assistants who, where known, are credited in brackets after the title. The prefix 'IHF' and adjoining number refer to the catalogue raisonné of Finlay's prints, published by the Graeme Murray Gallery, Edinburgh, in 1990 (and the 1992 supplement). Many of Finlay's works are in the form of printed texts and have been listed according to type of work (e.g. card, booklet, poster) rather than according to medium or technique. The sizes given are paper or card size. Finlay's printed works have been ascribed the prefix 'GMA A4', indicating that they were, in the past, acquired from a separate budget and not from the annual purchase grant. (The same conditions apply to the prints produced by the Wild Hawthorn Press, which Finlay helped establish.) Some Finlay material, such as exhibition catalogues and issues of the magazine *Poor. Old. Tired. Horse*, has not been recorded in this list.

SECTION THREE: ILLUSTRATIONS

This section contains a selection of some 900 illustrations, representing approximately one-fifth of the collection.

CATALOGUE

Norman Ackroyd

1938–

Celtic Sky
d 1975
Colour aquatint on paper (66/90)
45.4 x 41.4 (paper 76.3 x 56)
Purchased 1980
GMA 2160

Norman Adams

1927–

Moors near Scourie
d 1963
Watercolour, ink and pencil on paper
21.5 x 24.8
Purchased 1964
GMA 886

*Bathers in a Bright Light**
d 1975
Oil on canvas
152.7 x 203.7
Purchased 1979
GMA 2094

Robert Adams

1917–84

*Climbing Forms, Opus 166**
1962
Bronzed steel
74.5 x 54.8 x 18.5
Purchased 1986
GMA 2979

Triangular Forms
d 1962
Colour lithograph on paper (18/50)
57 x 32 (paper 75.5 x 57.8)
Purchased with funds given by two anonymous
donors 1963
GMA 838

Jankel Adler

1895–1949

*Hommage à Naum Gabo [Homage to Naum
Gabo]**
d 1946
Oil on canvas
112.5 x 86.8
Purchased 1978
GMA 1710

Jacob Afolabi

1940–

*Sango and Oya (The God of Thunder and his
Wife Oya)*
(from 'The Commonwealth Print Portfolio')
1978
Linocut on paper (54/65)
37 x 51 (paper 56.6 x 75.7)
Presented by the Canadian High Commission
1979
GMA 2118

Eileen Agar

1899–1991

*The Lotus Eater**
d 1939
Paper collage with watercolour and ink on paper
38.1 x 28.2
Purchased 1979
GMA 2079

*Slow Movement**
d 1970
Oil on canvas
151.2 x 151.2
Purchased 1975
GMA 1514

Sam Ainsley

1950–

Five Celebratory Banners
1984
Nylon with cotton binding
488 x 152 (outer two); 488 x 193 (inner three)
Commissioned 1984
GMA 2843

*Warrior Woman V: The Artist**
1986
Acrylic on canvas with cotton binding
381 x 142.5
Purchased 1987
GMA 3026

Reaping the Whirlwind
1987
Acrylic on canvas with cotton binding
760 x 1525
Commissioned 1987
GMA 3401

Craigie Aitchison

1926–

Landscape with Telegraph Poles
c 1951–52
Oil on hardboard
76.2 x 102.9
Purchased 1964
GMA 876

*Still Life No. 4**
1974
Oil on canvas
76.2 x 63.5
Purchased 1975
GMA 1501

Josef Albers

1888–1976

*Homage to the Square: R–NW IV**
d 1966
Oil on masonite
122 x 122
Purchased 1978
GMA 2030

Stanley Anderson

1884–1966

Le Marché, Falaise
1926
Drypoint on paper
19.3 x 26.7 (paper 27.4 x 39.5)
Purchased 1949
GMA 163

John de Andrea

1941–

*Model in Repose**
1981
Polyvinyl, painted in oil, and mixed media
58 x 74 x 55.5
Purchased 1981
GMA 2314

Michael Andrews

1928–

*Edinburgh (Old Town)**
d 1990–93
Oil on canvas
183 x 274.3
Purchased with assistance from the National Art
Collections Fund 1993
GMA 3697

Karel Appel

1921–

*Head over Landscape**
d 1958
Gouache on paper
57.1 x 77
Purchased 1962
GMA 808

*Danse d'espace avant la tempête [Dance in Space before the Storm]**
d 1959
Oil on canvas
129.5 x 161.9
Purchased 1962
GMA 815

Femme [Woman]
d 1960
Colour lithograph on paper (63/125)
76.1 x 56.5 (paper size)
Purchased 1961
GMA 790

Edward Ardizzone

1900–79

The Railway Station
(from the J. Lyons series 'Lithographs by Contemporary Artists, vol. I')
Published 1947
Colour lithograph on paper (after watercolour)
74.5 x 99 (paper size)
Presented by J. Lyons & Co. Ltd 1948
GMA 1198

Avigdor Arikha

1929–

T. Carmi
d 1971
Etching on paper (4/13)
17.9 x 12.9 (paper 33.4 x 25.8)
Purchased 1988
GMA 3392

Mirror with Self-Portrait and Press
d 1971
Etching on paper (19/30)
28.9 x 23.6 (paper 38.2 x 28.4)
Purchased 1988
GMA 3393

Samuel Beckett in Profile, Seated
d 1972
Etching on paper (15/18)
20.9 x 10.5 (paper 31.7 x 22.9)
Purchased 1988
GMA 3391

*Self-Portrait in Foreshortening**
d 1973
Aquatint on paper (8/15)
18 x 24 (paper 32 x 33)
Purchased 1988
GMA 3384

Self-Portrait with Open Mouth
d 1973
Aquatint on paper (1/20)
27.3 x 24.2 (paper 45 x 32.8)
Purchased 1988
GMA 3385

Three Apples and their Shadows
d 1973
Aquatint on paper (10/20)
24 x 18 (paper 49.7 x 32.3)
Purchased 1988
GMA 3386

David Sylvester Seated
d 1973
Aquatint on paper (22/25)
39.1 x 29.7 (paper 56.3 x 45.1)
Purchased 1988
GMA 3387

The Old Armchair
d 1973
Aquatint on paper (2/15)
27.4 x 24.2 (paper 45.6 x 39.9)
Purchased 1988
GMA 3388

Jacket and Tie in Foreshortening
d 1973
Aquatint on paper (6/6)
25.4 x 20.4 (paper 49.6 x 31)
Purchased 1988
GMA 3389

Le Chignon
d 1973
Aquatint on paper (1/12)
21 x 15 (paper 36.5 x 27.8)
Purchased 1988
GMA 3390

Sliced Bread
d 1974
Lithograph on paper (2/25)
48.1 x 32.6 (paper size)
Purchased 1988
GMA 3395

Stone
d 1975
Lithograph on paper (30/50)
28 x 42 (paper 44 x 57.5)
Purchased 1988
GMA 3378

View on the Jerusalem Wall from the Valley of Gehenna
d 1975
Lithograph on paper (22/30)
20 x 30 (paper 28.5 x 38.3)
Purchased 1988
GMA 3379

A Spoon
d 1975
Aquatint on paper (17/27)
17.9 x 12.9 (paper 32.1 x 23.9)
Purchased 1988
GMA 3382

The Right Hand of Dr Boris Dolto
d 1975
Etching on paper (1/20)
17.9 x 12.9 (paper 32.5 x 25)
Purchased 1988
GMA 3383

Hand
d 1976
Etching on paper (5/25)
17.9 x 13 (paper 33.1 x 24.9)
Purchased 1988
GMA 3381

Olives
d 1976
Etching on paper (9/13)
12.9 x 17.9 (paper 33.1 x 25.2)
Purchased 1988
GMA 3396

Jerusalem Cypresses and Lavender
d 1977
Lithograph on paper (31/75)
60 x 47 (paper 65.5 x 50.2)
Purchased 1988
GMA 3380

R. B. Kitaj
d 1983
Soft ground etching in two colours on paper (A.P. 8/10)
25.7 x 33.8 (paper 38 x 44.6)
Purchased 1988
GMA 3376

Catherine Deneuve
d 1984
Aquatint on paper (12/30)
47 x 35 (paper 66.1 x 50.8)
Purchased 1988
GMA 3377

Spectacles
d 1985
Aquatint on paper (A.P. 6/15)
13.5 x 9 (paper 37.8 x 28.3)
Purchased 1988
GMA 3375

Self-Portrait
d 1985
Aquatint on paper (A.P. 5/12)
19.7 x 19.7 (paper 32.6 x 30)
Purchased 1988
GMA 3394

Arman (Armand Fernandez)

1928–

*Violoncelle dans l'espace [Cello in Space]**
1967–68
Fragmented cello in polyester resin
127.9 x 48.6 x 14.6 (excluding metal base)
Purchased 1983
GMA 2793

William Armour

1903–79

The Plank Bridge
1932
Wood engraving on paper
15.4 x 19.1 (paper 18.8 x 23.8)
Purchased 1949
GMA 160

Ledlewan, Dunngoyne
1933
Wood engraving on paper
13.5 x 19.2 (paper 19.1 x 25.5)
Purchased 1949
GMA 161

Craigangawn Quarry, Stockiemuir
d 1933
Wood engraving on paper
16.5 x 20.2 (paper 21.8 x 26.8)
Purchased 1949
GMA 162

The Broomshed
d 1933
Wood engraving on paper
18 x 20.3 (paper 21.5 x 26.5)
Purchased 1982
GMA 2539

Davie
d 1935
Wood engraving on paper
20.4 x 14.9 (paper 31.3 x 22)
Purchased 1949
GMA 159

Head of a Girl
d 1935
Wood engraving on paper
16.5 x 11.5 (paper 21 x 17.7)
Purchased 1993
GMA 3678

John Armstrong

1893–1973

*Battle of the Rocking Horse**
d 1953
Tempera on paper laid on board
31.5 x 41.2
Bequeathed by Miss Elizabeth Watt 1989
GMA 3481

Jean Arp

1886–1966

*S'élèvant [Rising up]**
1962
Marble
176.5 x 44.5 x 44.5
Purchased 1970
GMA 1253

Constellation de cinq formes [Constellation with Five Forms]
1956
Colour lithograph on paper
54.6 x 38.5 (paper 65.2 x 50.3)
Purchased 1961
GMA 770

Conrad Atkinson

1940–

Wall Street Journal
d 1985
Screenprint on paper (20/50)
58.5 x 39.3 (paper 76.7 x 56.6)
Purchased 1986
GMA 2981

Frank Auerbach

1931–

Primrose Hill: High Summer*
1959
Oil on board
91.5 x 122
Purchased 1974
GMA 1302

Head of E.O.W. IV*
1961
Oil on plywood
59.8 x 56.8
Purchased 1976
GMA 1537

Primrose Hill: Spring Sunshine*
1961–62 / 1964
Oil on board
112.5 x 140
Presented by Miss Dorothy Claire Weicker 1984
GMA 2847

Tree at Tretire*
1975
Chalk, charcoal and gouache on paper (two sheets joined)
77 x 72.5
Presented by Miss Dorothy Claire Weicker 1984
GMA 2848

Head of G. B.
d 1966
Screenprint on paper (42/70)
79.5 x 57.4 (paper 101 x 70)
Purchased 1984
GMA 2849

Robert Sargent Austin

1895–1973

Study for the Engraving 'Comare Giulia'
d 1924
Pen and ink and watercolour on paper
12 x 18 (paper 28.3 x 19.5)
Bequeathed by Mr Kenneth Sanderson 1943
GMA 675

Study for the Engraving 'Donkeys of Selva'
c 1927
Pen and ink on paper
13.2 x 16.6 (paper 22.9 x 23.5)
Bequeathed by Sir David Young Cameron 1945
GMA 674

Man with a Crucifix [CD 45]
1924
Etching on grey paper (fifth state)
13.4 x 11.4 (paper 29.5 x 22.6)
Purchased 1949
GMA 43

The Stone Breaker [CD 57]
d 1925
Etching on paper (third state)
10.7 x 13.7 (paper 20.9 x 26.5)
Bequeathed by Sir David Young Cameron 1945
GMA 40

San Domenico, Perugia [CD 58]
d 1925
Etching on grey paper (third state)
9.4 x 13.8 (paper 18.6 x 21)
Purchased 1949
GMA 51

Woman Milking a Goat [CD 59]*
d 1925
Engraving on paper (final state)
11.5 x 11.9 (paper 18.4 x 19)
Purchased 1949
GMA 47

Woman of Scanno [CD 72]
d 1927
Engraving on paper (fourth state)
20.2 x 15.6 (paper 34 x 27.1)
Bequeathed by Sir David Young Cameron 1945
GMA 41

Woman Praying [CD 76]
d 1928
Engraving on paper (tenth state)
20.3 x 15.8 (paper 28.9 x 20.7)
Purchased 1949
GMA 53

The Wooden Bridge, Sottocastello [CD 85]
1929
Engraving on paper (fifth state)
15.9 x 12.2 (paper 27 x 20.2)
Purchased 1949
GMA 45

The Belfry [CD 88]
d 1930
Engraving on paper (fifth state, trial proof)
16.8 x 11.9 (paper 25 x 18.6)
Purchased 1949
GMA 44

The Wood Carriers [Post CD 93]
d 1932
Engraving on paper
20.1 x 15 (paper 29.2 x 23.2)
Purchased 1949
GMA 46

Woman Sleeping [Post CD 95]
1931–32
Engraving on paper (trial proof)
15.1 x 19 (paper 21.6 x 28.4)
Purchased 1949
GMA 52

Man and Scythe [Post CD 99]
d 1933
Engraving on paper
13.7 x 11.2 (paper 26.5 x 21.1)
Bequeathed by Mr Kenneth Sanderson 1943
GMA 39 A

Man and Scythe [Post CD 99]
d 1933
Engraving on paper
13.7 x 11.2 (paper 28.7 x 22.9)
Purchased 1949
GMA 39 B

Woman Cutting Grass [Post CD 100]
d 1933
Engraving on paper (trial proof)
11.6 x 9.6 (paper 25.5 x 20.5)
Purchased 1949
GMA 49

Hill Top Rest [Post CD 103]
1933–34
Engraving on paper
19.7 x 13.6 (paper 26.2 x 20.2)
Purchased 1949
GMA 48

The Bellringer's Wife [Post CD 107]
1934
Engraving on paper
15.2 x 10.6 (paper 24 x 18.6)
Purchased 1949
GMA 50

Young Mother [Post CD 112]
1936
Engraving on paper
13.2 x 10 (paper 24.2 x 18.7)
Purchased 1949
GMA 42

Women at Prayer (In Santa Serva II)
[Post CD 114]
d 1936
Engraving on paper
27.9 x 21.5 (paper 35.4 x 28)
Purchased 1949
GMA 54

[CD refers to the catalogue raisonné of Austin's prints by Campbell Dodgson (London 1930); and 'Post CD' to the supplement published by the Ashmolean Museum, Oxford (1980)]

Michael Ayrton

1921–75

The Acropolis of Cumae
c 1956
Colour lithograph on paper (49/50)
39 x 46.1 (paper 48.1 x 55.5)
Purchased 1960
GMA 741

Eugène Baboulène

1905–

Nature morte [Still Life]*
1957
Oil on canvas
60.3 x 73.3
Presented by Mrs Isabel M. Traill 1979
GMA 2141

William Baillie

1923–

Cocos Palms*
d 1964
Oil on canvas
76.2 x 101.6
Scott Hay Collection: presented 1967
GMA 1024

Donald Bain

1904–79

Jazz
d 1943
Watercolour and ink on paper
26.9 x 20.5
Purchased 1976
GMA 1593

A Glade in Angus
d 1944
Black and coloured chalk on paper
20.5 x 20.1
Purchased 1976
GMA 1594

Man Holding a Cigarette
c 1944
Watercolour and black chalk on paper
20.2 x 14.9
Purchased 1976
GMA 1597

The Children of Llyr*
d 1945
Oil on canvas
107 x 94
Purchased 1976
GMA 1587

Celtic Ballet: Forsaken Mermaid
d 1945
Watercolour, gouache and coloured chalk
on paper
28.6 x 30.2
Purchased 1976
GMA 1595

Still Life with Fruit
c 1945
Watercolour on paper
16.5 x 20.9
Purchased 1976
GMA 1601

Boulevard, Paris
d 1946
Watercolour and black chalk on paper
18 x 14.4
Purchased 1976
GMA 1596

Passageway, St-Paul-de-Vence
d 1947
Watercolour, pastel and black chalk on paper
29 x 27.1
Purchased 1976
GMA 1598

François Poulenc à St-Paul-de-Vence
d 1947
Ink on paper
21 x 19.4
Purchased 1976
GMA 1599

Dark Head
d 1972
Ink and white crayon on paper
16.3 x 13.9
Purchased 1976
GMA 1600

Robert Bain

Spirits of the Wood
Linocut on paper (25/100)
44.1 x 40.5 (paper 52.1 x 46.4)
Purchased 1976
GMA 1544

Edward Baird

1904–49

*Still Life**
d 1940
Oil on canvas
45.9 x 61
Purchased 1990
GMA 3535

Beck Balkan

1952–

Tropical Plant with Pineapple
1985
Aluminium, painted
246 x 158 x 55
Purchased 1985
GMA 2971

Yannik Ballif

1927–

L'Ile rousse [The Red Island]
c 1966
Colour etching on paper (A.P. 3)
72.7 x 56.7 (image and paper size)
Purchased 1967
GMA 1067

Balthus (Balthasar Klossowski de Rola)

1908–

*Le Lever [Getting up]**
1955
Oil on canvas
161 x 130.4
Purchased 1981
GMA 2311

John Rankine Barclay

1884–1962

The Towpath
Etching and drypoint on paper (2/50)
17.6 x 22.5 (paper 22 x 27.2)
Bequeathed by Mr Kenneth Sanderson 1943
GMA 55

Crowd Watching a Sunset behind a Bridge
Drypoint on paper
20.1 x 25.1 (paper 25.1 x 37.3)
Purchased 1949
GMA 56

Crowd Advancing
Drypoint on paper
20.2 x 25.1 (paper 24.8 x 37)
Purchased 1949
GMA 57

Peter Barker-Mill

1908–

Sting-Ray
exh. 1934
Colour linocut on tissue paper
30.6 x 24.9 (paper 40.9 x 27.7)
Provenance unrecorded
GMA 58

Ernst Barlach

1870–1938

Schreitende Frau (or *Schreitende Nonne*)
[*Walking Woman* (or *Walking Nun*)]*
1909
Porcelain, glazed
25 x 12.5 x 13.8
Purchased 1977
GMA 1664

Das Schlimme Jahr 1937 [*The Terrible Year
1937*]*
d 1936
Wood (oak)
142 x 31 x 28.5
Purchased with assistance from the National Art
Collections Fund (William Leng Bequest) 1987
GMA 3036

Die Wandlungen Gottes [*The Changing
Appearances of God*]
Published 1922
Book of seven woodcuts
31.6 x 44 (paper size)
Presented by Mr Keith Andrews 1963
GMA 837

Wilhelmina Barns-Graham

1912–

*White Rocks, St Mary's, Scilly Isles**
d 1953
Watercolour with oil monotype on paper
50.5 x 76.4
Purchased 1977
GMA 1697

*Zennor Rock – Rose II**
d 1953
Oil and pencil on wood
22.9 x 28.5
Bequeathed by Miss Elizabeth Watt 1989
GMA 3482

*March 1957 (Starbotton)**
d 1957
Oil on canvas
63.5 x 76.5
Purchased 1983
GMA 2778

Stuart Barrie

1925–

Derelict Pier
1965
Screenprint on paper (3/8)
38.1 x 25.3 (paper 47 x 33.4)
Purchased 1965
GMA 924

Georg Baselitz

1938–

Ohne Titel [*Untitled (Figure with Raised Arm)*]*
1982–84
Wood, painted
253 x 71 x 46
Purchased with assistance from the National Art
Collections Fund (William Leng Bequest) 1989
GMA 3530

Kopfkissen [*Pillow*]*
d 1987
Oil on canvas
200 x 162.2
Purchased 1988
GMA 3372

Grosser Kopf [*Large Head*]
1966
Colour woodcut with monotype on paper
48.3 x 40.5 (paper 50.1 x 40.9)
Purchased 1988
GMA 3374

Marius Bauer

1867–1932

Interior of Melrose Abbey
d 1928
Watercolour and pencil on paper
56.1 x 38.3
Purchased 1949
GMA 1196

Chariot Scene
Watercolour on paper
17.8 x 28.3
Purchased 1949
GMA 1194

A Chariot and Armed Men before a Tribune
of Babylonian Architecture
Sepia wash and gouache on paper
19 x 26.8 (paper 26.5 x 34)
Purchased 1949
GMA 1195

Een Ruiter [A Horseman] [w 14]
1887
Etching on paper
5.7 x 9.3 (paper 22.7 x 32.6)
Purchased 1949
GMA 1218

Binnenplaats Tesculari [Courtyard at Stamboul]
[w 25]
1888
Etching on paper
14.7 x 8.7 (paper 32.8 x 22.7)
Purchased 1949
GMA 1227

Voddenrapers [Ragpickers] [w 56]
1888
Drypoint on paper
12.5 x 11.2 (paper 32.8 x 22.5)
Purchased 1949
GMA 1219

Optocht [Cavalcade] [w 107]
1888
Etching on paper
11.9 x 10 (paper 33 x 22.7)
Purchased 1949
GMA 1225

Optocht [Cavalcade] [w 107]
1888
Etching on paper
11.9 x 10 (paper 33 x 22.8)
Presented by Mr Douglas Wood 1965
GMA 948

Een Turksche Koopman [A Turkish Merchant,
Damascus] [w 9]
1889
Etching on paper
17.5 x 12.1 (paper 32.9 x 22.7)
Purchased 1949
GMA 1233

Een Koperslager te Stamboel [A Brazier
at Stamboul] [w 28]
1889
Drypoint on paper
11.1 x 10.6 (paper 23.3 x 20)
Purchased 1949
GMA 1222

Een Turksche Bazaar [A Turkish Bazaar] [w 94]
1889
Drypoint on paper
17.1 x 11 (paper 32.8 x 22.6)
Purchased 1949
GMA 1226

Een Bazaar in Damascus [A Bazaar in Damascus]
[w 97]
1889
Etching on paper
11.5 x 7.4 (paper 32.7 x 22.7)
Purchased 1949
GMA 1229

Een Pasha [A Pasha] [w 106]
1889
Etching on paper
13.3 x 12.3 (paper 32.8 x 22.2)
Purchased 1949
GMA 1223

Een Straatje in Beyroet [A Street at Beyruth]
[w 109]
1889
Etching on paper
7.8 x 5.3 (paper 32.8 x 22.3)
Purchased 1949
GMA 1224

Een Ezeldrijver in Stamboel [A Donkey-Driver,
Stamboul] [w 2]
1890
Etching on paper
17.3 x 12.3 (paper 33 x 22.5)
Purchased 1949
GMA 1228

Oostersch Interieur [Oriental Interior] [w 32]
1890
Etching and drypoint on paper
12.7 x 15.8 (paper 22.3 x 32.6)
Presented by Mr Douglas Wood 1965
GMA 949

Op de Brug te Constantinopel [On the Bridge
at Constantinople] [w 121]
1890
Etching on paper
10.1 x 14.2 (paper 22.3 x 32.5)
Purchased 1949
GMA 1234

Een Sultan [A Sultan] [w 201]
1891
Etching on paper
41.5 x 37.3 (paper 52.8 x 44)
Purchased 1949
GMA 1241

Een Begrafenis te Cairo [A Funeral in Cairo]
[w 133]
1892
Etching on paper
21.2 x 27.2 (paper 32.5 x 45)
Presented by Mr Douglas Wood 1965
GMA 950

Mecca Pelgrims [Mecca Pilgrims] [w 134]
1892
Etching on paper
8.6 x 32.9 (paper 25 x 45)
Purchased 1949
GMA 1236

De Koningen van Sheba te Jeruzalem [The Queen
of Sheba at Jerusalem] [w 210]
1893
Etching on paper
32.5 x 32.7 (paper 62.1 x 49.9)
Provenance unrecorded
GMA 1240

Et le terrain résonnait sourdement sous ces
approches [And the Earth Trembled Deafeningly
at their Approach]
(for 'Akëdysséril' by P. Villiers de l'Isle-Adam)
[w 144]
1894
Etching on paper
16.8 x 25.5 (paper 39.3 x 51.1)
Purchased 1949
GMA 1235

Intocht van een Konig [Entry of a King] [w 213]
1894
Etching on paper
30.8 x 46.4 (paper 47.8 x 64.7)
Presented by Mr Douglas Wood 1965
GMA 952

Intocht van een Konig [Entry of a King] [w 213]
1894
Etching on paper
30.8 x 46.4 (paper 37 x 52.1)
Purchased 1949
GMA 1220

De Sphinx [The Sphinx] [w 218]
1895
Lithograph on paper
36 x 47 (paper 50.3 x 64.2)
Provenance unrecorded
GMA 1239

Bishop on a Horse
(for 'De Kroniek')
1898
Lithograph on paper
22.8 x 34.8 (paper 33 x 50.4)
Purchased 1949
GMA 1230

De Tooverdeur [*The Magic Door*] [w 37]
1899
Etching on paper
14.2 x 11.7 (paper 32.8 x 22.6)
Presented by Mr and Mrs Alexander Maitland
1953
GMA 1237

Aan de Bron [*At the Source*] [w 66]
1899
Etching on paper
16.8 x 11.7 (paper 32.5 x 22.8)
Presented by Mr and Mrs Alexander Maitland
1953
GMA 1238

Benares [w 232]
d 1899
Etching on paper
55.2 x 67.5 (paper 65.6 x 85.7)
Presented by Mr Douglas Wood 1965
GMA 954

Een Huwelijks-Optocht met Kameelen in Cairo
[*A Wedding Procession with Camels*] [w 126]
1900
Etching on paper
43.6 x 27.6 (paper 65.1 x 45.5)
Presented by Mr Douglas Wood 1965
GMA 951

Het Kremlin [*The Kremlin*] [w 135]
1900
Etching on paper
19.1 x 23.8 (paper 32.5 x 45)
Purchased 1949
GMA 1231

Jeruzalem [*Jerusalem*] [w 226]
d 1900
Etching on paper
33.7 x 76 (paper 51.1 x 96.8)
Bequeathed by Mr Kenneth Sanderson 1943
GMA 1242

Het Beleg van Constantinopel [*The Siege
of Constantinople*] [w 100]
1902
Etching on paper
1.7 x 10.4 (paper 22.3 x 32.8)
Purchased 1949
GMA 1232

Voorportaal van eene Moskee [*The Porch
of a Mosque*] [w 230]
1904
Etching on paper
67 x 56.3 (paper 95.6 x 77)
Purchased 1949
GMA 1243

Eene Begrafenis aan Ganges [*A Funeral
Ceremony on the Ganges*] [w 231]
1904
Etching on paper
56.1 x 67.8 (paper 74.5 x 93.2)
Presented by Mr Douglas Wood 1965
GMA 955

Een Oostersche Prins [*An Oriental Prince*]
[w 236]
d 1914
Etching on paper
54.3 x 64.6 (paper 76.6 x 91.4)
Presented by Mr Douglas Wood 1965
GMA 953

Elephant Procession
Drypoint on paper
16.8 x 23 (paper 29.5 x 36.8)
Purchased 1949
GMA 1221

[w refers to the catalogue raisonné of Bauer's
etchings and drypoints published by E. J. van
Wisselingh & Co. (Amsterdam 1927)]

Edward Bawden

1903–89

The Dolls at Home
(*from the J. Lyons series 'Lithographs by
Contemporary Artists, vol. I'*)
Published 1947
Colour lithograph on paper (after watercolour
and collage)
74.5 x 99 (paper size)
Presented by J. Lyons & Co. Ltd 1948
GMA 1199

Campions and Columbine
(for 'Signature', no. 4)
1947
Linocut on paper
91.5 x 62 (paper size)
Presented by the artist 1982
GMA 2584

*Masthead for the Lion and Unicorn Press (Royal
College of Art); Masthead for 'The Observer'*
1950s; 1961
Linocuts on paper
91.5 x 62 (paper size)
Presented by the artist 1982
GMA 2573

Six Designs for a London Transport Poster
1952
Linocuts on paper
91.5 x 62 (paper size)
Presented by the artist 1982
GMA 2582

*The Queen's Beasts (The White Horse of
Hanover; The White Greyhound of Richmond)**
1953
Linocuts on paper
62.5 x 91 (paper size)
Presented by the artist 1982
GMA 2572 A

*The Queen's Beasts (The Lion of England;
The Falcon of the Plantagenets)*
1953
Linocuts on paper
62 x 91.5 (paper size)
Presented by the artist 1982
GMA 2572 B

*The Queen's Beasts (The Griffin of Edward III;
A Griffin)*
1953
Linocuts on paper
62 x 91.5 (paper size)
Presented by the artist 1982
GMA 2572 C

Twelve Zodiac Signs for Gilbey's Drinks Mats
1954
Linocuts on paper
62 x 91.5 (paper size)
Presented by the artist 1982
GMA 2585

Five Untitled Designs
*(for 'The Sixpence that Rolled Away' by Louis
MacNeice)*
1956
Linocuts on paper
62 x 91.5 (paper size)
Presented by the artist 1982
GMA 2583

*Four Designs for Fortnum and Mason
Advertisements*
c 1956–59
Linocuts on paper
62 x 91.5 (paper size)
Presented by the artist 1982
GMA 2578 A

*Six Designs for Fortnum and Mason
Advertisements*
c 1956–59
Linocuts on paper
62 x 91.5 (paper size)
Presented by the artist 1982
GMA 2578 B

*Designs for 'De la Rue' Playing Cards (Jack,
Queen and King)*
1957
Linocuts on paper
62 x 91.5 (paper size)
Presented by the artist 1982
GMA 2575

*Five Heads (including Herodotus, Shakespeare
and Queen Victoria)*
1958 and after
Linocuts on paper
91.5 x 62 (paper size)
Presented by the artist 1982
GMA 2574

Five Geometric Designs
*(for 'The Histories of Herodotus
of Halicarnassus')*
1958
Linocuts on paper
62 x 91.5 (paper size)
Presented by the artist 1982
GMA 2592 D

Four Geometric Designs
(for 'The Histories of Herodotus
of Halicarnassus')
1958
Linocuts on paper
62 x 91.5 (paper size)
Presented by the artist 1982
GMA 2592 E

Five Geometric Designs
(for 'The Histories of Herodotus
of Halicarnassus')
1958
Linocuts on paper
62 x 91.5 (paper size)
Presented by the artist 1982
GMA 2592 F

Four Designs for Guinness Stout Advertisements
c 1960
Linocuts on paper
91 x 62.5 (paper size)
Presented by the artist 1982
GMA 2571 A

Four Designs for Guinness Stout Advertisements
c 1960
Linocuts on paper
91 x 62.5 (paper size)
Presented by the artist 1982
GMA 2571 B

Design for a Mural for the Liner 'Empress
of Canada' (Mountains and Tree)
1960
Linocut on paper
91 x 62.5 (paper size)
Presented by the artist 1982
GMA 2593 A

Design for a Mural for the Liner 'Empress
of Canada' (Mountains)
1960
Linocut on paper
62.5 x 91 (paper size)
Presented by the artist 1982
GMA 2593 B

Design for a Mural for the Liner 'Empress
of Canada' (Mountain Scenery)
1960
Linocut on paper
91 x 62.5 (paper size)
Presented by the artist 1982
GMA 2593 C

Design for a Mural for the Liner 'Empress
of Canada' (Hills)
1960
Linocut on paper
91 x 62.5 (paper size)
Presented by the artist 1982
GMA 2593 D

Design for a Mural for the Liner 'Empress
of Canada' (Mountains)
1960
Linocut on paper
91 x 62.5 (paper size)
Presented by the artist 1982
GMA 2593 E

Design for a Mural for the Liner 'Empress
of Canada' (Mountains)
1960
Linocut on paper
91 x 62.5 (paper size)
Presented by the artist 1982
GMA 2593 F

Design for a Mural for the Liner 'Empress
of Canada' (Mountains and Timber Cabin)
1960
Linocut on paper
62.5 x 91 (paper size)
Presented by the artist 1982
GMA 2593 G

Design for a Mural for the Liner 'Empress
of Canada' (Mountains)
1960
Linocut on paper
62.5 x 91 (paper size)
Presented by the artist 1982
GMA 2593 H

Design for a Mural for the Liner 'Empress of Canada' (Mountains and Lake)
1960
Linocut on paper
91 x 62.5 (paper size)
Presented by the artist 1982
GMA 2593 I

Design for a Mural for the Liner 'Empress of Canada' (Mountain and Timber Cabin)
1960
Linocut on paper
62.5 x 91 (paper size)
Presented by the artist 1982
GMA 2593 J

Design for a Mural for the Liner 'Empress of Canada' (Mountains)
1960
Linocut on paper
62.5 x 91 (paper size)
Presented by the artist 1982
GMA 2593 K

Design for a Mural for the Liner 'Empress of Canada' (Mountain Scenery and Timber House)
1960
Linocut on paper
62.5 x 91 (paper size)
Presented by the artist 1982
GMA 2593 L

Design for a Mural for the Liner 'Empress of Canada' (Cliffs and Timber House)
1960
Linocut on paper
62.5 x 91 (paper size)
Presented by the artist 1982
GMA 2593 M

Design for a Mural for the Liner 'Empress of Canada' (Timber Building and Rocks)
1960
Linocut on paper
62.5 x 91 (paper size)
Presented by the artist 1982
GMA 2593 N

Design for a Mural for the Liner 'Empress of Canada' (Fish and Rocks)
1960
Linocut on paper
62.5 x 91 (paper size)
Presented by the artist 1982
GMA 2593 O

Design for a Mural for the Liner 'Empress of Canada' (Tethered Horse, Timber House and Mountain Scenery)
1960
Linocut on paper
62.5 x 91 (paper size)
Presented by the artist 1982
GMA 2594 A

Design for a Mural for the Liner 'Empress of Canada' (Stone Houses, Cows and Mountain Scenery)
1960
Linocut on paper
62.5 x 91 (paper size)
Presented by the artist 1982
GMA 2594 B

Design for a Mural for the Liner 'Empress of Canada' (Large Timber House)
1960
Linocut on paper
62.5 x 91 (paper size)
Presented by the artist 1982
GMA 2595 A

Design for a Mural for the Liner 'Empress of Canada' (Four Timber Buildings)
1960
Linocut on paper
62.5 x 91 (paper size)
Presented by the artist 1982
GMA 2595 B

Design for a Mural for the Liner 'Empress of Canada' (Timber Church)
1960
Linocut on paper
91 x 62.5 (paper size)
Presented by the artist 1982
GMA 2595 C

Design for a Mural for the Liner 'Empress
of Canada' (Trees and Deer)
1960
Linocut on paper
91 x 62.5 (paper size)
Presented by the artist 1982
GMA 2595 D

Design for Wrapping Paper (Man in Kilt
and Thistle motifs)
c 1960
Colour linocut, white gouache and pencil
56 x 76 (paper size)
Presented by the artist 1982
GMA 2597 A

Design for Wrapping Paper (Deer in a Landscape)
c 1960
Colour linocut, pencil and collage on paper
56 x 76 (paper size)
Presented by the artist 1982
GMA 2597 B

Design for Wrapping Paper (Bagpipe Player)
c 1960
Colour linocut, white gouache, pencil and collage
on paper
56 x 76 (paper size)
Presented by the artist 1982
GMA 2597 C

Design for Wrapping Paper (Boats Crossing
the Water)
c 1960
Colour linocut on paper
56 x 76 (paper size)
Presented by the artist 1982
GMA 2597 D

Design for Wrapping Paper (Anglers and Deer
in a Landscape)
c 1960
Colour linocut, white gouache and pencil on paper
56 x 76 (paper size)
Presented by the artist 1982
GMA 2597 E

Design for Wrapping Paper (Deer and Trees)
c 1960
Colour linocut, white gouache and pencil on paper
56 x 76 (paper size)
Presented by the artist 1982
GMA 2597 F

Design for Wrapping Paper (Farm with Highland
Cattle)
c 1960
Colour linocut, pencil and collage on paper
56 x 76 (paper size)
Presented by the artist 1982
GMA 2597 G

Two Untitled Designs
(for 'Dunlopera: The Work and Workings
of the Dunlop Rubber Company')
1961
Linocuts on single sheet of paper
62.5 x 91 (paper size)
Presented by the artist 1982
GMA 2569 A

Five Untitled Designs
(for 'Dunlopera: The Work and Workings
of the Dunlop Rubber Company')
1961
Linocuts on single sheet of paper
62.5 x 91 (paper size)
Presented by the artist 1982
GMA 2569 B

Nine Untitled Designs
(for 'Dunlopera: The Work and Workings
of the Dunlop Rubber Company')
1961
Linocuts on single sheet of paper
62.5 x 91 (paper size)
Presented by the artist 1982
GMA 2569 C

Seven Untitled Designs
(mainly for 'Dunlopera: The Work and Workings
of the Dunlop Rubber Company')
1961
Linocuts on single sheet of paper
62.5 x 91 (paper size)
Presented by the artist 1982
GMA 2569 D

Endpaper Designs
(for 'Bawden in Portugal', published in 'Motif',
no. 9)
1962
Linocuts on single sheet of paper with part cut out
62.5 x 91 (paper size)
Presented by the artist 1982
GMA 2568 A

'Beja' and 'Lisbon'
(for 'Bawden in Portugal', published in 'Motif',
no. 9)
1962
Linocuts on single sheet of paper with part cut out
91 x 62.5 (paper size)
Presented by the artist 1982
GMA 2568 B

'Obidos' and statuary
(for 'Bawden in Portugal', published in 'Motif',
no. 9)
1962
Linocuts on single sheet of paper
91.5 x 62 (paper size)
Presented by the artist 1982
GMA 2568 C

'Evora' and 'Lamego'
(for 'Bawden in Portugal', published in 'Motif',
no. 9)
1962
Linocuts on single sheet of paper
91.5 x 62 (paper size)
Presented by the artist 1982
GMA 2568 D

Statues and Hedges
(for 'Bawden in Portugal', published in 'Motif',
no. 9)
1962
Linocut on paper
91 x 62.5 (paper size)
Presented by the artist 1982
GMA 2568 E

William I and Edward III
(for 'Associated Electrical Industries Calendar')
1964
Linocuts on single sheet of paper
62 x 91.5 (paper size)
Presented by the artist 1982
GMA 2577 A

Elizabeth I
(for 'Associated Electrical Industries Calendar')
1964
Linocut on paper
91.5 x 62 (paper size)
Presented by the artist 1982
GMA 2577 B

George IV
(for 'Associated Electrical Industries Calendar')
1964
Linocut on paper
91.5 x 62 (paper size)
Presented by the artist 1982
GMA 2577 C

Grasses in a Jug
1967
Linocut on paper
79.5 x 58 (paper size)
Presented by the artist 1982
GMA 2588

Church and Thunderstorm, Saffron Walden
Church
c 1975
Colour linocut on paper (A.P. 2nd ed. 3/50)
149 x 57 (paper 169.5 x 76.2)
Purchased 1982
GMA 2567

Two Designs for the Oxford University Almanac
Linocuts on single sheet of paper
91 x 62.5 (paper size)
Presented by the artist 1982
GMA 2570

Lion, Lion Cub, Elephant, Bird and Owl
Linocuts on single sheet of paper
91.5 x 62 (paper size)
Presented by the artist 1982
GMA 2576

Nine Designs for a Recruiting Poster
Linocuts on single sheet of paper
62 x 91.5 (paper size)
Presented by the artist 1982
GMA 2579 A

Nine Crowns (Designs for a Recruiting Poster)
Linocuts on single sheet of paper
62 x 91.5 (paper size)
Presented by the artist 1982
GMA 2579 B

Farming Motifs (Designs for an Irish Television
Series)
Linocuts on single sheet of paper
62 x 91.5 (paper size)
Presented by the artist 1982
GMA 2580

Nine Designs for Irish Postage Stamps
Linocuts on single sheet of paper
62 x 91.5 (paper size)
Presented by the artist 1982
GMA 2581

*Eleven Designs (including Ships, Boats, Cars,
Bus, Stevenson's 'Rocket' and Knights in
Combat)*
Linocuts on single sheet of paper
62 x 91.5 (paper size)
Presented by the artist 1982
GMA 2586

*Nine Designs for Westminster Abbey 900th
Anniversary Poster*
Linocuts on single sheet of paper
62 x 91.5 (paper size)
Presented by the artist 1982
GMA 2587

*'Greetings from the Bawdens' (Christmas Card
Design); A Moorish Scene (Cover for
'Architectural Review')*
Linocuts on single sheet of paper
62 x 91.5 (paper size)
Presented by the artist 1982
GMA 2589

Heraldic Device; A Geometric Design
Linocuts on single sheet of paper
91.5 x 62 (paper size)
Presented by the artist 1982
GMA 2590

*Design for Tiles for Tottenham Hale
Underground Station; Design for Tiles for
Highbury Underground Station*
Linocuts on single sheet of paper
91.5 x 62 (paper size)
Presented by the artist 1982
GMA 2591

Two Geometric Designs
Linocuts on single sheet of paper
91.5 x 62 (paper size)
Presented by the artist 1982
GMA 2592 A

Geometric Design
Linocut on paper
91.5 x 62 (paper size)
Presented by the artist 1982
GMA 2592 B

Geometric Design
Linocut on paper
91.5 x 62 (paper size)
Presented by the artist 1982
GMA 2592 C

Gilbert Bayes

1872–1953

*Knight on Horseback**
d 1913
Bronze
23.8 x 19.2 x 14 (excluding base)
Bequeathed by Sir David Young Cameron 1945
GMA 1

Penelope Beaton

1886–1963

Still Life with Decanter
c 1963
Watercolour and black chalk on paper
57 x 76
Scott Hay Collection: presented 1967
GMA 1025

Tarbert, Loch Fyne
Watercolour, gouache and pen and ink on paper
47 x 57.4
Bequeathed by Dr R. A. Lillie 1977
GMA 1993

Basil Beattie

1935–

Untitled
(from 'The London Suite')
d 1982
Screenprint on paper (11/75)
84 x 60.2 (image and paper size)
Purchased 1983
GMA 2749

Leonard Beaumont

1891–1986

The Club Hut
1932
Etching on paper (8/100)
24.8 x 20.9 (paper 28.5 x 22.9)
Purchased 1949
GMA 59

'To Hell with Tin Hats'
c 1933
Colour linocut on paper
20.6 x 25.2 (paper 23.6 x 32.4)
Purchased 1949
GMA 60

The Garden of Eden
c 1933
Colour linocut on paper
25.3 x 20.2 (paper 34.1 x 23.2)
Purchased 1949
GMA 62

Miners
c 1933–35
Colour linocut on paper
30.5 x 25.2 (paper 35.2 x 28.7)
Purchased 1949
GMA 61

Max Beckmann

1884–1950

*Tegeler Freibad [Swimming at Lake Tegel]**
d 1911
Lithograph on paper (9/40)
31.5 x 34.7 (paper 36.4 x 44.4)
Purchased 1984
GMA 2925

Die Hölle [Hell]
title page: Selbstbildnis [Self-Portrait]
  1) *Der Nachhauseweg [The Way Home]**
  2) *Die Strasse [The Street]*
  3) *Das Martyrium [The Martyrdom]*
  4) *Der Hunger [Hunger]*
  5) *Die Ideologen [The Ideologues]*
  6) *Die Nacht [The Night]**
  7) *Malepartus*
  8) *Das patriotische Lied [The Patriotic Song]*
  9) *Die Letzten [The Last Ones]*
  10) *Die Familie [The Family]*
1919
Portfolio of ten lithographs on paper and
lithographic title page (4/75)
Each approx. 87 x 61 (paper size)
Purchased 1981
GMA 2465

Trevor Bell

1930–

Tidal Spaces
d 1958
Colour lithograph on paper (23/30)
48.5 x 37.6 (paper 64 x 51.4)
Purchased 1960
GMA 742

John Bellany

1942–

*Allegory**
d 1964
Oil on hardboard (triptych)
212.4 x 121.8; 213.3 x 160; 212.5 x 121.8
Purchased 1988
GMA 3359

*My Father**
1966
Oil on hardboard
122 x 91.2
Purchased 1986
GMA 2987

*Kinlochbervie**
1966
Oil on hardboard (two sheets joined)
243.5 x 320
Purchased 1986
GMA 2988

*The Bereaved One**
1968
Oil on hardboard
91.5 x 91.4
Purchased 1986
GMA 2989

*Lap Dog**
c 1973
Oil on canvas
184.9 x 164.9
Purchased 1986
GMA 2990

*Mizpah**
d 1978
Oil on canvas
243.8 x 243.8
Purchased 1980
GMA 2197

*The Ventriloquist**
1983
Oil on canvas
173 x 153
Purchased 1984
GMA 2803

Self-Portrait with Lighthouse
d 1984
Watercolour and black chalk on paper
76.4 x 58.1
Presented by the artist 1988
GMA 3360

*Cockenzie**
1985
Watercolour and black chalk on paper
76.1 x 56.6
Presented by the artist 1988
GMA 3361

*Bel Ami**
d 1985
Watercolour and black chalk on paper
76 x 56.7
Presented by the artist 1988
GMA 3362

Self-Portrait
*(from 'The Addenbrookes Hospital Series')**
d 14 April 1988
Watercolour and black chalk on paper
57 x 38.6
Purchased 1990
GMA 3536

Self-Portrait
*(from 'The Addenbrookes Hospital Series')**
d 12 May 1988
Watercolour and black chalk on paper
77.5 x 56.9
Purchased 1990
GMA 3537

Self-Portrait
(from 'The Addenbrookes Hospital Series')
d 14 May 1988
Red chalk on paper
57 x 38.5
Purchased 1990
GMA 3538

My Hand
(from 'The Addenbrookes Hospital Series')
d 15 May 1988
Black chalk on paper
38.6 x 28.5
Purchased 1990
GMA 3539

Self-Portrait with Oxygen Mask
(*from 'The Addenbrookes Hospital Series'*)
d 19 May 1988
Watercolour and black chalk on paper
77 x 57
Purchased 1990
GMA 3540

Self-Portrait
(*from 'The Addenbrookes Hospital Series'*)
d 23 May 1988
Watercolour and black chalk on paper
57.2 x 38.7
Purchased 1990
GMA 3541

Self-Portrait
(*from 'The Addenbrookes Hospital Series'*)
d 12 June 1988
Watercolour and black chalk on paper
76.7 x 57.1
Purchased 1990
GMA 3542

Self-Portrait
(*from 'The Addenbrookes Hospital Series'*)
d 1988
Coloured crayon on paper
76.8 x 56.5
Purchased 1990
GMA 3543

Professor Sir Roy Calne
(*from 'The Addenbrookes Hospital Series'*)
d 1988
Black chalk on paper
77 x 56.8
Purchased 1990
GMA 3544

Untitled (Fish Totem)
d 1970
Etching on paper (10/75)
48.5 x 37 (paper 65 x 50)
Purchased 1986
GMA 2991

Untitled (Self-Portrait with Dog)
d 1971
Etching on paper (15/25)
26.5 x 23.6 (paper 65 x 50)
Purchased 1986
GMA 2992

Death Knell for John Knox
d 1971
Etching on paper (4/50)
20.8 x 17.8 (paper 41.6 x 34.6)
Purchased 1986
GMA 2993

Confessions of a Justified Sinner
d 1972
Etching on paper (3/50)
49.5 x 43.2 (paper 66.4 x 54.5)
Purchased 1986
GMA 2994

The Skate God
d 1972
Etching on paper (6/50)
35.7 x 28.6 (paper 61.3 x 49)
Purchased 1986
GMA 2995

Untitled (The Kiss)
d 1972
Etching on paper (10/30)
29.1 x 29 (paper 65 x 50)
Purchased 1986
GMA 2996

The Gambler
(*from 'The London Suite'*)
1982
Screenprint on paper
83.6 x 60.7 (image and paper size)
Purchased 1983
GMA 2750

Capercaillie Sings his Love Song
1985
Etching on paper (5/25)
16.8 x 24.5 (paper 31.5 x 45)
Purchased 1986
GMA 2997

Etoile
d 1986
Etching on paper (3/25)
33.2 x 24.5 (paper 53.6 x 37.7)
Purchased 1986
GMA 2998

Milne's Bar
d 1986
Etching on paper (4/50)
48.7 x 32.6 (paper 65 x 50)
Purchased 1986
GMA 2999

Sweet Promise
d 1986
Etching on paper (1/25)
49.5 x 32.8 (paper 63 x 45.4)
Purchased 1986
GMA 3000

Bonjour
d 1986
Etching on paper (2/50)
33 x 49 (paper 50 x 65)
Purchased 1986
GMA 3001

Eagle
(from 'The Scottish Bestiary')
Published 1986
Etching on paper (5/50)
45.2 x 30 (paper 76 x 56.5)
Purchased 1987
GMA 3019 L

Grouse
(from 'The Scottish Bestiary')
Published 1986
Etching on paper (5/50)
45 x 30 (paper 76 x 56.5)
Purchased 1987
GMA 3019 Q

Wildcat
(from 'The Scottish Bestiary')
Published 1986
Etching on paper (5/50)
45.6 x 29.6 (paper 76 x 56.5)
Purchased 1987
GMA 3019 S

Images Inspired by Ernest Hemingway's 'The Old Man and the Sea'
1987
Portfolio of fourteen prints: etching, aquatint and screenprint (4/60)
Each 75.7 x 56.8 or 56.8 x 75.7 (paper size)
Purchased 1988
GMA 3404

Untitled
(*unused proof for 'The Old Man and the Sea'*)
1987
Etching on paper
47.6 x 32.2 (paper 75 x 56.8)
Presented by Mr Charles Booth-Clibborn 1989
GMA 3625

Untitled
(*unused proof for 'The Old Man and the Sea'*)
1987
Etching on paper
32.4 x 42.7 (paper 75 x 56.8)
Presented by Mr Charles Booth-Clibborn 1989
GMA 3626

Untitled
(*unused proof for 'The Old Man and the Sea'*)
1987
Etching (red ink) on paper
47.9 x 32.1 (paper 75 x 56.8)
Presented by Mr Charles Booth-Clibborn 1989
GMA 3627

Untitled
(*unused proof for 'The Old Man and the Sea'*)
1987
Etching and aquatint on paper
47.8 x 32.5 (paper 75 x 56.8)
Presented by Mr Charles Booth-Clibborn 1989
GMA 3628

Untitled
(*unused proof for 'The Old Man and the Sea'*)
1987
Etching and aquatint (blue ink) on paper
47.9 x 32.6 (paper 75.2 x 57)
Presented by Mr Charles Booth-Clibborn 1989
GMA 3629

Untitled
(*unused proof for 'The Old Man and the Sea'*)
1987
Etching on paper
47.8 x 32.5 (paper 75.1 x 56.9)
Presented by Mr Charles Booth-Clibborn 1989
GMA 3630

Untitled
(*unused proof for 'The Old Man and the Sea'*)
1987
Etching and aquatint on paper
48 x 32.4 (paper 75.3 x 56.8)
Presented by Mr Charles Booth-Clibborn 1989
GMA 3631

Untitled (Self-Portrait, Addenbrookes Hospital)
d 1988
Etching and aquatint on paper (15/20)
121 x 112 (paper 135.5 x 120.5)
Purchased 1989
GMA 3464

One Singer One Song
(*from 'The Haymarket Print Suite'*)
Published 1990
Screenprint on paper (A.P.)
154 x 103 (paper 157 x 107)
Purchased 1990
GMA 3569

See also John BELLANY and Alan BOLD

John Bellany and Alan Bold

Bellany 1942– , Bold 1943–

A Celtic Quintet
Published 1983
Portfolio with five sugar aquatint etchings
by Bellany and poems by Bold (31/50)
Each 24.3 x 19.5 (paper 37.5 x 28.5)
Purchased 1983
GMA 2780

Haven
Published 1984
Portfolio with five lithographs by Bellany
and poems by Bold (27/50)
Each 38 x 28 (paper 50 x 35)
Purchased 1984
GMA 2928

Homage to MacDiarmid
Published 1985
Portfolio with five etchings by Bellany and poems
by Bold (5/50)
Each 24.5 x 19.3 (paper 36.7 x 28)
Purchased 1985
GMA 2963

Ira Belmont

1877–1964

An Expression from Variations (Enigma)
by Edward Elgar
d 1945
Oil on canvas
84.5 x 89
Presented by Mrs Elsie K. Belmont 1980
GMA 2231

Michael Bennett

1948–

Untitled
(*from 'The London Suite'*)
d 1982
Screenprint on paper (11/75)
60.2 x 85 (image and paper size)
Purchased 1983
GMA 2751

Nadia Benois

1896–1975

Still Life with Fruit
Oil on paper laid on board
27.5 x 37.7
Bequeathed by Dr R. A. Lillie 1977
GMA 1885

Frank Weston Benson

1862–1951

Four Ducks Swimming
d 1922
Drypoint on paper
19.9 x 14.9 (paper 31.9 x 24.7)
Purchased 1949
GMA 64

Heron at Rest
1923
Etching and drypoint on paper
30.2 x 19.9 (paper 39.2 x 28.7)
Purchased 1949
GMA 65

Geese over a Marsh
1925
Etching and drypoint on paper
19.8 x 24.7 (paper 28 x 29.5)
Purchased 1949
GMA 69

Salt Marshes
1927
Drypoint on paper
12.6 x 9.7 (paper 31.9 x 24.6)
Purchased 1949
GMA 63

Geese in Flight
Etching on paper
8.8 x 14 (paper 19.5 x 22.9)
Purchased 1949
GMA 66 A

Geese in Flight
Etching on paper
8.8 x 14 (paper 19.1 x 22.9)
Purchased 1949
GMA 66 B

Bald Pater
Drypoint on paper
19.6 x 24.8 (paper 28.2 x 32.6)
Purchased 1949
GMA 67

Cloudy Dawn
Etching on paper
25 x 30.1 (paper 32.5 x 40.7)
Purchased 1949
GMA 68

Tadek Beutlich

1922–

Two Insects
c 1963
Colour woodcut on paper (3/35)
51.4 x 78.8 (paper 66.9 x 92.9)
Purchased 1964
GMA 877

The Frog
c 1963
Colour woodcut on paper (6/24)
52.5 x 79.3 (paper 67.5 x 91.8)
Purchased 1964
GMA 878

Girl with Insect
c 1963
Woodcut (black ink) on paper (2/35)
82.2 x 60 (paper 97.8 x 68.6)
Purchased 1964
GMA 879

Joseph Beuys

1921–86

Three Pots for the Poorhouse – Action Object*
d 1974
Two blackboards with chalk, three cast iron pots,
cord
Boards 117.5 x 119.5, 120 x 119.2 ; pots 13 x 28.5
x 21 each
Purchased 1974
GMA 1318

Ohne die Rose tun wir's nicht [We can't do it without Roses]
1972
Poster
80 x 56
Purchased 1980
GMA 2234

Food for Thought
1977
Lithographic text and butter stain on paper
88.1 x 18.5 (paper size)
Purchased 1980
GMA 2235

Joseph Beuys: Conversation Pieces
1980
Poster
59.5 x 42
Purchased 1980
GMA 2236

What is to be Done 1984: Alternative Technology versus Nuclear Power
1980
Poster
101.5 x 68.2
Purchased 1980
GMA 2237

Joseph Beuys: Black and White Oil Conference
1974
1980
Poster
59 x 41.7
Purchased 1980
GMA 2238

Robert Bevan

1865–1925

*The Well at Mydlow, Poland**
c 1907
Charcoal and watercolour on paper
32.5 x 41.5
Purchased 1971
GMA 1255

*The Well at Mydlow, Poland (No. 2)**
1922
Oil on canvas
62.2 x 81.3
Purchased 1971
GMA 1244

Crocks
1924–25
Lithograph on paper (38/40)
29.5 x 35.3 (paper 38.2 x 50.7)
Purchased 1974
GMA 1303

Julius Bissier

1893–1965

*A.15 April 64**
d 1964
Tempera on batiste
44.5 x 58.8
Purchased 1970
GMA 1106

Roger Bissière

1888–1964

Le Jardin, Printemps [The Garden, Spring]
d 1955
Colour lithograph on paper (146/175)
56.5 x 40.3 (paper 66 x 50)
Provenance unrecorded
GMA 3429

Ion Bitzan

1924–

The Secret of Wholeness
d 1967
Collage with tissue paper and gold leaf on fabric
82 x 63.5
Purchased 1969
GMA 1093

Elizabeth Blackadder

1931–

Housesteads, Hadrian's Wall*
c 1960–61
Pen and ink, black chalk and pencil on paper
51 x 66.5
Bequeathed by Dr R. A. Lillie 1977
GMA 1888

Crovie
c 1961–63
Watercolour and pencil on paper
36.2 x 53.6
Bequeathed by Dr R. A. Lillie 1977
GMA 1886

Houses and Fields, Mykonos*
1962
Watercolour and gouache on paper
70 x 102.5
Purchased (Gulbenkian UK Trust Fund) 1963
GMA 839

Flowers on an Indian Cloth*
d 1965
Oil crayon on paper
102 x 77
Scott Hay Collection: presented 1967
GMA 1026

Garden, Vence
1966
Pen and ink on paper
25.2 x 35.4
Bequeathed by Keith Andrews 1990
GMA 3608

Untitled*
1967–68
Tapestry
144 x 237
Commissioned for the Gallery of Modern Art
by Mrs John Noble 1966
GMA 1105

End of Summer
d 1970
Gouache on paper (three pieces joined)
17.1 x 25.6
Bequeathed by Dr R. A. Lillie 1977
GMA 1887

Tuscan Landscape
c 1960
Colour lithograph on paper (35/50)
43.5 x 63.7 (paper 53.5 x 74)
Purchased 1960
GMA 743

Dark Hill, Fife
c 1960
Colour lithograph on paper (A.P.)
47.5 x 65.8 (paper 57 x 79.4)
Purchased 1960
GMA 759

Cats and Flowers
1980
Colour lithograph on paper (24/75)
62 x 83.7 (image and paper size)
Purchased 1980
GMA 2207

Still Life with Fan
d 1980
Colour lithograph on paper (5/75)
63 x 86 (image and paper size)
Purchased 1980
GMA 2208

Orchid
1985
Colour etching and aquatint on paper (4/50)
50.7 x 32.6 (paper 72.1 x 52.3)
Purchased 1986
GMA 2974

Peter Blake

1932–

Studio Tackboard
d 1972
Screenprint on paper (43/100)
97.5 x 136.6 (image and paper size)
Presented by Mme Andrée Stassart 1979
GMA 2103

Edmund Blampied

1886–1966

Two Draught Horses with Bareback Riders
Black chalk on paper
40.6 x 55.9
Purchased 1949
GMA 676

Abattoir: Man Sitting on a Dead Horse
Pen and ink, wash and pencil on paper
15.3 x 20 (paper size)
Purchased 1949
GMA 677

Weary [CD 16]
1913
Drypoint on paper
11.4 x 16.9 (paper 17.4 x 21.5)
Purchased 1949
GMA 82

Loading Seaweed [CD 19]
1913
Etching on paper
12.5 x 17.6 (paper 23.1 x 28.8)
Purchased 1949
GMA 72

At the Gate [CD 34]
1914
Drypoint on paper
10.1 x 14.8 (paper 22.9 x 29.1)
Purchased 1949
GMA 73

Sunday Morning Bathers [CD 45]
1920
Drypoint on paper
25 x 32.8 (paper 35.2 x 39.8)
Purchased 1949
GMA 79

'Fetch it!' [CD 46]
1920
Drypoint on paper
27.7 x 37.3 (paper 36.5 x 51.8)
Purchased 1949
GMA 76

The Stranger [CD 55]
1920
Drypoint on paper
25 x 32.5 (paper 33.1 x 45.8)
Purchased 1949
GMA 74

Dancing on the Seashore
by 1920
Drypoint on paper
17.2 x 25.1 (paper 26.2 x 38.4)
Purchased 1949
GMA 80

Wading [CD 58]
d 1920
Drypoint on paper
17.2 x 24.4 (paper 25.3 x 39.4)
Purchased 1949
GMA 81

Purring and Snoring [CD 62]
d 1921
Drypoint on paper
17.7 x 23.8 (paper 25 x 39.2)
Purchased 1949
GMA 78

The Sick Man [CD 65]
1921
Drypoint on paper
19.7 x 28.9 (paper 29.1 x 45.9)
Purchased 1949
GMA 77

Cider Drinkers [CD 93]
1925
Drypoint on paper (second state)
26 x 20.8 (paper 45.8 x 29.8)
Purchased 1949
GMA 75

Horses Watering
Lithograph on paper
26.4 x 39.6 (paper 33.5 x 50.7)
Purchased 1949
GMA 70

The Haycart
Lithograph on paper
24.9 x 34.5 (paper 33.5 x 50.7)
Purchased 1949
GMA 71

[CD refers to the catalogue raisonné of Blampied's etchings and drypoints by Campbell Dodgson (London 1926)]

Douglas Percy Bliss

1900–84

Barra
d 1924
Wood engraving on paper
10.8 x 15.4 (paper 15.8 x 18.7)
Purchased 1992
GMA 3666

Lachrymae Rerum
d 1925
Wood engraving on paper
16 x 10.4 (paper 20.8 x 19.1)
Purchased 1992
GMA 3665

*Lovers Sheltering from a Storm**
1926
Wood engraving on paper
10.5 x 16 (paper 12.8 x 20.1)
Purchased 1979
GMA 2081

*They Visit a Hermit
(for 'History of Rasselas, Prince of Abissinia'
by Dr Johnson)*
Published 1926
Wood engraving on paper
16.2 x 10.5 (paper 22.6 x 15)
Purchased 1982
GMA 2540

Morayshire Crofter
c 1929
Wood engraving on paper
10.2 x 15.7 (paper 23.9 x 31.3)
Purchased 1979
GMA 2082

Morayshire Shepherd
c 1929
Wood engraving on paper
10.2 x 15.9 (paper 15.9 x 26.5)
Purchased 1979
GMA 2083

Robert Henderson Blyth

1919–70

Don't Rev!
d 1943
Ink, watercolour and chalk on paper
28.6 x 38
Purchased 1987
GMA 3020

Troops on Manoeuvres in the Scottish Highlands
d 1943
Ink and watercolour on paper
28.5 x 37.7
Purchased 1987
GMA 3021

*Man and the Elements: Mountain Troops
Erecting a Bell Tent*
d 1943
Ink, watercolour and gouache on paper
28.7 x 38
Purchased 1987
GMA 3023

Mountain Troops being Briefed before Assault
d 1944
Ink, watercolour and gouache on paper
28.5 x 38
Purchased 1987
GMA 3024

War Landscape
d 1945
Gouache on paper
30.5 x 42.8
Purchased 1987
GMA 3022

*Holland (Troops on the Dutch Frontier)**
d 1945
Monotype on paper
15.9 x 20.3 (paper 22.5 x 28.8) (irregular)
Purchased 1987
GMA 3025

Farm on the Hill
c 1962
Watercolour and pastel on paper
67.3 x 75.4
Scott Hay Collection: presented 1967
GMA 1027

Alan Bold

1943–

Grass (Illuminated Poem)
d 1975
Ink, watercolour and gouache on paper
63.6 x 44.7
Purchased 1976
GMA 1528

Seeing (Illuminated Poem)
d 1975
Ink, watercolour and gouache on paper
63.7 x 44.7
Purchased 1976
GMA 1529

See also John BELLANY and Alan BOLD

David Bomberg

1890–1957

*Bargees**
c 1919
Brush and ink on paper
25.4 x 20.3
Presented by Mrs Dinora Davies-Rees and Mrs
Juliet Lamont through the Contemporary Art
Society 1987
GMA 3055

*Three Figures**
c 1919
Pen and ink, with brush and ink on verso,
on paper
32.5 x 20.2
Presented by Mrs Dinora Davies-Rees and Mrs
Juliet Lamont through the Contemporary Art
Society 1987
GMA 3056

*Self-Portrait**
d 1937
Oil on canvas
77.2 x 56.5
Purchased (Knapping Fund) 1967
GMA 994

*Vigilante**
d 1955
Oil on canvas
61 x 50.7
Purchased 1985
GMA 2944

*Ronda, Evening**
1956
Charcoal on paper
47 x 62.6
Purchased 1985
GMA 2945

Muirhead Bone

1876–1953

*The National Gallery and Bank of Scotland**
d 1910
Pencil on paper
12.9 x 16.9
Bequeathed by Sir James Caw 1950
GMA 682

San Silvestro, Rome
c 1912
Pencil on paper
33.1 x 20.3
Bequeathed by Sir Alexander Maitland 1965
GMA 938

Near Rome
c 1913
Pencil and watercolour on paper
13 x 21.1
Purchased 1949
GMA 685

Regent Street, Looking Towards Oxford Circus
d 1915
Pencil and wash on paper
15.8 x 24.1
Purchased 1979
GMA 2104

Cavalry and Wagons outside Albert, Somme
c 1917
Pencil and wash on paper
16.7 x 15.6
Provenance unrecorded
GMA 692

French Lane, Rollemourt
d 1917
Pencil and watercolour on paper
19.8 x 12.7
Provenance unrecorded
GMA 693

Warships on the Firth of Forth
d 1917
Pencil and watercolour on paper
19.6 x 29.2
Provenance unrecorded
GMA 694

Santillana at Night
c 1926
Black chalk on paper
24.1 x 17.8
Bequeathed by Sir Alexander Maitland 1965
GMA 940

Adriatic Coast
Pencil, black chalk and wash on paper
13.3 x 19.6
Bequeathed by Mr Kenneth Sanderson 1943
GMA 678

A House seen through Trees and Bushes
Pencil and pen and ink on paper
18 x 11
Bequeathed by Mr Kenneth Sanderson 1943
GMA 679

Street Scene
Pencil, pen and ink and wash on paper
21.8 x 17.2
Bequeathed by Mr Kenneth Sanderson 1943
GMA 680

Moonlight, Auxerre
Black crayon on paper
35.5 x 25.4
Bequeathed by Mr Kenneth Sanderson 1943
GMA 681

Vesuvius and the Bay of Naples, from Offshore
Pencil and watercolour on paper
15.8 x 25.3
Purchased 1949
GMA 683

Sailing Boats and Barge, Lisbon
Pencil and watercolour on paper
12.5 x 16.4
Purchased 1949
GMA 684

Tuscany – near Pisa
Pencil and watercolour on paper
14 x 20.9
Purchased 1949
GMA 686

Coastline near Cadiz
Pencil and watercolour on paper
20 x 35.4 (paper 25.2 x 35.4)
Purchased 1949
GMA 687

Landscape near Parma
Pencil and watercolour on paper
11.1 x 17.8
Purchased 1949
GMA 688

Monte Carlo
Pencil and watercolour on paper
13.3 x 19.2
Purchased 1949
GMA 689

Distant View of Wells Cathedral
Black chalk and watercolour on paper
11.3 x 17
Purchased 1949
GMA 690

West Coast Seascape
Pencil and watercolour on paper
21.7 x 30.8
Purchased 1949
GMA 691

Archway at Fonte*
Black chalk and watercolour on paper
22 x 25.5
Bequeathed by Sir Alexander Maitland 1965
GMA 936

Todi from the Rocca*
[verso: Sketch of a Tower]
Pastel on paper
24.3 x 36.5
Bequeathed by Sir Alexander Maitland 1965
GMA 937

The Basilica, Covadonga
Black chalk and wash on paper
28 x 38.4
Bequeathed by Sir Alexander Maitland 1965
GMA 939

Ballantrae
Black chalk on paper
27.2 x 38.1
Bequeathed by Dr R. A. Lillie 1977
GMA 1889

The Tapestries, Santiago di Compostella
Pencil and watercolour on paper
11.4 x 13.2
Bequeathed by Mr Alan Stark 1983
GMA 2775

Landscape Sketch, Lendalfoot (or Cottage among
Trees) [CD suppl. 9A]
1898
Drypoint on paper
9.7 x 6.7 (paper 16.2 x 10.5)
Provenance unrecorded
GMA 91

Glasgow International Exhibition: Entrance
from the Piazza [CD 100]
1901
Etching on paper
27.2 x 18 (paper 31.4 x 21.3)
Provenance unrecorded
GMA 94

Glasgow International Exhibition [CD 117A]
1901
Etching on paper
4.6 x 9.8 (paper 7.1 x 12.9)
Provenance unrecorded
GMA 93

Glasgow International Exhibition: The Russian
Section [CD 117B]
d 1901
Etching (brown ink) on paper
9.6 x 6.3 (paper 12.7 x 8.8)
Provenance unrecorded
GMA 95 A

Glasgow International Exhibition: The Russian
Section [CD 117B]
d 1901
Etching (black ink) on paper
9.6 x 6.3 (paper 13.9 x 8.8)
Provenance unrecorded
GMA 95 B

Glasgow International Exhibition: Annan's
Studio [CD 117E]
1901
Etching on paper
8.4 x 6.3 (paper 13.9 x 8.1)
Provenance unrecorded
GMA 90

Somerset House [CD 185]
1905
Drypoint on paper
30.4 x 28.8 (paper 35.3 x 32.9)
Bequeathed by Mr Thomas Barclay 1940
GMA 84

Demolition of St James's Hall: Interior [CD 196]
1906
Drypoint on paper
40.2 x 28.3 (paper 54.8 x 39.7)
Purchased 1949
GMA 89

Rye, from Camber [CD 205]
1907
Drypoint on paper
15.2 x 20.2 (paper 21.6 x 24)
Bequeathed by Mr Thomas Barclay 1940
GMA 85

Demolition of St James's Hall: Exterior [CD 207]
1907
Drypoint on paper
29.7 x 27.7 (paper 50.9 x 39.6)
Bequeathed by Mr Thomas Barclay 1940
GMA 86

St John's Wood [CD 208]
1907
Drypoint on paper
13.5 x 11.9 (paper 26.1 x 20)
Bequeathed by Mr Thomas Barclay 1940
GMA 87

A Tuscan Farm [CD 284]
1913
Drypoint on paper
13.9 x 10 (paper 27.7 x 20.8)
Provenance unrecorded
GMA 96

Building Ships: A Shipyard
(from the series 'The Great War: Britain's Efforts
and Ideals')
Published 1918
Lithograph on paper
47.1 x 36.5 (paper 50.5 x 40.3)
Presented by the Ministry of Information 1919
GMA 83 A

Building Ships: On the Stocks
(from the series 'The Great War: Britain's Efforts
and Ideals')
Published 1918
Lithograph on paper
35.5 x 46.2 (paper 40.4 x 50.5)
Presented by the Ministry of Information 1919
GMA 83 B

Building Ships: A Shipyard Seen from a Big
Crane
(from the series 'The Great War: Britain's Efforts
and Ideals')
Published 1918
Lithograph on paper
46.2 x 35.5 (paper 50.5 x 40)
Presented by the Ministry of Information 1919
GMA 83 C

Building Ships: A Workshop
(from the series 'The Great War: Britain's Efforts
and Ideals')
Published 1918
Lithograph on paper
36.5 x 47.6 (paper 40.2 x 51.5)
Presented by the Ministry of Information 1919
GMA 83 D

Building Ships: A Fitting-out Basin
(from the series 'The Great War: Britain's Efforts
and Ideals')
Published 1918
Lithograph on paper
46 x 35.5 (paper 50.5 x 40)
Presented by the Ministry of Information 1919
GMA 83 E

Building Ships: Ready for Sea
(from the series 'The Great War: Britain's Efforts
and Ideals')
Published 1918
Lithograph on paper
46.5 x 35.5 (paper 50.5 x 40.5)
Presented by the Ministry of Information 1919
GMA 83 F

Rabindranath Tagore [CD 371]
1920
Drypoint on paper
24.7 x 15 (paper 31 x 26)
Purchased 1949
GMA 92

Stockholm [CD 405]
1923
Drypoint on paper
22.7 x 28.8 (paper 31 x 38.9)
Purchased 1949
GMA 88

Autumn Evening, Lowestoft [CD 453]
1934
Drypoint on paper
20.1 x 32.6 (paper 33.6 x 48.6)
Purchased 1964
GMA 901

Railway Sheds, Marseilles [CD 473]
1937
Drypoint on paper
25.4 x 31.7 (paper 34.8 x 43)
Purchased 1964
GMA 902

[CD refers to the catalogue raisonné of Bone's
etchings and drypoints by Campbell Dodgson
(London 1909) and to the unpublished
supplement]

Phyllis Mary Bone

1896–1972

Red Deer – Mother and Son
c 1942
Plaster
32.5 x 39 x 16
Bequeathed by the artist 1972
GMA 1275 A

Red Deer – Mother and Son*
c 1942
Bronze
32.5 x 39 x 16
Bequeathed by the artist 1972
GMA 1275 B

Pierre Bonnard

1867–1947

Ruelle à Vernonnet [Lane at Vernonnet]*
c 1912–14
Oil on canvas
76 x 65.2
Purchased with funds given by Mrs Charles
Montagu Douglas Scott 1961
GMA 2932

Echappée sur la rivière, Vernon [View of the
River, Vernon]*
1923
Oil on canvas
48.3 x 45.7
Presented by Sir Alexander Maitland in memory
of his wife, Rosalind, 1960
GMA 2931

Edward Borein

1872–1945

Cowboy and Steer
Etching on paper
18.5 x 29.7 (paper 31.4 x 40.1)
Bequeathed by Dr Marinell Ash 1990
GMA 3531

Francisco Borès

1898–1972

Nude
c 1934–35
Black chalk on paper
103.5 x 74
Presented by Miss Elizabeth Watt 1960
GMA 760

Le Déjeuner [The Lunch]*
d 1935
Oil on canvas
26.1 x 30.6
Bequeathed by Miss Elizabeth Watt 1989
GMA 3483

Alfred Edward Borthwick

1871–1955

Toledo
1912
Pencil and watercolour on paper
28.8 x 38.7
Presented by Mrs A. E. Borthwick 1957
GMA 696

Lerida, Spain
1912
Pencil and watercolour on paper
29 x 38.9
Presented by Mrs A. E. Borthwick 1957
GMA 697

Derek Boshier

1937–

Plaza*
d 1965
Oil on two shaped canvases, attached by metal
struts
205.2 x 205.2
Purchased 1976
GMA 1539

Preparatory Study for 'Plaza'
1965
Ball-point pen on squared paper
20.1 x 14.5
Purchased 1980
GMA 2154 A

Preparatory Study for 'Plaza'
c 1965
Ball-point pen on squared paper
20.1 x 14.5
Purchased 1980
GMA 2154 B

Public Palette
d 1977
Screenprint and collage on paper (1/50)
43.6 x 77 (paper 55.7 x 82.7)
Purchased 1979
GMA 2108

Doris Boulton-Maude

exh. 1916–40

Hens in the Orchard
1936
Colour linocut on grey paper
22.1 x 25 (paper 29.4 x 31.9)
Provenance unrecorded
GMA 443

Emile-Antoine Bourdelle

1861–1929

*Petite bacchante aux jambes croisées [Small Bacchante with Crossed Legs]**
c 1906–10
Bronze with gilt patina
36.6 x 14.2 x 15
Bequeathed by Sir Alexander Maitland 1965
GMA 941

*La Vierge d'Alsace [The Virgin of Alsace]**
1919–21
Bronze
250.2 x 84 x 58.5
Purchased 1930
GMA 2

Mary Boyd

1910–

Cat
1933–34 (cast 1983)
Bronze
24.8 x 10.7 x 15
Presented by the artist 1984
GMA 2929

Mark Boyle

1934–

*Addison Crescent Study (London Series)**
1969
Painted fibreglass and mixed media
247 x 244 x 19
Purchased 1974
GMA 1304

*Skin Series No. 8**
1973
Black and white photograph on hardboard (two sheets joined)
183 x 183.4
Purchased 1974
GMA 1305

See also BOYLE FAMILY

Boyle Family

Mark Boyle 1934– , Joan Hills 1936– ,
Sebastian Boyle 1962– , Georgina Boyle 1964–

*Study from the Broken Path Series with Border Edging**
1986
Painted fibreglass and mixed media
182.7 x 305 x 12.5
Purchased 1986
GMA 3016

See also Mark BOYLE

Frank Brangwyn

1867–1956

*Assisi Woodland**
Oil on wood
43.3 x 31.3
Bequeathed by Mr Alan Stark 1983
GMA 2776

Meat Market, Hammersmith
1904
Woodcut on paper
20.5 x 18 (paper 30.5 x 22)
Purchased 1949
GMA 103

The Miraculous Draught
1910
Woodcut on paper
19.2 x 30.5 (paper 26.8 x 41.9)
Purchased 1949
GMA 98

The Nuns of Dixmiden
1912
Woodcut on paper
15.2 x 20.4 (paper 19.4 x 24.9)
Provenance unrecorded
GMA 105

The Forest
1913
Woodcut on paper
10.6 x 16.2 (paper 16.3 x 22.7)
Purchased 1949
GMA 104

Via Dolorossa (Jesus Falls beneath the Cross)
1916
Woodcut on paper
19.4 x 37.6 (paper 36.4 x 49.8)
Purchased 1949
GMA 97

The Dismantling of the 'Duncan'
c 1917
Lithograph on paper
25.6 x 36.4 (paper 31.9 x 42.3)
Purchased 1949
GMA 100

The Last of 'H.M.S. Britannia'
c 1917
Lithograph on paper
25.9 x 35.6 (paper 37 x 47)
Purchased 1949
GMA 102

Freedom of the Seas
(from the series 'The Great War: Britain's Efforts and Ideals')
Published 1918
Colour lithograph on paper
46 x 73.8 (paper 50.8 x 76)
Presented by the Ministry of Information 1919
GMA 106

Making Sailors: Youthful Ambition
(from the series 'The Great War: Britain's Efforts and Ideals')
Published 1918
Lithograph on paper
45.8 x 36 (paper 55 x 38.3)
Presented by the Ministry of Information 1919
GMA 3638 A

Making Sailors: "Duff"
(from the series 'The Great War: Britain's Efforts and Ideals')
Published 1918
Lithograph on paper
46.4 x 36.2 (paper 54.6 x 38.2)
Presented by the Ministry of Information 1919
GMA 3638 B

Making Sailors: Boat Drill
(from the series 'The Great War: Britain's Efforts and Ideals')
Published 1918
Lithograph on paper
46.5 x 36 (paper 54.3 x 38)
Presented by the Ministry of Information 1919
GMA 3638 C

Making Sailors: Going Aboard
(from the series 'The Great War: Britain's Efforts and Ideals')
Published 1918
Lithograph on paper
47.2 x 35.5 (paper 55 x 37)
Presented by the Ministry of Information 1919
GMA 3638 D

Making Sailors: The Look-Out
(*from the series 'The Great War: Britain's Efforts and Ideals'*)
Published 1918
Lithograph on paper
46 x 35.5 (paper 54.7 x 38)
Presented by the Ministry of Information 1919
GMA 3638 E

Making Sailors: The Gun
(*from the series 'The Great War: Britain's Efforts and Ideals'*)
Published 1918
Lithograph on paper
46.5 x 36.5 (paper 54.7 x 38)
Presented by the Ministry of Information 1919
GMA 3638 F

The Prize Fight (or *The Boxers*)
c 1919
Woodcut on paper (second state)
15.1 x 20.9 (paper 24.5 x 32.6)
Purchased 1965
GMA 921

Peace (or *Love amid Ruins*)
1920
Lithograph on paper
27.1 x 23.2 (paper 36.3 x 29)
Purchased 1949
GMA 99

The Storm (or *A Fair Wind*)
1923
Woodcut on paper
19.3 x 31.9 (paper 31.5 x 46.2)
Purchased 1949
GMA 108

Dyers (or *A Man Washing Cloth*)
c 1924–25
Lithograph on paper
25.3 x 20.4 (paper 31.5 x 25.6)
Purchased 1949
GMA 101

Georges Braque

1882–1963

Le Bougeoir [*The Candlestick*]*
1911
Oil on canvas
46.2 x 38.2
Purchased 1976
GMA 1561

Pal [*Pale Ale*]*
1911
Etching on paper (8/30)
45.7 x 32.8 (paper 56.5 x 45.3)
Purchased 1962
GMA 835

Raymond Breinin

1909–

*In the Forest**
d 1942
Oil on canvas
91.5 x 122
Purchased by U. S. subscription and presented through Lady Tennyson 1944
GMA 1002

Archie Brennan

1931–

Study for 'The Ali Tapestry'
d 1973
Ink and pencil on board
63.4 x 50.6
Presented anonymously 1984
GMA 2911

Study for 'The Ali Tapestry'
d 1973
Ink and pencil on board
63.5 x 50.8
Presented anonymously 1984
GMA 2912

Study for 'The Ali Tapestry'
d 1973
Pencil on board
63.5 x 50.8
Presented anonymously 1984
GMA 2913

Head of Muhammad Ali
d 1974
Aluminium
60.5 x 50.8 x 7.7
Presented anonymously 1984
GMA 2910

Norbertine Bresslern-Roth

1891–1978

Tigers
c 1925
Colour linocut on paper
20.9 x 22.9 (paper 24.6 x 25.5)
Purchased 1949
GMA 109 A

*The Attack**
c 1925
Colour linocut on paper
21.9 x 21.9 (paper 24.9 x 25.4)
Purchased 1949
GMA 109 B

James Bridie

See Osborne Henry MAVOR

Stanislaus Brien

exh. 1930–39

Mare and Foal
c 1933
Linocut on paper (28/50)
36.5 x 21.4 (paper 45 x 34)
Purchased 1949
GMA 111

Beur and Seal
c 1933
Linocut on paper (9/50)
36.7 x 21 (paper 45 x 34)
Purchased 1949
GMA 112

The Heron
c 1935
Linocut on paper (3/30)
28 x 21.4 (paper 33.6 x 25.7)
Bequeathed by Mr Kenneth Sanderson 1943
GMA 110

Gerald Leslie Brockhurst

1890–1978

Viba
d 1929
Etching on paper
21.4 x 17.2 (paper 37.9 x 28)
Bequeathed by Mr George Liston-Foulis 1958
GMA 114

*James McBey**
d 1931
Etching on paper
26.7 x 18.9 (paper 37.4 x 27.9)
Bequeathed by Mr George Liston-Foulis 1958
GMA 113

Horace Brodzky

1885–1969

Seated Nude
d 1917
Etching on paper
12.3 x 7.8 (paper 36.2 x 27.1)
Purchased 1986
GMA 3004

*The Wash Basin**
1919
Linocut on paper
19.8 x 14.5 (paper 38 x 29)
Purchased 1986
GMA 3005

Marcel Broodthaers

1924–76

La Tour visuelle [The Visual Tower] *
1966
Glass jars, wood and magazine illustrations
88.7 x 49.7 x 49.7
Purchased 1983
GMA 2794

James R. Brotchie

1909–56

Tuscan Landscape
d 1945
Watercolour, pen and ink and wash on paper
18.2 x 34.2
Presented by Mr David Baxandall 1991
GMA 3588

Helen Paxton Brown

1876–1956

Portrait of Jessie M. King *
Watercolour, ink and black chalk on paper
50.1 x 40.5
Purchased 1977
GMA 1698

Seated Woman
Watercolour and ink on paper
34.9 x 27.1
Purchased 1977
GMA 1699

March
Watercolour and ink on paper
24.2 x 23.8 (paper 39 x 28.1)
Purchased 1977
GMA 1700

'Comment ça va?'
Black chalk on paper
20 x 24.3
Purchased 1977
GMA 1701

Man with Portfolio
Pencil, coloured pencil and black chalk on paper
22.5 x 19.4
Purchased 1977
GMA 1702

Woman at an Easel
Black chalk on paper
21.9 x 19.2
Purchased 1977
GMA 1703

Woman with Portfolio
Pencil, coloured pencil and black chalk on paper
22.6 x 19.4
Purchased 1977
GMA 1704

'Quite impossible to paint with so many people around'
Black chalk on paper
23.3 x 26.5
Purchased 1977
GMA 1705

Man at an Easel
Black chalk on paper
23.5 x 26.4
Purchased 1977
GMA 1706

'Shade of what ho!'
Black chalk on paper
19.8 x 24.1
Purchased 1977
GMA 1707

Woman Painting in a Gallery
Black chalk on paper
20.7 x 26.5
Purchased 1977
GMA 1708

Man Painting Observed by Two Children
Black chalk on paper
22 x 24.9
Purchased 1977
GMA 1709

Roger Brown

1941–

*Misty Morning**
1975
Oil on canvas
183 x 183
Purchased 1981
GMA 2313

F. W. Bruce

A collection of paintings and graphic work,
presented by the artist's family, was accessioned
as archival material in 1982.

John R. Brundson

1933–

Flight out of Water
d 1962
Etching and aquatint on paper (9/50)
45.7 x 60.3 (paper 57.6 x 73.6)
Purchased with funds given by two anonymous
donors 1963
GMA 840

Purple Mist
d 1962
Etching and aquatint on paper (3/50)
45.3 x 60.8 (paper 56.9 x 73.4)
Purchased with funds given by two anonymous
donors 1963
GMA 841

Günter Brus

1938–

*Ohne Titel [Untitled]**
1965
Mixed media on board mounted on wood
77 x 77
Purchased 1987
GMA 3054

Gordon Bryce

1943–

Winter Landscape, Aberdeen
d 1976
Watercolour, gouache and black chalk on paper
51 x 73.7
Bequeathed by Dr R. A. Lillie 1977
GMA 1890

Fire
1965
Colour etching and aquatint on paper
60.5 x 45 (paper 67.2 x 50)
Purchased 1965
GMA 925

Sophie Brzeska

1872–1925

Landscape with Houses and Sun
Watercolour and gouache on paper
18.8 x 27.9
Presented by Jim Ede 1977
GMA 1626

Landscape with Trees
Watercolour and gouache on paper
19.5 x 27.9
Presented by Jim Ede 1977
GMA 1627

Alec Buckels

1892–1972

Fear
d 1923
Wood engraving on paper
10.2 x 9.8 (paper 21.3 x 12.9)
Purchased 1949
GMA 119

Music and Bells
1924
Wood engraving on paper (27/50)
10 x 7.6 (paper 14.2 x 11.5)
Purchased 1949
GMA 117

The Dew Pond
exh. 1929 (d 1931)
Wood engraving on paper (20/25)
14.4 x 16.9 (paper 19.5 x 27.7)
Bequeathed by Mr Kenneth Sanderson 1943
GMA 115

The Merry Men*
d 1932
Wood engraving on paper (1/25)
17.7 x 19.4 (paper 24 x 28)
Purchased 1949
GMA 116

The Storm
d 1933
Wood engraving on paper (1/25)
19.9 x 24.2 (paper 27.8 x 30.6)
Provenance unrecorded
GMA 120

Major Oak, Sherwood Forest
exh. 1935
Wood engraving on paper (posthumous edition
16/25)
30.4 x 35.5 (paper 40 x 47.4)
Purchased 1980
GMA 2209

Chanctonbury Ring
exh. 1935
Wood engraving on paper (posthumous edition
22/25)
18.5 x 25.9 (paper 28.2 x 36.5)
Purchased 1980
GMA 2210

Flint Mines
exh. 1936
Wood engraving on paper (posthumous edition
5/25)
18.8 x 22.8 (paper 24.4 x 27.1)
Purchased 1980
GMA 2211

Solitude
Wood engraving on paper (35/50)
7.5 x 7.5 (paper 12.9 x 11.9)
Purchased 1949
GMA 118

Burr Stones, Pottlebury
Wood engraving on paper (posthumous edition
17/25)
18.7 x 16.2 (paper 28.1 x 24.1)
Purchased 1980
GMA 2212

The Beck
Wood engraving on paper (posthumous edition
10/25)
11.5 x 14.5 (paper 15.8 x 19)
Purchased 1980
GMA 2213

Tillingbourne Brook
Wood engraving on paper (posthumous edition
6/25)
10 x 10.1 (paper 15.9 x 13.5)
Purchased 1980
GMA 2214

John Buckland Wright

See John Buckland WRIGHT

Rembrandt Bugatti
1885 1916

Le Faön [The Fawn]*
c 1909–10
Bronze
33.2 x 39 x 15
Purchased 1972
GMA 1264

Victor Burgin

1941–

Fiction Film
Published 1991
Portfolio of nine computer-generated duo-tone
screenprints on paper (17/35)
Each 75.5 x 95.2 (paper size)
Purchased 1992
GMA 3621

Jean D. Burns

1903–

The Meet
d 1933
Wood engraving on paper (1/30)
16.7 x 30.6 (paper 23 x 34)
Purchased 1949
GMA 121

Cumbernauld Glen
d 1934
Wood engraving on paper (2/30)
17.7 x 27.8 (paper 24.7 x 32.7)
Purchased 1949
GMA 1251

Cumbernauld Burn
d 1934
Wood engraving on paper (2/30)
17.7 x 27.8 (paper 26.5 x 33.1)
Purchased 1949
GMA 1252

Edward Burra

1905–76

*The Watcher**
c 1937
Watercolour and pencil on paper
102 x 67
Purchased 1970
GMA 1115

*Soldiers Resting in a Field**
1947
Watercolour and pencil on paper
68.5 x 101.2
Presented anonymously in memory of Terence
Rattigan 1984
GMA 2904

*Izzy Orts**
1955
Watercolour and pencil on paper
73.6 x 104.5
Purchased 1980
GMA 2147

Illustrated Letter
Pen and ink on paper
17.8 x 13.4
Presented anonymously in memory of the artist
1984
GMA 2909

Mac's Bar
c 1929
Woodcut on paper
16.3 x 11.1 (paper 18.9 x 13.1)
Presented anonymously in memory of the artist
1984
GMA 2908

Wednesday Night
1971–72
Etching on paper (38/75)
30 x 25 (paper 48 x 46.5)
Presented anonymously in memory of the artist
1984
GMA 2905

Drag Queen
1971–72
Etching on paper (38/75)
29.9 x 25 (paper 48 x 46.5)
Presented anonymously in memory of the artist
1984
GMA 2906

Mrs Pot
1971–72
Etching and aquatint on paper (38/75)
24.9 x 27 (paper 45.7 x 46.8)
Presented anonymously in memory of the artist
1984
GMA 2907

Alberto Burri

1915–

Combustione No. 3*
1965
Etching and aquatint on paper (48/80)
39.3 x 37.5 (paper 64.4 x 47.5)
Purchased 1966
GMA 986

Reg Butler

1913–81

Personage*
1949
Iron on stoneware base
24.3 x 7.4 x 5.5 (excluding base)
Purchased 1977
GMA 1661

Girl*
1957–58
Bronze (6/8)
177 x 60.5 x 60.5
Purchased 1962
GMA 809

Francis Campbell Boileau Cadell

1883–1937

The Model*
c 1912
Oil on canvas
127.2 x 101.6
Purchased 1947
GMA 3

Peggy in Blue and White*
d 1912
Oil on canvas
76.6 x 63.8
Bequeathed by Mr Gordon Binnie: received 1963
GMA 865

Still Life (The Grey Fan)*
c 1920–25
Oil on canvas
66 x 49.3
Purchased 1974
GMA 1311

Portrait of a Lady in Black*
c 1921
Oil on canvas
76.3 x 63.5
Bequeathed by Mr and Mrs G. D. Robinson through the National Art Collections Fund 1988
GMA 3350

Orange and Blue, Iona*
c 1925–30
Oil on canvas laid on board
37.2 x 44.5
Bequeathed by Dr R. A. Lillie 1977
GMA 1892

Iona Croft*
c 1925–30
Oil on canvas-board
37.7 x 45
Bequeathed by Dr R. A. Lillie 1977
GMA 1893

Aspidistra and Bottle on Table*
c 1930
Oil on canvas laid on board
76.2 x 60.9
Bequeathed by Mr and Mrs G. D. Robinson through the National Art Collections Fund 1988
GMA 3351

Melancholy Portrait of a Poet*
c 1934
Charcoal on paper
55.7 x 37.9
Bequeathed by Dr R. A. Lillie 1977
GMA 1891

James Cadzow

1881–1941

Scots Firs (Study for 'Wind and Rain')
d 1914
Pencil on paper
17.8 x 25.5
Presented by Mr William Cadzow
and Mr William Borland 1943
GMA 1170

Scots Firs
d 1914
Pencil on paper
17.8 x 25.4
Presented by Mr William Cadzow
and Mr William Borland 1943
GMA 1171

On Loch Lubnaig
d 1916
Pencil on paper
17.3 x 35.8
Presented by Mr William Cadzow
and Mr William Borland 1943
GMA 1177

The Broken Gate
d 1919
Pencil on paper
20.9 x 18.8
Presented by Mr William Cadzow
and Mr William Borland 1943
GMA 1172

Craig of Benderloch, Connel Ferry
d 1919
Pencil on paper
21 x 32.5
Presented by Mr William Cadzow
and Mr William Borland 1943
GMA 1176

Fir Foliage
d 1922
Pencil on paper
25.2 x 35.4
Presented by Mr William Cadzow
and Mr William Borland 1943
GMA 1169

Tower of Charlemagne, Tours
d 1925
Pencil on paper
27.8 x 15.3
Presented by Mr William Cadzow
and Mr William Borland 1943
GMA 1178

Place des Halles, Tours
d 1925
Pencil on paper
20 x 13.9
Presented by Mr William Cadzow
and Mr William Borland 1943
GMA 1179

A Street in Tours
d 1925
Pencil on paper
24 x 15.6
Presented by Mr William Cadzow
and Mr William Borland 1943
GMA 1180

Caen
d 1925
Pencil on paper
21.8 x 19.4
Presented by Mr William Cadzow
and Mr William Borland 1943
GMA 1181

Macduff Harbour
d 1928
Pencil on paper
22.8 x 32.5
Presented by Mr William Cadzow
and Mr William Borland 1943
GMA 1173

At Banff Harbour: Derelicts
d 1928
Pencil on paper
19.5 x 28.4
Presented by Mr William Cadzow
and Mr William Borland 1943
GMA 1175

Crags at Inchnadamph
d 1937
Pencil on paper
17.1 x 23.6
Presented by Mr William Cadzow
and Mr William Borland 1943
GMA 1174

Study of Trees
d 1922
Drypoint on paper (14/50)
24 x 20 (paper 29.2 x 26)
Presented by Mr William Cadzow
and Mr William Borland 1943
GMA 126

Craig of Benderloch, Connel Ferry
d 1940
Drypoint and etching on paper (second state)
20 x 29.7 (paper 28 x 41.7)
Presented by Mr William Cadzow
and Mr William Borland 1943
GMA 122

Loch Leven
d 1940
Drypoint and etching on paper (trial proof)
22.6 x 28.6 (paper 28.1 x 38.2)
Presented by Mr William Cadzow
and Mr William Borland 1943
GMA 123

The Keeper's Cottage
d 1940
Etching on paper
15.2 x 25 (paper 23.6 x 29.4)
Presented by Mr William Cadzow
and Mr William Borland 1943
GMA 125

Highland Landscape under Rain
Drypoint and etching on paper
12 x 28.2 (paper 19 x 35.2)
Presented by Mr William Cadzow
and Mr William Borland 1943
GMA 124

Alexander Calder
1898–1976

*The Spider**
c 1935–37
Metal, painted
104 x 89 x 0.7
Purchased 1976
GMA 1586

Robert Callender
1932–

*Abandoned Red Rudder**
1983
Cardboard, polystyrene and mixed media
300 x 61.3 x 65
Purchased 1985
GMA 2953

J. Bruce Cameron
fl. 1902–58

Marshland, Possilpark
Watercolour on paper laid on card
20.4 x 29.2
Presented by the artist 1958
GMA 698

The Glen near Dunbar
Watercolour, pen and ink and chalk on paper
17.7 x 20.4
Presented by the artist 1958
GMA 699

A Ruined Tower
Watercolour and pen and ink on paper
23.7 x 35.6 (paper 31.4 x 47.8)
Presented by the artist 1958
GMA 700

Landscape with Loch
[verso: *Trees and Hills*]
Watercolour and pen and ink on paper [verso: watercolour and pencil]
27.3 x 36.1
Presented by the artist 1958
GMA 701

A Ruined Castle
Black and coloured chalk on paper
33.9 x 26.5
Presented by the artist 1958
GMA 702

A Border Tower
Watercolour on paper
12.1 x 28.1
Presented by the artist 1958
GMA 703

A Ruined Castle
Etching on paper
12.8 x 16.8 (paper 20.5 x 26.5)
Presented by the artist 1958
GMA 127

A Stirlingshire Landscape
Etching on paper (trial proof)
5.2 x 16.4 (paper 10 x 20.9)
Presented by the artist 1958
GMA 128.3 A

A Stirlingshire Landscape
Etching on paper
5.2 x 16.4 (paper 13 x 20.2)
Presented by the artist 1958
GMA 128.3 B

A Stirlingshire Landscape
Etching on paper
5.2 x 16.4 (paper 7.8 x 19.9)
Presented by the artist 1958
GMA 128.3 C

Baldernoch Church
Etching on paper
5.7 x 8.5 (paper 9.1 x 13.8)
Presented by the artist 1958
GMA 129.2 A

Baldernoch Church
Etching on paper
5.7 x 8.5 (paper 9 x 12.2)
Presented by the artist 1958
GMA 129.2 B

An Ancient Fortress
Etching on paper
19 x 18.6 (paper 24.6 x 35.4)
Presented by the artist 1958
GMA 130.2 A

An Ancient Fortress
Etching on paper
18.9 x 18.4 (paper 24.7 x 26.1)
Presented by the artist 1958
GMA 130.2 B

Man Carrying a Basket
Etching on paper
22.5 x 16.4 (paper 38.7 x 24.6)
Presented by the artist 1958
GMA 131

Trees in a Landscape
Etching on paper
14 x 30.3 (paper 24.5 x 41)
Presented by the artist 1958
GMA 132.3 A

Trees in a Landscape
Etching on paper
14 x 30.3 (paper 24.5 x 36)
Presented by the artist 1958
GMA 132.3 B

Trees in a Landscape
Etching on paper
14 x 30.3 (paper 26 x 39.2)
Presented by the artist 1958
GMA 132.3 C

Bardowie
Etching on paper
6.6 x 16.1 (paper 20.6 x 26.7)
Presented by the artist 1958
GMA 133

Kingsbarns, Fife
Etching on paper
5 x 8.1 (paper 8.9 x 20.3)
Presented by the artist 1958
GMA 134.4 A

Kingsbarns, Fife
Etching on paper
5 x 8.1 (paper 10.5 x 13.2)
Presented by the artist 1958
GMA 134.4 B

Kingsbarns, Fife
Etching on paper
5 x 8.1 (paper 7 x 10)
Presented by the artist 1958
GMA 134.4 C

Kingsbarns, Fife
Etching on paper
5 x 8.1 (paper 8.5 x 13.2)
Presented by the artist 1958
GMA 134.4 D

Castle at the Water's Edge
Etching on paper
11.8 x 18.8 (paper 23.3 x 29.7)
Presented by the artist 1958
GMA 135

Trees by Water
Etching on paper
16 x 13.5 (paper 24 x 18)
Presented by the artist 1958
GMA 136.2 A

Trees by Water
Etching on paper
16 x 13.5 (paper 26.7 x 21.2)
Presented by the artist 1958
GMA 136.2 B

Working on the Land
Etching on paper
17 x 11 (paper 28.5 x 20)
Presented by the artist 1958
GMA 137.2 A

Working on the Land
Etching on paper
19 x 22.2 (paper 26.5 x 34)
Presented by the artist 1958
GMA 137.2 B

Landscape with House and Track
Etching on paper
17 x 27 (paper 29.9 x 31.7)
Presented by the artist 1958
GMA 138

The Training Ship 'Cumberland'
Etching on paper
14.2 x 23.4 (paper 26.5 x 41)
Presented by the artist 1958
GMA 139

Landscape with Road
Etching on paper
21 x 22.8 (paper 24.2 x 28)
Presented by the artist 1958
GMA 140

Three Trees near Water
Etching on paper
16.8 x 22.8 (paper 24 x 30)
Presented by the artist 1958
GMA 141

Church Tower, St Andrews
Etching on paper
21.6 x 15.1 (paper 38 x 25.5)
Presented by the artist 1958
GMA 142

Landscape with Trees
Etching on paper
19.2 x 24.8 (paper 24.5 x 31)
Presented by the artist 1958
GMA 143

Buildings on a Hillside
Etching on paper
17.8 x 13.7 (paper 25.5 x 19)
Presented by the artist 1958
GMA 144

Landscape with River and House
Etching on paper
16 x 20.9 (paper 18 x 25.3)
Presented by the artist 1958
GMA 145

Dunnottar Castle
Etching on paper
20 x 24.6 (paper 25.3 x 31.8)
Presented by the artist 1958
GMA 146

Near Craigallion
Etching on paper
18 x 25.3 (paper 26 x 40.4)
Presented by the artist 1958
GMA 147

Dr Livingstone's Birthplace, Blantyre
Etching on paper
18.6 x 26.5 (paper 26.8 x 41.7)
Presented by the artist 1958
GMA 148

Portrait of Joseph Conrad (after J. Craig Annan)
Etching on paper
22 x 15.7 (paper 29 x 23)
Presented by the artist 1958
GMA 149

Portrait of a Man
Etching on paper
35.6 x 21 (paper 38.3 x 25.3)
Presented by the artist 1958
GMA 150

Sombre Woods
Surface print on paper
42.8 x 20.5 (paper 45.4 x 32.2)
Presented by the artist 1958
GMA 151.3 A

Sombre Woods
Etching on paper
42.2 x 20 (paper 45.7 x 33)
Presented by the artist 1958
GMA 151.3 B

Sombre Woods
Etching on brown paper
42.8 x 20.6 (paper 50.8 x 29.1)
Presented by the artist 1958
GMA 151.3 C

Dog with Dead Chicken
Etching on paper
41.5 x 21.6 (paper 48.3 x 30)
Presented by the artist 1958
GMA 152

Castle by the Sea
Etching on paper
25.4 x 42.9 (paper 37 x 53.2)
Presented by the artist 1958
GMA 153.2 A

Castle by the Sea
Etching on paper
25.4 x 42.9 (paper 38.1 x 52.5)
Presented by the artist 1958
GMA 153.2 B

A Ruined Castle
Etching on paper
29 x 45 (paper 39.4 x 53.2)
Presented by the artist 1958
GMA 154.2 A

A Ruined Castle
Etching on paper
29 x 45.8 (paper 39.8 x 51.5)
Presented by the artist 1958
GMA 154.2 B

Ruin on the Coast
Etching on paper
23.6 x 34.9 (paper 30.2 x 40.5)
Presented by the artist 1958
GMA 155

Trees by Water
Etching on paper
42.7 x 25.5 (paper 48.1 x 31.5)
Presented by the artist 1958
GMA 156

The Sanctuary
Etching on paper
23.8 x 35 (paper 33 x 43.5)
Presented by the artist 1958
GMA 157

Ruined Castle on the Coast
Etching on paper
32.6 x 51.4 (paper 35.5 x 51.4)
Presented by the artist 1958
GMA 158.2 A

Ruined Castle on the Coast
Etching on paper
32.6 x 51.4 (paper 41.7 x 58.2)
Presented by the artist 1958
GMA 158.2 B

Steven Campbell

1953–

*A Man Perceived by a Flea**
1985
Oil on canvas
272 x 242
Purchased 1987
GMA 3049

*Elegant Gestures of the Drowned after Max Ernst**
1986
Oil on canvas
262 x 238.4
Purchased 1987
GMA 3296

Gesturing Hiker
1983
Woodcut on paper (two sheets joined) (20/20)
152.4 x 122.1 (paper 165 x 132.5)
Purchased 1989
GMA 3463

Frontispiece for 'The Scottish Bestiary'
Published 1986
Woodcut on paper (5/50)
56.5 x 39 (paper 76 x 56.5)
Purchased 1987
GMA 3019 A

Lobster
(from 'The Scottish Bestiary')
Published 1986
Woodcut on paper (5/50)
56.5 x 38.9 (paper 76 x 56.5)
Purchased 1987
GMA 3019 T

Hilda Carline

See Hilda SPENCER

Fionna Carlisle

1954–

Theresa's Place*
1984
Acrylic on paper
182 x 197.5
Purchased 1986
GMA 2985

Anita de Caro

1909–

Melody
d 1960
Watercolour, ink and gouache on a double sheet
of ruled music paper
35.3 x 54
Scott Hay Collection: presented 1967
GMA 1028

Anthony Caro

1924–

Table Piece CCCLXXXVIII*
1977
Steel, rusted and varnished
101.5 x 114.5 x 60
Purchased 1981
GMA 2464

Jorge Castillo

1933–

Maria Elena and Olga (2)*
d 1963
Oil on canvas
162 x 130.2
Purchased (Knapping Fund) 1967
GMA 995

Untitled
d 1966
Pen and ink, gouache and chalk on paper
96.8 x 67.2
Presented by Mrs Isabel M. Traill 1979
GMA 2142

Christopher Castle

1946–

Castlerigg – Music of the Stones
d 1978
Colour etching on paper (7/40)
44.5 x 39.1 (paper 75.8 x 56.2)
Purchased 1979
GMA 2109

Patrick Caulfield

1936–

*Parish Church**
d 1967
Oil on canvas
152.3 x 274.4
Purchased 1976
GMA 1536

Vase on Display
d 1970
Screenprint on paper (A.P.)
66 x 55.8 (paper 102.6 x 70.2)
Purchased 1984
GMA 2852

Portrait of a Frenchman
d 1971
Screenprint on paper (70/75)
63.5 x 53.3 (paper 103 x 70.2)
Purchased 1984
GMA 2850

Napkin and Onions
1972
Screenprint on paper (4/72)
86.8 x 66.3 (paper 100.4 x 74.6)
Purchased 1972
GMA 1265

Fig Branch
1972
Screenprint on paper (A.P.)
86.6 x 66.2 (paper 100 x 74.4)
Purchased 1984
GMA 2851

James Caw

1864–1950

Boys Bathing
Watercolour on paper
13.6 x 18.2
Bequeathed by the artist 1950
GMA 1182

Breakers
Pastel on paper
18.1 x 29
Bequeathed by the artist 1950
GMA 1183

A Country Road
Pastel on paper
22.5 x 30
Bequeathed by the artist 1950
GMA 1184

Trees in Blossom
Pastel on paper
31.6 x 22.8
Bequeathed by the artist 1950
GMA 1185

Seascape
Pastel on paper
14.5 x 24
Bequeathed by the artist 1950
GMA 1186

Trees by the Shore
Pastel on paper
17.7 x 28.7
Bequeathed by the artist 1950
GMA 1187

Arran Peaks
Pastel on paper
22.8 x 31.8
Bequeathed by the artist 1950
GMA 1188

Seascape
Watercolour on paper
15.8 x 23.3
Presented by Mrs R. I. Stirling 1965
GMA 1189

César (César Baldaccini)

1921–

*La Pacholette**
1966
Bronze (6/9)
86.4 x 96.5 x 72
Purchased 1970
GMA 1107

Compression*
d 1966
Compressed automobile parts
162 x 68.5 x 66
Purchased 1982
GMA 2505

Lynn Chadwick

1914–

Winged Figures*
1955
Bronze
55.9 x 33.5 x 30.5
Purchased 1960
GMA 761

Maquette for 'Moon of Alabama' II*
1957–58
Iron and composition
55.6 x 46.5 x 32
Purchased 1983
GMA 2764

William Chappell

1908–

Two Figures*
d 1925
Pencil on paper
33 x 25.5
Presented anonymously 1984
GMA 2922

Alan Charlton

1948–

Ten Grey Squares
d 1991
Portfolio of ten screenprints (32/35)
Each 58.4 x 58.4 (paper size)
Purchased 1992
GMA 3623

Ian Cheyne

1895–1955

Hell's Glen*
1928
Colour woodcut on paper (16/20)
25.2 x 29.8 (paper 28 x 32.1)
Purchased 1949
GMA 199

Glen Cluanie
1928
Colour woodcut on paper (17/20)
23.4 x 29.5 (paper 26.2 x 31.6)
Purchased 1949
GMA 205

Glen Cluanie
1928
Colour woodcut on paper
23.4 x 29.5 (paper 30.6 x 35.9)
Purchased 1988
GMA 3319

The Fishermen's Church
1930
Colour woodcut on paper (4/20)
25.5 x 26.7 (paper 31.5 x 31.3)
Purchased 1949
GMA 204

Spanish Hill Road
1931
Colour woodcut on paper (4/20)
22.2 x 29 (paper 25 x 31.5)
Purchased 1949
GMA 202

The Breakwater
1933
Colour woodcut on paper (3/20)
32.6 x 27.9 (paper 35.6 x 30.4)
Purchased 1949
GMA 206

Loch Duich
1934
Colour woodcut on paper
27.5 x 32.9 (paper 31.1 x 35.8)
Purchased 1949
GMA 200

Beeches in Glen Lyon
1937
Colour woodcut on paper
32.3 x 30 (paper 35.5 x 32.8)
Purchased 1949
GMA 203

Normandy Beach
1946
Colour woodcut on paper
24.6 x 27.8 (paper 30.3 x 33)
Purchased 1949
GMA 201

Arran Landscape
1946
Colour woodcut on paper
28.9 x 29.4 (paper 33 x 33.9)
Purchased 1949
GMA 207

Sandro Chia

1946–

Courageous Boys at Work*
d 1981
Oil and oil pastel on canvas
168.2 x 158
Purchased 1982
GMA 2503

Colin Cina

1943–

MH/37*
d 1973
Acrylic on canvas
228.6 x 274.4
Purchased 1974
GMA 1298

George Clausen

1852–1944

Filling Sacks (or *The Barn at Deer's Farm*)
c 1916
Etching and drypoint on paper
28.7 x 23.6 (paper 48.9 x 32.4)
Purchased 1949
GMA 210

The Reconstruction of Belgium
(from the series 'The Great War: Britain's Efforts
and Ideals')
d 1917 (published 1918)
Colour lithograph on paper
68 x 43.3 (paper 82.7 x 56)
Presented by the Ministry of Information 1919
GMA 208

Making Guns: Where the Guns are Made
(from the series 'The Great War: Britain's Efforts
and Ideals')
d 1917 (published 1918)
Lithograph on paper
35.4 x 45.7 (paper 37.8 x 50.5)
Presented by the Ministry of Information 1919
GMA 209 A

Making Guns: The Furnace
(from the series 'The Great War: Britain's Efforts
and Ideals')
d 1917 (published 1918)
Lithograph on paper
46 x 35 (paper 50.6 x 37.8)
Presented by the Ministry of Information 1919
GMA 209 B

Making Guns: The Great Hammer
(from the series 'The Great War: Britain's Efforts
and Ideals')
d 1917 (published 1918)
Lithograph on paper
35 x 45.5 (paper 38 x 50.7)
Presented by the Ministry of Information 1919
GMA 209 C

Making Guns: Turning a Big Gun
(*from the series 'The Great War: Britain's Efforts and Ideals'*)
d 1917 (published 1918)
Lithograph on paper
35 x 46 (paper 38.2 x 51)
Presented by the Ministry of Information 1919
GMA 209 D

Making Guns: The Radial Crane
(*from the series 'The Great War: Britain's Efforts and Ideals'*)
d 1917 (published 1918)
Lithograph on paper
35.3 x 46 (paper 40.5 x 50.6)
Presented by the Ministry of Information 1919
GMA 209 E

Making Guns: Lifting an Inner Tube
(*from the series 'The Great War: Britain's Efforts and Ideals'*)
d 1917 (published 1918)
Lithograph on paper
46 x 35.4 (paper 50.7 x 38)
Presented by the Ministry of Information 1919
GMA 209 F

Prunella Clough

1919–

*Yard at Night**
1959
Oil on canvas
61 x 91.5
Purchased 1975
GMA 1502

*Electrical Landscape**
1960
Oil on canvas
162 x 152.8
Purchased 1976
GMA 1535

*Mesh II**
1981
Oil on canvas
117 x 129.5
Purchased 1983
GMA 2744

Bernard Cohen

1933–

No. 3
d 1971
Screenprint on paper (6/50)
72.2 x 90.4 (paper size)
Purchased 1972
GMA 1266

Harold Cohen

1928–

*Conclave**
d 1963
Oil, tempera and pencil on canvas
249.2 x 295.3
Purchased 1975
GMA 1515

Richard Hamilton
d 1967
Screenprint on paper (9/40)
64.8 x 73.5 (paper 68.7 x 77.4)
Purchased 1984
GMA 2853 A

Richard I
d 1967
Screenprint on paper (9/40)
64.8 x 73.5 (paper 68.7 x 77.4)
Purchased 1984
GMA 2853 B

Richard II
d 1967
Screenprint on paper (9/40)
64.8 x 73.5 (paper 68.7 x 77.4)
Purchased 1984
GMA 2853 C

Richard III
d 1967
Screenprint on paper (9/40)
64.8 x 73.5 (paper 68.7 x 77.4)
Purchased 1984
GMA 2853 D

Richard IV
d 1967
Screenprint on paper (9/40)
64.8 x 73.5 (paper 68.7 x 77.5)
Purchased 1984
GMA 2853 E

Richard V
d 1967
Screenprint on paper (9/40)
64.8 x 73.5 (paper 68.7 x 77.4)
Purchased 1984
GMA 2853 F

Peter Coker

1926–

*Forest VIII**
1959
Oil on canvas
195 x 129.5
Purchased 1988
GMA 3417

Robert Colquhoun

1914–62

Study of a Male Nude
c 1937–38
Black chalk on paper
52.7 x 38
Purchased 1982
GMA 2476

Self-Portrait
c 1939–40
Pencil on paper
26.7 x 20.3
Purchased 1979
GMA 2110

Sacha
c 1939–40
Pencil on paper
30.2 x 20.8
Purchased 1979
GMA 2111

*The Dubliners**
1946
Oil on canvas
76.2 x 61
Purchased (Knapping Fund) 1963
GMA 842

*The Spectators**
d 1947
Watercolour on paper
73.6 x 55
Purchased 1983
GMA 2746

Man and Goat
d 1948
Carbon drawing on paper
55.8 x 45
Purchased 1983
GMA 2782

Figure on Horseback
c 1949 [?]
Monotype (black and orange ink) on paper
67.4 x 51.7
Purchased 1981
GMA 2295

Two Women and a Crab
d 1949
Carbon drawing on paper
36.8 x 52.5
Purchased 1983
GMA 2783

Siena Palio
d 1949
Monotype (black ink) on paper
46.6 x 56.6
Purchased 1983
GMA 2785

Head of a Woman
d 1949
Monotype (black, red and blue ink) on paper
47.6 x 41.1
Purchased 1983
GMA 2786

Man and Pig
d 1952
Carbon drawing on paper
46.2 x 34.3
Purchased 1980
GMA 2153

Bearded Man and Pig
d 1952
Carbon drawing on paper
47.5 x 36 (paper 57.2 x 44.5)
Purchased 1983
GMA 2781

Two Figures
c 1952
Carbon drawing with splashed ink on paper
41.9 x 32.2
Purchased 1983
GMA 2784

*Figures in a Farmyard**
d 1953
Oil on canvas
185.4 x 143.5
Purchased 1974
GMA 1306

Lear's Knight
(*Costume Design for 'King Lear'*)
1953
Gouache, watercolour and pencil on paper
38.2 x 21.7
Purchased 1974
GMA 1319

Edgar in Battle Dress
(*Costume Design for 'King Lear'*)*
d 1953
Gouache and pencil on paper
33.2 x 20.6
Presented by the Rev. Professor Moelwyn
Merchant 1990
GMA 3573

Regan in Battle Helmet, Coronet and Travel Cloak
(*Costume Design for 'King Lear'*)
d 1953
Gouache, gold paint and pencil on paper
37.2 x 20.6
Presented by the Rev. Professor Moelwyn
Merchant 1990
GMA 3574

Regan in Court Robe and Basic Costume
(*Costume Design for 'King Lear'*)
d 1953
Gouache, gold paint and pencil on paper
44.1 x 30.1
Presented by the Rev. Professor Moelwyn
Merchant 1990
GMA 3575

King Lear I: in the Palace
(*Costume Design for 'King Lear'*)
1953
Gouache, gold paint and pencil on paper
51 x 34
Purchased 1991
GMA 3591

Man with a Dead Bird
d 1954
Monotype (black ink) on paper
72 x 53
Purchased 1983
GMA 2787

Man at Table
c 1959
Colour monotype on paper
103.7 x 70
Purchased 1989
GMA 3453

Woman and Goat
1948
Colour lithograph on paper
39.1 x 28.1 (paper 51.3 x 33.3)
Purchased 1987
GMA 3310

Masked Figures and Horse
1953
Colour lithograph on paper
48.9 x 34.4 (paper 66.5 x 51)
Purchased 1987
GMA 3311

Head of Absalom
1959
Colour lithograph on paper (15/50)
53.4 x 40.6 (paper 79.5 x 67)
Purchased 1960
GMA 744

See also Robert COLQUHOUN and Robert MACBRYDE

Robert Colquhoun and Robert MacBryde

Colquhoun 1914–62, MacBryde 1913–66

Sword Dancer
(Costume Design for 'Donald of the Burthens')
1951
Carbon drawing and gouache on paper
50 x 37.4
Purchased 1974
GMA 1320

Peasant Woman
(Costume Design for 'Donald of the Burthens')
1951
Carbon drawing, ink and gouache on paper
38.2 x 27.1
Purchased 1974
GMA 1321

Calum Colvin

1961–

*Narcissus**
1987
Colour photograph (cibachrome print)
104 x 82.5
Purchased 1987
GMA 3047

Commonwealth Print Portfolio

Published 1978

See: Jacob AFOLABI, Dinny JAMPIJIMPA, Allen JONES, Walter JULE, KENOJUAK, Liu KUO-SUNG, Bea MADDOCK, William PEREHUDOFF, Barrington WATSON

Philip Connard

1875–1958

The Thames
Oil on canvas-board
17.5 x 25.3
Bequeathed by Dr R. A. Lillie 1977
GMA 1894

Stephen Conroy

1964–

*Healing of a Lunatic Boy**
1986
Oil on canvas
122 x 91.4
Purchased 1987
GMA 3039

*The Enthusiasts**
1987
Charcoal, pastel, gouache and varnish on paper
74.6 x 80.4 (paper size)
Purchased 1987
GMA 3040

John Kingsley Cook

1911–

Dilapidations No. 3: The City Church 1945
d 1946
Wood engraving on paper
23.2 x 15.5 (paper 33.6 x 24.8)
Purchased 1983
GMA 2789

Dilapidations No. 1: The Gutted Warehouse 1945
d 1946
Wood engraving on paper
22.8 x 15.2 (paper 33.4 x 24.4)
Purchased 1983
GMA 2790

Thomas Joshua Cooper

1946–

A Premonitional Work
1) *Guardians Gathering and Menacing,*
Gartocharn, Dunbartonshire, Scotland, 1983;
2) *Veiling Mask – An Indication, Patrick's Point,*
Humboldt County, California, 1981;
3) *Guardian Ghosting (Hupa Tribal Territory),*
Trinity River, Humboldt County, California,
1980
1980–83
Three black and white photographs (gelatin silver
prints)
Each 40.6 x 58
Purchased 1983
GMA 2798

A Quality of Dancing
1984
Three black and white photographs (gelatin silver
prints)
Each 39.7 x 57
Purchased 1986
GMA 2976

John Copley

1875–1950

A Judge of the Criminal Court [W 32]
1910
Colour lithograph on paper
40 x 46 (paper 48.5 x 63)
Bequeathed by Mr Kenneth Sanderson 1943
GMA 214

Musicians No. 1 [W 38]
1910
Lithograph on paper
20 x 44.7 (paper 32.9 x 52.7)
Purchased 1949
GMA 237

Nemi – Priests of the Sacred Grove [W 85]
1913
Lithograph on paper
56.5 x 41.5 (image and paper size)
Purchased 1949
GMA 215

The Sick King [W 105]
1914
Lithograph on paper (8/20)
33 x 33 (paper 40.5 x 39.2)
Purchased 1949
GMA 228

Le Monde où l'on s'amuse [W 108]*
1914
Lithograph on paper (4/25)
23.4 x 29 (paper 38.7 x 47.4)
Bequeathed by Mr Kenneth Sanderson 1943
GMA 211 A

Le Monde où l'on s'amuse [W 108]
1914
Lithograph on paper (8/20)
23.4 x 29 (paper 28.8 x 36.2)
Purchased 1949
GMA 211 B

Recruits [W 113]
1915
Lithograph on paper
36 x 41.8 (paper 39./ x 50.2)
Purchased 1949
GMA 250

The Pianist [W 138]
1916
Lithograph on paper
27.1 x 34.7 (paper 33.2 x 43.8)
Purchased 1949
GMA 246

Bearers (first version) [WS 141]
1917
Lithograph on paper
17.3 x 22.8 (paper 27.7 x 39.1)
Purchased 1949
GMA 235

Women Mourning [W 143]
1917
Lithograph on paper
27.3 x 36.2 (paper 32.2 x 42.2)
Purchased 1949
GMA 247

Three Ladies at the Opera [W 144]
1917
Lithograph on paper
47.5 x 24.5 (paper 53.6 x 38)
Bequeathed by Mr Kenneth Sanderson 1943
GMA 213 A

Three Ladies at the Opera [W 144]
1917
Lithograph on paper (third state)
47.5 x 24.5 (paper 54 x 34.8)
Purchased 1949
GMA 213 B

Tennis Players [W 149]
1918
Lithograph on paper
23.9 x 17.5 (paper 40.8 x 27.8)
Purchased 1949
GMA 227

Five Girls [W 150]
1918
Lithograph on paper
27.3 x 27.2 (paper 34.3 x 39.2)
Purchased 1949
GMA 240

Due Creature [W 157]
1919
Lithograph on paper
14.7 x 9.1 (paper 27 x 19)
Purchased 1949
GMA 225

Madonna Lavoratice [W 159]
1919
Lithograph on paper
16.8 x 14 (paper 40 x 29)
Purchased 1949
GMA 226

Maschio e Bambino Correnti [W 160]
1919
Lithograph on paper
22.2 x 16.5 (paper 29 x 36.2)
Purchased 1949
GMA 220

Madonna Giacente [W 164]
1919
Lithograph on paper
12.3 x 25.2 (paper 23.6 x 34.5)
Purchased 1949
GMA 222

Madonna col Figlio [W 165]
1919
Lithograph on paper
17.7 x 11.2 (paper 40.5 x 28)
Purchased 1949
GMA 223

Madonna ed Altra Donna [W 167]
1920
Lithograph on paper
14.1 x 22.8 (paper 27.2 x 39)
Purchased 1949
GMA 248

Madonna Nutrice [W 170]
1920
Lithograph on paper
13.8 x 15.2 (paper 33 x 24.4)
Purchased 1949
GMA 221

Al Piedo di Madonna [W 173]
1920
Lithograph on paper
29 x 13 (paper 40.8 x 24.8)
Purchased 1949
GMA 230

Spectators at a Tragic Play [W 178]
1920
Lithograph on paper
27.5 x 35.5 (paper 37.5 x 41.4)
Purchased 1949
GMA 243

Ladies at a Comedy [W 182]
1922
Lithograph on paper
27.2 x 34.5 (paper 34.5 x 40.5)
Purchased 1949
GMA 241

Men Lifting a Marble Slab [W 187]
1922
Lithograph on paper
27.4 x 35.4 (paper 33.4 x 40.8)
Purchased 1949
GMA 244

Mary and Elizabeth [W 190]
1923
Lithograph on paper
21.5 x 25.1 (paper 31.2 x 30.4)
Purchased 1949
GMA 224

Fog [W 191]
1923
Lithograph on paper
35 x 27.5 (paper 49.5 x 37.4)
Purchased 1949
GMA 239

The Scribes Disputing with Jesus [W 192]
1923
Lithograph on paper
33.6 x 45.5 (paper 43.2 x 58.9)
Purchased 1949
GMA 252

Precious Ointment [W 193]
1923
Lithograph on paper
34.6 x 30.6 (paper 45.6 x 38.2)
Purchased 1949
GMA 245

Shorn Sheep [W 194]
1923
Lithograph on paper
19 x 29 (paper 25.6 x 38.3)
Purchased 1949
GMA 242

Jesus Raised on the Cross [WS 197]
1924
Lithograph on paper
41 x 23.4 (paper 52 x 35.5)
Purchased 1949
GMA 231

Jesus Taken from the Cross [WS 198]
1924
Lithograph on paper
49.5 x 28.6 (paper 55 x 38.3)
Purchased 1949
GMA 216

Jesus and John [WS 199]
1924
Lithograph on paper
44.1 x 26.4 (paper 52.2 x 35.4)
Purchased 1949
GMA 233

Jesus Carried to the Tomb [W 200]
1924
Lithograph on paper
25.2 x 32.5 (paper 31 x 39.8)
Bequeathed by Mr Kenneth Sanderson 1943
GMA 212 A

Jesus Carried to the Tomb [W 200]
1924
Lithograph on paper
25.2 x 32.5 (paper 35.5 x 43.5)
Purchased 1949
GMA 212 B

The Horse Rake [W 203]
1924
Lithograph on paper
25 x 32.4 (paper 33.8 x 45.2)
Purchased 1949
GMA 238 A

The Horse Rake [W 203]
1924
Lithograph on paper (first state)
25 x 32.4 (paper 26.5 x 40)
Purchased 1949
GMA 238 B

Battastina and Carnations [C 25]
1927
Etching on paper
24 x 21.8 (paper 37.5 x 29.6)
Purchased 1949
GMA 218

Alassio [c 30]
1927
Etching on paper
30 x 21.6 (paper 38.7 x 29.9)
Bequeathed by Mr George Liston-Foulis 1958
GMA 253

Sunbathers, Alassio [ws 221]
1928
Lithograph on paper
21.6 x 31 (paper 34 x 42.2)
Purchased 1949
GMA 232

Gethsemane [ws 226]
1928
Lithograph on paper
19.5 x 21.5 (paper 40 x 29)
Purchased 1949
GMA 236 A

Gethsemane [ws 226]
1928
Lithograph on paper
19.5 x 21.5 (paper 39 x 33.7)
Purchased 1949
GMA 236 B

Jesus Nailed to the Cross [ws 227]
1928
Lithograph on paper
23.7 x 32.7 (paper 32.6 x 44)
Purchased 1949
GMA 234

Seen from an Omnibus [w 230]
1931
Lithograph on paper
27.6 x 16.8 (paper 45.2 x 29.2)
Purchased 1949
GMA 229

Lac Léman [ws 242]
1935
Lithograph on paper
34.5 x 52.8 (paper 43 x 58.2)
Purchased 1949
GMA 251

Racehorses [c 70]
1936
Etching on paper
27 x 22.6 (paper 38.2 x 26.8)
Purchased 1949
GMA 219

Polo Players [c 83]
1939
Etching on paper
37.3 x 27.7 (paper 42.8 x 34.2)
Purchased 1949
GMA 217

Quartet (second version) [c 89]
1939
Etching on paper
27.1 x 32.6 (paper 31.7 x 41.4)
Purchased 1949
GMA 249

[w refers to the catalogue raisonné of Copley's lithographs by Harold Wright (Chicago 1924); ws to the unpublished supplement; and c to Copley's unpublished list of his own etchings]

Lovis Corinth

1858–1925

Der Ritter [*The Knight*]*
1914
Drypoint on paper
14.7 x 10.8 (paper 29.3 x 23.1)
Presented by Mr Keith Andrews 1963
GMA 1197

Selbstbildnis an der Staffelei [*Self-Portrait at the Easel*]
1918
Drypoint on paper
24.6 x 16.1 (paper 34.2 x 23.7)
Purchased 1987
GMA 3315

Belle-Mère [*Mother-in-law*]
1920
Drypoint on paper
13.7 x 10.8 (paper 31.9 x 20.7)
Purchased 1987
GMA 3316

Kreuzigung [Crucifixion]
(Study for the Altarpiece in Tölz)
1921–22
Drypoint on paper
30 x 23.6 (paper 44.7 x 37.4)
Purchased 1987
GMA 3317

Totenklage [Pietà]
1921–22
Drypoint on paper
29 x 23 (paper 54 x 37.5)
Purchased 1987
GMA 3318

Sister Mary Corita

See Sister Mary Corita KENT

James Cosgrove

1939–

Number 4
c 1976
Monotype on paper
42.2 x 41.4 (paper size)
Purchased 1976
GMA 1543

Brigitte Coudrain

1934–

Sucrier et pavot [Sugar Bowl and Poppy]
1964
Colour aquatint and etching on paper (2/50)
39.3 x 44.8 (paper 50 x 65.6)
Purchased 1966
GMA 987

James Cowie

1886–1956

*Male Student (Study for 'A Portrait Group')**
c 1932–33
Coloured chalk and pencil on paper
56 x 33.6
Purchased 1975
GMA 1326

*Student and Plaster Cast**
c 1933
Black chalk on paper
50.5 x 36.8
Purchased 1975
GMA 1328

*Head of a Girl (Study for 'Falling Leaves')**
c 1933–34
Coloured chalk and pencil on paper
17.4 x 13.5
Purchased 1984
GMA 2815

*A Portrait Group**
1933 / c 1940
Oil on canvas
101.6 x 127.3
Purchased 1975
GMA 1325

*Playground, Bellshill**
c 1934
Pencil on paper
21.6 x 26.4
Purchased 1975
GMA 1331

Bellshill Art Room
c 1934
Black chalk and watercolour on paper
37.7 x 52.8
Bequeathed by Dr R. A. Lillie 1977
GMA 1895

Girl Lying Down (Study for 'Noon')
c 1938
Coloured chalk on brown paper
32.9 x 54.9
Purchased 1975
GMA 1327

*Still Life with Jug**
1940s
Pencil on paper
25.7 x 32.8 (paper 29.3 x 34.2)
Purchased 1975
GMA 1329

Studio Still Life
1940s
Black and white chalk on paper
25.8 x 20.5 (paper 40.2 x 32.9)
Purchased 1975
GMA 1330

*Composition**
1947
Oil on wood
46.3 x 45.5
Bequeathed by Sir William Oliphant Hutchison
1970
GMA 1167

*Study for a Backcloth for 'The Pirates
of Penzance'*
Pencil and watercolour on paper squared
for transfer
18.9 x 25.4
Bequeathed by Sir Alexander Maitland 1965
GMA 942

Edward Gordon Craig

1872–1966

*Waiting for 'The Marchioness'**
1899
Woodcut on paper laid on card
18.3 x 11.8 (card 30.9 x 23.3)
Purchased 1949
GMA 254

Wittenberg
d 1901
Woodcut on Japanese tissue paper
15 x 13.3 (paper 25.3 x 17.3)
Purchased 1949
GMA 255

Hecuba
(*a 'Black Figure'*)
d 1908
Woodcut on paper
39 x 26.9 (paper size)
Purchased 1949
GMA 256

Susan F. Crawford

1865–1918

Drummond Castle, Perthshire
c 1908
Etching on paper
27.8 x 14.8 (paper 37.2 x 24.3)
Purchased 1992
GMA 3658

John Craxton

1922–

*Man in a Garden**
d 1942
Pen and ink and ink wash on paper
44.4 x 54.5
Presented by the Patrons of the National Galleries
of Scotland 1987
GMA 3307

*Welsh Estuary Foreshore**
1943
Oil on burlap
112.3 x 180.3
Purchased 1972
GMA 1257

Landscape with the Elements
(*Cartoon for 'The Four Seasons' Tapestry*)*
1973–75
Tempera on canvas
204.5 x 262
Purchased 1985
GMA 2956

A. Pender Crichton

The Fair
d 1927
Wood engraving on paper
17.9 x 22.8 (paper 20.5 x 26.7)
Purchased 1949
GMA 257

William Crosbie

1915–

Heart Knife*
d 1934
Oil on canvas
60.3 x 43
Purchased 1978
GMA 1714

Study I
(An Exercise set by Léger)
c 1935
Gouache and watercolour on grey paper
37.6 x 28.4
Purchased 1978
GMA 2023

Recapitulation*
c 1940
Watercolour and ink on paper
38.1 x 28.5
Purchased 1989
GMA 3448

In Memoriam*
c 1948–50
Oil on canvas
122 x 169.4
Purchased 1980
GMA 2218

Victoria Crowe

1945–

Sheep and Fence
d 1976
Pencil, pen and ink and oil on paper
17.7 x 25.2
Bequeathed by Dr R. A. Lillie 1977
GMA 1896

William Crozier

1897–1930

Italian Landscape*
c 1927
Oil on plywood
45.2 x 60
Purchased 1989
GMA 3473

Study for 'Edinburgh (from Salisbury Crags)'*
c 1927
Oil on paper, laid on plywood
25.6 x 31.2
Purchased 1976
GMA 1592

Edinburgh (from Salisbury Crags)*
c 1927
Oil on canvas
71.1 x 91.5
Purchased 1942
GMA 7

Edinburgh in Snow*
c 1928
Oil on canvas
71.3 x 91.5
Presented by Miss Anna G. Blair in memory
of Mr R. K. Blair 1943
GMA 8

Tuscan Landscape
c 1930
Oil on canvas
41.1 x 46.2
Bequeathed by Miss Anna G. Blair 1952
GMA 9

William Crozier

1930–

Estuary, Wivenhoe, Essex
1959
Oil on paper
55.2 x 49.3
Presented anonymously 1984
GMA 2919

Burning Field, Essex*
d 1960
Oil on hardboard
91.4 x 76.9
Purchased (Gulbenkian UK Trust Fund) 1962
GMA 816

Trees by the Sea*
1985
Acrylic on canvas
106.5 x 114
Purchased 1985
GMA 2959

James M. Cumming

1922–91

Grey Kenneth
d 1960
Gouache on paper
41 x 49.2
Scott Hay Collection: presented 1967
GMA 1030

The Lewis Poacher*
d 1960
Gouache, pencil and collage on paper
76 x 50.8
Scott Hay Collection: presented 1967
GMA 1031

Weaving
c 1960
Oil on canvas
76.2 x 61
Scott Hay Collection: presented 1967
GMA 1034

The Callanish Man
1961
Oil on canvas
76.2 x 101.6
Scott Hay Collection: presented 1967
GMA 1032

Garry na-hine Women
c 1962
Oil on canvas
101.6 x 76.2
Scott Hay Collection: presented 1967
GMA 1033

Croft Table with Oil Lamp and Chimney
c 1963
Oil on canvas
71 x 91.5
Scott Hay Collection: presented 1967
GMA 1029

Ken Currie

1960–

Glasgow Triptych*
 1) *Template of the Future*
 2) *The Apprentices*
 3) *Young Glasgow Communists*
1986
Oil on canvas (three parts)
214 x 272.3; 217.6 x 277.8; 207 x 278.1
Purchased 1987
GMA 3012 A, B & C

Story from Glasgow
Published 1989
Portfolio of 97 linocuts (9/45)
Each image approx. 29 x 25 (paper 43 x 32.2)
Purchased 1990
GMA 3553

The Regime
d 1991
Etching on paper (6/40)
30.7 x 20.8 (paper 68.6 x 50.7)
Purchased 1992
GMA 3643

Rembrandt's Carcass
d 1991
Etching on paper (27/40)
41.6 x 30.6 (paper 68.6 x 50.7)
Purchased 1992
GMA 3644

The Age of Uncertainty
d 1992
Etching on paper (4/40)
29.8 x 41.9 (paper 50.7 x 68.6)
Purchased 1992
GMA 3645

Stanley Cursiter

1887–1976

The Regatta*
1913
Oil on canvas
50.4 x 60.8
Purchased 1987
GMA 3034

The Kame of Hoy*
d 1950
Oil on canvas
86.5 x 101.8
Bequeathed by Mr Thomas Godfrey Kirkness
1982
GMA 2711

The Lighthouse
d 1913
Lithograph on paper
39.1 x 25.1 (paper 45.7 x 31.6)
Purchased 1990
GMA 3565

Eric Fitch Daglish

1894–1964

Blossom and Bird Song
Wood engraving on paper
12.7 x 9.6 (paper 16.1 x 13.3)
Purchased 1949
GMA 258

Horia Damian

1922–

Untitled
d 1976
Lithograph on paper (A.P.)
70.6 x 102 (paper size)
Purchased 1977
GMA 1695

Untitled
d 1976
Lithograph on paper (A.P.)
70.8 x 101.8 (paper size)
Purchased 1977
GMA 1696

Allan d'Arcangelo

1930–

Landscape II
(from the portfolio 'Eleven Pop Artists, vol. II')
1965
Screenprint on vinyl
76.2 x 60.9 (vinyl sheet size)
Purchased 1975
GMA 1338

Michael Davey

1948–

Brogar Views
c 1976
Two dyeline prints on paper (A.P.)
Each 28.6 x 35.9 (paper 32.8 x 38)
Purchased 1976
GMA 1547

Line Work 1–9
1978
Suite of nine black and white photographs
Each 35.6 x 45.7 (paper 40.7 x 50.8)
Purchased 1978
GMA 2014

Alan Davie

1920–

Waving Machine
d 1948
Monotype on paper
24.9 x 20
Purchased 1993
GMA 3707

*Seascape Venice No. I**
d 1948
Monotype on paper
20.1 x 25.2
Purchased 1993
GMA 3708

Seascape Venice No. II
d 1948
Monotype on paper
20.4 x 24.6
Purchased 1993
GMA 3709

Spirit Dancer
d 1948
Monotype on paper
25 x 20
Purchased 1993
GMA 3710

The Flower that Flew to the Moon
d 1948
Monotype on paper
33.5 x 25
Purchased 1993
GMA 3711

Tobias and the Fish
d 1948
Monotype on paper
37 x 32.2
Purchased 1993
GMA 3712

*Jingling Space**
d 1950
Oil on masonite
122 x 152.5
Purchased (Knapping Fund) 1987
GMA 3308

*Seascape Erotic**
d 1955
Oil on masonite
160 x 241
Purchased 1968
GMA 1084

*Woman Bewitched by the Moon No. 2**
d 1956
Oil on hardboard
152.8 x 122
Purchased (Knapping Fund) 1987
GMA 3309

*The Horse that has Visions of Immortality No. 2**
d 1963
Oil on canvas
213.3 x 172.7
Purchased 1964
GMA 882

*Hallucination with a Red Headed Parrot**
d 1984
Oil on canvas
172.5 x 214
Presented by the artist 1988
GMA 3416

Celtic Dreamboat II
d 1965
Colour lithograph on paper (23/75)
51.3 x 76.8 (paper 57.2 x 80.6)
Purchased 1970
GMA 1118

Magic Pictures
(poster for an exhibition at The Scottish Gallery, Edinburgh)
d 1979
Colour lithograph on paper (5/65)
77.5 x 57
Presented by The Scottish Gallery 1980
GMA 2189

Magic Reader
1988
Portfolio of eighteen lithographs (27/45)
42.6 x 34.8 (paper size)
Purchased 1989
GMA 3465

Magic Reader
1988
Book of eighteen lithographs (21/50)
42.7 x 35.5 (page size)
Presented by Mr Charles Booth-Clibborn 1992
GMA 3668

Magic Circles
(*from 'The Haymarket Print Suite'*)
d 1989 (published 1990)
Screenprint on paper
152 x 101 (paper 157 x 107)
Purchased 1990
GMA 3567

Anthony Davies

1947–

Peter Grimes
d 1981
Suite of 25 etchings with aquatint on paper (A.P.)
Each 19.5 x 22.7 (paper 52 x 39)
Purchased 1982
GMA 2477

Bevan Davies

1941–

Scotland 1979
1979
Boxed set of ten black and white photographs
(2/20)
Each approximately 31.7 x 39.6 (paper 35.6 x 43)
Purchased 1981
GMA 2305

John Davies

1946–

*For the Last Time**
1970–72
Mixed media
Four figures, maximum height of each 181; 137;
82; 75
Purchased 1989
GMA 3450

Lawrence Daws

1927–

Tetraktys IV
d 1961
Gouache and black chalk on paper
60.3 x 76.2
Purchased 1962
GMA 810

Robert Delaunay

1885–1941

*L'Equipe de Cardiff [The Cardiff Team]**
1922–23
Oil and tempera on canvas
146.8 x 114.2
Purchased 1985
GMA 2942

Sonia Delaunay

1885–1979

*La Prose du transsibérien et de la petite Jehanne
de France [Trans-Siberian Prose]**
(with Blaise Cendrars)
d 1913
Pochoir and text on paper in hand-coloured
leather folder (no. 26); with separate pochoir
announcement of the edition
Open 199 x 35.5; announcement 9.1 x 34
Purchased 1980
GMA 2199

Sans titre [Untitled]
1960s
Colour etching and pochoir on paper
20 x 15.7 (paper 24.7 x 20.5)
Presented anonymously in memory of Terence
Rattigan 1984
GMA 2923

Richard Demarco

1930–

Arthur's Seat and Calton Hill from the Royal Botanic Garden
d 1967
Pen and ink, pencil and watercolour on paper
27.9 x 38
Purchased 1969
GMA 1094

'The Marques' Furling Sail
d 1979
Pen and ink on paper with paper additions
41.9 x 29.5
Purchased 1980
GMA 2240

'The Marques' Setting Sail
d 1979
Pen and ink on paper with paper additions
41.9 x 29.5
Purchased 1980
GMA 2241

'The Marques' under Full Sail
d 1979
Pen and ink on paper with paper additions
41.9 x 29.5
Purchased 1980
GMA 2242

Maurice Denis

1870–1943

Maternité à la fenêtre ouverte [*Maternity and Open Window*]
1926
Lithograph on paper (25/25)
27.7 x 19.8 (paper 48.5 x 32.3)
Purchased 1957
GMA 1020

Saint François d'Assise [*Saint Francis of Assisi*]
1926
Lithograph on paper (25/25)
24 x 19.5 (paper 50.7 x 32.5)
Purchased 1957
GMA 1021

Robyn Denny

1930–

*Glass 2 (From There)**
1971
Oil on canvas
274.3 x 365.8
Purchased 1975
GMA 1516

Paradise Suite
d 1969
Five screenprints on paper (A, 3/75; B, 3/75; C, 64/75; D, 8/75; E, 71/75)
Each 84.4 x 65.5 (image and paper size)
Purchased 1984
GMA 2854 A–E

André Derain

1880–1954

*Collioure**
1905
Oil on canvas
60.2 x 73.5
Purchased 1973
GMA 1280

George Devlin

1937–

Sea-edge Grasses II
c 1964
Chalk, watercolour and gouache on card
30.4 x 26.8
Purchased 1965
GMA 905

Jim Dine

1935–

Throat
(*from the portfolio 'Eleven Pop Artists, vol. II'*)
1965
Screenprint on paper (no. XXIV)
76.2 x 60.9 (image and paper size)
Purchased 1975
GMA 1332

A Tool Box
d 1966
Box of ten screenprints with collage on coloured
papers and acetate
Each 60.5 x 48 (image and paper size)
Purchased 1978
GMA 2072

Kenneth Dingwall

1938–

Grey Surface*
d 1979
Acrylic on canvas
160 x 213.5
Purchased 1980
GMA 2135

Otto Dix

1891 1969

Mädchen auf Fell [Nude Girl on a Fur]*
d 1932
Tempera and oil on canvas laid on wood
98.5 x 142.8
Purchased 1980
GMA 2195

Kartenspieler [Cardplayers]*
1920
Drypoint on paper (4/11)
32.9 x 28.3 (paper 46 x 32.3)
Purchased 1985
GMA 2960

J. B. Neumann
d 1922
Etching and drypoint on paper (13/50)
29.5 x 24 (paper 47.8 x 40.5)
Purchased 1982
GMA 2709

*Trichterfeld bei Dontrien von Leuchtkugeln
erhellt [Craterfield near Dontrien Lit by Flares]*
Published 1924
Etching on paper (26/70)
19.8 x 26.1 (paper 35.5 x 47.8)
Purchased 1978
GMA 2031

*Gastote (Templeux-la-Fosse, August 1916)
[Soldiers Killed by Gas (Templeux-la-Fosse,
August 1916)]**
Published 1924
Etching on paper
19.6 x 29.1 (paper 33.8 x 42.9)
Purchased 1978
GMA 2032

*Selbstbildnis im Profil beim Malen [Self-Portrait
in Profile, Painting]*
d 1966
Lithographic poster
53 x 51 (paper 80.4 x 57.4)
Presented anonymously
GMA 996

James Dixon

1887–?

The 'Wild Goose'
d 1946 [?]
Oil and pencil on paper laid on cardboard
38 x 60.5
Purchased (Knapping Fund) 1966
GMA 988

Michael Docherty

1947–

*An Object Fixed in Time**
d 1977
Wood and plaster
54.5 x 40.5 x 5.7
Purchased 1978
GMA 2013

Francis Dodd

1874–1949

St Mary-le-Strand, with Sky
1916
Etching and drypoint on paper
35.1 x 26.1 (paper 46 x 29)
Bequeathed by Mr George Liston-Foulis 1958
GMA 259

Marion Dorn

1899–1964

Sketchbook of Designs for Carpets and Papers
d 1938–39
Gouache and pencil on paper
25.3 x 36
Purchased 1981
GMA 2323

Pat Douthwaite

1939–

*The End of the World**
1970
Oil on canvas (triptych)
Each canvas 183 x 122
Purchased 1970
GMA 1117

*Death of Amy Johnson**
d 1976
Oil on canvas
152.5 x 152.5
Purchased 1977
GMA 1645

Woman in a Landscape
1974
Lithograph on paper (2/10)
41.4 x 62.2 (paper 60 x 83.5)
Purchased 1975
GMA 1343

The Sneer
d 1974
Lithograph on paper (4/10)
50.8 x 38.1 (paper 76 x 50.5)
Purchased 1975
GMA 1344

Japanese Lady with a Locust
1974
Lithograph on paper (3/10)
50.7 x 38.1 (paper 74 x 50.6)
Purchased 1975
GMA 1345

Nude in a Landscape
1974
Lithograph on paper (5/10)
60.2 x 45.4 (paper 76 x 56.2)
Purchased 1975
GMA 1346

Screaming Skeleton
d 1974
Lithograph on paper (7/10)
40.7 x 65.7 (paper 55.1 x 80.7)
Purchased 1975
GMA 1347

Jean Dubuffet

1901–85

*Villa sur la route [Villa by the Road]**
d 1957
Oil on canvas
81.3 x 100.3
Purchased (Knapping Fund) 1963
GMA 830

*Dispositif aux vaisselles [Dishwasher]**
d 1965
Vinyl on paper laid on canvas
99.5 x 69
Purchased 1980
GMA 2151

Marcel Duchamp

1887–1968

*La Boîte-en-valise [Box in a Suitcase]**
1935–41
Leather-covered case containing miniature
replicas and photographs of Duchamp's works
(De-luxe edition no. 2/20)
10 x 38 x 40.5 (closed)
Presented anonymously 1989
GMA 3472

Kenneth Duffy

1946–

Canyon
1979
Lithograph on paper (3/9)
46.5 x 31.2 (paper 52.4 x 35.7)
Purchased 1981
GMA 2315

Charles Dufresne

1876–1938

*L'Enlèvement d'Europe [The Rape of Europa]**
1924
Oil on paper laid on canvas
167.6 x 190.5
Presented by Mr A. J. McNeill Reid 1960
GMA 745

Edmund Dulac

1882–1953

Poland, a Nation
(from the series 'The Great War: Britain's Efforts
and Ideals')
d 1917 (published 1918)
Colour lithograph on paper
69.6 x 44.8 (paper 80.5 x 51)
Presented by the Ministry of Information 1919
GMA 3635

Victor Dupont

1875–

L'Attelage [Harnessed Horse]
Etching on paper
16.1 x 20 (paper 26.9 x 31.4)
Purchased 1949
GMA 260

Graham Durward

1956–

*The Incurable Romantic**
d 1983
Gouache on paper (two sheets joined)
153 x 247.5
Purchased 1983
GMA 2796

The Forest after Thinning
1983–85
Book of 32 etchings
25.4 x 27.5 (paper size)
Purchased 1987
GMA 3031

Joan Eardley

1921–63

Italian Peasant Sitting on the Ground
1948–49
Black chalk on paper laid on card
52.6 x 48.7
Purchased 1980
GMA 2224

Seine Boat*
c 1949
Oil on canvas
61.5 x 51
George and Isobel Neillands Collection: presented
1988
GMA 3322

Street Kids*
c 1949–51
Oil on canvas
102.9 x 73.7
Purchased with funds given by an anonymous
donor 1964
GMA 887

An Old Woman Sewing
c 1950
Black crayon on paper
56.1 x 44.3
Purchased 1978
GMA 2024

Sleeping Nude*
1955
Oil on canvas
76 x 155.2
Presented by Mrs Irene Eardley 1964
GMA 897

A Stove*
c 1955
Oil on canvas laid on hardboard
95.5 x 79
Purchased 1984
GMA 2801

Sea and Snow, Catterline
c 1958
Oil on hardboard
18.2 x 33
George and Isobel Neillands Collection: presented
1988
GMA 3323

Seeded Grasses and Daisies, September*
1960
Oil, grasses and seedheads on hardboard
121.9 x 133.3
Purchased with funds given by an anonymous
donor 1964
GMA 889

Harvest
1960–61
Oil and grit on hardboard
118.1 x 118.1
Scott Hay Collection: presented 1967
GMA 1035

The Wave*
1961
Oil and grit on hardboard
121.9 x 188
Purchased (Gulbenkian UK Trust Fund) 1962
GMA 791

Summer Fields
c 1961
Oil and grasses on hardboard
106 x 105
Scott Hay Collection: presented 1984
GMA 2940

Children and Chalked Wall 3*
1962–63
Oil, newspaper and metal foil on canvas
61 x 68.6
Purchased 1963
GMA 853

Catterline in Winter*
c 1963
Oil on hardboard
120.7 x 130.8
Purchased 1964
GMA 888

*Boats on the Shore**
c 1963
Oil on hardboard
101.6 x 115.6
Scott Hay Collection: presented 1967
GMA 1036

Landscape with Oxen Ploughing
Black ink on paper
45.9 x 38.6
Presented by the artist's sister, Mrs P. M. Black,
1987
GMA 3058

A Pair of Oxen
Pastel on grey paper
48 x 62.8
Presented by the artist's sister, Mrs P. M. Black,
1987
GMA 3059

Mule Harnessed to a Cart, Italy
[verso: *Street Scene*]
Pastel on paper [verso: pen and ink and pastel]
47.8 x 63.2
Presented by the artist's sister, Mrs P. M. Black,
1987
GMA 3060

*Fishing Nets Hung up to Dry and Boat
on the Shore*
Black chalk on paper (two pieces joined)
48.8 x 77.6
Presented by the artist's sister, Mrs P. M. Black,
1987
GMA 3061

Italian Street Scene with a Man and a Mule
Pastel on paper
55.9 x 74.3
Presented by the artist's sister, Mrs P. M. Black,
1987
GMA 3062

Arcaded Street Front
Pastel, pen and ink and watercolour on paper
48.1 x 63.6
Presented by the artist's sister, Mrs P. M. Black,
1987
GMA 3063

*Detail of the Façade of Santa Maria Novella,
Florence*
Blue ball-point pen on grey paper
21.6 x 28
Presented by the artist's sister, Mrs P. M. Black,
1987
GMA 3064

A Wooden Door
Pastel on paper
10.1 x 13.1
Presented by the artist's sister, Mrs P. M. Black,
1987
GMA 3065

Row of Houses with Shuttered Windows
Pen and black ink on paper
12.7 x 20.3
Presented by the artist's sister, Mrs P. M. Black,
1987
GMA 3066

Detail of a Façade with Archway
Pen and blue ink on paper
12.7 x 10
Presented by the artist's sister, Mrs P. M. Black,
1987
GMA 3067

Ponte dei Greci, Venice
Pastel on paper
26.1 x 37.1
Presented by the artist's sister, Mrs P. M. Black,
1987
GMA 3068

Front View of a Saddled Donkey
Black chalk on grey paper
22.1 x 28
Presented by the artist's sister, Mrs P. M. Black,
1987
GMA 3069

Back View of a Saddled Donkey
Black chalk on grey paper
22.1 x 28
Presented by the artist's sister, Mrs P. M. Black,
1987
GMA 3070

Study of the Base of a Statue
Black chalk on paper
13.1 x 25.4
Presented by the artist's sister, Mrs P. M. Black,
1987
GMA 3071

Study of a Statue of a Bearded Man
Black chalk on paper
24.2 x 23.1
Presented by the artist's sister, Mrs P. M. Black,
1987
GMA 3072

The Scuola Grande di San Marco, Venice
Black chalk on grey paper
28.6 x 22.8
Presented by the artist's sister, Mrs P. M. Black,
1987
GMA 3073

*Church of Santa Maria Formosa and the Scuola
Grande di San Marco, Venice*
Black chalk on paper
28.3 x 22.1
Presented by the artist's sister, Mrs P. M. Black,
1987
GMA 3074

*Church of San Giovanni Grisostomo, Venice,
with Well and Market Stall*
Black chalk on grey paper
22.9 x 17
Presented by the artist's sister, Mrs P. M. Black,
1987
GMA 3075

*Left Side of the Church of San Giovanni
Grisostomo, Venice, with Well and Market Stall*
Black chalk on grey paper
22.8 x 15.2
Presented by the artist's sister, Mrs P. M. Black,
1987
GMA 3076

Bell-Tower, Venice
Black chalk on squared paper
12 x 16.6
Presented by the artist's sister, Mrs P. M. Black,
1987
GMA 3077

Church Exterior, Venice
Black chalk on paper
13.2 x 10.6
Presented by the artist's sister, Mrs P. M. Black,
1987
GMA 3078

Long-Horned Ox
Black chalk on paper
22 x 28
Presented by the artist's sister, Mrs P. M. Black,
1987
GMA 3079

Two Oxen Harnessed to a Cart
Blue ball-point pen on paper
20 x 22
Presented by the artist's sister, Mrs P. M. Black,
1987
GMA 3080

Figure on a Horse-Drawn Cart
Black chalk on blue paper
21.4 x 27.5 (irregular)
Presented by the artist's sister, Mrs P. M. Black,
1987
GMA 3081

*Three Sketches of Mules with Saddles, Harness
and Panniers*
Blue ball-point pen on paper
22.1 x 28
Presented by the artist's sister, Mrs P. M. Black,
1987
GMA 3082

Sketches of a Mule and Cart
Blue ball-point pen on grey paper
22 x 28
Presented by the artist's sister, Mrs P. M. Black,
1987
GMA 3083

Sketches of a Mule and Cart
Blue ball-point pen on paper (two pieces joined)
15.8 x 29
Presented by the artist's sister, Mrs P. M. Black,
1987
GMA 3084

Street Market
Pastel on paper
10.2 x 12.7
Presented by the artist's sister, Mrs P. M. Black,
1987
GMA 3085

Tree-Lined Avenue
Black chalk on paper
12.6 x 10.2
Presented by the artist's sister, Mrs P. M. Black,
1987
GMA 3086

Cart Loaded with Farm Produce
Black chalk on blue paper
14.7 x 15.7
Presented by the artist's sister, Mrs P. M. Black,
1987
GMA 3087

Young Man Playing a Guitar
Black chalk on blue paper
21.6 x 13.7
Presented by the artist's sister, Mrs P. M. Black,
1987
GMA 3088

Two Figures on Steps at Entrance to a Building
[verso: Church Interior]
Black chalk on paper
11.2 x 12.3
Presented by the artist's sister, Mrs P. M. Black,
1987
GMA 3089

Sketches of Women, Men and Wheelbarrow
Blue ball-point pen on paper
18.5 x 12.5
Presented by the artist's sister, Mrs P. M. Black,
1987
GMA 3090

Man in a Coat, Hat and Scarf
Black chalk on grey paper
13.1 x 8.3
Presented by the artist's sister, Mrs P. M. Black,
1987
GMA 3091

Figure Seated by an Altar
Black chalk on paper
10.9 x 8.2
Presented by the artist's sister, Mrs P. M. Black,
1987
GMA 3092

Old Man with Pipe and Hat, Hands in Pockets
Blue ball-point pen on paper
9.5 x 8.3
Presented by the artist's sister, Mrs P. M. Black,
1987
GMA 3093

Street Market Scene
Black chalk on paper (two pieces joined)
28.5 x 26.1
Presented by the artist's sister, Mrs P. M. Black,
1987
GMA 3094

Two Women with Shawls over their Heads
Black chalk on paper
13.4 x 11.2
Presented by the artist's sister, Mrs P. M. Black,
1987
GMA 3095

Woman in a Headscarf
Black chalk on paper (torn fragment)
6.7 x 11
Presented by the artist's sister, Mrs P. M. Black,
1987
GMA 3096

Gondola Seen from Above
Black chalk on graph paper
11.9 x 7.3
Presented by the artist's sister, Mrs P. M. Black,
1987
GMA 3097

Man with Two Walking-Sticks
Black chalk on grey paper
10.4 x 6.9
Presented by the artist's sister, Mrs P. M. Black,
1987
GMA 3098

Woman Sewing
Black chalk on grey paper
13 x 9.3
Presented by the artist's sister, Mrs P. M. Black,
1987
GMA 3099

Woman with a Baby, Begging
Black chalk on grey paper
18.2 x 14.7
Presented by the artist's sister, Mrs P. M. Black,
1987
GMA 3100

A Group of Figures, One Standing and Five Seated
Black chalk on paper
11.4 x 13.5
Presented by the artist's sister, Mrs P. M. Black,
1987
GMA 3101

Studies of Women in a Church
Black chalk on paper (pink telegram form)
19.5 x 13.9
Presented by the artist's sister, Mrs P. M. Black,
1987
GMA 3102

Standing Female Nude
Black chalk on paper
58.5 x 40.1
Presented by the artist's sister, Mrs P. M. Black,
1987
GMA 3103

Seated Male Nude
Black chalk on paper
41.1 x 33.2
Presented by the artist's sister, Mrs P. M. Black,
1987
GMA 3104

Seated Female Nude
Black and brown chalk on paper
53.5 x 40
Presented by the artist's sister, Mrs P. M. Black,
1987
GMA 3105

Seated Male Nude
Black chalk on paper
45.6 x 32
Presented by the artist's sister, Mrs P. M. Black,
1987
GMA 3106

Standing Male Nude in Trunks
Black chalk on paper
42.1 x 36
Presented by the artist's sister, Mrs P. M. Black,
1987
GMA 3107

Seated Female Nude
Black chalk on paper
53.5 x 36.9
Presented by the artist's sister, Mrs P. M. Black,
1987
GMA 3108

Female Nude on the Ground
Black and white chalk on wallpaper
75 x 52.2
Presented by the artist's sister, Mrs P. M. Black,
1987
GMA 3109

Female Nude in an Armchair
Black chalk and ink on paper
75.9 x 52.5
Presented by the artist's sister, Mrs P. M. Black,
1987
GMA 3110

Female Nude in an Armchair
Black and red chalk on paper
59 x 62
Presented by the artist's sister, Mrs P. M. Black,
1987
GMA 3111

Female Nude Lying Down
Pastel on paper
55.3 x 75.7
Presented by the artist's sister, Mrs P. M. Black,
1987
GMA 3112

Seated Man in a Shirt and Blue Neckerchief
Pastel on paper
91.3 x 58.5
Presented by the artist's sister, Mrs P. M. Black,
1987
GMA 3113

Old Italian Woman Sewing
[verso: *Horse with Nosebag and Blanket*]
Black chalk on paper
29.2 x 49.8
Presented by the artist's sister, Mrs P. M. Black,
1987
GMA 3114

Man Playing a Guitar, Italy
Black chalk and pastel on paper
100 x 74.2
Presented by the artist's sister, Mrs P. M. Black,
1987
GMA 3115

Back View of Seated Woman in a Shawl
[verso: *Two Women, Buildings and Hillside*]
Watercolour, ink and crayon on paper
86.6 x 56.2
Presented by the artist's sister, Mrs P. M. Black,
1987
GMA 3116

Man in a Cap, Lying on the Ground
Black chalk on paper
55.5 x 64.5
Presented by the artist's sister, Mrs P. M. Black,
1987
GMA 3117

Young Man Playing an Accordion
Black chalk on paper
66.2 x 42.2
Presented by the artist's sister, Mrs P. M. Black,
1987
GMA 3118

Old Woman by a Fire
Watercolour, black ink and chalk on paper-backed
canvas (two sheets joined)
67.5 x 98.2
Presented by the artist's sister, Mrs P. M. Black,
1987
GMA 3119

Two Studies of Figures
Blue ball-point pen on paper
18.4 x 11.4
Presented by the artist's sister, Mrs P. M. Black,
1987
GMA 3120

Five Studies of Figures
Blue ball-point pen on paper
18.4 x 12.4
Presented by the artist's sister, Mrs P. M. Black,
1987
GMA 3121

Two Women in Shawls, Seen from Behind
Black chalk on grey paper
22.8 x 13.8
Presented by the artist's sister, Mrs P. M. Black,
1987
GMA 3122

Seated Woman
Blue ball-point pen and blue chalk on blue paper
11.8 x 14.2
Presented by the artist's sister, Mrs P. M. Black,
1987
GMA 3123

Three Men in a Café or Bar
Black chalk on paper
12.8 x 10
Presented by the artist's sister, Mrs P. M. Black,
1987
GMA 3124

Four Men on a River Bank by a Bridge
Black chalk on paper
10.1 x 12.6
Presented by the artist's sister, Mrs P. M. Black,
1987
GMA 3125

Group of Three Women
Pastel on paper
10.2 x 13.2
Presented by the artist's sister, Mrs P. M. Black,
1987
GMA 3126

Man in a Doorway, with a Bundle under his Arm
Black chalk on paper
13.2 x 10.2
Presented by the artist's sister, Mrs P. M. Black, 1987
GMA 3127

Man in a Cap
Black chalk on paper
12.7 x 10.1
Presented by the artist's sister, Mrs P. M. Black, 1987
GMA 3128

Head of an Old Man
Black chalk on paper
12.9 x 10
Presented by the artist's sister, Mrs P. M. Black, 1987
GMA 3129

Old Woman Seated at a Pew
Black chalk on squared paper
8.2 x 11.5
Presented by the artist's sister, Mrs P. M. Black, 1987
GMA 3130

Pot on an Open Fire and Figure
Pastel on paper
10 x 12.8
Presented by the artist's sister, Mrs P. M. Black, 1987
GMA 3131

Two Figures, one Carrying Bags
Pastel on paper
12.9 x 10.1
Presented by the artist's sister, Mrs P. M. Black, 1987
GMA 3132

Two Men in Caps
Pastel on paper
13.3 x 10.3
Presented by the artist's sister, Mrs P. M. Black, 1987
GMA 3133

Man in Shirtsleeves at an Easel, Seen from Behind
Pastel on paper
22.6 x 17.7
Presented by the artist's sister, Mrs P. M. Black, 1987
GMA 3134

Four Figures
Pastel on paper
13 x 10.2
Presented by the artist's sister, Mrs P. M. Black, 1987
GMA 3135

A Group of Children
Pastel on paper
17.4 x 11.3
Presented by the artist's sister, Mrs P. M. Black, 1987
GMA 3136

A Group of Children Playing on the Ground
Pastel on paper (two pieces joined)
24.1 x 17.4
Presented by the artist's sister, Mrs P. M. Black, 1987
GMA 3137

Man Standing, his Hands in Jacket Pockets
Pastel on paper
17.3 x 11.3
Presented by the artist's sister, Mrs P. M. Black, 1987
GMA 3138

Three Figures
Pastel on paper
22.4 x 14
Presented by the artist's sister, Mrs P. M. Black, 1987
GMA 3139

Man in a Cap – Interior
Black chalk on paper (four sheets joined)
13.7 x 22.2 (irregular)
Presented by the artist's sister, Mrs P. M. Black, 1987
GMA 3140

Man on the Ground Playing a Guitar
Pastel and pencil on paper
12 x 13.3
Presented by the artist's sister, Mrs P. M. Black,
1987
GMA 3141

Woman in a Doorway and Child Seated on a Kerb
Pastel on paper
22.4 x 14
Presented by the artist's sister, Mrs P. M. Black,
1987
GMA 3142

Two Mothers Watching Children Playing
Pastel on paper
12.1 x 27
Presented by the artist's sister, Mrs P. M. Black,
1987
GMA 3143

Child with Pram
Pastel on paper
17.5 x 14.8
Presented by the artist's sister, Mrs P. M. Black,
1987
GMA 3144

War Veteran
[verso: *Inscription*]
Black chalk on index card
12.6 x 7.6
Presented by the artist's sister, Mrs P. M. Black,
1987
GMA 3145

Seated Woman Wearing a Headscarf
Black chalk on paper
10.2 x 13.2
Presented by the artist's sister, Mrs P. M. Black,
1987
GMA 3146

Two Men in Raincoats
Blue ball-point pen on paper
12.6 x 10.1
Presented by the artist's sister, Mrs P. M. Black,
1987
GMA 3147

Study of a Woman and Detail of the Fringe of a Shawl
[verso: *Woman in a Shawl*]
Blue ball-point pen on paper [verso: black chalk]
12.8 x 10.2
Presented by the artist's sister, Mrs P. M. Black,
1987
GMA 3148

Tenements and Yard
Blue ball-point pen on paper
12.2 x 20
Presented by the artist's sister, Mrs P. M. Black,
1987
GMA 3149

View of Tenements
[verso: *Figures by a Pawnbroker's Sign*]
Blue ball-point pen on paper [verso: black chalk]
11.1 x 16.2
Presented by the artist's sister, Mrs P. M. Black,
1987
GMA 3150

Three Studies of Figures
Pastel on paper
16.6 x 20.3
Presented by the artist's sister, Mrs P. M. Black,
1987
GMA 3151

Gable End of a Tenement and Telegraph Poles
Pastel with watercolour on paper
25.3 x 20.3
Presented by the artist's sister, Mrs P. M. Black,
1987
GMA 3152

Two Doorways and a Window at Street Level
Pastel on paper
11.8 x 17.4
Presented by the artist's sister, Mrs P. M. Black,
1987
GMA 3153

Study of Doors
Pastel on paper
13.9 x 22.4
Presented by the artist's sister, Mrs P. M. Black,
1987
GMA 3154

Street Doorways
Pastel on paper
20.3 x 25.3
Presented by the artist's sister, Mrs P. M. Black,
1987
GMA 3155

Rooftop Seen Between Two Buildings
Pastel on paper
22.2 x 13.7
Presented by the artist's sister, Mrs P. M. Black,
1987
GMA 3156

Street Scene with Lamps
Blue ball-point pen on paper
12.6 x 19
Presented by the artist's sister, Mrs P. M. Black,
1987
GMA 3157

Houses and Cottages with Cart
Black chalk and pastel on paper (five
sheets joined)
13.8 x 22.1 (irregular)
Presented by the artist's sister, Mrs P. M. Black,
1987
GMA 3158

Backs of Tenements
Black chalk and pastel on paper
14.4 x 13.9
Presented by the artist's sister, Mrs P. M. Black,
1987
GMA 3159

Shop Front
Pastel on paper
12.5 x 9.9
Presented by the artist's sister, Mrs P. M. Black,
1987
GMA 3160

Glasgow Street with Bunting for the Coronation,
1953
Pastel on paper
17.7 x 22.7
Presented by the artist's sister, Mrs P. M. Black,
1987
GMA 3161

Bunting for the Coronation, 1953
Pen and red ink on paper
17.7 x 22.8
Presented by the artist's sister, Mrs P. M. Black,
1987
GMA 3162

Boy in Torn Shirt and Blue Sleeveless Jumper
Pastel on ruled paper
33 x 21.2
Presented by the artist's sister, Mrs P. M. Black,
1987
GMA 3163

Head of a Child
Pastel on index card
12.7 x 7.6
Presented by the artist's sister, Mrs P. M. Black,
1987
GMA 3164

Study of a Girl
Black chalk and pastel on paper
22.1 x 13.8
Presented by the artist's sister, Mrs P. M. Black,
1987
GMA 3165

Study of a Child in a Pink Jumper
Pastel on paper
22.5 x 14
Presented by the artist's sister, Mrs P. M. Black,
1987
GMA 3166

Profile of a Boy with Black Hair
[verso: Two Seated Children Playing]
Pastel on paper [verso: black chalk]
22.8 x 18.1
Presented by the artist's sister, Mrs P. M. Black,
1987
GMA 3167

Child's Head, Seen from Behind
Pastel on paper
22.8 x 18
Presented by the artist's sister, Mrs P. M. Black,
1987
GMA 3168

Half-Length Study of a Boy
Ink, pastel and watercolour on pink paper
32.6 x 47.6
Presented by the artist's sister, Mrs P. M. Black,
1987
GMA 3169

Seated Boy and Head of a Red-Haired Boy
Black chalk, pastel and wash on pink paper
62.7 x 47.8
Presented by the artist's sister, Mrs P. M. Black,
1987
GMA 3170

*Two Children Seated on the Ground, Reading
Comics*
Black chalk and pastel on paper
47.8 x 37.3
Presented by the artist's sister, Mrs P. M. Black,
1987
GMA 3171

Boy Seated on the Ground, Reading
Black chalk and pastel on paper
52.2 x 31.1
Presented by the artist's sister, Mrs P. M. Black,
1987
GMA 3172

Boy Reclining on the Ground
Black chalk on paper
12.6 x 20.2
Presented by the artist's sister, Mrs P. M. Black,
1987
GMA 3173

*Study of a Boy in Blazer and Shorts, Seen from
Behind*
Black chalk on paper
22.2 x 13.7
Presented by the artist's sister, Mrs P. M. Black,
1987
GMA 3174

Study of a Figure
Black chalk on paper
12.6 x 20.2
Presented by the artist's sister, Mrs P. M. Black,
1987
GMA 3175

Study of a Boy in a Blazer
Black chalk on paper
22.2 x 13.8
Presented by the artist's sister, Mrs P. M. Black,
1987
GMA 3176

Study of a Boy in Blazer and Shorts
Black chalk on paper
17.7 x 11.2
Presented by the artist's sister, Mrs P. M. Black,
1987
GMA 3177

Two Studies of a Boy
Pen and black ink on paper
12.7 x 10.1
Presented by the artist's sister, Mrs P. M. Black,
1987
GMA 3178

Boy Holding a Ball
Pen and black ink on paper (two pieces joined)
21.5 x 10.8
Presented by the artist's sister, Mrs P. M. Black,
1987
GMA 3179

*Five Studies of Children and Detail of a Church
Steeple*
[verso: *Woman's Head*]
Pen and black ink and red chalk on paper [verso:
pen and black ink and watercolour]
17.7 x 25.3
Presented by the artist's sister, Mrs P. M. Black,
1987
GMA 3180

Girl in a Frock
Pen and black ink on paper
28 x 20
Presented by the artist's sister, Mrs P. M. Black,
1987
GMA 3181

Two Girls and a Boy
[verso: *Two Heads and a Hand*]
Pen and black ink on paper
17.7 x 25.3
Presented by the artist's sister, Mrs P. M. Black,
1987
GMA 3182

Study of a Boy in Jumper and Shorts
Black chalk and pastel on paper
22.9 x 18
Presented by the artist's sister, Mrs P. M. Black, 1987
GMA 3183

Study of a Crouching Child, Seen from Behind
Pastel on paper
14.1 x 11.1
Presented by the artist's sister, Mrs P. M. Black, 1987
GMA 3184

Study of a Boy in Blazer and Shorts, Seen from Behind
Pastel on paper
17.8 x 11.4
Presented by the artist's sister, Mrs P. M. Black, 1987
GMA 3185

Study of a Boy in Shirt, Blazer and Tie
Black chalk on paper
22.2 x 13.7
Presented by the artist's sister, Mrs P. M. Black, 1987
GMA 3186

Study of a Girl in a Pleated Dress
Pastel on paper
17.8 x 11.4
Presented by the artist's sister, Mrs P. M. Black, 1987
GMA 3187

Study of a Girl in a Gymslip
Pastel on paper
22 x 13.8
Presented by the artist's sister, Mrs P. M. Black, 1987
GMA 3188

Study of the Legs and Shorts of a Seated Boy
Pastel on paper
10.2 x 12.8
Presented by the artist's sister, Mrs P. M. Black, 1987
GMA 3189

Study of a Boy in Blazer and Shorts
Pastel on paper
16.3 x 12.8
Presented by the artist's sister, Mrs P. M. Black, 1987
GMA 3190

Study of a Child in Shorts
Pastel on paper
18.2 x 22.9
Presented by the artist's sister, Mrs P. M. Black, 1987
GMA 3191

Study of a Child in Jumper and Shorts
Pastel on paper
31 x 26.3
Presented by the artist's sister, Mrs P. M. Black, 1987
GMA 3192

Two Seated Children
Pastel, ink and watercolour on paper
17.6 x 14.2 (paper 30 x 17.3)
Presented by the artist's sister, Mrs P. M. Black, 1987
GMA 3193

Boy in a Blazer, Leaning against a Wall
Pastel on paper
17.7 x 11.4
Presented by the artist's sister, Mrs P. M. Black, 1987
GMA 3194

Boy on a Bicycle
Pastel on paper (three sheets joined)
20.1 x 27.3
Presented by the artist's sister, Mrs P. M. Black, 1987
GMA 3195

Girl in Front of a Tenement
[verso: *Sketches of Figures*]
Pastel on paper
17.5 x 14
Presented by the artist's sister, Mrs P. M. Black, 1987
GMA 3196

Girl in a Blue Cardigan and Pink Dress
Pastel on paper (two pieces joined)
27.6 x 15.4
Presented by the artist's sister, Mrs P. M. Black,
1987
GMA 3197

Girl in a Summer Dress
Pastel on paper (two pieces joined)
31 x 15.2
Presented by the artist's sister, Mrs P. M. Black,
1987
GMA 3198

Two Girls
Pastel on paper
23.8 x 35.6
Presented by the artist's sister, Mrs P. M. Black,
1987
GMA 3199

Head of a Girl
Pastel on sandpaper
30.4 x 25.3
Presented by the artist's sister, Mrs P. M. Black,
1987
GMA 3200

Child's Head with One Eye Closed
Pastel on sandpaper
30.5 x 25.3
Presented by the artist's sister, Mrs P. M. Black,
1987
GMA 3201

The Macaulay Children at a Window
Pastel on paper
5.5 x 12 (paper 12.6 x 16.6)
Presented by the artist's sister, Mrs P. M. Black,
1987
GMA 3202

*Head of a Boy (Andrew Macaulay), his Hand
on his Cheek*
Pastel on paper
23.4 x 15
Presented by the artist's sister, Mrs P. M. Black,
1987
GMA 3203

*Head of a Boy (Andrew Macaulay), Sucking his
Thumb*
Pastel on paper
23.4 x 15
Presented by the artist's sister, Mrs P. M. Black,
1987
GMA 3204

*Head of a Boy (Andrew Macaulay), his Hand on
his Chin*
Pastel on paper
23.4 x 15
Presented by the artist's sister, Mrs P. M. Black,
1987
GMA 3205

Head of a Boy (Andrew Macaulay)
Pastel on paper
25.1 x 17.7
Presented by the artist's sister, Mrs P. M. Black,
1987
GMA 3206

Head of a Boy (Martin Macaulay)
Pastel on paper
17.7 x 25.3
Presented by the artist's sister, Mrs P. M. Black,
1987
GMA 3207

Head of a Girl (Madeleine Macaulay)
Pastel on paper
34 x 38
Presented by the artist's sister, Mrs P. M. Black,
1987
GMA 3208

Five Studies of a Baby
Pastel on paper
56 x 38.2
Presented by the artist's sister, Mrs P. M. Black,
1987
GMA 3209

Head of a Girl
Gouache and pastel on paper laid on board
37.6 x 37.4
Presented by the artist's sister, Mrs P. M. Black,
1987
GMA 3210

A Girl
Watercolour, gouache and black chalk on paper
69.8 x 36.6
Presented by the artist's sister, Mrs P. M. Black,
1987
GMA 3211

Study of Figures
Gouache on paper
38.2 x 55.8
Presented by the artist's sister, Mrs P. M. Black,
1987
GMA 3212

Children Playing in a Street (Compositional Study)
Watercolour and gouache on paper
38 x 55.8
Presented by the artist's sister, Mrs P. M. Black,
1987
GMA 3213

Children Playing in a Street (Compositional Study)
Blue ball-point pen on blue paper (two sheets joined)
13.5 x 22.5
Presented by the artist's sister, Mrs P. M. Black,
1987
GMA 3214

Children Playing in a Street (Compositional Study)
Pen and black ink on pink paper
17.2 x 23.7
Presented by the artist's sister, Mrs P. M. Black,
1987
GMA 3215

Children Playing in a Street (Compositional Study)
Pen and black ink on pink paper
17.4 x 24.1
Presented by the artist's sister, Mrs P. M. Black,
1987
GMA 3216

Children Playing in a Street (Compositional Study)
Pen and black ink on pink paper
16 x 24.6
Presented by the artist's sister, Mrs P. M. Black,
1987
GMA 3217

Cove and Wooded Hillside
Black chalk on paper
10.1 x 13.1
Presented by the artist's sister, Mrs P. M. Black,
1987
GMA 3218

Harnessed Horse
Black ink on paper
35.5 x 45.7
Presented by the artist's sister, Mrs P. M. Black,
1987
GMA 3219

Row of Dead Crows Strung up
Black ink and wash on paper
46.6 x 63.1
Presented by the artist's sister, Mrs P. M. Black,
1987
GMA 3220

Horses at a Showground
Pen and blue ink on paper
11.4 x 17.6
Presented by the artist's sister, Mrs P. M. Black,
1987
GMA 3221

Back Gardens with Washing Hung out in the Rain
Pen and black ink on paper
17.6 x 22.4
Presented by the artist's sister, Mrs P. M. Black,
1987
GMA 3222

Promenade with Donkey Rides
Black ink on paper
11.4 x 15.1
Presented by the artist's sister, Mrs P. M. Black,
1987
GMA 3223

Studies of Reclining Figures
Black ink on paper
11.3 x 15.2
Presented by the artist's sister, Mrs P. M. Black,
1987
GMA 3224

Horse in Fancy Harness at a Showground
Pen and blue ink on paper
19.2 x 17.7
Presented by the artist's sister, Mrs P. M. Black,
1987
GMA 3225

View from Ringside at a Showground
Blue ink on paper (two pieces joined)
11.4 x 22.8
Presented by the artist's sister, Mrs P. M. Black,
1987
GMA 3226

Horses and Marquee at a Showground
Blue ink on paper
11.4 x 17.6
Presented by the artist's sister, Mrs P. M. Black,
1987
GMA 3227

Horses at a Showground
Blue ink on paper
11.4 x 17.6
Presented by the artist's sister, Mrs P. M. Black,
1987
GMA 3228

Back View of a Line of Horses
Blue ink on paper
11.4 x 17.6
Presented by the artist's sister, Mrs P. M. Black,
1987
GMA 3229

Sketch of Figures
Black ink on paper
17.6 x 22.4
Presented by the artist's sister, Mrs P. M. Black,
1987
GMA 3230

A Group of Figures
Black ink on paper
17.6 x 22.4
Presented by the artist's sister, Mrs P. M. Black,
1987
GMA 3231

A Group of Figures
Black ink on paper
17.6 x 22.4
Presented by the artist's sister, Mrs P. M. Black,
1987
GMA 3232

Crew in a Fishing Boat in a Harbour, Arbroath
Black ink on paper
17.5 x 22.8
Presented by the artist's sister, Mrs P. M. Black,
1987
GMA 3233

Harbour Scene, Arbroath
Blue ink on paper
11.5 x 17.5
Presented by the artist's sister, Mrs P. M. Black,
1987
GMA 3234

Boats in a Harbour, Seen from Above, Arbroath
Black ink on paper
17.5 x 22.7
Presented by the artist's sister, Mrs P. M. Black,
1987
GMA 3235

Fishing Nets Hung up in a Harbour, Arbroath
Pen and blue ink on paper (three sheets joined)
14.5 x 25.5 (irregular)
Presented by the artist's sister, Mrs P. M. Black,
1987
GMA 3236

Boats Moored near a Harbour Wall, Arbroath
Pen and black ink on paper (three sheets joined)
11.5 x 31.8
Presented by the artist's sister, Mrs P. M. Black,
1987
GMA 3237

*Study of Fishing Nets Hung from the Mast
of a Boat, Arbroath*
Pen and black ink on paper
12.5 x 20
Presented by the artist's sister, Mrs P. M. Black,
1987
GMA 3238

Fishing Nets Hung from the Mast of a Boat
in Harbour, Arbroath
Pen and blue ink on paper
11.5 X 17.5
Presented by the artist's sister, Mrs P. M. Black,
1987
GMA 3239

Study of Fishing Nets and Rigging
Black ink on paper
17.5 X 23
Presented by the artist's sister, Mrs P. M. Black,
1987
GMA 3240

Study of Fishing Nets and Rigging
Black ink on paper
12.5 X 20
Presented by the artist's sister, Mrs P. M. Black,
1987
GMA 3241

Study of the Prow of a Boat with Coils of Rope
Black ink on paper
17.5 X 22.8
Presented by the artist's sister, Mrs P. M. Black,
1987
GMA 3242

Fishing Nets Hung up
Pen and black ink on paper
17.1 X 21.7
Presented by the artist's sister, Mrs P. M. Black,
1987
GMA 3243

Fishing Nets Hung up
Pastel on yellow paper (two sheets joined)
21.5 X 38.5
Presented by the artist's sister, Mrs P. M. Black,
1987
GMA 3244

Fishing Boats Moored in a Harbour
Watercolour on paper
25.1 X 20.1
Presented by the artist's sister, Mrs P. M. Black,
1987
GMA 3245

The Sea at Catterline
Pastel on paper (two sheets joined)
13.2 X 34.2
Presented by the artist's sister, Mrs P. M. Black,
1987
GMA 3246

The Sea at Catterline
Pastel on paper (four pieces joined)
29.5 X 35.3
Presented by the artist's sister, Mrs P. M. Black,
1987
GMA 3247

Stormy Sea
Pastel on paper (two sheets joined)
21.2 X 26.8 (irregular)
Presented by the artist's sister, Mrs P. M. Black,
1987
GMA 3248

Waves Breaking on the Shore
Pastel on paper
13.5 X 17.7
Presented by the artist's sister, Mrs P. M. Black,
1987
GMA 3249

Waves Breaking on the Shore
Pastel on paper
20.2 X 25.2
Presented by the artist's sister, Mrs P. M. Black,
1987
GMA 3250

Sun in Stormy Sky over Catterline
Pastel on paper
20.2 X 25.2
Presented by the artist's sister, Mrs P. M. Black,
1987
GMA 3251

Stormy Sky over Catterline Sea Shore
Pastel on paper (two sheets joined)
12.5 X 29.7
Presented by the artist's sister, Mrs P. M. Black,
1987
GMA 3252

View of Catterline from Harvest Fields
Black chalk on paper
9.4 x 12.6
Presented by the artist's sister, Mrs P. M. Black,
1987
GMA 3253

Catterline Village and Foreshore
Black chalk on paper
9.4 x 12.6
Presented by the artist's sister, Mrs P. M. Black,
1987
GMA 3254

Catterline Cottages
Pastel on paper
11.2 x 17.1
Presented by the artist's sister, Mrs P. M. Black,
1987
GMA 3255

Stormy Sky over Catterline
Pastel on paper
20.2 x 25.2
Presented by the artist's sister, Mrs P. M. Black,
1987
GMA 3256

Row of Cottages, Catterline
Black ink and watercolour on paper
20.2 x 25.1
Presented by the artist's sister, Mrs P. M. Black,
1987
GMA 3257

Sea Shore
Pastel on paper
10 x 12.6
Presented by the artist's sister, Mrs P. M. Black,
1987
GMA 3258

Landscape at Comrie, Perthshire
Watercolour, ink and pastel on paper
11.9 x 25.2 (unfolded paper 20.2 x 25.2)
Presented by the artist's sister, Mrs P. M. Black,
1987
GMA 3259

Landscape at Comrie, Perthshire
Watercolour, ink and pastel on paper
12.4 x 25.2 (unfolded paper 20.2 x 25.2)
Presented by the artist's sister, Mrs P. M. Black,
1987
GMA 3260

Huts and Trees by the Sea
Watercolour and ink on paper (two sheets joined)
13.8 x 17.4
Presented by the artist's sister, Mrs P. M. Black,
1987
GMA 3261

Cornfield and Wide Horizon
Pastel on paper
18.1 x 13.5
Presented by the artist's sister, Mrs P. M. Black,
1987
GMA 3262

Cows by a Tree in a Field
Pastel and gouache on green paper
18.9 x 29.1
Presented by the artist's sister, Mrs P. M. Black,
1987
GMA 3263

Landscape of Flat Fields
Pastel on paper (three sheets joined)
23.5 x 30.5 (irregular)
Presented by the artist's sister, Mrs P. M. Black,
1987
GMA 3264

Field with Wild Flowers
Gouache on grey paper
49.7 x 64.5
Presented by the artist's sister, Mrs P. M. Black,
1987
GMA 3265

Green Corn and Flowers at a Field's Edge
Watercolour, gouache and ink on paper
24.7 x 32.5
Presented by the artist's sister, Mrs P. M. Black,
1987
GMA 3266

Autumn Flowers and Seed-Heads
Pastel and oil on paper (three sheets joined)
25 x 22.6 (irregular)
Presented by the artist's sister, Mrs P. M. Black,
1987
GMA 3267

Field of Corn and Haystacks
Pastel on sandpaper
30.5 x 25.2
Presented by the artist's sister, Mrs P. M. Black,
1987
GMA 3268

Harvest Field with Stooks of Corn
Black chalk on paper
11.4 x 17.7
Presented by the artist's sister, Mrs P. M. Black,
1987
GMA 3269

Harvest Field with Stooks of Corn
Black chalk on paper
11.4 x 17.7
Presented by the artist's sister, Mrs P. M. Black,
1987
GMA 3270

Studies of Sheep
Pastel on paper
17.4 x 30.2
Presented by the artist's sister, Mrs P. M. Black,
1987
GMA 3271

Sheep Feeding in a Field of Turnips
Black ink and watercolour on grey paper
49.6 x 64.6
Presented by the artist's sister, Mrs P. M. Black,
1987
GMA 3272

Boy with a Saddled Black Horse
Pastel on invoice paper
13 x 20.7
Presented by the artist's sister, Mrs P. M. Black,
1987
GMA 3273

Back View of a Saddled Brown Horse
Pastel on invoice paper
13 x 20.7
Presented by the artist's sister, Mrs P. M. Black,
1987
GMA 3274

Study of Two Horses
Pastel on invoice paper
12.9 x 20.7
Presented by the artist's sister, Mrs P. M. Black,
1987
GMA 3275

Figure with Two Saddled Horses
Pastel on paper
13.2 x 21
Presented by the artist's sister, Mrs P. M. Black,
1987
GMA 3276

Study of Two Horses
Pastel on invoice paper
12.9 x 20.7
Presented by the artist's sister, Mrs P. M. Black,
1987
GMA 3277

Study of a Saddled Black Horse
Pastel on invoice paper
12.9 x 20.7
Presented by the artist's sister, Mrs P. M. Black,
1987
GMA 3278

Study of a Horse with Saddle and Bridle
Pastel on invoice paper
12.9 x 20.7
Presented by the artist's sister, Mrs P. M. Black,
1987
GMA 3279

A Young Heifer
Black chalk on paper
11.2 x 17.6
Presented by the artist's sister, Mrs P. M. Black,
1987
GMA 3280

Chair Strewn with Clothes
[verso: *Figure, Wearing a Cap*]
Black ink, red chalk and wash on paper [verso:
black ink and wash]
63.3 x 52.2
Presented by the artist's sister, Mrs P. M. Black,
1987
GMA 3281

Interior with Cupboard, Table and Chair
Pen and black ink on paper
38 x 44
Presented by the artist's sister, Mrs P. M. Black,
1987
GMA 3282

Kitchen Sink and Cupboard
Pen and black ink on paper
26.3 x 24.3
Presented by the artist's sister, Mrs P. M. Black,
1987
GMA 3283

*Tabletop with Oil Lamp, Candlestick and
Crockery*
Pen and black ink on paper
24.3 x 26.4
Presented by the artist's sister, Mrs P. M. Black,
1987
GMA 3284

Cast-Iron Weighing Machine
Pen and black ink on paper
60.5 x 42.5
Presented by the artist's sister, Mrs P. M. Black,
1987
GMA 3285

Corner of a Scullery
[verso: *Large Seated Woman*]
Pen and black ink on paper
49.2 x 32.6
Presented by the artist's sister, Mrs P. M. Black,
1987
GMA 3286

An Oil Lamp
Pen and black ink on paper
27.8 x 21.5
Presented by the artist's sister, Mrs P. M. Black,
1987
GMA 3287

Cast-Iron Upright Cylinder Stove
Black ink and watercolour on paper
32.4 x 18.5
Presented by the artist's sister, Mrs P. M. Black,
1987
GMA 3288

Kitchen-Range Door
Pen and black ink on paper
17.4 x 20.6
Presented by the artist's sister, Mrs P. M. Black,
1987
GMA 3289

Trees
Pastel on paper
11.1 x 17.5
Presented by the artist's sister, Mrs P. M. Black,
1987
GMA 3290

Black Sky with Blue Sea
Pastel on paper
20.1 x 25.3
Presented by the artist's sister, Mrs P. M. Black,
1987
GMA 3291

Children Grouped Around a Man and Cart
Pastel on paper
11.2 x 17.6
Presented by the artist's sister, Mrs P. M. Black,
1987
GMA 3292

Girl Skipping in Front of Tenements
Black chalk on paper
22.8 x 17.8
Presented by the artist's sister, Mrs P. M. Black,
1987
GMA 3293

Small Girl Walking
Black chalk on paper
12.5 x 10
Presented by the artist's sister, Mrs P. M. Black,
1987
GMA 3294

Sketchbook of Sheep Studies
Sketchbook of twelve sheets, with sketches on 17
sides; black chalk on paper
24.3 x 26.2
Presented by the artist's sister, Mrs P. M. Black,
1987
GMA 3295

Saucepan on a Primus Stove
Watercolour and gouache on paper
38.3 x 28
Presented by the artist's sister, Mrs P. M. Black,
1987
GMA 3314

Yellow Sky and Gas Lamps
Pastel on paper (four sheets joined)
14.5 x 44.5
George and Isobel Neillands Collection: presented
1988
GMA 3324

A Girl
Pastel on paper
22.4 x 17
George and Isobel Neillands Collection: presented
1988
GMA 3325

Harvest Field with Stooks of Corn
Black chalk on paper
11.4 x 17.8
Presented by the artist's sister, Mrs P. M. Black,
1987
GMA 3415

Maud Ede

Salt Unloading, Venice
Etching and aquatint on paper
17.9 x 23.9 (paper 22 x 30.4)
Presented by Jim Ede 1977
GMA 1605

Evening in San Giorgio, Venice
Etching and aquatint on paper
12.1 x 16.2 (paper 22.2 x 30.8)
Presented by Jim Ede 1977
GMA 1606

Rio San Giuseppe, Venice
Etching and aquatint on paper
11.8 x 15.9 (paper 21.9 x 30.5)
Presented by Jim Ede 1977
GMA 1607

San Francesco in Deserto, Venice
Etching and aquatint on paper
11.5 x 16.3 (paper 22.2 x 31.1)
Presented by Jim Ede 1977
GMA 1608

Sails Drying, Redoutare in the Distance, Venice
Etching and aquatint on paper
24.6 x 17.9 (paper 31 x 22)
Presented by Jim Ede 1977
GMA 1609

Georg Ehrlich

1897–1966

View of Chipping Camden
1944–46
Pen and ink and wash on paper
31.8 x 50.3
Presented by the estate of the artist through the
Scottish Arts Council 1988
GMA 3412

Lying Cow
c 1948
Bronze (1/6)
16.5 x 55 x 21
Purchased 1968
GMA 1085

Mother and Child
d 1949
Brown chalk and ink on paper
50 x 32.6
Presented by the estate of the artist through the
Scottish Arts Council 1988
GMA 3414

The Prodigal Son and his Mother
1954–55
Bronze
67 x 61.5 x 32.5
Presented by Mrs Bettina Ehrlich 1983
GMA 2780

*Age and Youth**
c 1961
Bronze (1/6)
32.3 x 38.9 x 3
Presented by Mrs Bettina Ehrlich 1972
GMA 1273

Study for 'Age and Youth'
c 1961
Pencil, pen and ink and ink wash on paper
19.5 x 20.8
Purchased 1973
GMA 1282

Study for 'Age and Youth'
c 1961
Pen and ink and ink wash on paper
29.5 x 20.8
Purchased 1973
GMA 1283

Study for 'Age and Youth'
c 1961
Pen and ink and ink wash on paper
20.8 x 29.5
Purchased 1973
GMA 1284

Study for 'Age and Youth'
c 1961
Pen and ink and ink wash on paper
20.8 x 29.5
Purchased 1973
GMA 1285

Study for 'Age and Youth'
c 1961
Pen and ink and ink wash on paper
20.8 x 29.5
Purchased 1973
GMA 1286

Study for 'Age and Youth'
c 1961
Pen and ink and ink wash on paper
20.8 x 29.5
Purchased 1973
GMA 1287

Study for 'Age and Youth'
c 1961
Pen and ink and ink wash on paper
20.8 x 29.5
Purchased 1973
GMA 1288

Study for 'Age and Youth'
c 1961
Pen and ink and ink wash on paper
29.5 x 20.8
Purchased 1973
GMA 1289

Study for 'Age and Youth'
c 1961
Pen and ink and ink wash on paper
29.4 x 20.8
Purchased 1973
GMA 1290

Study for 'Age and Youth'
c 1961
Ink wash on paper
20.8 x 29.5
Purchased 1973
GMA 1291

Study for 'Age and Youth'
c 1961
Ink wash on paper
29.6 x 20.8
Purchased 1973
GMA 1292

*Horse's Head**
1963–64
Bronze (2/6)
23.6 x 45 x 16
Purchased 1971
GMA 1246

Bull
d 1964
Pen and ink, red chalk and wash on paper
23.6 x 33
Presented by the estate of the artist through the
Scottish Arts Council 1988
GMA 3411

Garden, 15 St Peter's Square, London
Pen and ink, ink wash and watercolour on paper
31.4 x 48.1
Presented by the estate of the artist through the
Scottish Arts Council 1988
GMA 3413

Eleven Pop Artists, vol. II
(Portfolio, published 1965)

See Allan D'ARCANGELO, Jim DINE, Allen
JONES, Gerald LAING, Roy LICHTENSTEIN, Peter
PHILLIPS, Mel RAMOS, James ROSENQUIST,
Andy WARHOL, John WESLEY, Tom
WESSELMANN

Ger van Elk
1941–

The Missing Persons: Lunch II*
d 1976
Retouched colour photograph mounted on
aluminium sheet
98.1 x 111.1
Purchased 1982
GMA 2508

Clifford Ellis and Rosemary Ellis
Clifford, 1907–85, Rosemary 1910–

Teignmouth
(from the J. Lyons series 'Lithographs by
Contemporary Artists, vol. I')
Published 1947
Colour lithograph on paper (after gouache)
72.5 x 97.5 (paper 74.7 x 99)
Presented by J. Lyons & Co. Ltd 1948
GMA 1200

James Ensor
1860–1949

Cortège infernal [Infernal Procession]
d 1887
Etching on paper
21.9 x 26.9 (paper 34.5 x 46.6)
Purchased 1979
GMA 2098

L'Entrée du Christ à Bruxelles [The Entry
of Christ into Brussels]*
d 1896
Etching on paper
24.8 x 35.6 (paper 35 x 47.2)
Purchased 1981
GMA 2285

Jacob Epstein
1880–1959

Baby Asleep*
c 1904
Bronze
13.2 x 9.8 x 14.8
Bequeathed by Sir David Young Cameron 1945
GMA 12

The Risen Christ*
1917–19
Bronze (unique cast)
218.5 x 54.5 x 56
Purchased 1969
GMA 1092

Albert Einstein*
1933
Bronze
43.5 x 30 x 25.5
Presented by the children of James Watt and his
wife Menie, in their memory 1958
GMA 13

Consummatum Est*
1936–37
Alabaster
61 x 223.5 x 81
Purchased 1981
GMA 2304

Betty Cecil*
1938
Bronze
52.7 x 42 x 34.5
Bequeathed by Sir Alexander Maitland 1965
GMA 943

Head of Marie Tracey*
1938
Bronze
40.8 x 29.5 x 34.3
Bequeathed by Miss Elizabeth Watt 1989
GMA 3484

Max Ernst

1891–1976

Mer et soleil [Sea and Sun]*
d 1925
Oil on canvas
54 x 37
Purchased 1970
GMA 1119

Le Grand amoureux I [The Great Lover I]*
1926
Oil and black crayon on canvas
100.3 x 81.2
Purchased 1980
GMA 2134

La Forêt [The Forest]*
c 1928
Oil on canvas
54.2 x 65.5
Presented by Miss E. M. Dolbey 1980
GMA 2217

Danseuses [Dancers]
1950
Lithograph on paper (145/200)
49.5 x 32.6 (paper 56.4 x 38.1)
Purchased 1962
GMA 792

Merlyn Evans

1910–73

Thunderbird
d 1957
Aquatint on paper (23/50)
73.5 x 54.7 (paper 89.8 x 66.2)
Purchased 1960
GMA 746

Walker Evans

1903–75

Country Church, South Carolina
1936
Black and white photograph (gelatin silver print)
(posthumous print 1/75)
24 x 18.9 (paper 35.3 x 27.8)
Purchased 1980
GMA 2203

Sharecropper (Floyd Burroughs), Hale County, Alabama
1936
Black and white photograph (gelatin silver print)
(posthumous print 1/75)
24 x 19 (paper 35.4 x 27.9)
Purchased 1980
GMA 2204

Sharecropper's Kitchen, Hale County, Alabama
1936
Black and white photograph (gelatin silver print)
(posthumous print 1/75)
24.1 x 19 (paper 35.4 x 28)
Purchased 1980
GMA 2205

Sharecropper's Family, Hale County, Alabama
1936
Black and white photograph (gelatin silver print)
(posthumous print 4/75)
19.1 x 24.1 (paper 27.9 x 29.9)
Purchased 1980
GMA 2206

John Everett

exh. 1908–36

Luynes
Aquatint on paper
16.4 x 21.5 (paper 26.2 x 34.8)
Purchased 1949
GMA 261

Stormy Sea
Aquatint on paper
24.8 x 35.1 (paper 29.7 x 39.7)
Purchased 1949
GMA 262

David Shanks Ewart

1901–65

*The Return**
d 1927
Oil on canvas
127 x 76.5
Purchased 1980
GMA 2222

Chao Ling Fang

1914–

Lotus
1960
Brush and ink on paper
183 x 94.5
Purchased 1968
GMA 1077

Frederick Arthur Farrell

1882–1935

Cathedral Gateway, Ypres
d 1917
Pencil and watercolour on paper
20.5 x 12.9
Provenance unrecorded
GMA 695

Bernard Faucon

1950–

Le Banquet [*The Banquet*]
d 1978 (printed 1988)
Colour photograph (38/40)
30.5 x 30.3 (paper 37 x 32.6)
Purchased 1988
GMA 3403

Première communion [*First Communion*]
d 1979 (printed 1988)
Colour photograph
30.5 x 30.4 (paper 36.8 x 32.5)
Purchased 1988
GMA 3402

Jean Fautrier

1898–1964

La Chope [*The Tankard*]
d 1946
Colour etching and aquatint on paper (10/25)
26.6 x 35 (paper 37 x 52.3)
Purchased 1985
GMA 2961

Pericle Fazzini

1913–87

Nudo di schiena [*Recumbent Nude from Behind*]
Lithograph on paper (5/50)
45.7 x 65.7 (paper size)
Purchased 1968
GMA 1078

Lyonel Feininger

1871–1956

*Gelmeroda III**
1913
Oil on canvas
100.5 x 80
Purchased 1985
GMA 2951

John Duncan Fergusson

1874–1961

*Nude**
c 1898–1904
Oil on board
13.9 x 11.3
Presented anonymously in memory of Vivien
Leigh 1984
GMA 2920

*The Toreador**
c 1901–03
Watercolour and gouache on paper
16.3 x 11.8
Presented by Miss Violet Couper 1962
GMA 793

*Dieppe, 14 July 1905: Night**
d 1905
Oil on canvas
76.8 x 76.8
Purchased 1978
GMA 1713

*Portrait of Anne Estelle Rice**
d 1908
Oil on board
66.5 x 57.5
Purchased 1971
GMA 1247

*Twilight, Royan**
d 1910
Oil on board
27 x 34.9
Bequeathed by Dr R. A. Lillie 1977
GMA 1897

*Tin Openers**
c 1918
Black chalk and watercolour on paper
51 x 38.1
Purchased 1974
GMA 1350

*Eástre (Hymn to the Sun)**
1924 (cast 1971)
Brass
41.8 x 22 x 22.5
Purchased 1972
GMA 1263

*The Log Cabin Houseboat**
d 1925
Oil on canvas
76.2 x 66
Purchased 1966
GMA 974

*In the Patio: Margaret Morris Fergusson**
1925
Oil on canvas
71.2 x 61.1
Bequeathed by Mr and Mrs G. D. Robinson
through the National Art Collections Fund 1988
GMA 3352

Margaret Morris Fergusson

1891–1980

*Red Roofs (Dieppe)**
1922
Oil on board
35.5 x 27.3
Purchased 1984
GMA 2846

Ian Hamilton Finlay

1925–

*Beware of the Lark**
(with Michael Harvey)
1974
Stone
23 x 43 x 39
Purchased 1993
GMA 3706

*Sundial: Umbra Solis non Aeris**
(with Michael Harvey)
1975
Slate and metal rod
125.7 x 118.4 x 18.1
Commissioned 1975
GMA 1520

*Et in Arcadia Ego**
(with John Andrew)
1976
Stone
28.1 x 28 x 7.6
Purchased 1976
GMA 1583

*Conning Tower Draughts**
(with Susan Goodricke)
1976
24 ceramic draughts on tiled wooden base
Ceramic draughts, each 4.7 x 8.7 x 5.4 (7.5 h. with
lid reversed); base 29 x 92 x 120
Purchased 1976
GMA 1584

*Coastal Boy (Fishing Boat: A534)**
(with Peter Grant)
1977
Wood, painted
26 x 244.5 x 6.5
Purchased 1992
GMA 3603

*Nature over again after Poussin**
(with Sue Finlay, Nicholas Sloan, David Paterson
& Wilma Paterson)
1979–80
Eleven black and white photographs, each in
halves mounted separately on perspex; recorded
flute music
Each half print 49.5 x 29.2
Purchased 1981
GMA 2293

*Prints, cards and booklets by Ian Hamilton
Finlay, see* APPENDIX. *Also see* WILD
HAWTHORN PRESS

Beth Fisher

1944–

*Fear for My Children
(from the 'Canopy' series)**
d 1987
Four monoprints on paper
Four panels, each 182.8 x 60.8
Purchased 1990
GMA 3584

Dan Flavin

1933–

*Monument to V. Tatlin**
1975
Fluorescent lights
305 x 61 x 12
Purchased 1983
GMA 2799

Ian Fleming

1906–

*Puente de Alcantara, Toledo (Alcantara Bridge,
Toledo)*
1930
Engraving on paper
26.6 x 35.5 (paper 33.6 x 45.7)
Purchased 1982
GMA 2544

*Gethsemane**
1931
Engraving on paper
34 x 44.3 (paper 37 x 48.2)
Purchased 1982
GMA 2545

*Spanish Village**
c 1934
Etching and drypoint on paper (first state)
18.9 x 21.4 (paper 23.9 x 25.5)
Purchased 1982
GMA 2543

Glasgow School of Art
c 1935 (printed c 1984)
Etching on paper
21.3 x 15 (paper 38 x 28.5)
Purchased 1984
GMA 2835

Portrait of the Artist
d 1937
Etching on paper
30.4 x 25.2 (paper 42.2 x 31.2)
Purchased 1984
GMA 2834

Air-Raid Shelters, Maryhill
1942 (printed 1992)
Etching on paper
21.2 x 14.8 (paper 33.2 x 23)
Purchased 1992
GMA 3659

Industrial Landscape, Glasgow
d 1946
Drypoint on paper
27.8 x 33.8 (paper 33.5 x 38.4)
Purchased 1982
GMA 2542

Port Dundas, Glasgow
c 1946 / c 1956
Etching and drypoint on paper (12/20)
19.8 x 30 (paper 37 x 45)
Purchased 1984
GMA 2836

Frank Morley Fletcher

1866–1949

Girl Reading (or *The Bookworm*)*
by 1904
Colour woodcut on paper
19 x 15.6 (paper 24.6 x 20.8)
Purchased 1949
GMA 266

Landscape with Two Figures
by 1906
Woodcut on paper
35.3 x 18 (paper 39.6 x 22.4)
Purchased 1949
GMA 264

Canal Landscape with Two Figures
Colour woodcut on paper
20.6 x 25.4 (paper 23.7 x 28.6)
Purchased 1949
GMA 263

The Orange Seller
Colour woodcut on paper
15.7 x 21 (paper 19.7 x 25.4)
Purchased 1949
GMA 265

Robert Purves Flint

1883–1947

High Tide, Margate
d 1925
Watercolour and pen and ink on paper
28.2 x 38.8
Bequeathed by Dr R. A. Lillie 1977
GMA 1899

Genoa
Watercolour and pencil on paper
23.6 x 37.3
Bequeathed by Dr R. A. Lillie 1977
GMA 1898

William Russell Flint

1880–1969

*Provençal Landscape**
Watercolour on paper
25.2 x 35.5
Presented by Mrs Isabel M. Traill 1979
GMA 2143

Erik Forrest

Interior
d 1950
Etching on paper
14.7 x 22.5 (paper 21.3 x 29.4)
Purchased 1982
GMA 2546

Rose Frain

1940–

Royne descosse: A Distillation
1992
Box containing handmade paper with embedding,
photographic images with texts and one pencil
drawing
5.5 x 27.8 x 35 (box size)
Purchased (Knapping Fund) 1993
GMA 3671

Helen Frankenthaler

1928–

Saturn*
d 1963
Acrylic on canvas
264.2 x 119.5
Purchased 1972
GMA 1258

Claud Lovat Fraser

1890–1921

The Market
c 1912
Watercolour and black chalk on paper
21.1 x 34.2
Presented anonymously in memory of Terence
Rattigan 1984
GMA 2915

Barnett Freedman

1901–58

People
(from the J. Lyons series 'Lithographs by
Contemporary Artists, vol. I')
Published 1947
Colour lithograph on paper (after pen and ink and
watercolour)
72.2 x 97.7 (paper 74.3 x 99)
Presented by J. Lyons & Co. Ltd 1948
GMA 1201

Annie French

1872–1965

Title Page Design for 'Goblin Market'
by Christina Rossetti*
c 1912–13
Pen and ink, brush and ink and gold paint,
on paper (three pieces joined)
27.7 x 17.5
Presented by Mr Stanley Cursiter 1943
GMA 710

Princess Melilot
d 1941
Pen and ink and pencil on paper
22 x 18
Presented by Mr Stanley Cursiter 1943
GMA 712

Cinderella and the Ugly Sisters*
Pen and ink, watercolour and gold paint on
vellum
23.5 x 21.5
Presented by the artist 1943
GMA 708

The Little Boy Tells Tales of the Outer World to
the Little Brown Men: An Unwritten Fairy Tale
Pen and ink and brush and ink on paper, cut out
and laid on paper
Diameter 21.4 (laid on paper 32 x 25)
Presented by Mr Stanley Cursiter 1943
GMA 709

Puddie Fishing under the Waterfall:
An Unwritten Fairy Tale
Pen and ink and watercolour on paper
Diameter 21.5 (paper 29.8 x 25.2)
Presented by Mr Stanley Cursiter 1943
GMA 711

Lucian Freud

1922–

Two Men*
1987–88
Oil on canvas
106.7 x 75
Purchased 1988
GMA 3410

Lawrence Gowing
1982
Etching on paper (7/10)
17.6 x 15.2 (paper 33.2 x 27.8)
Purchased 1983
GMA 2741

Lord Goodman in his Yellow Pyjamas
1987
Etching and watercolour on paper (23/50)
31 x 39.7 (paper 48 x 55.4)
Purchased 1988
GMA 3355

Girl Sitting
1987
Etching on paper (15/50)
52.7 x 69.9 (paper 61.3 x 77.8)
Purchased 1988
GMA 3356

Elisabeth Frink

1930–93

Bird*
1959
Bronze
38 x 37.2 x 25.3
Presented by Mrs M. E. B. Scott Hay 1970
GMA 1108

Clifford Frith

1924–

Fun Fair
(from the J. Lyons series 'Lithographs by
Contemporary Artists, vol. 1)
Published 1947
Colour lithograph on paper (after gouache)
72.5 x 96.5 (paper 74.5 x 98)
Presented by J. Lyons & Co. Ltd 1948
GMA 1202

Hester Frood

1882–1971

Porte Gayole, Boulogne
Etching and drypoint on paper
14.2 x 11.2 (paper 20.4 x 13.5)
Bequeathed by Sir David Young Cameron 1945
GMA 267

Norman Gateway
Etching on paper
13.8 x 13.2 (paper 23.8 x 20.9)
Bequeathed by Sir David Young Cameron 1945
GMA 268

Landscape with Farm Buildings
Etching and drypoint on paper
10.3 x 18.8 (paper 13.6 x 21)
Bequeathed by Sir David Young Cameron 1945
GMA 269

Landscape with a Ruined Castle (I)
Etching on paper
18 x 26.3 (paper 22 x 29.2)
Bequeathed by Sir David Young Cameron 1945
GMA 270

Old City Street with Shops
Etching on paper
25.2 x 12.6 (paper 31.7 x 17.6)
Bequeathed by Sir David Young Cameron 1945
GMA 271

Landscape with Ruined Castle (II)
Etching on paper
21.2 x 26.4 (paper 24.3 x 28.8)
Bequeathed by Sir David Young Cameron 1945
GMA 272

Interior of a Barn
Etching on paper
25.2 x 17.7 (paper 27 x 18.9)
Bequeathed by Sir David Young Cameron 1945
GMA 273

Terry Frost

1915–

*Black and White Movement on Blue and Green II**
d 1951–52
Oil on canvas
111.8 x 86.3
Purchased 1974
GMA 1299

*Grey Figure**
d 1957
Oil on board
121.9 x 121.9
Purchased 1962
GMA 794

Brown Figure, Newbattle
d 1957
Colour lithograph on paper (27/30)
44.2 x 56.5 (paper 56 x 70.3)
Purchased 1960
GMA 747

Red and Black on Grey
d 1968
Screenprint on paper (17/75)
55.2 x 69.5 (paper 68.6 x 101.6)
Purchased 1984
GMA 2855

Moonship
d 1972
Colour lithograph on paper (A.P.)
103.5 x 64.4 (paper 105.5 x 75.2)
Purchased 1984
GMA 2856

Roger Fry

1866–1934

*White Road with Farm**
c 1912
Oil on canvas
64.8 x 80.6
Purchased 1975
GMA 1500

Hamish Fulton

1946–

*A Four Day Walk across the Border Country of England and Scotland, West Coast to East Coast from the Solway Firth to Holy Island, Early Spring 1977**
1977
Three black and white photographs joined and mounted on card with transfer-text
Photographs 50.3 x 204.5; card 96 x 244
Purchased 1980
GMA 2201

*Lightning over Liathach: A Five Day Hill Walk in June, Wester Ross, Scotland, 1980**
1980
Two black and white photographs mounted on card with transfer-text
Photographs 141 x 42.5; card 162 x 58.5
Purchased 1981
GMA 2306

Fourteen Works
1982–89 (published 1989)
Portfolio of fourteen offset lithographs
From 46.5 x 111 to 104.2 x 88 (paper size)
Purchased 1990
GMA 3555

Ethel Gabain

1883–1950

Le Petit déjeuner
1912
Lithograph on paper (second state)
40 x 28.9 (paper 52.2 x 38)
Purchased 1949
GMA 275

Rochester Proposing to Jane (for 'Jane Eyre')
1922 (published 1924)
Lithograph on paper
25.1 x 17.4 (paper 37.1 x 27.7)
Purchased 1949
GMA 274

Naum Gabo

1890–1977

*Spiral Theme**
1941
Celluloid on perspex base
6.8 x 16.8 x 11.3; base 0.2 x 15.9 x 15.6
Purchased 1986
GMA 2978

Edward Gage

1925–

*Self-Portrait**
d 1951
Watercolour, gouache and ink on paper
56.4 x 39.2
Purchased 1988
GMA 3363

Portrait Study of Hugh MacDiarmid
c 1954
Black crayon on paper
24 x 14.9
Purchased 1988
GMA 3364

Sketches of Hugh MacDiarmid
c 1954
Pencil on paper
24 x 14.9
Purchased 1988
GMA 3365

*Hugh MacDiarmid: Drunk Man Looks at the
Thistle*
(for 'The Radio Times')
d 1954 / 1962
Ink over pencil on scraperboard
12.8 x 20.3 (scraperboard 15.2 x 22.8)
Purchased 1988
GMA 3366

Drama Fringe
(for 'The Radio Times')
d 1956
Ink over pencil on scraperboard with paper
addition
11.3 x 10.2 (scraperboard 13.9 x 12.7)
Purchased 1988
GMA 3370

Master Mariner
(for 'The Radio Times')
d 1956
Ink over pencil on scraperboard
10.2 x 10.5 (scraperboard 12.7 x 12.6)
Purchased 1988
GMA 3371

Under Milk Wood
(for 'The Radio Times')
d 1957 / 1964
Ink over pencil on scraperboard
6.5 x 30.5 (scraperboard 8.9 x 33)
Purchased 1988
GMA 3368

Old Verily
(for 'The Radio Times')
d 1959
Ink over pencil on scraperboard
13.5 x 17.2 (scraperboard 16 x 19.7)
Purchased 1988
GMA 3367

Heart of the Parish
(for 'The Radio Times')
d 1959
Ink over pencil on scraperboard
12.7 x 12.9 (scraperboard 15.2 x 15.2)
Purchased 1988
GMA 3369

Paul Gangolf

1879–1940

Factories from Greenwich Pier
d 1931
Watercolour and pencil on paper
18.1 x 26
Presented by Jim Ede 1977
GMA 1622

Pavement Artist
Gouache on paper
10.9 x 15.1
Presented by Jim Ede 1977
GMA 1623

Indian Musicians at the Victoria and Albert Museum
d 1931
Etching on paper (7/40)
9.5 x 13.8 (paper 33.1 x 25.5)
Presented by Jim Ede 1977
GMA 1612

Near Greenwich Pier
d 1931
Etching on paper (3/40)
12.6 x 19 (paper 33.5 x 30.9)
Presented by Jim Ede 1977
GMA 1617

Indian on a Rug
d 1931
Etching on paper (3/40)
12 x 10 (paper 32.5 x 25.4)
Presented by Jim Ede 1977
GMA 1619

Rotten Row, London
d 1931
Etching on paper (17/25)
13 x 16.5 (paper 33.5 x 30.7)
Presented by Jim Ede 1977
GMA 1620

Change of Address Card
d 1931
Woodcut on paper (2/4)
10.5 x 12.5 (paper 15.7 x 21)
Presented by Jim Ede 1977
GMA 1624

Euston Road, London
d 1932 and 1934
Etching on paper
15.6 x 19.6 (paper 23 x 28.8)
Presented by Jim Ede 1977
GMA 1615

Gerona (A Street of Houses)
d 1933
Etching on paper (A.P.)
12.6 x 16.5 (paper 24.5 x 24)
Presented by Jim Ede 1977
GMA 1610

San Feliu (Boat Entering the Harbour)
d 1933 and 1934
Etching on paper (A.P.)
10.6 x 15.7 (paper 23.3 x 27.8)
Presented by Jim Ede 1977
GMA 1611

Arabian Riders
d 1934
Etching on paper (A.P.)
10 x 13 (paper 15.8 x 22.9)
Presented by Jim Ede 1977
GMA 1616

An Execution (1001 Nights)
Etching on paper
9.2 x 8 (paper 37.5 x 28.2)
Presented by Jim Ede 1977
GMA 1613

Paris, marché aux puces [Paris, Flea market]
Etching on paper
12 x 15.7 (paper 28.3 x 32.2)
Presented by Jim Ede 1977
GMA 1614

'The Rat' (A Lion-tamer)
Etching on paper
10 x 12 (paper 29.6 x 28.1)
Presented by Jim Ede 1977
GMA 1618

Village Hindou, Paris [Hindu Village, Paris]
Etching on paper
10 x 15 (paper 32.2 x 27.8)
Presented by Jim Ede 1977
GMA 1621

Exhibition Notice (Tiger)
Linocut on brown paper
9 x 12 (paper 11.3 x 14.6)
Presented by Jim Ede 1977
GMA 1625

Henri Gaudier-Brzeska
1891–1915

Head of an Idiot*
c 1912 (posthumous cast)
Bronze
18 x 14.5 x 16.8
Purchased 1977
GMA 1668

Standing Female Nude
c 1913
Pen and ink on paper
38.3 x 25.2
Presented by the Kettle's Yard Collection,
Cambridge, 1966
GMA 958

Female Nude Seated on the Ground
c 1913
Pen and ink on paper
25.5 x 38.8
Presented by the Kettle's Yard Collection,
Cambridge, 1966
GMA 959

Woman in a Long Dress*
c 1913
Black chalk on paper
25.1 x 19.1
Presented by the Kettle's Yard Collection,
Cambridge, 1966
GMA 960

Figure*
c 1914
Pencil on paper
33.7 x 21
Presented by the Kettle's Yard Collection,
Cambridge, 1966
GMA 961

Bird Swallowing a Fish*
1914 (posthumous cast)
Bronze
32 x 60.5 x 29.5
Purchased 1980
GMA 2150

William Gear
1915–

Fantôme blanc*
d January 1948
Gouache on paper
39 x 56.8
Purchased 1987
GMA 3300

Landscape*
d March 1949
Oil on canvas
73.5 x 92.5
Purchased 1974
GMA 1300

Interior*
d August 1949
Oil on canvas
73 x 60.3
Purchased 1987
GMA 3297

Pink Interior
d January 1949
Monotype with gouache and ink on paper
50 x 65.5
Purchased 1987
GMA 3301

Feu: Drawing – Black on Red No. 4
d 1949
Gouache and ink on paper
36.4 x 44.4
Purchased 1987
GMA 3302

Coucher de soleil*
d January – February 1950
Oil on canvas
54.4 x 73.9
Purchased 1987
GMA 3298

Marine Finistère No. 2
d August 1950
Oil on canvas
65.4 x 54.6
Purchased 1987
GMA 3299

*Autumn Landscape**
d September 1950
Oil on canvas
100.9 x 73.3
Purchased 1974
GMA 1301

*White Interior**
d December 1954
Oil on canvas
81.3 x 100.3
Purchased with funds given by an anonymous
donor 1964
GMA 890

Paso Doble
d 1959
Monotype on paper
37.6 x 50.8 (paper 52 x 63.5)
Purchased 1993
GMA 3713

*Broken Yellow**
d 1967
Oil on canvas
182.9 x 182.9
Purchased 1974
GMA 1307

Landscape
d 1949
Lithograph on paper (A.P.)
24.5 x 38.2 (paper 32.7 x 49.8)
Presented by the artist 1978
GMA 2016

Landscape
d 1949
Lithograph on paper (13/30)
15.6 x 23.6 (paper 25 x 32.6)
Presented by the artist 1978
GMA 2017

Black Element
d 1950
Lithograph on paper (13/25)
40.3 x 28.1 (paper 48.8 x 32.5)
Presented by the artist 1978
GMA 2018

Trellis
d 1952
Colour lithograph on paper (19/25)
28.2 x 40 (paper 38.5 x 56.2)
Presented by the artist 1978
GMA 2019

Alberto Giacometti

1901–66

*Objet désagréable, à jeter [Disagreeable Object,
to be Disposed of]**
1931
Wood
19.6 x 31 x 29
Purchased 1990
GMA 3547

*Femme égorgée [Woman with her Throat Cut]**
1932 (cast 1949)
Bronze (5/5)
22 x 87.5 x 53.5
Purchased 1970
GMA 1109

*Atelier aux deux seaux [Studio with Two
Buckets]*
1955
Etching on paper (29/50)
26.4 x 21.3 (paper 50.2 x 38.3)
Purchased 1962
GMA 795

Robert Gibbings

1889–1958

The Retreat from Serbia
d 1916
Colour wood engraving on paper
17.8 x 17.8 (paper 25.6 x 21.8)
Provenance unrecorded
GMA 277

Evening at Gaza
d 1918
Colour wood engraving on paper
26.9 x 13 (paper 33.6 x 17.7)
Provenance unrecorded
GMA 278

Melleha, Malta
d 1919
Wood engraving on buff paper
Diameter 19.3 (paper 22.5 x 20.9)
Purchased 1949
GMA 1602

Buildings and Smoking Chimneys
c 1920
Wood engraving on paper (11/50)
20.7 x 20.5 (paper 32.4 x 23.6)
Provenance unrecorded
GMA 276

Clear Waters*
1920
Wood engraving on paper
24.6 x 13.5 (paper 29.1 x 16.8)
Purchased 1949
GMA 1603

Illustration for 'The Lives of Gallant Ladies'
by Brantôme
Published 1924
Wood engraving on paper
11.3 x 13 (paper 20.2 x 26.5)
Purchased 1978
GMA 2005

Tailpiece for 'A Mirror for Witches'
by Esther Forbes
Published 1928
Wood engraving on paper
Diameter 5.8 (paper 20.8 x 13)
Purchased 1978
GMA 2006

Frontispiece for 'A Mirror for Witches'
by Esther Forbes
Published 1928
Wood engraving on paper
8.7 x 8.4 (paper 21.1 x 18.6)
Purchased 1978
GMA 2008

'The Bounty'
(for 'The Journal of James Morrison')
Published 1935
Wood engraving on paper
10.5 x 12 (paper 19.4 x 20.3)
Purchased 1978
GMA 2007

September: Pigs on a Farm
(for 'The Twelve Months' by Llewelyn Powys)
Published 1937
Wood engraving on paper
5.2 x 10 (paper 10.6 x 13.5)
Purchased 1978
GMA 2003

Cows on a Farm
(for 'The Twelve Months' by Llewelyn Powys)
Published 1937
Wood engraving on paper
5 x 8.5 (paper 13.5 x 21)
Purchased 1978
GMA 2004

Carole Gibbons

1935–

The Bride
c 1965
Coloured chalk and gouache on brown paper
50.7 x 40.5
Purchased 1965
GMA 912

Gilbert and George

Gilbert Proesch 1943 , George Passmore 1942–

Exhausted*
d 1980
Sixteen-part photographic work (each part dyed
and framed)
242 x 202 (assembled)
Purchased 1982
GMA 2507

David Gilbert

1928–

Study for Cross, No. 3
1963
Wood (burnt larch)
107 x 29.5 x 31
Purchased with funds given by an anonymous
donor 1964
GMA 891

William Giles

1872–1939

Our Lady's Birds
1908
Colour woodcut on paper
25.8 x 41.6 (paper 29.3 x 45.7)
Provenance unrecorded
GMA 284

*The Passing of the Crescent, Umbria**
1910
Colour woodcut on paper
24.7 x 37.4 (paper 33.9 x 42.1)
Provenance unrecorded
GMA 282

*The Last Glint of a Summer's Day, Vejle Fjord,
Denmark*
c 1920
Colour relief-etching on paper (7/50)
41 x 26.8 (paper 49 x 32.2)
Provenance unrecorded
GMA 280

The Raven
by 1926
Colour relief-etching on paper
14.6 x 20.5 (paper 17 x 23.7)
Provenance unrecorded
GMA 279

Landscape with Sunset Sky
Colour relief-etching on paper
32.6 x 24.3 (paper 38.6 x 28.3)
Provenance unrecorded
GMA 281

Landscape with Birds
Woodcut on paper
2.3 x 9.2 (paper 4.3 x 11.8)
Provenance unrecorded
GMA 283

Eric Gill

1882–1940

*Talitha Cumi (Maiden I say unto Thee, Arise)**
c 1909
Slate
40.3 x 125.5 x 2.7
Purchased 1978
GMA 2021

*Christ on the Cross**
c 1913
Hoptonwood stone, partly painted
31.2 x 14 x 3.5
Bequeathed by Sir David Young Cameron 1945
GMA 14

Christmas Greetings [P 8]
1908
Wood engraving on paper
3.5 x 7.3 (paper 7.3 x 11.8)
Bequeathed by Sir David Young Cameron 1945
GMA 311

Book-Plate for Stephen Pepler [P 11]
1911
Wood engraving in red and black on paper
9.5 x 8.1 (paper 12.8 x 10.3)
Bequeathed by Sir David Young Cameron 1945
GMA 339

The Trinity with Chalice [P 22]
d 1913
Wood engraving on paper
10 x 6.3 (paper 17.5 x 10.3)
Bequeathed by Sir David Young Cameron 1945
GMA 306

The Slaughter of the Innocents [P 18]
1914
Wood engraving on paper
6.1 x 5
Bequeathed by Sir David Young Cameron 1945
GMA 297

Hog and Wheatsheaf (The Hampshire House
Bakery) [P 31]
1915
Wood engraving on paper
Diameter 13.7 (paper 27.8 x 22.2)
Bequeathed by Sir David Young Cameron 1945
GMA 333

Dumb-Driven Cattle [P 36]
1915
Wood engraving on paper
9.2 x 8.2 (paper 12.8 x 10.9)
Bequeathed by Sir David Young Cameron 1945
GMA 341

'No. 27': A Man Seated in his Garden [P 37]
1915
Wood engraving on paper
7.8 x 8.2 (paper 11.2 x 10.8)
Bequeathed by Sir David Young Cameron 1945
GMA 355

The Money-Bag and the Whip [P 38]
1915
Wood engraving on paper
10.1 x 8.2 (paper 15 x 11.8)
Bequeathed by Sir David Young Cameron 1945
GMA 342

Five Stalks of Leaves [P 39]
1915
Wood engraving on paper
5.1 x 8 (paper 10.8 x 12.8)
Bequeathed by Sir David Young Cameron 1945
GMA 315

The Purchaser [P 40]
1915
Wood engraving on paper
12.6 x 8.1 (paper 19.1 x 14.4)
Bequeathed by Sir David Young Cameron 1945
GMA 354

Ship (Progress) [P 41]
1915
Wood engraving on paper
5 x 6.4 (paper 13.8 x 9.9)
Bequeathed by Sir David Young Cameron 1945
GMA 299

The Happy Labourer [P 42]
1915
Wood engraving on paper
13.5 x 8.2 (paper 19.1 x 12.5)
Bequeathed by Sir David Young Cameron 1945
GMA 357

Devil's Tails [P 43]
1915
Wood engraving on paper
4.1 x 5.6 (paper 10.4 x 12.6)
Bequeathed by Sir David Young Cameron 1945
GMA 316

Christ Crucified, Chalice and Host [P 45]
1915
Wood engraving (gold on black paper) (second
state)
13 x 8.3 (paper 13.4 x 8.9)
Bequeathed by Sir David Young Cameron 1945
GMA 362

Christ Crucified, Chalice and Host [P 45]
1915
Wood engraving on paper (second state)
13.1 x 8.3 (paper 25.7 x 21.9)
Bequeathed by Sir David Young Cameron 1945
GMA 363

Triangular Device [P 47]
1915
Wood engraving on paper
5.3 x 8.1 (paper 8.6 x 13)
Bequeathed by Sir David Young Cameron 1945
GMA 313

Two Wood Engravings
   1) Semi-circular Device [P 77]
   2) Calvary [P 44]
1) 1916; 2) 1915
Wood engravings on one sheet of paper
1) 2.9 x 9.1; 2) 2.8 x 8.1 (paper 11 x 11.3)
Bequeathed by Sir David Young Cameron 1945
GMA 300

Flight into Egypt [P 52]
1916
Wood engraving on paper
5.9 x 5 (paper 13 x 7.5)
Bequeathed by Sir David Young Cameron 1945
GMA 310

A Ship (Book-Plate for C. L. Rutherston) [P 55]
1916
Wood engraving on paper
5.8 x 8 (paper 7 x 11.7)
Bequeathed by Sir David Young Cameron 1945
GMA 301

Hand Holding a Book (Book-Plate for Everard
Meynell) [P 59]
1916
Wood engraving on paper
3 x 2.8 (paper 5 x 11.6)
Bequeathed by Sir David Young Cameron 1945
GMA 298

Gravestone with Angel ('Old Freeman') [P 61]
1916
Wood engraving on paper
2.6 x 3 (paper 9.7 x 12.8)
Bequeathed by Sir David Young Cameron 1945
GMA 286

St Michael and the Dragon [P 66]
1916
Wood engraving on paper
6.9 x 5 (paper 9.3 x 16.2)
Bequeathed by Sir David Young Cameron 1945
GMA 338

Adeste Fideles [P 72]
1916
Wood engraving on paper
5.1 x 5 (paper 19.4 x 14.7)
Bequeathed by Sir David Young Cameron 1945
GMA 287

Three Kings (Stella Duce Magi) [P 73]
1916
Wood engraving on paper
5.1 x 5 (paper 19.1 x 13.7)
Bequeathed by Sir David Young Cameron 1945
GMA 288

The Manger (Splendorem Aeternum) [P 74]
1916
Wood engraving on paper
5 x 5 (paper 19 x 11.6)
Bequeathed by Sir David Young Cameron 1945
GMA 294

Cantet Nunc Io [P 75]
1916
Wood engraving on paper
5.1 x 5 (paper 19.3 x 11.1)
Bequeathed by Sir David Young Cameron 1945
GMA 289

Madonna and Child with Gallows (with text
'Verbum Caro Factum Est...') [P 82]
d 1916
Wood engraving on paper
7.4 x 5.5 (paper 19.2 x 11.5)
Bequeathed by Sir David Young Cameron 1945
GMA 347

Madonna and Child with Crucifix [P 113]
1916
Wood engraving on paper
5 x 4.3 (paper 19 x 9.9)
Bequeathed by Sir David Young Cameron 1945
GMA 293

Five Wood Engravings
    1) Initial 'S' with Church [P 62]
    2) Chalice and Host with Candles [P 53]
    3) Hog in Triangle [P 58]
    4) 'D', 'P' and Cross [P 64]
    5) Chalice and Host [P 65]
1916
Wood engravings on one sheet of paper
1) 2.5 x 2.5; 2) 3.1 x 2.6; 3) 1.9 x 2.9; 4) 3.1 x 1.1;
5) 3.7 x 1.8 (paper 19.5 x 12.6)
Bequeathed by Sir David Young Cameron 1945
GMA 340

Five Illustrations from 'Concerning Dragons'
    1) Child and Nurse [P 67]
    2) Child in Bed [P 68]
    3) Child and Ghost [P 69]
    4) Child and Spectre [P 70]
    5) Dragon [P 88]
1916
Wood engravings on one sheet of paper
1) 3.7 x 3.8; 2) 3.7 x 3.7; 3) 3.7 x 3.8; 4) 3.8 x 3.6;
5) 3.3 x 4 (paper 18.4 x 14)
Bequeathed by Sir David Young Cameron 1945
GMA 356

'Concerning Dragons' (pamphlet)
  1) St Michael and the Dragon [P 66]
  2) Child and Nurse [P 67]
  3) Child in Bed [P 68]
  4) Child and Ghost [P 69]
  5) Child and Spectre [P 70]
  6) 'D', 'P' and Cross [P 64]
Published 1916
Pamphlet with wood engravings
14.5 x 11.4 (pamphlet size)
Bequeathed by Sir David Young Cameron 1945
GMA 358

'Adeste Fideles: A Christmas Hymn' (pamphlet)
  1) Madonna and Child and Chalice [P 76,
printed in red]
  2) Adeste Fideles [P 72]
  3) Three Kings [P 73]
  4) The Manger [P 74]
  5) Cantet Nunc Io [P 75]
  6) 'D', 'P' and Cross [P 64]
1916
Pamphlet with wood engravings
19.5 x 13.5 (pamphlet size)
Bequeathed by Sir David Young Cameron 1945
GMA 365

Four Wood Engravings
  1) Lettering with a Nib [P 71]
  2) Circular Device [P 78]
  3) Stalk with Leaves [P 109]
  4) Flower [P 139]
1) 1916; 2) 1916; 3) 1917; 4) 1918
Wood engravings on one sheet of paper
1) 2.3 x 4.3; 2) diameter 3.8; 3) 2.3 x 2.7;
4) diameter 1.6 (paper 14.4 x 11.8)
Bequeathed by Sir David Young Cameron 1945
GMA 319

Epiphany [P 84]
1917
Wood engraving on paper
4.2 x 6.2 (paper 8.3 x 12.5)
Bequeathed by Sir David Young Cameron 1945
GMA 302 A

Epiphany [P 84]
1917
Wood engraving on paper
4.2 x 6.2 (paper 5.6 x 7.4)
Purchased 1949
GMA 302 B

Parlers [P 85]
1917
Wood engraving on paper
4 x 5.8 (paper 9.3 x 12.8)
Bequeathed by Sir David Young Cameron 1945
GMA 305

Palm Sunday [P 86]
1917
Wood engraving on paper
4.1 x 6.3 (paper 9.3 x 12.7)
Bequeathed by Sir David Young Cameron 1945
GMA 303

Adam and Eve [P 87]
1917
Wood engraving on paper
3.2 x 5.8 (paper 10.4 x 13)
Bequeathed by Sir David Young Cameron 1945
GMA 318

'St George for England' (pamphlet featuring
'St George and the Dragon' [P 90])
1917 (published 1918)
Pamphlet with wood engraving
4.7 diameter; 25.7 x 19.8 (pamphlet size)
Bequeathed by Sir David Young Cameron 1945
GMA 336

Paschal Lamb (Agnus Redemit Oves) [P 92]
1917
Wood engraving on paper
Diameter 4.6 (paper 7.8 x 13.2)
Bequeathed by Sir David Young Cameron 1945
GMA 304

The Last Judgement [P 107]
1917
Wood engraving on paper
4.5 x 5.6 (paper 15.5 x 14.4)
Bequeathed by Sir David Young Cameron 1945
GMA 296

Initial Letter 'O' with Speedwell [P 110]
1917
Wood engraving on paper
3 x 2.8 (paper 12.8 x 6.5)
Bequeathed by Sir David Young Cameron 1945
GMA 309 A

Initial Letter 'O' with Speedwell (with in memoriam text for Olof Alice Johnston) [P 110]
1917
Wood engraving on paper
8.3 x 6.1 (paper 14.1 x 12.5)
Bequeathed by Sir David Young Cameron 1945
GMA 309 B

The Holy Face [P 111]
1917
Wood engraving on paper
7.7 x 5.7 (paper 19.3 x 13.2)
Bequeathed by Sir David Young Cameron 1945
GMA 295

Executioner's Axe and Block [P 135]
1917
Wood engraving on paper
3.6 x 3.5 (paper 8.5 x 11.6)
Bequeathed by Sir David Young Cameron 1945
GMA 312

Hangman's Rope [P 136]
1917
Wood engraving on paper
3 x 2.2 (paper 7.7 x 9.3)
Bequeathed by Sir David Young Cameron 1945
GMA 314

Spirit and Flesh [P 137]*
1917
Wood engraving on paper
5.8 x 5.8 (paper 7.1 x 7.1)
Bequeathed by Sir David Young Cameron 1945
GMA 317

View of Ditchling [P 138]
1918
Wood engraving on paper
2 x 5.8 (paper 9.8 x 12.8)
Bequeathed by Sir David Young Cameron 1945
GMA 290

Crucifix: En Ego [P 148]
1918
Wood engraving on paper
4.7 x 3.8 (paper 5.1 x 4.1)
Bequeathed by Sir David Young Cameron 1945
GMA 292

Welsh Dragon [P 150]
1919
Wood engraving on paper (printed in red)
2 x 2.8 (paper 3.8 x 3.8)
Bequeathed by Sir David Young Cameron 1945
GMA 337

Christ and the Money-Changers [P 152]
1919
Wood engraving on paper
5.2 x 7.9 (paper 7.4 x 8.8)
Bequeathed by Sir David Young Cameron 1945
GMA 291 A

Christ and the Money-Changers [P 152]
1919
Wood engraving on paper
5.2 x 7.9 (paper 8.8 x 10.7)
Purchased 1949
GMA 291 B

Hand and Cross [P 161]
1920
Wood engraving on paper
1.5 x 0.8 (paper 2.5 x 1.4)
Bequeathed by Sir David Young Cameron 1945
GMA 325

'Three Poems by Ananda Coomaraswamy' (pamphlet)
  1) *Welsh Dragon* [P 150, printed in red]
  2) *New England Woods* [P 163]
  3) *Invitation* [P 164])
1920
Pamphlet with wood engraving and woodcuts
26.8 x 19 (pamphlet size)
Bequeathed by Sir David Young Cameron 1945
GMA 322

The Lion (or She Loves Me Not) [P 179]
1921
Wood engraving on paper
5.6 x 7.7 (paper 9.4 x 12.2)
Bequeathed by Sir David Young Cameron 1945
GMA 348

Westward Ho! [P 185]
1921
Wood engraving on paper
12.7 x 9 (paper 19 x 12.8)
Bequeathed by Sir David Young Cameron 1945
GMA 323

On the Tiles [P 191]
1921
Wood engraving on paper
8.3 x 7 (paper 13 x 11.2)
Bequeathed by Sir David Young Cameron 1945
GMA 361

Nude Crucifix [P 192]
1922
Wood engraving on paper
11.4 x 3.9 (paper 13.4 x 6.4) (irregular)
Bequeathed by Sir David Young Cameron 1945
GMA 330

Girl in Bath I [P 194]
1922
Wood engraving on paper
10.4 x 10.3 (paper 13.5 x 12)
Bequeathed by Sir David Young Cameron 1945
GMA 350

The Plait (Portrait of Petra, the Artist's
Daughter) [P 195]
1922
Wood engraving on paper
16.5 x 9.7 (paper 17.9 x 13.1)
Bequeathed by Sir David Young Cameron 1945
GMA 346

Clare (Portrait of Mrs H. D. C. Pepler) [P 196]
1922
Wood engraving on paper
16.6 x 11.6 (paper 18.4 x 12.3)
Bequeathed by Sir David Young Cameron 1945
GMA 345

Crucifix with Crown of Thorns [P 197]
1922
Wood engraving on paper (final state)
20.1 x 7.8 (paper 22.7 x 8.7)
Bequeathed by Sir David Young Cameron 1945
GMA 328

St Sebastian [P 200]
1922
Wood engraving on paper
10.7 x 4 (paper 12.9 x 5.1)
Bequeathed by Sir David Young Cameron 1945
GMA 329

Divine Lovers [P 201]
1922
Wood engraving on paper (second state)
8.2 x 6.6 (paper 13 x 10.2)
Bequeathed by Sir David Young Cameron 1945
GMA 353

Shuttle and Web [P 202]
1922
Wood engraving on paper
1.6 x 1.9 (paper 2.6 x 4.7)
Bequeathed by Sir David Young Cameron 1945
GMA 367

St Martin (Book-Plate for Thomas Lowinsky)
[P 207]
1922
Wood engraving on paper
9.5 x 7 (paper 12.3 x 7.8)
Bequeathed by Sir David Young Cameron 1945
GMA 331

Hair Combing [P 208]*
1922
Wood engraving on paper
10.2 x 6.4 (paper 12.9 x 8.6)
Bequeathed by Sir David Young Cameron 1945
GMA 351

Madonna and Child [P 209]
1922
Wood engraving on paper
9 x 6.6 (paper 10.1 x 7.7)
Bequeathed by Sir David Young Cameron 1945
GMA 332

St Luke (Book-Plate for Thomas and Ruth
Lowinsky) [P 210]
1922
Wood engraving on paper (printed from 2 blocks)
10.9 x 5.6 (paper 12.9 x 8.2)
Bequeathed by Sir David Young Cameron 1945
GMA 360

St Martin [P 212]
1922
Wood engraving on paper
3.6 x 3.1 (paper 7.1 x 5)
Bequeathed by Sir David Young Cameron 1945
GMA 308

St George and the Dragon [P 213]
1922
Wood engraving on paper
3.6 x 4.7 (paper 7.7 x 6.7)
Bequeathed by Sir David Young Cameron 1945
GMA 343

Nuptials of God [P 214]
1922
Wood engraving on paper
6.5 x 5.1 (paper 7.9 x 6.5)
Bequeathed by Sir David Young Cameron 1945
GMA 334

Madonna and Child with Arms Outstretched
(Sedes Sapientiæ) [P 215]
1922
Wood engraving on paper
6.8 x 3 (paper 9.3 x 4.2)
Bequeathed by Sir David Young Cameron 1945
GMA 307

Madonna and Child Enthroned [P 216]
1923
Wood engraving on paper
10.9 x 5.4 (paper 11.5 x 6.3)
Bequeathed by Sir David Young Cameron 1945
GMA 335

Girl in Bath II [P 218]
1923
Wood engraving on paper
10.6 x 10.6 (paper 12 x 11.7)
Purchased 1949
GMA 366

Hound of St Dominic [P 225]
1923
Woodcut on paper
16.5 x 24.2 (paper 18.1 x 25.6)
Bequeathed by Sir David Young Cameron 1945
GMA 364

Crown of Thorns [P 252]
1923
Wood engraving on paper
2 x 2 (paper 3.1 x 3.2)
Bequeathed by Sir David Young Cameron 1945
GMA 324

Torso of a Woman [P 257, with black border]
1923
Wood engraving on paper
9 x 2.1 (paper 11.7 x 3.8)
Bequeathed by Sir David Young Cameron 1945
GMA 349

Crucifix, Robed [P 258]
1923
Wood engraving on paper
7.9 x 4.8 (paper 9.8 x 6.8)
Bequeathed by Sir David Young Cameron 1945
GMA 326

Mary at the Sepulchre [P 262]
1923
Wood engraving on paper
7.3 x 5.5 (paper 10.2 x 7.9)
Bequeathed by Sir David Young Cameron 1945
GMA 359

Adam [P 265]
1923
Wood engraving on paper
10.1 x 2.5 (paper 12.8 x 4.3)
Bequeathed by Sir David Young Cameron 1945
GMA 352

Eve [P 266]
1923
Wood engraving on paper
10.2 x 2.6 (paper 12.5 x 4.3)
Bequeathed by Sir David Young Cameron 1945
GMA 344

Madonna and Child [P 268]
1923
Wood engraving on paper
7.2 x 5.1 (paper 9.6 x 7.4)
Bequeathed by Sir David Young Cameron 1945
GMA 327

[P refers to the catalogue raisonné of Gill's
engravings by J. F. Physick (Victoria and Albert
Museum, London, 1960)]

William Gillies

1898–1973

Sunshine, Cramond*
c 1916–21
Oil on canvas
35.7 x 46
Bequeathed by Dr R. A. Lillie 1977
GMA 1717

Unfinished Study for an Annunciation (after
Florentine School, 15th Century)
c 1924
Watercolour, gum arabic, gouache and black
chalk on paper
87.6 x 50.5
Bequeathed by Dr R. A. Lillie 1977
GMA 1718

Woodland Path
d 1926
Watercolour and pencil on paper
28.2 x 36.1
Bequeathed by Keith Andrews 1990
GMA 3609

On the Tyne, The Long Cram, Haddington
[verso: Trees]
d 1927
Watercolour and gouache on paper
41 x 48./
Bequeathed by Dr R. A. Lillie 1977
GMA 1765

Morning Light, Kirkcudbright Farm
c 1929
Watercolour and pencil on paper
26.9 x 35.2
Bequeathed by Dr R. A. Lillie 1977
GMA 1775

Near Kirkcudbright
d 1929
Watercolour and pencil on paper
26.9 x 35
Bequeathed by Dr R. A. Lillie 1977
GMA 1776

Border Landscape
Early 1930s
Oil on plywood
25.8 x 41.6
Bequeathed by Dr R. A. Lillie 1977
GMA 1732

Morar
d 1931
Watercolour and gum arabic on paper
38.2 x 55.7
Bequeathed by Dr R. A. Lillie 1977
GMA 1808

Skye Hills from near Morar*
c 1931
Watercolour and gouache on board
37.6 x 55.8
Bequeathed by Dr R. A. Lillie 1977
GMA 1833

Near Durisdeer*
c 1932
Oil on canvas
63.4 x 76
Bequeathed by Dr R. A. Lillie 1977
GMA 1747

A Pool
d 1932
Watercolour and black chalk on paper
27.8 x 38
Bequeathed by Dr R. A. Lillie 1977
GMA 1819

Milton
d 1933
Watercolour on paper
46.1 x 55.9
Bequeathed by Dr R. A. Lillie 1977
GMA 1805

The Street
c 1933
Watercolour and gouache on paper
50.5 x 63.1
Bequeathed by Dr R. A. Lillie 1977
GMA 1854

The Dark Pond
c 1934
Watercolour on paper
50.4 x 63.6
Bequeathed by Dr R. A. Lillie 1977
GMA 1818

Poppies in a Yellow Vase
d 1934
Oil on canvas
91.5 x 61.5
Bequeathed by Dr R. A. Lillie 1977
GMA 1821

*The Harbour**
c 1934–37
Oil on canvas
76.5 x 91.5
Bequeathed by Dr R. A. Lillie 1977
GMA 1766

Head of the Glen
Mid – late 1930s
Watercolour and pencil on paper
55.5 x 73.5
Bequeathed by Dr R. A. Lillie 1977
GMA 1770

*In Ardnamurchan**
c 1936
Watercolour and gouache on paper
50.6 x 63
Bequeathed by Dr R. A. Lillie 1977
GMA 1723

Loch Carron
c 1936
Watercolour on paper
50 x 63.2
Bequeathed by Dr R. A. Lillie 1977
GMA 1797

Autumn So Early
c 1937
Watercolour on paper
25.3 x 35.4
Bequeathed by Dr R. A. Lillie 1977
GMA 1726

Suilven, Wester Ross
d 1937
Watercolour and gouache on paper
50.7 x 64
Bequeathed by Dr R. A. Lillie 1977
GMA 1856

*Poppies and Cretonne Cloth**
c 1937–40
Oil on canvas
91.5 x 71
Bequeathed by Dr R. A. Lillie 1977
GMA 1820

Rhynie
[verso: *Study of a Tree*]
Late 1930s – early 1940s
Watercolour on paper [verso: black chalk]
56.2 x 76.7
Bequeathed by Dr R. A. Lillie 1977
GMA 1823

French Harbour
c 1938
Watercolour on paper
48 x 63
Scott Hay Collection: presented 1967
GMA 1037

Crofts, Bonar Bridge
c 1938
Watercolour and pen and ink on paper
66.5 x 79
Bequeathed by Dr R. A. Lillie 1977
GMA 1731

Laide
c 1938
Pen and ink on paper
25.9 x 42.1
Bequeathed by Dr R. A. Lillie 1977
GMA 1785

Spinningdale
c 1938–39
Watercolour, gouache and pen and ink on paper
50 x 63.2
Bequeathed by Dr R. A. Lillie 1977
GMA 1804

Samuelston
d 1939
Watercolour and pen and ink on paper
62.6 x 48
Bequeathed by Dr R. A. Lillie 1977
GMA 1831

Temple Street
Early 1940s
Pen and ink and brush and ink on paper
20.9 x 51
Bequeathed by Dr R. A. Lillie 1977
GMA 1868

The Village (Temple)
Early 1940s
Brown ink and wash on paper
24.5 x 40.3
Bequeathed by Dr R. A. Lillie 1977
GMA 1869

Temple Village
Early 1940s
Oil on canvas
61 x 91.5
Bequeathed by Dr R. A. Lillie 1977
GMA 1870

The Wooded Road
Early 1940s
Pen and ink and ink wash on paper
25.1 x 36.6
Bequeathed by Dr R. A. Lillie 1977
GMA 1881

Summer
c 1940 45
Oil on canvas
56 x 76.5
Bequeathed by Dr R. A. Lillie 1977
GMA 1857

Wooded Road (near Temple)
Early – mid 1940s
Pen and ink and wash on paper
26.9 x 40.8
Bequeathed by Dr R. A. Lillie 1977
GMA 1882

Outskirts of a Border Town (Darnick)
[verso: Street Scene]
1940s
Pencil on paper
10.6 x 14.8
Bequeathed by Dr R. A. Lillie 1977
GMA 1733

Border Village, Darnick
1940s
Pencil on paper
10.6 x 14.8
Bequeathed by Dr R. A. Lillie 1977
GMA 1810

The Village Letter-Box
1940s
Watercolour, gouache and pencil on paper
50.6 x 68.7
Bequeathed by Dr R. A. Lillie 1977
GMA 1878

Studies of Cattle
c 1940s – 1950s
Pen and ink on paper
24.2 x 35.4
Bequeathed by Dr R. A. Lillie 1977
GMA 1744

Aultbea
c 1941
Pencil on paper
12.1 x 20.8
Bequeathed by Dr R. A. Lillie 1977
GMA 1724

Flowers on a Sideboard*
c 1941
Oil on canvas
80 x 124
Bequeathed by Dr R. A. Lillie 1977
GMA 1759

Back Garden, Temple
c 1941
Pen and ink on paper
15.6 x 22.1
Bequeathed by Dr R. A. Lillie 1977
GMA 1861

The Road between Temple and Middleton
c 1941
Watercolour, gouache and pen and ink on paper
42 x 53.2
Bequeathed by Dr R. A. Lillie 1977
GMA 1866

Still Life, Breton Pot
c 1942
Oil on canvas
76.2 x 91.4
Bequeathed by Dr R. A. Lillie 1977
GMA 1840

Early Morning, Temple
c 1942
Oil on canvas
54 x 69
Bequeathed by Dr R. A. Lillie 1977
GMA 1860

Winter Afternoon, Temple
c 1942
Watercolour, gouache and pen and ink on paper
34.2 x 51.1
Bequeathed by Dr R. A. Lillie 1977
GMA 1873

The Tulip Vase
c 1942–44
Oil on canvas
91.5 x 76
Bequeathed by Dr R. A. Lillie 1977
GMA 1876

Still Life with Roses
c 1943
Oil on canvas
66.5 x 56.2
Bequeathed by Dr R. A. Lillie 1977
GMA 1849

Temple Street
c 1943
Crayon on paper
37.6 x 60.6
Bequeathed by Dr R. A. Lillie 1977
GMA 1867

Castleton
c 1944
Watercolour and gouache on paper
37.2 x 44.7
Bequeathed by Dr R. A. Lillie 1977
GMA 1743

Farm in Winter
c 1944
Pen and brown ink on paper
25.8 x 37
Bequeathed by Dr R. A. Lillie 1977
GMA 1754

Midlothian Village
c 1944
Oil on canvas
61.5 x 92
Bequeathed by Dr R. A. Lillie 1977
GMA 1803

Trees in the Gloaming
d 1944
Watercolour and gouache on paper
46.3 x 55.6
Bequeathed by Dr R. A. Lillie 1977
GMA 1875

Manse with Chickens (Temple)
Mid-1940s
Pen and ink on paper
14.1 x 39.4
Bequeathed by Dr R. A. Lillie 1977
GMA 1800

Studio Table
Mid-1940s
Oil on canvas
85 x 48
Bequeathed by Dr R. A. Lillie 1977
GMA 1855

Temple
Mid-1940s
Oil on canvas
56.5 x 68.7
Bequeathed by Dr R. A. Lillie 1977
GMA 1858

Landscape with Houses, Temple
Mid-1940s
Watercolour and gouache on paper
50.6 x 63.7
Bequeathed by Dr R. A. Lillie 1977
GMA 1865

Temple, Winter Street
Mid-1940s
Oil on board
37.7 x 52
Bequeathed by Dr R. A. Lillie 1977
GMA 1874

The Garden, Sunset
d 1945
Watercolour and pencil on paper
68.6 x 96
Scott Hay Collection: presented 1967
GMA 1038

Anstruther Harbour
1945
Oil on canvas
50.5 x 66.2
Bequeathed by Dr R. A. Lillie 1977
GMA 1721

Fishing Boats, Anstruther Harbour
c 1945
Oil on board
48 x 60.5
Bequeathed by Dr R. A. Lillie 1977
GMA 1722

The Pond
c 1945–48
Watercolour, gouache and pen and ink on paper
68.5 x 53
Bequeathed by Dr R. A. Lillie 1977
GMA 1817

Roadway, Blue Sky
c 1945–50
Oil on canvas
37 x 40.3
Bequeathed by Dr R. A. Lillie 1977
GMA 1825

Still Life on a Blue Cloth
c 1945–50
Oil on canvas
44 x 55
Bequeathed by Dr R. A. Lillie 1977
GMA 1838

Dykehead, Glen Prosen
d 1946
Watercolour and pencil on paper
31.6 x 50.8
Bequeathed by Dr R. A. Lillie 1977
GMA 1748

Floors Castle
1946
Watercolour, pen and ink and pencil on paper
18.1 x 22.7
Bequeathed by Dr R. A. Lillie 1977
GMA 1757

Flowers in a Pot
1946
Pen and ink on paper
50.5 x 40.5
Bequeathed by Dr R. A. Lillie 1977
GMA 1758

Gifford
c 1946
Pencil on paper
28.7 x 41.3
Bequeathed by Dr R. A. Lillie 1977
GMA 1764

Kirriemuir, the Roods
c 1946
Watercolour, pen and ink and pencil on paper
23.5 x 30.7
Bequeathed by Dr R. A. Lillie 1977
GMA 1777

Kirriemuir
1946
Pen and ink on paper
25.7 x 36.5
Bequeathed by Dr R. A. Lillie 1977
GMA 1778

Kirriemuir, Houses on a Slope
1946
Pen and ink on paper
28.3 x 38.4
Bequeathed by Dr R. A. Lillie 1977
GMA 1779

Main Street, Kirriemuir
c 1946
Watercolour and pencil on paper
23.5 x 30.6
Bequeathed by Dr R. A. Lillie 1977
GMA 1780

North Muir, Kirriemuir
c 1946
Watercolour and pencil on paper
10.6 x 14.8
Bequeathed by Dr R. A. Lillie 1977
GMA 1781

The Red House, Kirriemuir
d 1946
Watercolour and pen and ink on paper
23.6 x 30.7
Bequeathed by Dr R. A. Lillie 1977
GMA 1782

The Two Churches, Kirriemuir
1946
Watercolour, gum arabic and pencil on paper
47.9 x 61.7
Bequeathed by Dr R. A. Lillie 1977
GMA 1783

Wind above Kirriemuir
d 1946
Watercolour and pen and ink on paper
23.9 x 31.2
Bequeathed by Dr R. A. Lillie 1977
GMA 1784

Balmacara
1947
Watercolour and pencil on paper
24 x 27.1
Bequeathed by Dr R. A. Lillie 1977
GMA 1727

Balmacara
[verso: *Balmacara*]
c 1947
Watercolour and pencil on paper [verso: pencil]
24.6 x 31.5
Bequeathed by Dr R. A. Lillie 1977
GMA 1728

Winter, Carrington
d 1947
Watercolour, gouache and pencil on paper
20.4 x 25.9
Bequeathed by Dr R. A. Lillie 1977
GMA 1737

Winter, Carrington
c 1947
Oil on board
62.5 x 77
Bequeathed by Dr R. A. Lillie 1977
GMA 1738

Eilean Donan Castle, Loch Duich
c 1947
Oil on canvas
25.3 x 60.8
Bequeathed by Dr R. A. Lillie 1977
GMA 1750

Letterfearn
c 1947
Oil on canvas
56 x 71.5
Bequeathed by Dr R. A. Lillie 1977
GMA 1787

Letterfearn
c 1947
Oil on canvas
58 x 76
Bequeathed by Dr R. A. Lillie 1977
GMA 1788

Letterfearn
c 1947
Pen and ink on paper
25.3 x 36.5
Bequeathed by Dr R. A. Lillie 1977
GMA 1789

The Boats, Letterfearn
c 1947
Pen and ink on paper
25.3 x 36.5
Bequeathed by Dr R. A. Lillie 1977
GMA 1790

Dusk at Letterfearn
c 1947
Oil on canvas
49 x 61.2
Bequeathed by Dr R. A. Lillie 1977
GMA 1791

View of Village, Letterfearn (with Nets)
c 1947
Pen and ink on paper
25.3 x 36.5
Bequeathed by Dr R. A. Lillie 1977
GMA 1792

The Rainbow, Letterfearn
c 1947
Watercolour on paper
51.6 x 63.5
Bequeathed by Dr R. A. Lillie 1977
GMA 1793

Summer Afternoon, Letterfearn
c 1947
Oil on canvas
47 x 53
Bequeathed by Dr R. A. Lillie 1977
GMA 1794

View of Village, Letterfearn
c 1947
Pen and ink on paper
25.3 x 36.5
Bequeathed by Dr R. A. Lillie 1977
GMA 1795

The Gyles, Pittenweem
c 1947
Watercolour and pen and ink on paper
47.9 x 62.2
Bequeathed by Dr R. A. Lillie 1977
GMA 1814

Snow from the Studio Window (The Gordon
Children)
c 1947
Oil on canvas
62 x 82.5
Bequeathed by Dr R. A. Lillie 1977
GMA 1834

Hawksnest Farm
Late 1940s
Oil on canvas
51 x 61
Bequeathed by Dr R. A. Lillie 1977
GMA 1768

Hawksnest Farm
Late 1940s
Watercolour and pencil on paper
25.4 x 59
Bequeathed by Dr R. A. Lillie 1977
GMA 1769

Harbour, Pittenweem
Late 1940s
Pen and ink on paper with pencil colour notes
47.7 x 62.4
Bequeathed by Dr R. A. Lillie 1977
GMA 1815

Rainy Day, Pittenweem
Late 1940s
Oil on canvas
56.2 x 76.8
Bequeathed by Dr R. A. Lillie 1977
GMA 1816

Snow, Temple
Late 1940s
Watercolour on paper
33.9 x 50.8
Bequeathed by Dr R. A. Lillie 1977
GMA 1871

Anstruther from the Harbour Wall
1948
Watercolour, gouache and pen and ink on paper
47.8 x 63.2
Bequeathed by Dr R. A. Lillie 1977
GMA 1719

Anstruther Harbour
c 1948
Watercolour and pen and ink on paper
47.7 x 63.2
Bequeathed by Dr R. A. Lillie 1977
GMA 1983

Anstruther
c 1948
Watercolour and pen and ink on paper
22.7 x 62.4
Bequeathed by Dr R. A. Lillie 1977
GMA 1720

South Esk
c 1948
Oil on canvas
46 x 58
Bequeathed by Dr R. A. Lillie 1977
GMA 1835

The South Esk in Arniston Grounds
1948
Oil on canvas
38.5 x 48.4
Bequeathed by Dr R. A. Lillie 1977
GMA 1836

Spring Evening
c 1948
Oil on canvas
37.1 x 77
Bequeathed by Dr R. A. Lillie 1977
GMA 1837

Still Life, Pot with Evergreen Leaves
c 1948
Oil on canvas
53.5 x 68
Bequeathed by Dr R. A. Lillie 1977
GMA 1848

Back of the Artist's House, Temple
c 1948
Pen and ink on paper
45.4 x 57.5
Bequeathed by Dr R. A. Lillie 1977
GMA 1859

The Fishing Boat
d 1949
Watercolour and pen and ink on paper
24.5 x 31.2
Bequeathed by Dr R. A. Lillie 1977
GMA 1756

'The Protect Me III' (St Monance)
d 1949
Pen and ink on paper
36 x 56.1
Bequeathed by Dr R. A. Lillie 1977
GMA 1767

Rosebery Reservoir
c 1949
Watercolour and gum arabic on paper
38.3 x 57
Bequeathed by Dr R. A. Lillie 1977
GMA 1827

*St Monance**
c 1949
Watercolour and chalk on paper
24.7 x 31.5
Bequeathed by Dr R. A. Lillie 1977
GMA 1829

St Monance from the Harbour
c 1949
Watercolour and pen and ink on paper (two
sheets joined)
24.6 x 39.9
Bequeathed by Dr R. A. Lillie 1977
GMA 1830

Winter, Temple (Back of Houses)
c 1949
Watercolour and pen and ink on paper
50.2 x 67.1
Bequeathed by Dr R. A. Lillie 1977
GMA 1872

Carrington, Church and Houses
c 1950
Watercolour and pen and ink on paper
45.3 x 56.8
Bequeathed by Dr R. A. Lillie 1977
GMA 1736

Gardenstown Harbour
c 1950
Watercolour, gouache and pen and ink on paper
48.2 x 61.7
Bequeathed by Dr R. A. Lillie 1977
GMA 1760

Gardenstown Old Cemetery
d 1950
Watercolour and pencil on paper
24.7 x 31.7
Bequeathed by Dr R. A. Lillie 1977
GMA 1761

Gardenstown – Red Cliff
c 1950
Watercolour and pencil on paper
24.7 x 31.6
Bequeathed by Dr R. A. Lillie 1977
GMA 1762

Valley past Heriot
d 1950
Watercolour, gouache and pen and ink on paper
36 x 55.4
Bequeathed by Dr R. A. Lillie 1977
GMA 1771

Wooded Landscape, Lothian
d 1950
Watercolour and pen and ink on paper
47.9 x 63
Bequeathed by Dr R. A. Lillie 1977
GMA 1798

The Peebles Train
c 1950
Oil on canvas
46 x 56.5
Bequeathed by Dr R. A. Lillie 1977
GMA 1811

The Pentlands, Winter
c 1950–52
Watercolour and pencil on paper
25.5 x 35.5
Bequeathed by Dr R. A. Lillie 1977
GMA 1813

Hay Time, Temple
Early 1950s
Watercolour and gouache on paper
55 x 67.2
Bequeathed by Dr R. A. Lillie 1977
GMA 1864

Autumn Crocus
c 1950s
Coloured crayon on paper
33.2 x 29
Bequeathed by Dr R. A. Lillie 1977
GMA 1725

Boats, Low Tide
c 1950s
Pen and ink on paper
27.8 x 34.5
Bequeathed by Dr R. A. Lillie 1977
GMA 1730

North of Broughton
1950s
Pencil on paper
25.4 x 35.4
Bequeathed by Dr R. A. Lillie 1977
GMA 1735

Coldingham
1950s
Pencil on paper
25.5 x 35.2
Bequeathed by Dr R. A. Lillie 1977
GMA 1745

Early Evening
1950s
Watercolour and pencil on paper
39.3 x 57.1
Bequeathed by Dr R. A. Lillie 1977
GMA 1749

Road near Loanhead
1950s
Pencil on paper
17.7 x 22.7
Bequeathed by Dr R. A. Lillie 1977
GMA 1796

Stormy Loch
1950s
Pencil on paper
11.2 x 17.5
Bequeathed by Dr R. A. Lillie 1977
GMA 1850

Gattonside
c 1951
Pen and ink and ink wash on paper
25.1 x 36.5
Bequeathed by Dr R. A. Lillie 1977
GMA 1763

Near Howgate
d 1951
Watercolour and pencil on paper
25.2 x 35.4
Bequeathed by Dr R. A. Lillie 1977
GMA 1772

Farm on the Meldons Road
d 1951
Watercolour and pencil on paper
37.5 x 55.6
Bequeathed by Dr R. A. Lillie 1977
GMA 1802

March, Moorfoot
d 1951
Watercolour and pencil on paper
66.3 x 55
Bequeathed by Dr R. A. Lillie 1977
GMA 1806

Moray Harbour
d 1951
Watercolour, gouache and ink on paper
48.2 x 61.5
Bequeathed by Dr R. A. Lillie 1977
GMA 1809

Pennan
c 1951
Watercolour, gouache and pen and ink on paper
25.2 x 35.2
Bequeathed by Dr R. A. Lillie 1977
GMA 1812

Near Romanno Bridge
c 1951
Watercolour and pencil on paper
25.3 x 35.4
Bequeathed by Dr R. A. Lillie 1977
GMA 1826

Still Life, Pears and Green Jug
c 1951
Oil on canvas
51.2 x 62
Bequeathed by Dr R. A. Lillie 1977
GMA 1846

Winter
d 1951
Watercolour and pencil on paper
25.5 x 35.5
Bequeathed by Dr R. A. Lillie 1977
GMA 1880

The Blue Jug
c 1952
Oil on canvas
71.5 x 92
Bequeathed by Dr R. A. Lillie 1977
GMA 1729

Still Life, Goblet, White Jug and Honesty
d 1952
Oil on canvas
37.7 x 52.4
Bequeathed by Dr R. A. Lillie 1977
GMA 1844

Still Life with Penguin Books
c 1952
Oil on canvas
40 x 32.5
Bequeathed by Dr R. A. Lillie 1977
GMA 1847

Peebleshire Landscape
c 1952
Oil on canvas
69.2 x 84
George and Isobel Neillands Collection: presented
1988
GMA 3327

Landscape above Stow
c 1952–54
Oil on canvas
45.5 x 61
Bequeathed by Dr R. A. Lillie 1977
GMA 1853

Border Valley (with Train)
c 1953
Charcoal and ink wash on paper
35.4 x 42.4
Bequeathed by Dr R. A. Lillie 1977
GMA 1734

Still Life, Lamplight*
c 1953
Oil on canvas
61.5 x 73.5
Bequeathed by Dr R. A. Lillie 1977
GMA 1845

Hills above Stow
c 1953
Oil on canvas
30.8 x 41
Bequeathed by Dr R. A. Lillie 1977
GMA 1852

Double Still Life*
c 1954
Oil on canvas
59.6 x 130
Scott Hay Collection: presented 1967
GMA 1040

Still Life with Blue Vase
c 1954
Oil on canvas
41 x 53.5
Bequeathed by Dr R. A. Lillie 1977
GMA 1839

Still Life, Dried Flowers and Grasses
Mid-1950s
Oil on canvas
71 x 83.3
Bequeathed by Dr R. A. Lillie 1977
GMA 1841

Kenmore
Mid – late 1950s
Watercolour and black chalk on paper
24.5 x 31.7
Bequeathed by Dr R. A. Lillie 1977
GMA 1773

Eyemouth (Boats with Nets)
c 1955–56
Watercolour and pencil on paper
23.4 x 35.6
Bequeathed by Dr R. A. Lillie 1977
GMA 1751

Eyemouth
c 1955–56
Pencil on paper
25.3 x 35.4
Bequeathed by Dr R. A. Lillie 1977
GMA 1752

Fisherman's Cove, Eyemouth
c 1955–56
Black chalk on paper
25.4 x 45.6
Bequeathed by Dr R. A. Lillie 1977
GMA 1753

Beached Boats, Kippford
d 1956
Watercolour, pen and ink and pencil on paper
27.8 x 38
Bequeathed by Dr R. A. Lillie 1977
GMA 1774

St Abbs, Nets
c 1956
Watercolour and pencil on paper
25.4 x 35.5
Bequeathed by Dr R. A Lillie 1977
GMA 1828

Below Stow
d 1956
Watercolour and pencil on paper
24 x 27.4
Bequeathed by Dr R. A. Lillie 1977
GMA 1851

White Boats in the Bay
d 1956
Watercolour and gouache on paper
50.1 x 67.3
Bequeathed by Dr R. A. Lillie 1977
GMA 1879

Below Heriot, other Side of the River
d 1956
Watercolour and pencil on paper
24.7 x 31.5
Bequeathed by Dr R. A. Lillie 1977
GMA 1883

The Roadman's House, Lyne
d 1957
Watercolour and black chalk on paper
25.6 x 35.3
Bequeathed by Dr R. A. Lillie 1977
GMA 1799

Sandy Knowes
d 1957
Pencil on paper
25.5 x 35.4
Bequeathed by Dr R. A. Lillie 1977
GMA 1832

Upland Harvest
d 1957
Watercolour and pencil on paper
25.4 x 35.4
Bequeathed by Dr R. A. Lillie 1977
GMA 1877

Wooded Hillside
1957
Oil on hardboard
95.7 x 80.5
George and Isobel Neillands Collection: presented
1988
GMA 3326

Fields and River
Late 1950s
Oil on canvas
64 x 87
Bequeathed by Dr R. A. Lillie 1977
GMA 1755

The Meldons
Late 1950s
Pencil on paper
13 x 17.7
Bequeathed by Dr R. A. Lillie 1977
GMA 1801

Cartmel
d 1958
Watercolour and pencil on paper
25.4 x 35.5
Bequeathed by Dr R. A. Lillie 1977
GMA 1739

Cartmel
1958
Pencil on paper
25.5 x 56.2
Bequeathed by Dr R. A. Lillie 1977
GMA 1740

Cartmel
1958
Pencil on paper
25.3 x 45.5
Bequeathed by Dr R. A. Lillie 1977
GMA 1741

Cartmel Priory
1958
Watercolour and pencil on paper
25.7 x 53.6
Bequeathed by Dr R. A. Lillie 1977
GMA 1742

Dreva
d 1959
Watercolour, gouache and pencil on paper
34 x 51.2
Bequeathed by Dr R. A. Lillie 1977
GMA 1746

Still Life, Flowers on a Round Stool
c 1959
Oil on canvas
53.7 x 37.5
Bequeathed by Dr R. A. Lillie 1977
GMA 1842

Summer, Moorfoot
d 1960
Watercolour and pencil on paper
25.2 x 35.5
Bequeathed by Dr R. A. Lillie 1977
GMA 1807

Road to the Farm
d 1960
Watercolour and pencil on paper
25.4 x 35.4
Bequeathed by Dr R. A. Lillie 1977
GMA 1824

Still Life with Four Jugs
c 1960
Oil on canvas
102 x 92
Bequeathed by Dr R. A. Lillie 1977
GMA 1843

Landscape
c 1960s
Watercolour and chalk on paper
25.9 x 56.6
Bequeathed by Dr R. A. Lillie 1977
GMA 1786

The Loch, Portmore
1960s
Watercolour and pencil on paper
24 x 27.2
Bequeathed by Dr R. A. Lillie 1977
GMA 1822

Studio Interior
1960s
Oil on canvas
81.1 x 107.5
Bequeathed by Dr R. A. Lillie 1977
GMA 1884

The Garden, Temple
1962
Pencil on paper
41.8 x 58.4
Bequeathed by Dr R. A. Lillie 1977
GMA 1863

From the Garden, Temple
d 1963
Watercolour and black chalk on paper
25.5 x 35.4
Bequeathed by Dr R. A. Lillie 1977
GMA 1862

Still Life with Black Fishes*
1965
Oil on canvas
78 x 104
Scott Hay Collection: presented 1967
GMA 1039

Fay Godwin

1931–

Single Standing Stone, Prenteg Road (Drovers' Roads, Wales)
1977
Black and white photograph (gelatin silver print)
32.2 x 27.6
Presented by the M. S. Ackerman Foundation
1977
GMA 1694

Henri Goetz

1909–89

Untitled
d 1949
Lithograph on paper (23/33)
44 x 30.4 (paper 56.2 x 38)
Presented by Mr William Gear in memory of his wife 1989
GMA 3529

Natalya Goncharova

1881–1962

Rabbi with Cat*
c 1912
Oil on canvas
100.2 x 92
Purchased with funds given by two anonymous donors 1962
GMA 796

*Backdrop Design for 'Le Coq d'or' Act II**
d 1913 (possibly executed 1914)
Watercolour on paper
65.8 x 99.6
Purchased with funds given by two anonymous
donors 1962
GMA 797

*The Forest**
c 1913
Oil on canvas
53.8 x 81
Purchased 1977
GMA 1674

*Costume Design for One of the Three Kings
in 'La Liturgie'**
1915
Watercolour, pencil and metallic paper, on paper
62.2 x 47.6
Purchased with funds given by two anonymous
donors 1962
GMA 798

*Two Figures**
c 1916–20
Pencil and crayon on paper
36.3 x 25.8
Presented by Jim Ede 1977
GMA 1642

Julio González
1876–1942

*L'Arlequin [Harlequin]**
c 1929–30 (posthumous cast)
Bronze
40.8 x 27.5 x 29.5
Purchased 1972
GMA 1259

Antony Gormley
1950–

*Present Time**
1986–88
Lead over fibreglass and plaster
340 x 193 x 35.5
Purchased with assistance from the Henry Moore
Foundation 1990
GMA 3561

Body and Soul
d 1990
Portfolio of nine etchings (5/25)
Each 30 x 40 (paper 50 x 58.1)
Purchased 1991
GMA 3590

Sylvia Gosse
1881–1968

Un petit lapin de garenne [A Small Wild Rabbit]
Etching on paper
5.4 x 10.4 (paper 13.2 x 19.8)
Bequeathed by Sir David Young Cameron 1945
GMA 368

Henryk Gotlib
1890–1966

*Nude by Garden Door**
1942
Oil on canvas
76.5 x 63.5
Purchased 1970
GMA 1120

Seated Nude
d 1964
Charcoal on paper
121 x 99.5
Purchased 1970
GMA 1260

*Nude**
1964–65
Oil on canvas
127 x 101.5
Purchased 1970
GMA 1121

An Angel and Robbie
Charcoal on pink paper
115.6 x 83.8
Presented by Mrs Janet Gotlib 1970
GMA 1297

Adolph Gottlieb

1903–74

Green Halo
1966
Colour lithograph on paper (12/50)
61 x 45.6 (paper size)
Purchased 1984
GMA 2859

Flying Lines
d 1967
Lithograph on paper (27/75)
76 x 56 (paper size)
Purchased 1984
GMA 2857

Figure Eight
d 1967
Colour lithograph on paper (10/75)
45.7 x 61 (paper size)
Purchased 1984
GMA 2858

Karl Otto Götz

1914–

Gilgamesch III
d 1946
Monotype on paper
38.5 x 57.4 (paper 43 x 61)
Presented by Mr William Gear 1987
GMA 3321

Duncan Grant

1885–1978

*Vanessa Bell Painting**
1915 (incorrectly dated 1913)
Oil on canvas
76.2 x 55.9
Purchased 1965
GMA 900

*Farmhouse among Trees**
d 1928
Oil on canvas
38.3 x 46.8
Presented by Mrs Isabel M. Traill 1979
GMA 2144

Still Life
(*from the J. Lyons series 'Lithographs by Contemporary Artists, vol. I'*)
Published 1947
Colour lithograph on paper (after oil)
74.5 x 99 (paper size)
Presented by J. Lyons & Co. Ltd 1948
GMA 1203

Eileen Gray

1878–1976

*Untitled**
c 1940–42
Paper and card collage with ink, gouache and chalk on paper
46.5 x 31.7
Purchased 1977
GMA 1662

The Great War: Britain's Efforts and Ideals

(Series of portfolios published 1918)

See Muirhead BONE, Frank BRANGWYN, George CLAUSEN, Edmund DULAC, Maurice GREIFFENHAGEN, Archibald Standish HARTRICK, Ernest JACKSON, Augustus JOHN, Eric KENNINGTON, Gerald MOIRA, Christopher NEVINSON, William NICHOLSON, Charles PEARS, Charles RICKETTS, William ROTHENSTEIN, Charles SHANNON, Claude SHEPPERSON, Edmund SULLIVAN

Emilio Greco

1913–

Anna*
d 1954
Bronze
63.5 x 26.5 x 31 (excluding base)
Bequeathed by Miss Elizabeth Watt 1989
GMA 3486

Danzatrice [Dancer]*
c 1955
Bronze
34.4 x 19.5 x 12 (excluding base)
Bequeathed by Miss Elizabeth Watt 1989
GMA 3485

Barbara Greg

1900–83

Beach Huts
exh. 1932
Wood engraving on paper
17.5 x 20 (paper 25.1 x 27.5)
Purchased 1949
GMA 369

The Garden
exh. 1932
Wood engraving on paper
13.4 x 14.2 (paper 18.3 x 19.7)
Purchased 1949
GMA 373

Diana and Actaeon
exh. 1934
Wood engraving on paper
10 x 12.5 (paper 14.9 x 19.3)
Purchased 1949
GMA 372

Illustration for 'Composite Man'
exh. 1938
Wood engraving on paper
16.6 x 10.9 (paper 27.4 x 19)
Purchased 1982
GMA 2547

Essex Farm
Wood engraving on paper
16.5 x 19.8 (paper 26.7 x 27.4)
Purchased 1949
GMA 370

Europa*
Wood engraving on paper
10.5 x 13.2 (paper 16.4 x 18.9)
Purchased 1949
GMA 371

Lower Lydbrook
Wood engraving on paper
20.3 x 19 (paper 25.9 x 25.3)
Purchased 1949
GMA 374

Maurice Greiffenhagen

1862–1931

*The Restoration of Alsace-Lorraine to France
(from the series 'The Great War: Britain's Efforts and Ideals')*
d 1917 (published 1918)
Colour lithograph on paper
70 x 44.5 (paper 77 x 51.3)
Presented by the Ministry of Information 1919
GMA 3634

Frederick Griggs

1876–1938

The Quay [FAC 15]
d 1915–16
Etching on paper (third state)
16.6 x 20.2 (paper 23.2 x 35.7)
Purchased 1949
GMA 375

Laneham [FAC 30]
d 1923
Etching on paper (fourth state)
12.8 x 12 (paper 24.9 x 20.5)
Bequeathed by Mr George Liston-Foulis 1958
GMA 376

Tattershall [FAC 45]·
1930
Etching on paper (fourth state)
17.5 x 26 (paper 29.6 x 40.6)
Bequeathed by Mr George Liston-Foulis 1958
GMA 380

Lanterns of Sarras [FAC 47]*
1932
Etching on paper (fourth state)
25.6 x 18 (paper 26.6 x 18.5)
Bequeathed by Mr George Liston-Foulis 1958
GMA 379

Fotheringhay [FAC 48]
d 1932
Etching on paper (second state)
17.1 x 23.7 (paper 17.6 x 23.7)
Bequeathed by Mr George Liston-Foulis 1958
GMA 381

Memory of Clavering [FAC 51]
d 1934
Etching on paper (fourth state)
14.7 x 23.7 (paper 15.6 x 24.1)
Bequeathed by Mr George Liston-Foulis 1958
GMA 378

Netherton Chapel [FAC 53]
1935
Etching on paper (fifth state)
12.5 x 11 (paper 19.2 x 16.8)
Bequeathed by Mr George Liston-Foulis 1958
GMA 377

[FAC refers to the catalogue raisonné of Griggs's prints by Francis Adams Comstock (Boston & Oxford 1966)]

Anthony Gross

1905–84

Herne Bay Pier
(*from the J. Lyons series 'Lithographs by Contemporary Artists, vol. I'*)
Published 1947
Colour lithograph on paper (after gouache)
74.5 x 99 (paper size)
Presented by J. Lyons & Co. Ltd 1948
GMA 1204

Children and Wheelbarrow
1955
Etching on paper (16/50)
45.1 x 53.8 (paper 56.5 x 68.3)
Purchased 1960
GMA 748

The Valley No. 1
1956
Etching on paper (trial proof)
41.5 x 60 (paper 54.4 x 72)
Presented by the Hon. Robert Erskine 1960
GMA 749

Rudolf Grossman

1882–1941

*Portrait of Hubert Renfro Knickerbocker**
c 1923–24
Black and red chalk and ink on paper
38 x 29 3
Presented by Mr Lutz Riester to mark the keepership of Mr Douglas Hall 1987
GMA 3032

George Grosz

1893–1959

*Die Besitzkröten [Toads of Property]**
1920
Pen and ink on paper
52.7 x 41.1
Purchased 1979
GMA 2102

James Guthrie

1874–1952

Group of Buildings
Pen and ink and wash on card
22.4 x 28.8
Presented by Mr F. M. S. Winand 1963
GMA 843

Hideo Hagiwara

1913–

Ancient Song No. 2
d 1965
Wood engraving on paper (16/50)
90 x 60.7 (paper 99 x 66.4)
Purchased 1966
GMA 989

Philip Hagreen

1890–1988

Sunset
d 1920
Wood engraving on paper (13/50)
10.2 x 8 (paper 13.2 x 10)
Purchased 1949
GMA 382

The Earl Haig

1918–

Bungalow, Sulmona Camp
1943
Pen and ink on paper
24.5 x 35.9
Bequeathed by Dr R. A. Lillie 1977
GMA 1900

White Hawthorn
1959
Oil on canvas
61 x 76.2
Scott Hay Collection: presented 1967
GMA 1041

*The Tweed at Mertoun**
1968
Oil on canvas
86.3 x 112.1
Purchased 1973
GMA 1293

Farmhouse, Orzes
1990
Watercolour, ink and pencil on paper
32.3 x 49.7
Purchased 1991
GMA 3593

Maggi Hambling

1945–

*The Holyrood**
d 1987
Oil on canvas
61 x 56.2
Purchased 1988
GMA 3397

Richard Hamilton

1922–

*Desk**
[verso: *unfinished collage*]
d 1964
Oil and collage on photograph, laid on panel
62.5 x 89
Purchased 1980
GMA 2155

Reaper (i)
1949
Etching and sugar aquatint on paper (3/25)
19.9 x 27.7 (paper 26.7 x 35.7)
Purchased 1980
GMA 2156

Interior
1964–65
Screenprint on paper (5/50)
49 x 63.9 (paper 56.8 x 78.4)
Purchased 1978
GMA 2073

Portrait of the Artist by Francis Bacon
1970–71
Screenprint and collotype on paper (113/140)
55 x 49.9 (paper 82 x 69.2)
Purchased 1978
GMA 2075

I'm Dreaming of a Black Christmas
1971
Screenprint and collotype on paper (62/150)
50.6 x 76 (paper 75 x 100)
Purchased 1978
GMA 2074

Release
1972
Screenprint and collage on paper (86/150)
68.2 x 86 (paper 70 x 94.2)
Purchased 1978
GMA 2076

Duane Hanson

1925–

*Tourists**
1970
Polyester resin and fibreglass, painted in oil, and
mixed media
Man 152 x 80.5 x 31; woman 160 x 44 x 37
Purchased 1979
GMA 2132

Gwen Hardie

1962–

*Head I**
d 1985
Oil on canvas
190 x 170
Purchased 1993
GMA 3718

*Fist I**
d 1986
Oil on canvas
158 x 220.5
Purchased 1987
GMA 3038

*Dance**
1989
Paper, glue, acrylic, wire and iron rods
227 x 320 x 10
Purchased 1990
GMA 3551

Martin Hardie

1875–1952

Kirkcudbright Castle
d 1950
Watercolour over black chalk on paper
26 x 37.8
Presented by Mrs Madeleine Hardie and Dr Frank
Hardie 1963
GMA 844

Suffolk
Watercolour on paper
14.9 x 22.5
Provenance unrecorded
GMA 713

The Incoming Tide
1923
Drypoint on paper
11.5 x 28 (paper 22.2 x 43.2)
Presented by Mrs Madeleine Hardie and Dr Frank
Hardie 1963
GMA 845

Archibald Standish Hartrick

1864–1950

Illustration for 'The Ghost and The Exciseman'
d 1902
Black chalk with white gouache on card
26.5 x 36.7
Purchased 1949
GMA 714

Joseph Pennell
by 1910
Lithograph on paper
26.5 x 38.8 (paper 28.9 x 44.9)
Purchased 1949
GMA 384

Women's Work: On the Land – Ploughing
(from the series 'The Great War: Britain's Efforts
and Ideals')
Published 1918
Lithograph on paper
47 x 35.9 (paper 50.7 x 40.4)
Presented by the Ministry of Information 1919
GMA 383 A

Women's Work: On the Railways – Engine and
Carriage Cleaners
(from the series 'The Great War: Britain's Efforts
and Ideals')
Published 1918
Lithograph on paper
46.5 x 35.7 (paper 50.6 x 40.4)
Presented by the Ministry of Information 1919
GMA 383 B

Women's Work: In the Towns – A Bus
Conductress
(from the series 'The Great War: Britain's Efforts
and Ideals')
Published 1918
Lithograph on paper
47 x 36 (paper 51.4 x 40.6)
Presented by the Ministry of Information 1919
GMA 383 C

Women's Work: On Munitions – Skilled Work
(from the series 'The Great War: Britain's Efforts
and Ideals')
Published 1918
Lithograph on paper
46.5 x 35.8 (paper 50.7 x 40)
Presented by the Ministry of Information 1919
GMA 383 D

Women's Work: On Munitions – Dangerous
Work, Packing T. N. T.
(from the series 'The Great War: Britain's Efforts
and Ideals')
Published 1918
Lithograph on paper
46.3 x 35.3 (paper 50.7 x 40.3)
Presented by the Ministry of Information 1919
GMA 383 E

Women's Work: On Munitions – Heavy Work,
Drilling and Casting
(from the series 'The Great War: Britain's Efforts
and Ideals')
Published 1918
Lithograph on paper
46.5 x 35.7 (paper 51 x 40)
Presented by the Ministry of Information 1919
GMA 383 F

J. Harvey-Bloom

fl. 1930–60

A Mill on the Mole
exh. 1936
Wood engraving on paper
12.7 x 17.8 (paper 19.1 x 27.6)
Purchased 1982
GMA 2541

Wládysláw Hasior

1928–

Nailed to the Stars*
1972
Mixed media on cloth
155 x 312.5
Presented anonymously 1972
GMA 1267

Black Angel
d 1972
Mixed media on cloth
137 x 353
Presented anonymously 1972
GMA 1268

Joan Hassall

1906–88

Comus and the Lady
c 1934–35
Wood engraving on paper (24/50)
15.2 x 10.2 (paper 22.7 x 17.5)
Purchased 1949
GMA 386

Title Page for 'Devil's Dyke' by Christopher Hassall
1936
Wood engraving on paper (11/20)
19.1 x 12.1 (paper 27.3 x 19.6)
Purchased 1949
GMA 387

The Stricken Oak
(for 'Portrait of a Village' by Francis Brett Young)
1937
Wood engraving on paper (16/20)
15.2 x 10.7 (paper 22.3 x 14.1)
Bequeathed by Mr Kenneth Sanderson 1943
GMA 385

Book-Plate for Kathleen Finlay Horsman
1946
Colour wood engraving on card
7.5 x 6.1 (card 10.1 x 7.6)
Purchased 1982
GMA 2548

Anthony Hatwell

1931–

King and Queen*
1962
Wood construction, painted
198 x 96 x 76
Purchased 1988
GMA 3354

Seated Girl*
d 1967
Charcoal on paper
75.5 x 56.2
Purchased 1988
GMA 3357

Girl in a Long Dress Tying her Hair*
d 1967
Charcoal on paper
76 x 56.3
Purchased 1988
GMA 3358

Henri Hayden

1883–1970

Fay-le-Bac
d 1968
Colour lithograph on paper (58/75)
38.1 x 51.3 (paper 50.6 x 66.1)
Purchased 1969
GMA 1095

Nature morte brune [Brown Still Life]
d 1968
Colour lithograph on brown paper (66/75)
35 x 52.6 (paper 49.5 x 65)
Purchased 1969
GMA 1096

The Haymarket Print Suite

Published 1990

See John BELLANY, Alan DAVIE, Bruce McLEAN, Adrian WISZNIEWSKI

Stanley William Hayter

1901–88

Footprint (Hayter's Firstborn's Foot)
d 1940
Etching on paper
6.9 x 9.9 (paper 25.6 x 16.6)
Presented by Jim Ede 1979
GMA 2107

*Tropic of Cancer**
d 1949
Engraving, scorper and soft-ground etching on paper (28/50)
55.4 x 69.5 (paper 68.9 x 84.4)
Presented by Mr William Wilson 1961
GMA 771

Adrian Heath

1920–92

Abstract: Black, Yellow, and Grey
d 1959
Colour lithograph on paper (15/30)
58.3 x 79.3 (paper size)
Purchased 1960
GMA 750

Hein Heckroth

1901–70

Joie-de-vivre
d 1933
Pen and ink on paper
21.3 x 27.6
Presented by Jim Ede 1977
GMA 1644

Jean Hélion

1904–87

*Nu accoudé [Nude Leaning on her Elbows]**
d 1948
Charcoal on paper
103 x 73
Purchased 1987
GMA 3305

Barbara Hepworth

1903–75

*Dyad**
1949
Himalayan rosewood
118 x 40.5 x 22
Purchased 1963
GMA 854

*Conversation with Magic Stones**
1973
Bronze (2/4)
Six parts, maximum height of each 282; 274; 269; 93; 86; 80
Accepted by H. M. Government in lieu of death duties 1977; allocated 1978
GMA 2000

Josef Herman

1911–

*Outside the Fish and Chip Shop**
1946
Watercolour, pastel and black chalk on paper laid on board
55.9 x 76.8
Purchased (Knapping Fund) 1965
GMA 913

*Miners (Study for Festival of Britain Mural)**
d 1951
Oil on paper laid on board
52.5 x 121.3
Purchased 1972
GMA 1269

Snooker Players
d 1982
Oil on canvas
122 x 91.5
Purchased 1983
GMA 2743

Dusk
1965
Colour lithograph on paper (17/70)
51 x 75 (paper 57.5 x 80.5)
Purchased 1984
GMA 2860

Peasant in Fields: Figure against a Dark Sky
1965
Colour lithograph on paper (68/70)
53 x 70 (paper 57.9 x 80.5)
Purchased 1984
GMA 2861

In the Mountains
1965
Colour lithograph on paper (21/70)
52 x 71 (paper 57.5 x 80.7)
Purchased 1984
GMA 2862

Gertrude Hermes

1901–83

The Yolk
1954 (printed 1975)
Wood engraving on paper
35.7 x 30.5 (paper 53.5 x 43.7)
Presented by the artist's son and daughter 1991
GMA 3594

Stonehenge
1963 (printed 1975)
Wood engraving on paper
25.5 x 35.5 (paper 43.8 x 53.5)
Presented by the artist's son and daughter 1991
GMA 3595

Patrick Heron

1920–

Red Painting, July 25, 1963 *
d 1963
Oil on canvas
121.9 x 152.4
Purchased 1977
GMA 1675

Four Blues, Two Discs
d 1970
Screenprint on paper (18/100)
59.8 x 78.3 (paper 70.8 x 102.5)
Purchased 1984
GMA 2863

Interlocking Scarlet and Pink in Deep Green
d 1970
Screenprint on paper (16/100)
59.3 x 78.5 (paper 71 x 102)
Purchased 1984
GMA 2864

Three Reds in Green and Magenta in Blue
d 1970
Screenprint on paper (9/100)
59.2 x 78 (paper 70 x 101.5)
Purchased 1984
GMA 2865

Anthony Hill

1930–

Relief Construction (F 1) *
1966
Aluminium and steel on vulkide
91.5 x 91.5
Presented by the Peter Stuyvesant Foundation
1977
GMA 1686

Derek Hill

1916–

Bernard Berenson's Housekeeper
c 1949–54
Oil on wood
23.5 x 17.3
Bequeathed by Dr R. A. Lillie 1977
GMA 1901

Tristram Hillier

1905–83

*La Confiserie**
c 1931
Oil on plywood
57.2 x 57.2
Bequeathed by Miss Elizabeth Watt 1989
GMA 3487

*Pylons**
1933
Oil on canvas
92 x 60.3
Bequeathed by Miss Elizabeth Watt 1989
GMA 3488

*Quantoxhead**
d 1946
Oil on wood
15.1 x 25.4
Bequeathed by Miss Elizabeth Watt 1989
GMA 3489

Roger Hilton

1911–75

*June 1953**
d 1953
Oil on canvas
91.4 x 71.1
Purchased with assistance from an anonymous
donor 1963
GMA 831

*January 1954**
d 1954
Oil on canvas
125 x 102
Purchased 1981
GMA 2289

*Palisade**
d 1959
Oil on canvas
152.4 x 137.5
Purchased 1974
GMA 1312

*Dancing Woman**
d 1963
Oil and black chalk on canvas
152.5 x 127
Purchased 1981
GMA 2463

Andrew Healey Hislop

1887–1954

Harlequin
Etching and drypoint on paper
26 x 20 (paper 44.5 x 29.3)
Purchased 1982
GMA 2549

Ivon Hitchens

1893–1979

*The Verandah**
1943
Oil on canvas
41.4 x 75.1
Bequeathed by Miss Elizabeth Watt 1989
GMA 3491

*Tangled Pool, No. 10**
1946
Oil on canvas
53.5 x 84
Purchased 1966
GMA 975

Sunflowers and Blue Jar *
c 1947
Oil on canvas
66.3 x 56.2
Bequeathed by Miss Elizabeth Watt 1989
GMA 3490

River Rother, Dark Evening *
1951
Oil on canvas
46 x 108.7
Presented by the Peter Stuyvesant Foundation
1977
GMA 1688

David Hockney
1937–

Rocky Mountains and Tired Indians *
1965
Acrylic on canvas
170.4 x 252.8
Purchased 1976
GMA 1538

The Diploma
d 1962
Etching and aquatint on paper (12/50)
40.5 x 28 (paper 56.8 x 39)
Purchased with funds given by two anonymous
donors 1963
GMA 846

The Beginning
d 1966
Etching on paper (32/75)
35 x 22.4 (paper 56.4 x 40)
Purchased 1976
GMA 1270

Maureen Hodge
1941–

A Hill For My Friend
1976
Tapestry
179 x 165.5
Purchased 1979
GMA 2112

Eliot Hodgkin
1905–87

Quinces *
d 1969
Tempera on hardboard
15.7 x 19.7
Bequeathed by Miss Elizabeth Watt 1989
GMA 3492

Leaves *
d 1970
Tempera on hardboard
28 x 28.2
Bequeathed by Miss Elizabeth Watt 1989
GMA 3493

Howard Hodgkin
1932–

Portrait of Mrs Rhoda Cohen *
1962
Oil on canvas
91 x 91
Presented by the Contemporary Art Society 1980
GMA 2131

For Bernard Jacobson
1979
Lithograph and gouache on black paper (two
sheets joined) (4//80)
105 x 125
Purchased 1980
GMA 2157

Frances Hodgkins
1869–1947

Chairs and Pots *
c 1939
Gouache and watercolour on paper
72.3 x 54.9
Bequeathed by Miss Elizabeth Watt 1989
GMA 3494

*Lilies and Still Life**
c 1940
Watercolour and pencil on paper
46.7 x 35.3
Bequeathed by Miss Elizabeth Watt 1989
GMA 3495

Ferdinand Hodler

1853–1918

*Thunersee mit Stockhornkette [Lake Thun and the Stockhorn Mountains]**
d 1910
Oil on canvas
83 x 105.4
Purchased 1975
GMA 1523

Cliff Holden

1919–

Figure
d 1954
Screenprint on paper (19/25)
72 x 43.2 (paper 76.2 x 56.2)
Purchased 1963
GMA 855

Edgar Holloway

1914–

Mansion House, Nazeing
d 1931
Drypoint on paper
20.2 x 15.1 (paper 29.4 x 23)
Purchased 1949
GMA 388

Self-Portrait No. 2
d 1931
Drypoint on paper
15.2 x 10.7 (paper 19.8 x 17.5)
Purchased 1949
GMA 391

Herbert Read
1934
Etching on paper (8/25)
22.4 x 18.8 (paper 29.1 x 23.2)
Purchased 1982
GMA 2551

*Alec Buckels**
d 1934
Etching on paper (31/35)
23.9 x 16.3 (paper 29.5 x 23.5)
Purchased 1986
GMA 3003

William Wilson I
1935
Etching on paper
24.8 x 17.5 (paper 29.2 x 22.9)
Purchased 1949
GMA 390

Turban (Self-Portrait No. 8)
c 1937
Etching on paper (16/30)
12.7 x 10.3 (paper 19.2 x 15.4)
Purchased 1949
GMA 389

William Wilson II
1937
Etching on paper (first state)
21.3 x 20.1 (paper 28.5 x 22.4)
Purchased 1982
GMA 2550

In a Railway Carriage (Portrait of the Artist's Father)
c 1937
Etching with black chalk on paper
18.3 x 21 (paper 21.2 x 27.4)
Purchased 1982
GMA 2552

Summer 1984 (Self-Portrait No. 18)
1984
Etching and aquatint on paper (14/50)
20.4 x 16 (paper 33.7 x 26)
Purchased 1986
GMA 3002

Andrew Holmes

1947–

White Western Star
d 1979
Screenprint on paper (91/100)
49.7 x 74 (paper 76.8 x 99.7)
Purchased 1982
GMA 2701

Charles Holmes

1868–1936

Black Hill, Liddesdale
[verso: *Sketch of Hills*]
d 1919
Watercolour and black chalk on paper
25.9 x 34.7
Bequeathed by Sir James and Lady Caw 1951
GMA 715

Evening Landscape
Watercolour and black chalk on paper
24 x 34.8
Bequeathed by Mr Kenneth Sanderson 1943
GMA 716

George Hooper

1910–

Hotel Entrance
(from the J. Lyons series 'Lithographs by
Contemporary Artists, vol. I')
Published 1947
Colour lithograph on paper (after gouache)
74.5 x 99 (paper size)
Presented by J. Lyons & Co. Ltd 1948
GMA 1205

Gordon House

1932–

Series 40 A
d 1965
Screenprint on paper (50/50)
40.2 x 40.2 (paper 76.2 x 58.8)
Purchased 1984
GMA 2867 A

Series 40 B
d 1965
Screenprint on paper (44/50)
40.2 x 40.2 (paper 76.2 x 58.8)
Purchased 1984
GMA 2867 B

Series of Six Screenprints
A) *Ladder Box*
B) *Multi-case*
C) *Vertical Screen*
D) *Drop Initials*
E) *Quoined Chase*
F) *Mitred Matrix*
d 1970
Six screenprints on paper: A) (9/75); B) (10/75); C)
(9/75); D) (7/75); E) 8/75); F) (7/75)
A) 50.2 x 50; B) 50 x 50.2; C) 50 x 50.7; D) 49.8 x
50.1; E) 50 x 50.2; F) 50 x 50.2 (Each on paper 76 x
56.3)
Purchased 1984
GMA 2866 A–F

John Houston

1930–

Flowers in a Landscape*
d 1960
Watercolour on paper
67.6 x 104.5
Scott Hay Collection: presented 1967
GMA 1042

Birds, Flowers and Dark Sun
c 1962
Oil on canvas
86.4 x 112.1
Purchased (Gulbenkian UK Trust Fund) 1962
GMA 818

*Bathers**
d 1965 / 1966
Oil on canvas
122 x 122
Purchased 1966
GMA 976

A Garden in Summer III
d 1970
Gouache and watercolour on paper
17.5 x 40.4
Bequeathed by Keith Andrews 1990
GMA 3610

Sunset over the Sea
d 1980
Colour lithograph on paper (4/75)
51.5 x 72.4 (paper 56.4 x 76.4)
Purchased 1988
GMA 3320

James Howie

1931–

*City Painting**
d 1964
Synthetic resin and oil on canvas
203.2 x 162.6
Purchased with funds given by an anonymous
donor 1964
GMA 892

Bitter Circle
d 1965
Etching on paper (1/6)
38.8 x 36.5 (paper 48.4 x 45.6)
Purchased 1965
GMA 926

Peter Howson

1958–

*Heroic Dosser**
1986
Monotype with oil and crayon on paper
104.5 x 75.7
Purchased 1987
GMA 3013

*Head of Saint Anthony**
d 1986
Crayon, chalk and pen and ink on paper
30.5 x 22.9
Purchased 1987
GMA 3014

*Just Another Bloody Saturday**
1987
Oil on canvas
211 x 274.7
Purchased 1987
GMA 3041

*Heroic Dosser**
1987
Oil on canvas
198.5 x 213.5
Presented anonymously through the British
American Arts Association 1989
GMA 3460

Man with Cigarette
d 1982
Colour lithograph on paper (28/50)
44.5 x 35.8 (paper 62.4 x 53.2)
Purchased 1986
GMA 2975

Four Scottish Scenes
d 1982
Colour lithograph on paper (27/40)
59 x 43 (paper 67.2 x 51.7)
Purchased 1987
GMA 3029

Fieldmouse
(*from 'The Scottish Bestiary'*)
Published 1986
Screenprint on paper (5/50)
55 x 36.8 (paper 76 x 56.5)
Purchased 1987
GMA 3019 C

Moth
(*from 'The Scottish Bestiary'*)
Published 1986
Screenprint on paper (5/50)
54.5 x 36.7 (paper 76 x 56.5)
Purchased 1987
GMA 3019 P

Stag
(*from 'The Scottish Bestiary'*)
Published 1986
Screenprint on paper (5/50)
55 x 36.7 (paper 76 x 56.5)
Purchased 1987
GMA 3019 R

Johnie
(*from the series 'Saracen Heads'*)
d 1987
Etching on paper (A.P. VIII)
33 x 24.7 (paper 56 x 38)
Purchased 1987
GMA 3050

Ned
(*from the series 'Saracen Heads'*)
d 1987
Etching on paper (A.P. VIII)
32.5 x 24.6 (paper 56.7 x 38.2)
Purchased 1987
GMA 3051

Maxwell
(*from the series 'Saracen Heads'*)
d 1987
Etching on paper (A.P. VIII)
33.3 x 24.7 (paper 56.5 x 38)
Purchased 1987
GMA 3052

Peter
(*from the series 'Saracen Heads'*)
d 1987
Etching on paper (A.P. VIII)
32.5 x 24.8 (paper 56.5 x 38)
Purchased 1987
GMA 3053

A Hero of the People
Published 1987
Portfolio of sixteen linocuts (30/40)
55 x 38.5 (page size)
Purchased 1988
GMA 3405

The Noble Dosser
d 1988
Screenprint on paper (19/30)
151 x 102 (paper 151 x 107)
Purchased 1988
GMA 3406

The Heroic Dosser
d 1988
Screenprint on paper (19/30)
149 x 101.5 (151 x 106.8)
Purchased 1988
GMA 3407

The Bodybuilder
d 1988
Screenprint on paper (30/30)
151 x 101 (paper 151 x 106.8)
Purchased 1988
GMA 3408

John Hoyland

1934–

Large Green (Swiss)
d 1968
Colour lithograph on paper (21/75)
49.5 x 77.6 (paper 63.6 x 90)
Purchased 1984
GMA 2868

Small Red
d 1968
Colour lithograph on paper (30/75)
46.5 x 68.6 (paper 56 x 76)
Purchased 1984
GMA 2870

Blues, Reds
d 1969
Screenprint on paper (A.P.)
60 x 91.5 (paper 70.5 x 101)
Purchased 1984
GMA 2869

John Hubbard

1931–

After the Snow, 4*
d 1963
Oil on board
78 x 55.8
Purchased 1963
GMA 856

Karl Hubbuch

1891–1979

Zwei Modelle [Two Models]*
c 1926
Black chalk and coloured crayon on paper (eight
pieces joined together)
77 x 65
Purchased 1985
GMA 2957

Myriam III (In Profile)
1951
Woodcut on paper
32.8 x 29 (paper 43 x 52)
Purchased 1987
GMA 3033

Ian Hughes

1958–

Apperception (I)*
d 1987
Oil on canvas
152.7 x 152.4
Purchased 1987
GMA 3048

The Ship of Fools (I)
d 1988
Monoprint on photograph
59 x 40.5
Purchased 1988
GMA 3440

The Ship of Fools (II)
d 1988
Monoprint on photograph
59 x 40.5
Purchased 1988
GMA 3441

Blair Hughes-Stanton

1902–81

Flowers
(for 'Birds, Beasts and Flowers' by D. H.
Lawrence)*
d 1930
Wood engraving on paper (6/12)
22.7 x 13.3 (paper 34.3 x 21.8)
Purchased 1949
GMA 393

Alexis Hunter

1948–

Approach to Fear III: Taboo Demystify (1–4)*
d 1976
Colour photographs on four card panels
Each 100.7 x 25 (card 120 x 37)
Purchased 1980
GMA 2202

George Leslie Hunter

1879–1931

Still Life*
c 1920–25
Oil on board
45.7 x 50.8
Purchased 1942
GMA 19

Figures on a Quay, Largo*
c 1920–25
Oil on wood, laid on board
29.5 x 35.6
Bequeathed by Dr R. A. Lillie 1977
GMA 1905

Still Life with Anemones and Fruit
c 1920–25
Oil on board
40.5 x 35.2
Bequeathed by Dr R. A. Lillie 1977
GMA 1909

A Hilly Landscape
d 1921
Pen and ink on paper
15.3 x 25.2
Presented by Mr W. Dodd 1948
GMA 718

Venice
d 1922
Pen and ink on paper
25.8 x 36
Bequeathed by Dr R. A. Lillie 1977
GMA 1912

Cottages, Fife*
c 1923–24
Oil on wood
26.2 x 34.7
Bequeathed by Dr R. A. Lillie 1977
GMA 1903

Cottages, Fife
c 1923–24
Oil on wood
29.5 x 39.5
Bequeathed by Dr R. A. Lillie 1977
GMA 1908

Stubble Field*
c 1923–24
Oil on canvas
64 x 77
Bequeathed by Dr R. A. Lillie 1977
GMA 1911

Still Life with Flowers and Fruit*
[verso: Still Life with Flowers and Bananas]
c 1923–26
Oil on plywood
45.7 x 38
Bequeathed by Dr R. A. Lillie 1977
GMA 1906

Boats and Houses
c 1923–27
Pen and ink and coloured crayon on paper
22.8 x 29
Bequeathed by Dr R. A. Lillie 1977
GMA 1902

Juan-les-Pins*
c 1927–29
Ink and coloured crayon on paper
32 x 41.3
Bequeathed by Dr R. A. Lillie 1977
GMA 1907

Still Life with Gladioli*
c 1927–30
Oil on canvas
82.3 x 66.9
Purchased 1975
GMA 1348

Reflections, Balloch*
c 1929–30
Oil on canvas
63.5 x 76.2
Presented by Mr William McInnes 1933
GMA 18

Still Life*
c 1930
Oil on canvas
51 x 61.2
Purchased 1945
GMA 20

*Still Life, Stocks**
c 1930
Oil on canvas
56 x 45.8
Bequeathed by Dr R. A. Lillie 1977
GMA 1910

*Still Life of Apples, Plate and Knife**
Pen and ink on paper
21.1 x 26.8
Bequeathed by Mr Kenneth Sanderson 1943
GMA 717

Fifeshire Village
Watercolour and pen and ink on brown paper
22.2 x 34.8
Bequeathed by Dr R. A. Lillie 1977
GMA 1904

Margaret Hunter
1948–

*Whisper ...**
1988
Acrylic on paper
134.7 x 100.4
Purchased 1988
GMA 3418

*Precious Belonging**
1988
Acrylic on paper collage laid on board
122.1 x 92.1
Purchased 1988
GMA 3419

Peter Hurd
1904–

*Anselmo's House**
d 1941
Tempera on wood
55.2 x 91.5
Presented by Mr Richard Peto through Lady
Tennyson 1945
GMA 1003

Leslie Hurry
1909–78

*Death Mask of Mary Queen of Scots**
d 1946
Ink, watercolour and coloured crayon on paper
(in frame incorporating nails, painted gold)
26.3 x 31.3
Purchased 1986
GMA 3006

Isobel Wylie Hutchison
fl. 1897–1939

Arctic Landscape
d 1933
Watercolour and black chalk on paper
26.8 x 37.7
Presented by Miss Dorothea Hamilton 1970
GMA 1160

William Oliphant Hutchison
1889–1970

In Ross-Shire
d 1949
Oil on canvas-board
23.6 x 30.3
Bequeathed by Dr R. A. Lillie 1977
GMA 1913

*Oak Tree and Windmill**
Oil on canvas
61 x 45.7
Presented by Lady Hutchison 1971
GMA 1214

The Black Shore, Southwold
Oil on canvas-board
22.9 x 30.5
Presented by Lady Hutchison 1971
GMA 1215

Paul Huxley

1938–

No. 8
d 1973
Screenprint on paper (144/150)
59.8 x 59.8 (paper 73.3 x 73.3)
Purchased 1984
GMA 2871

Henry Inlander

1925–83

Yellow Landscape*
d 1965
Oil on canvas
99.4 x 145
Purchased 1966
GMA 945

Callum Innes

1962–

Six Identified Forms*
d 1992
Oil on canvas
220 x 190
Purchased (Knapping Fund) 1993
GMA 3670

Albert Irvin

1922–

Battle Bridge
(from 'The London Suite')
d 1982
Screenprint on paper (11/75)
60.9 x 83.7 (image and paper size)
Purchased 1983
GMA 2752

Donald Jackson

1955–

Lewis Burn, Kielder Forest
d 1982
Black and white photograph (gelatin silver print)
24.3 x 19.1
Purchased 1984
GMA 2927

Ernest Jackson

1872–1945

United Defence against Aggression
(from the series 'The Great War: Britain's Efforts
and Ideals')
Published 1918
Colour lithograph on paper
63.5 x 43.8 (paper 76.2 x 50.2)
Presented by the Ministry of Information 1919
GMA 3633

Dinny Jampijimpa

Women Dreaming
(from 'The Commonwealth Print Portfolio')
d 1978
Screenprint and lithograph on paper (35/36)
66 x 45.6 (paper 75.3 x 55.7)
Presented by the Canadian High Commission
1979
GMA 2119

Alexei Jawlensky

1864–1941

Frauenkopf [Head of a Woman]*
c 1911
Oil on millboard laid on plywood
52.2 x 50.2
Purchased 1964
GMA 896

Augustus John

1878–1961

*Grace Westry**
c 1897
Red chalk on paper
20.6 x 18.5
Bequeathed by Dr Dorothea Walpole
and Mr R. H. Walpole 1963
GMA 860

*Head of a Girl**
d 1906
Pencil on paper
35.4 x 25.2
Bequeathed by Sir David Young Cameron 1945
GMA 719

*Woman Standing**
c 1907–08
Watercolour, gouache and pencil on paper
40.6 x 28.8
Bequeathed by Dr Dorothea Walpole
and Mr R. H. Walpole 1963
GMA 861

*Woman in a Landscape**
c 1911–12
Oil on canvas-board
40.6 x 33
Bequeathed by Dr Dorothea Walpole
and Mr R. H. Walpole 1963
GMA 862

Tête Farouche (or *Portrait of the Artist*)
c 1900
Etching on paper (14/25)
21.3 x 17.1 (paper 28.4 x 22.5)
Purchased 1949
GMA 1190

The Dawn
(from the series 'The Great War: Britain's Efforts
and Ideals')
d 1917 (published 1918)
Colour lithograph on paper
46 x 69 (paper 51 x 80.5)
Presented by the Ministry of Information 1919
GMA 3637

Gwen John

1876–1939

*A Sleeping Nun**
c 1914–18
Gouache, watercolour and black chalk on paper
31.5 x 24
Purchased 1976
GMA 1530

*A Young Nun**
c 1915–20
Oil on canvas
65.1 x 49
Purchased 1970
GMA 1116

Walter R. H. Johnson

d. 1935

Promontory
c 1930–35
Wood engraving on paper (43/50)
12.1 x 15.5 (paper 20.2 x 22.9)
Presented by Dr Henry Roland 1984
GMA 2930

Alan Johnston

1945–

Untitled
(from the suite 'From the Mountain to the
Plain')*
1978
Pencil on paper
187.3 x 39.5
Purchased 1978
GMA 2009

Untitled
(from the suite 'From the Mountain to the Plain')
1978
Pencil on paper
187.3 x 39.5
Purchased 1978
GMA 2010

Untitled
(*from the suite 'From the Mountain to the Plain'*)
1978
Pencil on paper
187.3 x 39.5
Purchased 1978
GMA 2011

Untitled
(*from the suite 'From the Mountain to the Plain'*)
1978
Pencil on paper
187.3 x 39.5
Purchased 1978
GMA 2012

Colin Johnstone

1960–

Warrior Shield
d 1980
Etching on paper (1/5)
81 x 55 (paper 97 x 67)
Purchased 1981
GMA 2316

William Johnstone

1897–1981

Summer, Selkirk*
c 1927 / c 1938 / c 1951 (d 1927)
Oil on canvas
101.6 x 101.6
Purchased 1969
GMA 1100

Study for 'A Point in Time'*
c 1928
Oil on hardboard
45.8 x 50.8
Bequeathed by Mrs Hope Montagu Douglas Scott
1990
GMA 3562

A Point in Time*
c 1929 / 1937
Oil on canvas
137.2 x 243.8
Presented by Mrs Hope Montagu Douglas Scott
1971
GMA 1254

Portrait of Mrs J. E. Winand*
c 1945
Oil on canvas
51 x 38.4
Presented by Mr F. Winand 1982
GMA 2712

Embryonic*
1972–73
Plaster on plasterboard
122.2 x 91.5
Bequeathed by Mrs Hope Montagu Douglas Scott
1990
GMA 3563

Celebration of Earth, Air, Fire and Water*
d 1974
Oil on canvas
137.2 x 242
Purchased 1974
GMA 1313

*Twenty Poems by Hugh MacDiarmid with
Twenty-one Lithographs by William Johnstone*
Published 1977
Portfolio with 21 lithographs (21/50)
Page size 39.6 x 28.7; lithographs each 36 x 25.2
Purchased 1978
GMA 3656

*Lithographs by William Johnstone with Poems
by Edwin Muir*
Published 1981
Portfolio with 21 lithographs (50/50)
32.2 x 51.5 (paper size, folded in centre)
Purchased 1981
GMA 2307

Allen Jones

1937–

Pour les lèvres
(from the portfolio 'Eleven Pop Artists, vol. II')
d 1965
Screenprint on paper (no.25)
76.2 x 60.9 (paper size)
Purchased 1975
GMA 1337

Spice
d 1971
Colour lithograph on paper (64/75)
89.5 x 52 (image and paper size)
Purchased 1984
GMA 2872

Untitled
(from 'The Commonwealth Print Portfolio')
d 1977 (published 1978)
Colour lithograph on paper (49/65)
56 x 75.5 (image and paper size)
Presented by the Canadian High Commission
1979
GMA 2120

David Jones

1895–1974

*View from No.1 Elm Row, Hampstead**
c 1927
Pencil on paper
30.9 x 23.2
Presented by Jim Ede 1977
GMA 1641

*Northumberland Fields**
c 1930
Watercolour and pencil on paper
49.9 x 62.2
Purchased 1970
GMA 1165

*Princess with Longboats**
c 1948–49
Chalk, coloured crayon and pencil on buff paper
40.9 x 32.9
Purchased 1976
GMA 1533

*Glass Chalice with Flowers and Mug**
c 1950
Watercolour, gouache and pencil on paper
78.2 x 58.7
Purchased 1976
GMA 1532

*In Principio Erat Verbum ...**
c 1951
Watercolour over pencil on paper
35.9 x 32.6
Purchased 1976
GMA 1531

The Wounded Knight
c 1930
Drypoint on paper
20.1 x 15.7 (paper 29 x 23.1)
Presented by Mr William Wilson 1953
GMA 1022

'He Frees the Waters in Helyon'
1932
Wood engraving on paper
15.2 x 24.6 (paper 28.7 x 38)
Presented by Mr A. J. Hyne 1980
GMA 2145

Trevor Jones

1945–

For Soon
(from 'The London Suite')
d 1982
Screenprint on paper (11/75)
83.5 x 61.2 (image and paper size)
Purchased 1982
GMA 2753

Donald Judd

1928–

*Progression**
d 1978
Chartreuse anodised aluminium and galvanised
steel
13 x 190.5 x 12.7
Purchased 1982
GMA 2504

Walter Jule

1940–

Untitled
(*from 'The Commonwealth Print Portfolio'*)
d 1978
Photo-screenprint and lithograph on paper (13/
65)
57 x 76.8 (image and paper size)
Presented by the Canadian High Commission
1979
GMA 2121

Wassily Kandinsky

1866–1944

*Improvisation 19**
1911
Woodcut on paper
15 x 18.5 (paper 28 x 27.7)
Purchased 1982
GMA 2710

*Kleine Welten III [Small Worlds III]**
d 1922
Colour lithograph on paper
27.7 x 23 (paper 31.9 x 25.5)
Purchased 1983
GMA 2779

Alexander Kanoldt

1881–1939

Olevano VIII
d 1926
Lithograph on paper (23/50)
33.4 x 29 (paper 55.7 x 40)
Presented by the Staatliche Graphische
Sammlung, Munich 1981
GMA 2470

Anish Kapoor

1954–

*Untitled**
1983
Cement, polystyrene, gesso and pigment
130 x 92 x 98
Presented by the Contemporary Art Society
(Henry Moore Foundation Grant) 1986
GMA 2954

Kim Kempshall

1934–

Flight
d 1965
Colour etching on paper (2/20)
63.5 x 50.5 (paper 74.2 x 55.8)
Purchased 1965
GMA 927

George Kennethson

1910–

Sea Study
c 1974
Alabaster
45 x 41.6 x 12.5
Presented by Jim Ede 1978
GMA 1716

Eric Kennington

1888–1960

Making Soldiers: Bayonet Practice
*(from the series 'The Great War: Britain's Efforts
and Ideals')*
Published 1918
Lithograph on paper
46.5 x 35.9 (paper 51.3 x 40)
Presented by the Ministry of Information 1919
GMA 394 A

Making Soldiers: The Gas Mask
*(from the series 'The Great War: Britain's Efforts
and Ideals')*
Published 1918
Lithograph on paper
47 x 36 (paper 51.1 x 41)
Presented by the Ministry of Information 1919
GMA 394 B

Making Soldiers: Ready for Service
*(from the series 'The Great War: Britain's Efforts
and Ideals')*
Published 1918
Lithograph on paper
46.5 x 36 (paper 51 x 39.5)
Presented by the Ministry of Information 1919
GMA 394 C

Making Soldiers: Into the Trenches
*(from the series 'The Great War: Britain's Efforts
and Ideals')**
Published 1918
Lithograph on paper
46.3 x 36 (paper 50.8 x 39.5)
Presented by the Ministry of Information 1919
GMA 394 D

Making Soldiers: Over the Top
*(from the series 'The Great War: Britain's Efforts
and Ideals')*
Published 1918
Lithograph on paper
46.5 x 36.2 (paper 51 x 39.8)
Presented by the Ministry of Information 1919
GMA 394 E

Making Soldiers: Bringing in Prisoners
*(from the series 'The Great War: Britain's Efforts
and Ideals')*
Published 1918
Lithograph on paper
45.9 x 36 (paper 51.5 x 40.3)
Presented by the Ministry of Information 1919
GMA 394 F

Kenojuak

1927–

Owl with Seagulls
(from 'The Commonwealth Print Portfolio')
d 1978
Stonecut and stencil on paper (58/65)
57 x 76 (paper size)
Presented by the Canadian High Commission
1979
GMA 2122

Sister Mary Corita Kent

1918–86

Pentecost
Serigraph on paper
39.6 x 54.6 (paper 48.3 x 61.4)
Presented by Mr and Mrs J. H. Macdonell 1961
GMA 784

Treasure Hidden in a Field
Serigraph on paper
39.7 x 55 (paper 48.4 x 61)
Presented by Mr and Mrs J. H. Macdonell 1961
GMA 785

A Covert of Cypress for its Walls
Serigraph on paper
56 x 75 (paper 61 x 83.8)
Presented by Mr and Mrs J. H. Macdonell 1961
GMA 786

Rockwell Kent

1882–1971

To God
(from the portfolio 'Drawings by Rockwell Kent')
Published 1924
Wood engraving on paper
18 x 13.8 (paper 22.8 x 17.7)
Purchased 1965
GMA 922

Far Horizon
1932
Wood engraving on paper (posthumous print 54/100)
13.9 x 17.7 (paper 23.6 x 28.1)
Presented by the Rockwell Kent Legacies 1978
GMA 2037

Greenland Swimmer
1932
Wood engraving on paper (posthumous print 53/100)
13.7 x 17.6 (paper 26.7 x 25)
Presented by the Rockwell Kent Legacies 1978
GMA 2038

John Keppie

1862–1945

Church, Montreuil
d 1931
Pencil on paper
17.5 x 24.7
Purchased 1978
GMA 2025

Farmhouse and Buildings
d 1934
Pencil on paper
17.1 x 24.7
Purchased 1978
GMA 2026

Mary Kessell

1914–78

The Flight into Egypt
(from the J. Lyons series 'Lithographs by Contemporary Artists, vol. I')
Published 1947
Colour lithograph on paper (after oil)
72.4 x 98 (paper 74.5 x 99)
Presented by J. Lyons & Co. Ltd 1948
GMA 1206

Jessie Marion King

1875–1949

*The Fisherman Watched over by Mermaids**
c 1913
Pen and ink and watercolour, heightened with silver paint, on vellum
37.6 x 50.4
Purchased 1977
GMA 1672

*Design for One Wall of a Child's Nursery**
1913
Watercolour, gouache and pencil on board
35.7 x 61.8
Purchased 1977
GMA 1673

*Princess Melilot**
c 1916–17
Pen and ink on vellum laid on board
32.4 x 21.2
Bequeathed by Mr Kenneth Sanderson 1943
GMA 720

Phillip King

1934–

*Small Wall Sculpture**
d 1974
Painted aluminium (2/6)
135.2 x 60 x 22
Purchased 1974
GMA 1314

Ernst Ludwig Kirchner

1880–1938

Japanisches Theater [Japanese Theatre]*
[verso: Interior with Nude Woman and Man]*
c 1909 [verso c 1924]
Oil on canvas
113.7 x 113.7
Purchased 1965
GMA 911

Weisse Tänzerin in Kleinem Variété [White
Dancer in a Cabaret]*
1914
Lithograph on paper (second state)
59.6 x 50.4 (paper 65.2 x 50.4)
Purchased 1984
GMA 2924

John Kirkwood

1947–

Industrial Landscape
1980
Etching and watercolour on paper (4/4)
49.1 x 44.5 (paper 75 x 54.3)
Purchased 1981
GMA 2317

R. B. Kitaj

1932–

If Not, Not*
1975–76
Oil and black chalk on canvas
152.4 x 152.4
Purchased 1976
GMA 1585

Actor (Richard)*
1979
Pastel and charcoal on paper
76.8 x 49.2
Purchased 1988
GMA 3373

Truman in the White House
1966
Screenprint on paper (30/70)
55.4 x 79.5 (paper 68.7 x 102.5)
Purchased 1984
GMA 2873

Revolt on the Clyde (Hugh MacDiarmid)
1967
Screenprint on paper (8/70)
64.7 x 52.2 (image and paper size)
Purchased 1984
GMA 2874

Glue Words
1967
Screenprint with collage on paper (50/70)
83.8 x 58.3 (image and paper size)
Purchased 1984
GMA 2875

Bacon I
1968
Screenprint on paper (36/70)
47.4 x 104 (image and paper size)
Purchased 1984
GMA 2876

Ctric News Topi
1968
Screenprint on paper (44/70)
98.9 x 62.4 (paper 104.1 x 70.4)
Purchased 1984
GMA 2877

Die Gute Alte Zeit
1969
Screenprint with collage on paper (28/70)
98.5 x 63.5 (paper 104 x 68.5)
Purchased 1984
GMA 2878

A Life
1975
Lithograph on buff paper (12/50)
73.5 x 53 (image and paper size)
Purchased 1980
GMA 2226

Paul Klee

1879–1940

Gespenst eines Genies [Ghost of a Genius]*
d 1922
Oil transfer and watercolour on paper laid on card
50 x 35.4
Purchased 1979
GMA 2106

Drohender Schneesturm [Threatening
Snowstorm]*
d 1927
Pen and coloured inks and watercolour on paper
laid on card
49.9 x 31.6
Bequeathed by Miss Anna G. Blair in memory
of Mr R. K. Blair 1952
GMA 1015

Seiltänzer [Tightrope Walker]*
d 1923
Colour lithograph on paper
44 x 26.8 (paper 52.2 x 38)
Purchased 1960
GMA 762

Rechnender Greis [Old Man Calculating]*
1929
Etching on paper
29.7 x 23.8 (paper 52.5 x 43)
Purchased 1979
GMA 2095

Gustav Klimt

1862–1918

Stehende Frau mit durchsichtigem Gewand
[Standing Woman with Transparent Drapery]*
c 1902
Black chalk on paper
45.3 x 31.9
Purchased 1971
GMA 1249

Schwangere mit Mann nach links: Studie zu
'Hoffnung I' [Pregnant Woman with Man: Study
for 'Hoffnung I']*
c 1903–04
Black chalk on paper
44.7 x 30.6
Purchased 1985
GMA 2946

Max Klinger

1857–1920

Paraphrase über den Fund eines Handschuhes
[On the Finding of a Glove] Opus VI
  1) Ort [Place]
  2) Handlung [Action]*
  3) Wünsche [Yearnings]
  4) Rettung [Rescue]
  5) Triumph
  6) Huldigung [Homage]
  7) Ängste [Fears]
  8) Ruhe [Repose]
  9) Entführung [Abduction]
  10) Amor
First published 1881 (this 5th edition 1924)
Portfolio of ten etchings (two also with aquatint)
and title page
40 x 50 (folio size); image and paper size variable
Purchased 1986
GMA 2980

Dramen [Dramas] Opus IX
  1) In Flagranti
  2) Ein Schritt [A Step]
  3) Eine Mutter I [A Mother I]
  4) Eine Mutter II [A Mother II]
  5) Eine Mutter III [A Mother III]
  6) Im Walde [In the Forest]
  7) Ein Mord [A Murder]*
  8) Märztage I [March Days I]
  9) Märztage II [March Days II]
  10) Märztage III [March Days III]
First published 1883 (this 6th edition 1922)
Portfolio of ten etchings (six also with aquatint)
and title page
56 x 47.5 (paper size); image size variable
Purchased 1983
GMA 2768

Danuta Kluza

1926–

Le Jardin [*The Garden*]
Etching on paper (4/10)
75 x 45 (paper 79.4 x 53.3)
Purchased 1966
GMA 990

Laura Knight

1877–1970

Dressing Room No. 3 [BW 6]
1923
Etching on paper
25.2 x 17.5 (paper 40.2 x 26.5)
Purchased 1949
GMA 395

Spanish Dancer No. 1 [BW 8]*
1923
Etching and aquatint on paper
27 x 21.7 (paper 46.3 x 29.6)
Purchased 1949
GMA 397

A Quarrel [BW 11]
1923
Etching and aquatint on paper (A.P.)
22.4 x 17.5 (paper 39.3 x 26.3)
Purchased 1949
GMA 400

Spanish Dancer No. 2 [BW 19]
1923
Etching and aquatint on paper
26.2 x 21.2 (paper 46.1 x 28)
Purchased 1949
GMA 398

Swing Boats [BW 22]
1923
Etching and aquatint on paper (A.P.)
25 x 17.5 (paper 45.7 x 29)
Purchased 1949
GMA 399

Dancer Resting [BW 24]
1923
Etching and aquatint on paper (A.P.)
17.6 x 12.6 (paper 31.8 x 23.1)
Purchased 1949
GMA 396

Bank Holiday [BW 25]
1923
Etching and aquatint on paper (A.P.)
26.7 x 21.2 (paper 38.3 x 29.2)
Purchased 1949
GMA 401

[BW refers to the catalogue raisonné of Knight's prints by G. F. Bolling and V. A. Withington (Aldershot 1993)]

Jack Knox

1936–

*Aftermath**
c 1960
Oil on hardboard
104.1 x 129.6
Purchased 1971
GMA 1168

*Bajazet Encag'd**
c 1962
Oil on canvas
90.8 x 90.8
Purchased 1963
GMA 867

*How It Is**
d 1968
P. V. A., oil, pastel and black chalk on canvas
152 x 152
Purchased 1987
GMA 3010

*Three Piles of Cherries**
c 1978
P. V. A. on canvas
30.2 x 71
Bequeathed by Mr Alan Stark 1983
GMA 2773

West Highland Way*
1982
Oil on canvas
152.5 x 182.5
Purchased 1987
GMA 3009

Dove
(from 'The Scottish Bestiary')
Published 1986
Lithograph over screenprint on paper (5/50)
53.5 x 35.5 (paper 76 x 56.5)
Purchased 1987
GMA 3019 D

Nuckelavee
(from 'The Scottish Bestiary')
Published 1986
Lithograph over screenprint on paper (5/50)
53.5 x 35.5 (paper 76 x 56.5)
Purchased 1987
GMA 3019 I

Whale
(from 'The Scottish Bestiary')
Published 1986
Lithograph over screenprint on paper (5/50)
53.5 x 35.5 (paper 76 x 56.5)
Purchased 1987
GMA 3019 N

Oskar Kokoschka

1886–1980

Alma Mahler*
c 1913
Black chalk on paper
39.2 x 31.5
Purchased 1987
GMA 3037

Zrání (Summer)*
1938–40
Oil on canvas
68.3 x 89.2
Presented by the Czechoslovak Government in Exile 1942
GMA 21

Kathleen, Countess of Drogheda*
d 1940
Coloured pencil on paper
56.5 x 38.2
Presented by Mrs Olda Kokoschka 1989
GMA 3451

The Crucified Christ Helping the Hungry Children*
d 1945
Black and red chalk on paper
44.8 x 33.7
Purchased 1962
GMA 811

Die träumenden Knaben [The Dreaming Boys]*
1908 (published 1917)
Book with eight colour lithographs and three black and white lithographs (215/275)
24.1 x 29.5 (page size)
Purchased 1990
GMA 3552

Selbstbildnis von zwei Seiten als Maler [Self-Portrait as a Painter from Two Aspects]*
1923
Colour lithographic poster
127.8 x 91 (paper size)
Purchased 1990
GMA 3557

The Crucified Christ Helping the Hungry Children ('En Memoria de los Niños de Viena')*
1945–46
Lithograph on paper
76.2 x 51 (paper size)
Presented by Mrs Olda Kokoschka 1990
GMA 3549

The Greyhound
1952
Colour lithograph on paper (142/200)
50 x 64.4 (paper size)
Purchased 1961
GMA 772

Käthe Kollwitz

1867–1945

*Gesenkter Frauenkopf [Woman with Bowed Head]**
1905
Etching and soft ground on paper
37.6 x 31.7 (paper 60 x 44.9)
Purchased 1979
GMA 2096

*Bewaffnung in einem Gewölbe [Arming in a Cellar]**
1906 (published 1921)
Etching and soft ground on paper
49.8 x 32.9 (paper 64 x 48)
Purchased 1979
GMA 2097

Leon Kossoff

1926–

*Portrait of Father**
1978
Oil on board
123 x 97.5
Purchased 1979
GMA 2105

Marian Kratochwil

1906–

Leather-bound volume containing 115 drawings and one print, made while serving with the Polish Army in Scotland
d 1940–47
Mainly pencil, black chalk or ink on paper
41.3 x 30.5
Presented by the artist 1979
GMA 2117 A

Leather-bound volume containing 143 drawings and one print, made while serving with the Polish Army in Scotland
d 1944–47
Mainly pencil, black chalk or ink on paper
41.3 x 30.5
Presented by the artist 1979
GMA 2117 B

View of Dalkeith from the North
d 1945
Oil on canvas laid on wood
20.3 x 29.5
Presented by the artist 1986
GMA 2977

Liu Kuo-sung

1932–

*Floating Mountains
(from 'The Commonwealth Print Portfolio')*
1978
Silkscreen and lithograph on paper (13/65)
72.8 x 52.2 (paper 75.7 x 56.4)
Presented by the Canadian High Commission 1979
GMA 2123

Jean-Emile Laboureur

1877–1943

Le 14 juillet sur le front anglais [The 14th July on the English Front]
d 1917
Etching on paper
24.8 x 26.5 (paper 51 x 40)
Purchased 1992
GMA 3657

Edwin La Dell

1914–70

Hastings
(from the J. Lyons series 'Lithographs by
Contemporary Artists, vol. I')
Published 1947
Colour lithograph on paper (after oil)
72.5 x 97.5 (paper 74.8 x 99)
Presented by J. Lyons & Co. Ltd 1948
GMA 1207

Gerald Laing

1936–

*Pyramid**
1971
Polished mild steel (two parts)
62.4 x 62.2 x 26.6
Purchased 1975
GMA 1503

*Galina 3**
1974
Bronze
28 x 27.5 x 24
Purchased 1975
GMA 1504

The Human Condition II
d 1979
Bronze (6/10)
60.5 x 32 x 31
Purchased 1982
GMA 2500

Slide
(from the portfolio 'Eleven Pop Artists, vol. II')
1965
Screenprint and collage on styrene (no. 25)
76 x 60.9 (paper size)
Purchased 1975
GMA 1339

Pendulum
d 1968
Screenprint on paper (A.P.)
80 x 36.3 (paper 88.8 x 58.5)
Purchased 1975
GMA 1506

Headers
d 1968
Screenprint and alufoil on paper (25/75)
58.7 x 73.8 (paper size)
Purchased 1975
GMA 1507

Follow Me
d 1968
Screenprint and alufoil on paper (A.P.)
58.5 x 73.8 (paper size)
Purchased 1975
GMA 1508

Three Axes
d 1968
Screenprint and alufoil on paper (A.P.)
58.6 x 73.8 (paper size)
Purchased 1975
GMA 1509

C. T. Strokers
d 1968
Screenprint on paper (A.P.)
74 x 42.9 (paper 88.8 x 58.6)
Purchased 1975
GMA 1510

*Just Another Pretty Face**
d 1968
Screenprint on paper (A.P.)
76.3 x 39.4 (paper 89 x 58.6)
Purchased 1975
GMA 1511

Field
1973
Screenprint on paper (5/20)
56 x 69.5 (paper size)
Purchased 1975
GMA 1505

The United States Pyramid – Dawn
d 1973
Colour lithograph on paper (6/10)
38 x 53.7 (paper 49.5 x 62.9)
Purchased 1975
GMA 1512

The United States Pyramid – Dusk
d 1973
Colour lithograph on paper (6/10)
38 x 53.7 (paper 49.5 x 63.5)
Purchased 1975
GMA 1513

Margaret Laing

d. 1970

In the Studio
1937
Colour lithograph on paper
46 x 32.5 (paper 54.5 x 40.6)
Purchased 1982
GMA 2555

The Jazz Band
Lithograph on paper
30.7 x 25.1 (paper 38.3 x 25.2)
Purchased 1982
GMA 2553

Boys Shrimping
Lithograph on paper (4/24)
22.3 x 27.4 (paper 25.3 x 38.6)
Purchased 1982
GMA 2554

John Gascoyne Lake

1903–75

Les Lecques Bay
(*from the J. Lyons series 'Lithographs by Contemporary Artists, vol. I'*)
Published 1947
Colour lithograph on paper (after watercolour)
72.4 x 97.6 (paper 74.5 x 98.6)
Presented by J. Lyons & Co. Ltd 1948
GMA 1208

William Lamb

1893–1951

An Old Man Reading a Newspaper (or 'The Daily News')*
c 1930s (cast 1969)
Bronze
56 x 28 x 36
Purchased 1969
GMA 1104

Colin Lanceley

1938–

Bluebeard's Castle
d 1968
Screenprint on paper (A.P. 27/30)
96 x 63.2 (paper 103 x 71.4)
Purchased 1984
GMA 2879

Some are More Equal than Others
d 1969
Screenprint on paper (8/150)
76.5 x 56 (paper 80.5 x 60.5)
Purchased 1984
GMA 2880

Peter Lanyon

1918–64

Solo Flight*
d 1960
Oil on masonite
121.5 x 183
Purchased 1983
GMA 2742

Ginger Hill*
d 1961
Oil on canvas
123 x 76
Purchased 1981
GMA 2290

Mikhail Larionov

1881–1964

*Soldier in a Wood**
c 1911
Oil on canvas
84.5 x 91.4
Purchased with funds given by two anonymous
donors 1962
GMA 799

*Costume Design for 'Les Contes Russes'**
d 1915
Watercolour and pencil on paper
63.4 x 43.7
Purchased with funds given by two anonymous
donors 1962
GMA 800

William M. Larkins

1901–74

Underwood Street, Whitechapel
1922
Etching on paper
7.4 x 7.9 (paper 19.6 x 27)
Purchased 1949
GMA 402

Manorbier Castle
1924
Etching on paper
10 x 10.5 (paper 25.7 x 19.8)
Purchased 1949
GMA 403

Jean-Baptiste L'Arrivé

1875–1928

Jeune athlète [Young Athlete]
c 1908
Marble
173 x 71 x 52
Purchased 1911
GMA 1004

*Vierge et enfant [Virgin and Child]**
c 1910
Bronze
49 x 14.5 x 11
Bequeathed by Sir David Young Cameron 1945
GMA 1005

Elie Lascaux

1888–1969

*L'Eglise de Puteaux [The Church at Puteaux]**
1927
Oil on canvas
61.3 x 46.1
Bequeathed by Miss Elizabeth Watt 1989
GMA 3496

Henri Laurens

1885–1954

*Femme debout à la draperie au bras levé
[Standing Woman with Drapery, Arm Raised]**
1928
Bronze (2/6)
38 x 13.8 x 10.5
Purchased 1969
GMA 1101

Alfred Kingsley Lawrence

1893–1975

*Portrait of a Woman**
d 1925
Black chalk on paper
50 x 35.5
Bequeathed by Sir David Young Cameron 1945
GMA 721

Miss Mayo
d 1926
Pencil on paper
63.2 x 46.9
Bequeathed by Sir David Young Cameron 1945
GMA 722

The Pioneer
d 1918
Etching on paper (first state)
23.7 x 21.4 (paper 29.6 x 23.6)
Bequeathed by Sir David Young Cameron 1945
GMA 404

Eileen Lawrence
1946–

*Naples, Serpent, Fascine**
d 1983–84
Watercolour, oil and sand on handmade paper,
laid on paper
183 x 160
Purchased 1985
GMA 2958

*The Blood of the Peacock**
1986
Watercolour, Indian ink and gold leaf on paper,
folded inside wooden cover
53 x 224 fully extended ; wooden cover 55.8 x 24
Purchased 1987
GMA 3011

Medicine Bag
c 1975
Etching on paper (16/20)
24.6 x 24.8 (paper 47.2 x 37.5)
Purchased 1976
GMA 1548

Allan Lawson
1948–

Homage to Rauschenberg
d 1975
Screenprint with collage on paper (1/6)
38.2 x 50 (paper 43.8 x 55)
Purchased 1976
GMA 1545

Homage to Jasper Johns
d 1975
Screenprint with collage on paper (1/6)
38.2 x 50 (paper 44 x 55.3)
Purchased 1976
GMA 1546

Christopher Le Brun
1951–

*Sir Bedivere**
d 1982–83
Oil on canvas
229 x 245
Purchased 1984
GMA 2833

Seven Lithographs
Published 1989
Portfolio of seven lithographs (21/35)
Each 91.5 x 76 (image and paper size)
Purchased 1989
GMA 3467

Fernand Léger
1881–1955

*Femme et nature morte [Woman and Still Life]**
d 1921
Oil on canvas
65.5 x 92
Purchased 1966
GMA 962

*Le Tronc d'arbre sur fond jaune [Tree Trunk on
Yellow Ground]**
d 1945
Oil on canvas
112.5 x 127
Purchased 1981
GMA 2310

*Etude pour 'Les Constructeurs': l'équipe au repos
[Study for 'The Constructors': The Team at Rest]**
d 1950
Oil on canvas
162 x 129.5
Purchased 1984
GMA 2845

Le Profil à la corde: étude pour 'Les
Constructeurs' [Man in Profile with Rope: Study
for 'The Constructors']*
1950 or 1951
Ink and black chalk on paper
64.5 x 49.7
Purchased 1985
GMA 2955

Wilhelm Lehmbruck

1881–1919

Mädchenkopf, sich umwendend [Head of a Girl
Looking over her Shoulder]*
1913–14 (posthumous cast)
Terracotta
39.5 x 27 x 18.5
Purchased 1993
GMA 3731

Clare Leighton

1898–1989

Women Washing Clothes
Wood engraving on paper (11/50)
13.9 x 18.7 (paper 18 x 24.5)
Purchased 1949
GMA 405

Auguste Lepère

1849–1918

L'Abreuvoir au Pont-Marie, Paris [The Watering
Place at the Pont-Marie, Paris]
d 1902
Etching on paper
15.3 x 23.2 (paper 22.7 x 30.3)
Purchased 1949
GMA 406

Cecil Mary Leslie

1900–80

Robing of the Empress
1923
Aquatint on paper
35.4 x 30.2 (paper 43.6 x 38.6)
Presented by Mrs P. Hunter Blair 1985
GMA 2967

Endymion
1927
Aquatint on paper (5/10)
35.1 x 25.2 (paper 45.1 x 34.2)
Presented by Mrs P. Hunter Blair 1985
GMA 2966

The Son and Heir
c 1929
Etching and aquatint on paper (5/15)
35.4 x 25.5 (paper 42.8 x 29.4)
Presented by Mrs P. Hunter Blair 1985
GMA 2968

The Running of the Deer
c 1950
Aquatint on paper
15.1 x 20.3 (paper 31.7 x 38.8)
Presented by Mrs P. Hunter Blair 1985
GMA 2969

Percy Wyndham Lewis

1882–1957

A Reading of Ovid (Tyros)*
1920–21
Oil on canvas
165.2 x 90.2
Purchased 1977
GMA 1685

Seated Figure*
c 1921
Oil on canvas
75.7 x 63
Presented by Mrs Karina Williamson 1988
GMA 3428

Portrait of Edwin Evans*
1922–23
Oil on canvas
149 x 107.8
Purchased 1968
GMA 1079

Sol LeWitt

1928–

*Five Modular Structures (Sequential
Permutations on the Number Five)**
1972
Wood, enamel paint
Each structure 62 x 98 x 62
Purchased 1974
GMA 1308

*Tear R 106 – From Midpoint of Left Side to
Middle of the Page*
d 1973
Torn paper with pencil inscription
41.9 x 41.9
Presented by Mr E. J. Power 1974
GMA 1323

Double Composite
1971
Screenprint on paper (48/60)
101.5 x 77.8 (paper size)
Presented by Mr E. J. Power 1974
GMA 1322

Roy Lichtenstein

1923–

In the Car*
d 1963
Magna on canvas
172 x 203.5
Purchased 1980
GMA 2133

Reverie
(*from the portfolio 'Eleven Pop Artists, vol. II'*)
1965
Screenprint on paper (no. 24)
68.5 x 58 (paper 76.2 x 60.9)
Purchased 1975
GMA 1335

Robert Lillie

1867–1949

Beach Scene
d 1906
Watercolour on paper
17.2 x 24.8
Bequeathed by Dr R. A. Lillie 1977
GMA 1994

Kim Lim

1936–

Blue Disc
d 1970
Aquatint on paper (7/10)
Diameter 17.8 (paper 41.1 x 41)
Purchased 1984
GMA 2881

Silver Engraving
d 1973
Engraving on paper (3/20)
42 x 25.5 (paper 64 x 50.2)
Purchased 1984
GMA 2882

Henry Lintott

1877–1965

Sussex Downs
c 1927
Oil on plywood
28.2 x 37.1
Bequeathed by Dr R. A. Lillie 1977
GMA 1914

Jacques Lipchitz

1891–1973

*Figure assise [Seated Figure]**
c 1916–17
Bronze (1/7)
78 x 29.2 x 29
Purchased (Knapping Fund) 1968
GMA 1091

El Lissitzky

1890–1941

*1° Kestnermappe Proun [Proun. 1st Kestner
Portfolio]**
Published 1923
Portfolio of six lithographs (two with collage),
cover and title page (16/50)
Each sheet 60 x 44 (sheet 6 44 x 60)
Purchased 1983
GMA 2767

William Littlejohn

1929–

*Still Life, Harbour and Bird*ˣ
1964–66
Oil and pencil on canvas
127 x 127
Purchased 1966
GMA 991

The London Suite

(Portfolio, published 1982)

See Basil BEATTIE, John BELLANY, Michael
BENNETT, Albert IRVIN, Trevor JONES, Michael
MOON, Terry SETCH, Harry THUBRON, John
WALKER, Gary WRAGG

Richard Long

1945–

*Stone Line**
1980
Slate
10 x 183 x 1067
Purchased 1980
GMA 2196

L. S. Lowry

1887–1976

*Canal and Factories**
d 1955
Oil on canvas
61 x 76.3
Purchased 1975
GMA 1349

*Industrial Scene
(from the J. Lyons series 'Lithographs by
Contemporary Artists, vol. I')*
Published 1947
Colour lithograph on paper (after oil)
72.2 x 97.5 (paper 74.5 x 98.6)
Presented by J. Lyons & Co. Ltd 1948
GMA 1209

Ernest S. Lumsden

1883–1948

*Paris en construction No. 1: Tour de Sacré-Coeur
de Montmartre*
d 1907
Etching on paper
21.7 x 14.5 (paper 25.8 x 19.5)
Purchased 1989
GMA 3456

Paris en construction No. 5
d 1907
Etching on paper
21.5 x 12.6 (paper 25 x 18)
Purchased 1989
GMA 3455

Loch Torridon
d 1909
Etching on paper
22.1 x 12.6 (paper 25.9 x 19.7)
Presented by Mr and Mrs Alexander Maitland
1953
GMA 412

*James McBey**
1920
Etching on paper (49/50)
25.2 x 29.3 (paper 29.2 x 34.8)
Bequeathed by Mr Kenneth Sanderson 1943
GMA 407

Augustus John
d 1921
Etching and drypoint on paper (3/26)
30.1 x 25.4 (paper 36.2 x 29.6)
Bequeathed by Mr Kenneth Sanderson 1943
GMA 409

Frank Brangwyn
d 1921
Etching on paper (28/30)
30.4 x 24.9 (paper 40.7 x 29.9)
Bequeathed by Mr Kenneth Sanderson 1943
GMA 410

William Rothenstein
d 1921
Etching and drypoint on paper
30.3 x 25.2 (paper 40.9 x 32.1)
Bequeathed by Mr Kenneth Sanderson 1943
GMA 411

Marius Bauer
d 1928
Etching on paper
33.2 x 25.9 (paper 39.7 x 30.5)
Bequeathed by Mr Kenneth Sanderson 1943
GMA 408

Boston Harbour, Lincolnshire
d 1934
Etching on paper
37.6 x 25.2 (paper 45.5 x 32.6)
Purchased 1982
GMA 2556

Elder Street, Edinburgh
d 1939
Etching on paper
25.2 x 20.2 (paper 38.1 x 25.7)
Purchased 1982
GMA 2557

J. Lyons Series 'Lithographs by Contemporary Artists, vol. I'

(Portfolio, published 1947)

See Edward ARDIZZONE, Edward BAWDEN, Clifford and Rosemary ELLIS, Barnett FREEDMAN, Clifford FRITH, Duncan GRANT, Anthony GROSS, George HOOPER, Mary KESSELL, Edwin LA DELL, John Gascoyne LAKE, L. S. LOWRY, John NASH, William SCOTT, Ruskin SPEAR, Carel WEIGHT

James McBey

1883–1959

Zaandijk [MH 73]
d 1910
Etching on paper (no. 28)
10.2 x 17.6 (paper 19.5 x 30.4)
Bequeathed by Mr George Liston-Foulis 1958
GMA 418

The Banderillas [MH 107]
d 1911
Drypoint on paper (no. 19)
15 x 20.2 (paper 18 x 23.2)
Bequeathed by Mr George Liston-Foulis 1958
GMA 417

The Skylark [MH 117]
d 1912
Etching and drypoint on paper (no. 39)
16.2 x 30.2 (paper 25.1 x 42)
Purchased 1961
GMA 421

Beggars, Tetuan, No. 2 [MH 134]
d 1912
Etching on paper
17 x 13.7 (paper 24.3 x 18.8)
Purchased with funds from the Cowan Smith
Bequest 1962
GMA 819

A Moroccan Market (Tetuan) [MH 136]
d 1913
Etching on paper (no. 50)
15.1 x 27.9 (paper 21.3 x 34)
Purchased with funds from the Cowan Smith
Bequest 1962
GMA 820

The Approach to Tetuan [MH 137]
d 1913
Etching on paper (no. 45)
13.8 x 25.2 (paper 17.7 x 28.6)
Purchased with funds from the Cowan Smith
Bequest 1962
GMA 821

The Ford [MH 140]
d 1913
Etching on paper (no. 40)
13.8 x 24 (paper 17.5 x 27.7)
Purchased 1961
GMA 419

A Fishing Harbour (Stonehaven) [MH 145]
d 1913
Etching on paper (no. 9)
13.8 x 20.3 (paper 16.1 x 23.6)
Purchased 1961
GMA 420

The Isle of Ely [MH 162]
d 1915
Etching and drypoint on paper
20.6 x 34.1 (paper 24.6 x 37.7)
Purchased 1961
GMA 422

The Carpenter of Hesdin [MH 178]
d 1917
Drypoint on paper
19.7 x 30.5 (paper 23.5 x 33.9)
Purchased 1949
GMA 414

Margot as Lopokova [MH 189]
d 1920
Drypoint on paper
30.1 x 21.4 (paper 35.9 x 25.2)
Purchased with funds from the Cowan Smith
Bequest 1962
GMA 822

Dust, Beersheba, November 1917 [MH 193]
d 1920
Etching and drypoint on paper (no. 47)
23.1 x 39.3 (paper 32.2 x 45.7)
Purchased 1949
GMA 413

The Moonlight Attack, Jelil [MH 200]
d 1920
Etching and drypoint on paper (no. 47)
22.7 x 39.1 (paper 29.3 x 43.2)
Purchased 1949
GMA 415

New York, March 1930 (East River Sunset) [Post
MH 270]*
1934
Etching and drypoint on paper (no. 23)
20.8 x 35.3 (paper 31.9 x 45.6)
Bequeathed by Mr George Liston-Foulis 1958
GMA 416

[MH refers to the catalogue raisonné of McBey's
etchings and drypoints by Martin Hardie (London
1925)]

Robert MacBryde

1913–66

*Still Life**
c 1947
Oil on canvas
41.5 x 87
Bequeathed by Miss Elizabeth Watt 1989
GMA 3497

*The Chess Player**
c 1947–50
Oil on canvas
76.2 x 51.3
Bequeathed by Mr Alan Stark 1983
GMA 2772

*Two Women Sewing**
c 1948
Oil on canvas
100.3 x 143.5
Purchased 1976
GMA 1588

*Still Life with Cucumber**
1948
Oil on canvas
38.6 x 53.8
Purchased 1987
GMA 3306

*Still Life – Fish on a Pedestal Table**
c 1950
Oil on canvas
61.3 x 50.9
Purchased with funds given by Mrs J. Kennedy
1966
GMA 946

Woman at a Table
1948
Colour lithograph on paper
38 x 30.2 (paper 44.6 x 34)
Purchased 1983
GMA 2788

Still Life with Oil Lamp
c 1948–50
Colour lithograph on paper
39 x 53.7 (paper 46.3 x 58.7)
Purchased 1987
GMA 3313

Woman with a Drum
1949
Colour lithograph on paper
50 x 32.5 (paper 66.4 x 50.3)
Purchased 1987
GMA 3312

See also Robert COLQUHOUN and Robert
MACBRYDE

Charles McCall
1907–89

*William McCall**
d 1935
Oil on canvas
102 x 65.4
Presented by Mrs Mitzi McCall 1991
GMA 3592

William McCance
1894–1970

*Heavy Structures in a Landscape Setting**
c 1922
Pen and ink and ink wash on paper
18 x 22.9 (irregular)
Purchased 1988
GMA 3432

*Heavy Structures in a Landscape Setting**
d 1922
Oil on canvas with irregular, seven-sided, shaped
hardboard sheet, painted white, laid on top
71.2 x 91.7 (maximum visible canvas surface 68.8
x 83.5)
Purchased 1992
GMA 3612

*Abstract Cat**
c 1922–24
Clayslip, glazed
9.4 x 15.2 x 8.6
Presented by Dr Margaret McCance 1992
GMA 3620

*Agnes Miller Parker**
d 1925
Black chalk on paper
38 x 50.8
Purchased 1988
GMA 3433

*Portrait of Joseph Brewer**
d 1925
Oil on canvas
76.3 x 61.3
Purchased 1989
GMA 3446

*Joseph Brewer**
d 1925
Black chalk on paper
50.7 x 37.3
Presented by Dr Margaret McCance 1989
GMA 3471

*Study for a Colossal Steel Head**
d 1926
Black chalk on paper
53.8 x 37.8
Purchased 1988
GMA 3439

Hiroshima (or *Atom Horizon*)*
d 1947
Oil on hardboard
44 x 61
Purchased 1992
GMA 3613

View from an Egg
d 1962
Ink, watercolour and wax crayon on paper
25 x 18
Presented by Mr James Coxson 1985
GMA 2943

Mediterranean Hill Town
d 1923
Linocut on brown paper
18.2 x 12.8 (paper 24.3 x 16.3)
Purchased 1988
GMA 3431

Tree Trunk Composition
c 1924
Linocut on linen
18.2 x 24.3 (linen 19.9 x 26.4)
Purchased 1992
GMA 3614

The Piper (or *Highland Fantasia*)
c 1924–28
Linocut on paper
16 x 8
Purchased 1992
GMA 3616

The Engineer, his Wife and Family
1925
Linocut (black ink) on paper
10.4 x 6.7 (paper 13.9 x 8.9)
Purchased 1988
GMA 3434

The Engineer, his Wife and Family
1925
Linocut (black ink) on paper
10.4 x 6.7 (paper 11.1 x 7.3)
Purchased 1988
GMA 3435

The Engineer, his Wife and Family
d 1925
Linocut (blue ink over black ink) on paper
9.5 x 6.6 (paper and image size)
Purchased 1988
GMA 3436

The Engineer, his Wife and Family
1925
Linocut (green ink over purple ink) on paper
12 x 7.6 (paper and image size)
Purchased 1988
GMA 3437

The Engineer, his Wife and Family
d 1925
Linocut (green ink over purple ink) on paper
11.3 x 7.7 (paper and image size)
Purchased 1988
GMA 3438

Moloch of the Machine (or *Machine Gods*)
c 1928
Linocut (white ink) on black paper
10.7 x 15 (paper 18.2 x 18.9)
Purchased 1992
GMA 3615

David McClure

1926–

Picador on a Frightened Horse
1959
Black chalk and wash on paper
43.5 x 56.5
Bequeathed by Keith Andrews 1990
GMA 3606

*Figure and Flowers**
d 1963
Oil on canvas
75.7 x 91.2
Purchased 1963
GMA 869

Arbirlot by Sunlight
d 1966
Oil on canvas
50.8 x 61.4
Bequeathed by Dr R. A. Lillie 1977
GMA 1921

Malcolm McCoig

1941–

Isobel
c 1965
Etching and aquatint on paper
37.8 x 37.8 (paper 47.1 x 43.3)
Purchased 1965
GMA 928

Archibald W. MacDonald

1906–

View from a Window
d 1931
Etching on paper
25.3 x 20 (paper 37.9 x 25.6)
Purchased 1982
GMA 2558

Tom MacDonald

1914–85

*Clown before the Mirror**
d 1963
Oil on canvas
76.2 x 61
Purchased 1964
GMA 880

Rory McEwen

1932–82

*Untitled (Grey Plate Glass, Series 1968, No. 4)**
1968
Grey plate glass and metal
203 x 51 x 25.5
Purchased 1968
GMA 1086

Bardrochat
d 1978
Watercolour on vellum
68.7 x 61
Presented by the artist's family in accordance
with his wishes 1983
GMA 2792

*Datchet Road, Eton**
d 1979
Watercolour on vellum
55.5 x 45.8
Purchased 1980
GMA 2136

Beetle
d 1972
Etching on paper (12/50)
9.8 x 8.8 (paper 28.6 x 25.9)
Purchased 1984
GMA 2807

Moth and Leaf
d 1972
Etching on paper (13/50)
16.5 x 15 (paper 40.8 x 34)
Purchased 1984
GMA 2808

Onion
d 1972
Etching on paper (31/50)
26.3 x 17.8 (paper 56 x 42.6)
Purchased 1984
GMA 2809

Single Violet
d 1972
Etching on paper (31/50)
42.3 x 33.6 (paper 68.8 x 56)
Purchased 1984
GMA 2810

Violet and Leaves
d 1972
Etching on paper (31/50)
42.4 x 33.8 (paper 68.8 x 56.3)
Purchased 1984
GMA 2811

Rose
d 1972
Etching on paper (31/50)
33.8 x 42.5 (paper 56.1 x 68)
Purchased 1984
GMA 2812

Pomegranates
d 1972
Etching on paper (31/50)
33.8 x 42.5 (paper 56.1 x 68)
Purchased 1984
GMA 2813

Shell
d 1972–73
Etching and aquatint on paper (31/50)
42.6 x 33.7 (paper 68.8 x 56.2)
Purchased 1984
GMA 2814

Brian McGeogh

1948–

Blast
d 1980
Portfolio of 75 linocuts (6/20)
Each 30.5 x 23 (paper 59.7 x 41.9)
Purchased 1981
GMA 2294

David Mach

1956–

Matchead*
1986
Burnt matches, glue
45.5 x 20.5 x 15
Presented by the Contemporary Art Society
(Henry Moore Foundation Grant) 1989
GMA 3468

Dying for It*
1989
Glass bottles, water, dye and emulsion paint, on
board base
22.5 x 300 x 207 (excluding base)
Commissioned 1989
GMA 3469

Keith McIntyre

1959–

Lochwood Oaks*
[verso: *untitled sketch*]
d 1985
Charcoal on paper
57.5 x 78
Purchased 1986
GMA 3015

Tracy MacKenna

1963–

Objects 5,6,7
1989
Brass, steel, zinc and rubber bands
9 x 11.5 x 2; 10.5 x 10.3 x 3.3; 8 x 14.3 x 3.5
Purchased 1989
GMA 3458

Objects 8,9,10*
1989
Copper, zinc, tin, rubber bands and rivets
11.7 x 9 x 2.5; 10 x 10 x 5; 8.7 x 12.6 x 4
Purchased 1989
GMA 3461

*Sinners (Unexplored Routes)**
1990
Galvanised steel, copper, rubber, rivets, solder and tacks
224 x 24.5 x 21.5
Purchased with funds bequeathed by Miss Elizabeth Watt 1990
GMA 3585

*Sinners (Unexplored Routes)**
1990
Galvanised steel, copper, rubber, rivets and solder
223.5 x 63 x 21
Purchased with funds bequeathed by Miss Elizabeth Watt 1990
GMA 3586

Tom Mackenzie

1947–

Untitled
c 1975
Etching on paper
25.1 x 20 (paper 33 x 29.6)
Purchased 1976
GMA 1540

Untitled
c 1975
Screenprint on paper
29.5 x 25 (paper 51.7 x 38)
Purchased 1976
GMA 1541

George Mackie

1920–

Portsoy
d 1968
Watercolour, pen and ink, gouache and pencil on paper
44.1 x 56.5
Bequeathed by Dr R. A. Lillie 1977
GMA 1918

Deeside Cottage
d 1968
Watercolour and pen and ink on paper
46.3 x 58.5
Bequeathed by Dr R. A. Lillie 1977
GMA 1920

Norwegian Flag
d 1969
Watercolour and black chalk on paper
36.5 x 49.6
Bequeathed by Dr R. A. Lillie 1977
GMA 1917

'Dogger Shore'
d 1975
Watercolour and pencil on paper
16.7 x 24.7
Bequeathed by Dr R. A. Lillie 1977
GMA 1915

'Jerome Letzer' and 'Viking Shore'
d 1975
Watercolour, gouache and pencil on paper
16.9 x 24.7
Bequeathed by Dr R. A. Lillie 1977
GMA 1916

'Rig Sailor' and 'King Supplier'
d 1975
Watercolour, gouache and pencil on paper
16.7 x 24.7
Bequeathed by Dr R. A. Lillie 1977
GMA 1919

Charles Rennie Mackintosh

1868–1928

*Revolving Bookcase for Hous'hill, Nitshill, Glasgow**
1904
Wood, painted
122 x 46 x 46
Purchased 1989
GMA 3447

Mont Alba*
c 1924–27
Watercolour on paper
38.7 x 43.8
Purchased 1990
GMA 3533

Robert Maclaurin

1961–

Amongst the Turkish Wilderness*
d 1988
Oil on canvas
153 x 168
Purchased 1988
GMA 3420

Under the Armenian Bridge*
d 1988
Oil on canvas
168 x 153
Purchased 1988
GMA 3421

Bruce McLean

1944–

Landscape Painting*
d 1968
Colour photograph with transfer-text
31.2 x 31
Purchased 1990
GMA 3572

People Who Make Art in Glass Houses, Work*
1969 / 1970
Two black and white photographs, one with
transfer-text
Two panels, each 123.5 x 92.5
Purchased 1980
GMA 2223 A & B

Untitled Blue*
c 1980
Acrylic and oil pastel on photographic paper
164 x 137.2
Presented by the Contemporary Art Society 1983
GMA 2777

Five Banners for the Exhibition 'Scottish Art
Since 1900'
1989
Mixed media
488 x 152 (outer two); 488 x 193 (inner three)
Commissioned 1989
GMA 3477

Design for 'Scottish Art Since 1900' Banners
1989
Collage, watercolour and pencil on paper
42.6 x 76.1
Acquired through the commission of GMA 3477,
1989
GMA 3478

Design for 'Scottish Art Since 1900' Banners
1989
Collage, watercolour and pencil on paper
41 x 109.9
Acquired through the commission of GMA 3477,
1989
GMA 3479

Green Peace Piece
1989
Monoprint on paper
100 x 127 (paper 124 x 150)
Purchased 1989
GMA 3480

A Certain Smile (A New Front Door?)
d 1980
Photo-screenprint on paper (8/50)
101.7 x 123.4 (paper size)
Purchased 1985
GMA 2947

Dreamwork
(with text by Mel Gooding)
Published 1985
Book with sixteen screenprints (15/140)
40 x 30.4 (page size)
Purchased 1985
GMA 2970

Spider
(from 'The Scottish Bestiary')
Published 1986
Screenprint on paper (5/50)
36.8 x 36 (paper 76 x 56.5)
Purchased 1987
GMA 3019 F

Salmon
(from 'The Scottish Bestiary')
Published 1986
Screenprint on paper (5/50)
33 x 32.3 (paper 76 x 56.5)
Purchased 1987
GMA 3019 G

Stoor Worm
(from 'The Scottish Bestiary')
Published 1986
Screenprint on paper (5/50)
37 x 36.8 (paper 76 x 56.5)
Purchased 1987
GMA 3019 K

Wish You were Here (Phew what a Scorcher)
(from 'The Haymarket Print Suite')
Published 1990
Screenprint on paper
152 x 101 (paper 157 x 107)
Purchased 1990
GMA 3568

John McLean

1939–

Escalator*
d 1988
Acrylic on canvas
185.7 x 89
Purchased 1989
GMA 3476

Talbert McLean

1906–92

Ochre*
1973
P. V. A. on canvas
165 x 142.6
Purchased 1973
GMA 1294

Will Maclean

1941–

The Ring-Net (Ring-Net Herring Fishing on the West Coast of Scotland)
1973–78
375 items, including photographs, drawings, watercolours and documentary material
Purchased 1978
GMA 2130

Bard McIntyre's Box*
d 1984
Mixed-media assemblage
60 x 45.8 x 7.3
Purchased 1986
GMA 2973

A Night of Islands; Ten Etchings from Gaelic Poems and Prose
Published 1991
Portfolio of ten colour etchings with ten poems in Gaelic and English (20/40)
75.4 x 54.3 (paper size)
Purchased 1992
GMA 3622

George Mackley

1900–83

Chestnuts
1944
Wood engraving on paper
10 x 7.5 (paper 15.2 x 13)
Presented by Monica Poole in accordance with the artist's wishes, 1993
GMA 3688

Summer Flowers
1944
Wood engraving on card
10.2 x 8 (card 11.3 x 8.9)
Presented by Monica Poole in accordance with the artist's wishes, 1993
GMA 3689

Open Gate
1945
Wood engraving on paper
10 x 8 (paper 15.9 x 13.3)
Presented by Monica Poole in accordance with the
artist's wishes, 1993
GMA 3682

The House by the Lake
1952
Wood engraving on paper (6/75)
13 x 15.1 (paper 18.8 x 25.1)
Presented by Monica Poole in accordance with the
artist's wishes, 1993
GMA 3679

Litter Basket
1963
Wood engraving on paper
10 x 8 (paper 18.7 x 12.6)
Presented by Monica Poole in accordance with the
artist's wishes, 1993
GMA 3683

The Boat Inn
(for 'British Waterways')
1967
Wood engraving on paper
5.1 x 6.4 (paper 9.6 x 12.8)
Presented by Monica Poole in accordance with the
artist's wishes, 1993
GMA 3684

Old Lock at Brentford
(for 'British Waterways')
1967
Wood engraving on paper
5.1 x 6.4 (paper 9.9 x 12.6)
Presented by Monica Poole in accordance with the
artist's wishes, 1993
GMA 3685

Painting the Boat
(for 'British Waterways')
1967
Wood engraving on paper
5.1 x 6.5 (paper 7.2 x 9.9)
Presented by Monica Poole in accordance with the
artist's wishes, 1993
GMA 3686

Entrance to the Grand Canal
(for 'British Waterways')
1967
Wood engraving on paper
5.2 x 6.5 (paper 8.5 x 10.6)
Presented by Monica Poole in accordance with the
artist's wishes, 1993
GMA 3687

Haybarns at Eemdijk
Wood engraving on paper
10.2 x 12.8 (paper 15.6 x 21)
Presented by Monica Poole in accordance with the
artist's wishes
GMA 3680

Weir
Wood engraving on paper
7.5 x 12.8 (paper 16.1 x 18)
Presented by Monica Poole in accordance with the
artist's wishes, 1993
GMA 3681

Lords and Ladies
Wood engraving on paper
12.6 x 15 (paper 21.2 x 23.6)
Presented by Monica Poole in accordance with the
artist's wishes, 1993
GMA 3690

Iain Macnab

1890–1967

*The Waterfront, Calvi, Corsica**
1930
Wood engraving on paper (7/40)
25.3 x 20.2 (paper 31.8 x 26)
Purchased 1979
GMA 2084

Sardine Fishermen
1930
Wood engraving on paper (4/40)
11.1 x 9.6 (paper 17 x 12.6)
Purchased 1979
GMA 2089

Landscape near Cassis
1930
Wood engraving on paper (4/30)
10.3 x 10.7 (paper 16.8 x 21)
Purchased 1979
GMA 2090

Cassis
1933
Wood engraving on paper (3/40)
9.9 x 15 (paper 16.6 x 23.4)
Purchased 1979
GMA 2085

Las Lavanderas
1936
Wood engraving on paper (11/50)
12.7 x 17.3 (paper 16.6 x 21.6)
Purchased 1979
GMA 2088

The Quayside, Whitby Harbour
1937
Wood engraving on paper
29.1 x 24 (image and paper size)
Purchased 1979
GMA 2091

The Haunted Olive Grove
1939
Wood engraving on paper (5/9)
12.2 x 10.3 (paper 19 x 13.8)
Purchased 1979
GMA 2087

London Snow
1955
Wood engraving on paper
20.2 x 12.5 (paper 32.7 x 22.7)
Purchased 1979
GMA 2086

Ronda Bridge, Spain
1961
Wood engraving on paper (trial proof)
25.2 x 20.2 (paper 35.3 x 28.8)
Purchased 1979
GMA 2092

Ronda Bridge, Spain
1961
Wood engraving on paper (trial proof)
25.2 x 20.2 (paper 35.5 x 28.8)
Purchased 1979
GMA 2093

Three Men at a Table
Wood engraving on paper
12.6 x 22.9 (paper 15.9 x 26.3)
Purchased 1949
GMA 438

Caroline McNairn

1955–

*Looking Outside**
d 1987
Oil on canvas
182.9 x 182.9
Purchased 1989
GMA 3474

William MacTaggart

1903–81

*Snow, near Lasswade**
c 1928
Oil on wood
50.5 x 60.7
Purchased 1968
GMA 1087

Sketchbook
(*30 drawings*)
d 1928–30
Charcoal, pencil, watercolour and ink on paper
28 x 22
Presented by the executors of the artist 1981
GMA 2325

*The Old Mill, East Linton**
c 1942
Oil on canvas
51 x 76.2
Bequeathed by Dr R. A. Lillie 1977
GMA 1922

Fields at Pontarmé
c 1948 / c 1964
Oil on hardboard
51.4 X 71.2
Scott Hay Collection: presented 1967
GMA 1043

Roses
d 1959
Oil on board
53.4 X 40.6
Bequeathed by Miss Tertia Liebenthal 1970
GMA 1110

On the Esk
d 1961
Oil on board
71.1 X 91.5
Scott Hay Collection: presented 1967
GMA 1045

*Poppies against the Night Sky**
c 1962
Oil on hardboard
76.2 x 63.5
Scott Hay Collection: presented 1967
GMA 1046

*Nocturne**
1963
Oil on canvas
86.4 x 111.7
Purchased (Gulbenkian UK Trust Fund) 1963
GMA 847

Cornfields
d 1964
Oil on hardboard
63.5 x 76.2
Scott Hay Collection: presented 1967
GMA 1044

*The Wigtown Coast**
d 1968
Oil on canvas
86.2 x 111.5
Purchased 1983
GMA 2740

Sketchbook
(*7 drawings*)
Pencil and pastel on paper
24 X 15.2
Presented by the executors of the artist 1981
GMA 2326

Sketchbook
(*4 drawings*)
Pastel and charcoal on paper
29.2 X 19
Presented by the executors of the artist 1981
GMA 2327

Sketchbook
(*20 drawings*)
Charcoal, pencil and ink on paper
26 x 19.6
Presented by the executors of the artist 1981
GMA 2328

Sketchbook
(*13 drawings*)
Charcoal on paper
35 X 24.7
Presented by the executors of the artist 1981
GMA 2329

Sketchbook
(*14 drawings*)
Charcoal and chalk on paper
35.5 X 25.1
Presented by the executors of the artist 1981
GMA 2330

Sketchbook
(*27 drawings*)
Charcoal and ink on paper
35.5 X 25.1
Presented by the executors of the artist 1981
GMA 2331

Sketchbook
(*34 drawings*)
Charcoal, chalk and pencil on paper
35.5 X 24.7
Presented by the executors of the artist 1981
GMA 2332

Bea Maddock

1934–

Canberra Eclipse
(from 'The Commonwealth Print Portfolio')
d 1977 (published 1978)
Etching on paper (27/65)
50.4 x 36.8 (paper 75.7 x 56.5)
Presented by the Canadian High Commission
1979
GMA 2124

René Magritte

1898–1967

Le Drapeau noir [The Black Flag]*
1937
Oil on canvas
54.2 x 73.7
Purchased 1972
GMA 1261

La Représentation [Representation]*
1937
Oil on canvas laid on plywood
48.8 x 44.5 (frame 54 x 49.2)
Purchased 1990
GMA 3546

Aristide Maillol

1861–1944

Eve à la pomme [Eve with the Apple]*
1899
Bronze (1/6)
58.4 x 20.7 x 12
Purchased 1955
GMA 2941

Femme au berceau, bras droit levé au dessus de
l'epaule [Woman in a Cradle, Right Arm Raised
above the Shoulder] [G 267]
Published 1925
Lithograph on paper (third state, 25/25)
14.5 x 19.3 (paper 32.4 x 49.4)
Purchased 1957
GMA 439

Femme au berceau, bras droit levé au dessus de
l'epaule [Woman in a Cradle, Right Arm Raised
above the Shoulder] [G 267]
Published 1925
Lithograph (sanguine ink) on paper (first state,
16/35)
14.5 x 19.3 (paper 32 x 50)
Purchased 1962
GMA 801

Femme nue de dos, bras droit relevé au dessus de
la tête [Female Nude from Behind, Right Arm
Raised above the Head] [G 271]
Published 1925
Lithograph (sanguine ink) on paper (third state,
25/25)
30 x 11.5 (paper 49.9 x 32.4)
Purchased 1957
GMA 441

Femme de dos, drapée [Woman from Behind,
with Drapery] [G 272]
Published 1925
Lithograph on paper (third state, 25/25)
27.7 x 13 (paper 49.2 x 32.2)
Purchased 1957
GMA 442

Junon [G 274]
Published 1925
Lithograph (sanguine ink) on paper (third state,
25/25)
20.5 x 25.3 (paper 32.2 x 49.7)
Purchased 1957
GMA 440

[G refers to the catalogue raisonné of Maillol's
prints by Marcel Guérin (Geneva 1963)]

Roy de Maistre

1894–1968

The Lacemaker's Lamp*
c 1953
Oil on board
78.7 x 61.1
Presented by Miss Elizabeth Watt 1969
GMA 1099

Man Ray
1890–1976

Involute*
d 1917
Mixed-media collage on card laid on laminated
board
61.5 x 46.5
Purchased 1978
GMA 2064

Giacomo Manzú
1908–91

Scultore nello Studio [Sculptor in the Studio]
1957
Etching on paper (20/50)
12 x 17.8 (paper 25.1 x 32.8)
Purchased 1961
GMA 773

Franz Marc
1880–1916

Geburt der Pferde [Birth of Horses]*
1913
Colour woodcut on paper
21.6 x 14.5 (paper 35 x 24.7)
Purchased 1985
GMA 2949

Jean Marchand
1883–1941

Le Lac [The Lake]*
c 1910
Oil on canvas
56.5 x 67
Purchased 1969
GMA 1097

Herman Maril
1908–86

Going to the Blacksmith*
d 1936
Oil on canvas-board
30.5 x 40.1
Bequeathed by Miss Elizabeth Watt 1989
GMA 3498

John Marin
1870–1953

Downtown, The El
d 1921
Etching on paper
17.6 x 22.4 (paper 21.3 x 26.2)
Purchased 1980
GMA 2128

Marino Marini
1901–80

Pomona*
1949
Bronze
170 x 80.5 x 58
Presented by Lady Hay 1978
GMA 2027

Figura Seduta [Seated Figure]
(for 'Marino Marini' by Filippo de Pissis)
1941
Lithograph on paper (27/100)
33.2 x 25.1
Purchased 1962
GMA 802

Cavalier fond gris [Rider on a Grey Ground]
1957
Colour lithograph on paper (40/50)
57.5 x 40.3 (paper 65.3 x 48.7)
Purchased 1962
GMA 803

Kenneth Martin

1905–84

*Screw Mobile**
1959
Phosphor bronze
62.5 x 56 x 56
Presented by the Executors of the estate of the
late Mr Ashley Havinden 1976
GMA 1590

Marcello Mascherini

1906–83

*Danzatrice [Dancer]**
c 1958
Bronze
32.6 x 12 x 7
Bequeathed by Miss Elizabeth Watt 1989
GMA 3499

André Masson

1896–1987

*La Rivière en hiver [The River in Winter]**
1951
Oil on canvas
128.5 x 65.8
Purchased (Knapping Fund) 1967
GMA 1068

Têtes de chevaux [Horses' Heads]
1934
Etching on paper (1/10)
29.8 x 24 (paper 54 x 43.8)
Purchased 1977
GMA 1683

Henri Matisse

1869–1954

*Jeannette II**
1910
Bronze (4/6)
26.5 x 22.5 x 24
Purchased 1978
GMA 1995

La Séance de peinture (or *La Leçon de peinture*)
[*The Painting Session* (or *The Painting Lesson*)]*
1919
Oil on canvas
73.4 x 92.2
Bequeathed by Sir Alexander Maitland 1965
GMA 929

Nu assis (or *'Le Grand bois'*) [*Seated Nude* (or
'The Large Woodcut')]*
1906
Woodcut on paper (27/50)
47.5 x 38.3 (paper 58 x 46.1)
Purchased 1961
GMA 787

*Jazz**
Published 1947
Portfolio with twenty pochoir plates and text
(189/270)
42 x 65.5 (opened page size)
Purchased 1981
GMA 2284

Carlo Mattioli

1911–

*Ritratto di Giorgio Morandi [Portrait of
Giorgio Morandi]*
Colour lithograph on paper (45/50)
64.6 x 46.2
Purchased 1968
GMA 1080

Osborne Henry Mavor (James Bridie)

1888–1951

Persian Boy
d 1918
Watercolour and black chalk on paper
35.6 x 26
Presented by Mrs O. H. Mavor 1961
GMA 778

Man in Folk Costume
c 1918
Watercolour on paper
32.3 x 19.6
Presented by Mrs O. H. Mavor 1961
GMA 3587

Subaltern of Volunteer Army, Baku
d 1920
Pen and ink over pencil on paper
29.3 x 23.5
Presented by Mrs O. H. Mavor 1961
GMA 779

Church Dignitary Drinking Port
d 1939
Watercolour on paper
33 x 20.1
Presented by Mrs O. H. Mavor 1961
GMA 780

The Train
d 1939
Watercolour on paper
20 x 32.9
Presented by Mrs O. H. Mavor 1961
GMA 782

Gallstone Leaving the Common Duct
c 1939–42
Watercolour on paper
20.1 x 32.8
Presented by Mrs O. H. Mavor 1961
GMA 777

*The Angel and the Vice**
d 1942
Watercolour on paper
17.6 x 25.5
Presented by Mrs O. H. Mavor 1961
GMA 776

Mr Attlee on the Crest of a Wave
d 1945
Watercolour on paper
22.5 x 31.6
Presented by Mrs O. H. Mavor 1961
GMA 781

Mary Queen of Scots at Linlithgow
d 1946
Watercolour on paper
30.4 x 53.2
Presented by Professor Ronald Mavor 1983
GMA 2791

John Maxwell

1905–62

*View from a Tent**
[verso: *Woman and Child (unfinished)*]
d 1933
Oil on plywood
76.2 x 91.5
Purchased 1966
GMA 977

*Fish Market**
d 1934
Oil on canvas
71.5 x 96
Bequeathed by Dr R. A. Lillie 1977
GMA 1906

Still Life with Stuffed Birds
d 1934
Oil on canvas
91.5 x 61
Purchased 1982
GMA 2475

Landscape with Houses and Ancient Bridge
c 1934
Oil on canvas laid on hardboard
30.8 x 16.3
George and Isobel Neillands Collection: presented
1988
GMA 3329

Harbour with Three Boats*
d 1934
Oil on canvas
71.3 x 87.7
George and Isobel Neillands Collection: presented
1988
GMA 3342

A Head
d 1936
Watercolour, gouache and pen and ink on paper
27.9 x 14
George and Isobel Neillands Collection: presented
1988
GMA 3337

The Pleasures of the Snow*
c 1936
Pen and ink and wash on paper
33 x 25
George and Isobel Neillands Collection: presented
1988
GMA 3338

Strange Garden
d 1937
Watercolour and pen and ink on paper
43.9 x 61.3
Presented by Mr Hubert Wellington 1963
GMA 870

Requiem for a Decayed Affection*
d 1937
Watercolour, gouache and ink on board
50.8 x 63.2
Bequeathed by Sir David Milne 1974
GMA 1324

Figure in a Garden
1937
Watercolour and pen and ink on paper
43.4 x 61.5
Presented by Mr Hubert Wellington 1963
GMA 3662

Music and Nature Studies
c 1938
Pen and ink on paper
25.3 x 19
George and Isobel Neillands Collection: presented
1988
GMA 3333

Self-Portrait*
[verso: Nude in an Interior]
c 1937–39
Oil on plywood
86 x 59 [verso: 59 x 86]
George and Isobel Neillands Collection: presented
1988
GMA 3346

The Circus*
d 1941
Watercolour, ink and gouache on paper
12.2 x 13
George and Isobel Neillands Collection: presented
1988
GMA 3335

Flower Piece
d 1944
Watercolour, gouache, pen and ink and pencil
on paper
57.5 x 39.5
Bequeathed by Mr Alan Stark 1983
GMA 2771

St Abb's Head
[verso: Sketch of Two Plants, squared up]
c 1944
Pen and ink on paper [verso: pencil and wash]
23.1 x 28.6
George and Isobel Neillands Collection: presented
1988
GMA 3330

A Comic Figure Holding a Shepherd's Crook
c 1944
Pen and ink and pencil on paper
22.3 x 15.4
George and Isobel Neillands Collection: presented
1988
GMA 3334

A Shepherd (Happy Birthday Drawing)
d 1944
Pen and ink on paper
22.1 x 14
George and Isobel Neillands Collection: presented
1988
GMA 3336

Autumn Woods
d 1944
Gouache and pen and ink on paper laid on board
39.6 x 54.1
George and Isobel Neillands Collection: presented
1988
GMA 3343

Winter Landscape
d 1948
Watercolour and pen and ink on paper
57.5 x 74.6
George and Isobel Neillands Collection: presented
1988
GMA 3344

Figure with Flowers
d 1949
Watercolour, gouache and ink on paper
60.6 x 46.2
George and Isobel Neillands Collection: presented
1988
GMA 3340

Flowers by Night
1949
Watercolour and pen and ink on paper
44.5 x 48.7
Bequeathed by Mrs Hope Montagu Douglas Scott
1990
GMA 3564

Ventriloquist*
d 1952
Oil on canvas
68.6 x 55.9
George and Isobel Neillands Collection: presented
1988
GMA 3347

Fruit
d 1953
Watercolour and ink on paper
34.1 x 57.2
George and Isobel Neillands Collection: presented
1988
GMA 3339

Nudes and Flowers*
d 1953
Watercolour, gouache and ink on paper
44.5 x 55.8
George and Isobel Neillands Collection: presented
1988
GMA 3341

Sombre Landscape
d 1953
Watercolour, gouache and ink on paper
48 x 78.6
George and Isobel Neillands Collection: presented
1988
GMA 3345

Harvest Moon
d 1959
Watercolour and pencil on paper
57 x 79.6
Purchased 1960
GMA 756

Nude in a Mythical Landscape
d 1960
Pen and ink and wash on paper
23.5 x 29.5
Bequeathed by Keith Andrews 1990
GMA 3607

Farm near Dalbeattie
Pencil on paper
24.3 x 35 4
Bequeathed by Dr R. A. Lillie 1977
GMA 1923

Landscape near Dalbeattie
[verso: Landscape with Cattle]
Pencil on paper
24.5 x 35.5
Bequeathed by Dr R. A. Lillie 1977
GMA 1924

Mill near Dalbeattie
Pencil on paper
24.5 x 35.5
Bequeathed by Dr R. A. Lillie 1977
GMA 1925

The Square, Dalbeattie
Red chalk on paper
17.7 x 25.5
George and Isobel Neillands Collection: presented
1988
GMA 3331

George Mayer-Marton

1897–1960

Boats under the Spire
d 1950
Watercolour and ink on paper
38.5 x 58.8
Presented by Mrs C. Friend 1973
GMA 1276

Remembering the Danube*
d 1952
Oil on canvas
49.3 x 66.2
Presented by Mrs C. Friend 1973
GMA 1277

Margaret Mellis

1914–

Relief Construction in Wood*
1941
Wood relief, pencil
36.4 x 37.3
Purchased 1983
GMA 2745

*White Painting (with Red, Blue, Violet and
Ochre)**
1964
Oil on hardboard
122 x 101.6
Purchased 1975
GMA 1499

Bernard Meninsky

1891–1950

Girl with a Book*
d 1924
Oil on paper laid on board
47.8 x 23.7
Bequeathed by Miss Elizabeth Watt 1989
GMA 3501

Fish with Lemons*
c 1948
Gouache on paper
38 x 56.1
Bequeathed by Miss Elizabeth Watt 1989
GMA 3500

Thomas Buford Meteyard

1865–1928

Autumn, Scituate, Mass., U. S. A.
Oil on canvas
38 x 56.2
Bequeathed by Dr R. A. Lillie 1977
GMA 1927

Jean Metzinger

1883–1956

Paysage [Landscape]*
c 1921
Oil on canvas
60 x 81.3
Purchased 1970
GMA 1111

Alastair Michie

1921–

The Far Side of the Field*
d 1964
Acrylic on board
43.2 x 58
Scott Hay Collection: presented 1967
GMA 1047

David Michie

1928–

*Houses in a Fife Village**
1961
Oil on board
51 x 61
Bequeathed by Dr R. A. Lillie 1977
GMA 1928

*Houses on a Hill, Lisbon**
1963
Oil on hardboard
71 x 91.5
Scott Hay Collection: presented 1967
GMA 1048

Seaside Afternoon
1964
Oil on canvas
66 x 101.6
Scott Hay Collection: presented 1967
GMA 1049

Jack Miller

1945–

Bureau Jacques Klein, Decorateur
1973
Photolithograph on paper (1/6)
30.2 x 39 (paper 50 x 63.6)
Purchased 1976
GMA 1558

Los Angeles South
d 1975
Photolithograph on paper (A.P.)
32.1 x 49.7 (paper 51 x 63.6)
Purchased 1976
GMA 1559

Hollywood
d 1975
Photolithograph on paper (A.P.)
36.2 x 52.9 (paper 50.9 x 63.6)
Purchased 1976
GMA 1560

John MacLaughlin Milne

1885–1957

*Landscape, Sutherland**
c 1930–35
Oil on canvas
91.3 x 121.5
Bequeathed by Mr W. W. Friskin 1967
GMA 1069

John Milne

1931–78

Resurgence
d 1976
Polished bronze (1/9)
45.4 x 19.5 x 14
Presented by Lord Erskine of Rerrick 1977
GMA 1658

Malcolm Milne

1887–1954

Landscape near San Giovanni Manzano
c 1916–17
Pen and ink over pencil on paper
18.9 x 25.5
Purchased 1968
GMA 1088

Valley with Vineyards near San Giovanni Manzano
c 1916–17
Watercolour and pen and ink on paper
18.9 x 25.6
Purchased 1968
GMA 1089

Flowers in a Jar
c 1923
Watercolour on paper
40.7 x 24.3
Purchased 1968
GMA 1090

Keith Milow

1945–

Cross No. 88*
1978
Fibreglass, wood and polyester resin
101 X 75 X 19.2
Purchased 1983
GMA 2763

Joan Miró

1893–1983

Maternité [Maternity]*
d 1924
Oil on canvas
92.1 X 73.1
Purchased with assistance from the National
Heritage Memorial Fund, the National Art
Collections Fund (William Leng Bequest) and
members of the public, 1991
GMA 3589

Peinture [Painting]*
d 1925
Oil and black chalk on canvas
140 X 113.5
Purchased 1979
GMA 2078

Astrologie III [Astrology III]
1953
Colour lithograph on paper (30/100)
39.6 x 29.6 (paper size)
Purchased 1962
GMA 804

Józef Młynarski

1925–

Powstanie Warszawskie 1944 [The Warsaw
Insurrection 1944]
1960
Folio of twenty etchings with aquatint plus
title page
Each image approx. 17.6 x 24.5 or 24.5 x 17.6
(paper 24 x 33.5 or 33.5 x 24)
Presented by Count Jan Tarnowski through the
National Library of Scotland 1964
GMA 898

The Defence of Warsaw, Czerniakowski Outpost,
1944
1965
Etching and aquatint on paper
24 x 60.3 (paper 52.5 x 85.5)
Presented by the artist 1966
GMA 963

Warsaw Street Scene
Drypoint on paper
4.7 x 6.2 (image and paper size)
Presented by Count Jan Tarnowski through the
National Library of Scotland 1964
GMA 899 A

Warsaw Street Scene
Drypoint on paper
5.6 x 7.4 (image and paper size)
Presented by Count Jan Tarnowski through the
National Library of Scotland 1964
GMA 899 B

Warsaw Street Scene
Drypoint on paper
6 x 9.1 (image and paper size)
Presented by Count Jan Tarnowski through the
National Library of Scotland 1964
GMA 899 C

Warsaw Street Scene
Drypoint on paper
6.6 x 9.6 (image and paper size)
Presented by Count Jan Tarnowski through the
National Library of Scotland 1964
GMA 899 D

After Amedeo Modigliani

1884–1920

Portrait of Jeanne Hébuterne
Oil on canvas
81.3 x 54.6
Presented by Sir Alexander Maitland in memory
of his wife, Rosalind, 1960
GMA 966

Alexander Moffat

1943–

Ian Hamilton Finlay*
d 1975
Coloured chalk on paper
54 x 40.1
Presented by Mr Philip Wright 1976
GMA 1591

Gwen Hardie (2)*
d 1987
Oil on canvas
152.5 x 122
Purchased 1989
GMA 3454

László Moholy-Nagy

1895–1946

Sil I*
d 1933
Oil and incised lines on silberit
50 x 20
Purchased 1977
GMA 1663

Gerald Moira

1867–1959

The Restoration of Serbia
(from the series 'The Great War: Britain's Efforts
and Ideals')
d 1917 (published 1918)
Colour lithograph on paper
69 x 44.4 (paper 80.5 x 55.8)
Presented by the Ministry of Information 1919
GMA 3632

Piet Mondrian

1872–1944

Composition*
d 1932
Oil on canvas
45.3 x 45.3
Purchased 1982
GMA 2502

Walter Thomas
Monnington

1902–76

Sketch for Mural in St Stephen's Hall,
Westminster (The English and Scottish
Commissioners Present the Articles of Agreement
for the Union to Queen Anne, 1707)*
c 1924
Oil and pencil on canvas laid on wood
78.1 x 113.7
Bequeathed by Sir David Young Cameron 1945
GMA 24

Helen Monro Turner

See Helen Monro TURNER

Nicholas Monro

1936–

Dancers
d 1970
Screenprint on paper (7/75)
80.5 x 67.4 (paper 101.5 x 70)
Purchased 1984
GMA 2883

Jeremy Moon

1934–73

7/73*
d 1973
Oil on canvas
98 x 103.5 (irregular)
Purchased 1974
GMA 1309

Michael Moon

1937–

Kautilyia (from 'The London Suite')
1982
Screenprint on paper (11/75)
83.7 x 61 (paper and image size)
Purchased 1983
GMA 2754

John Mooney

1948–

Design for a Tapestry
1981–82
Watercolour on paper
64.3 x 91.6
Purchased 1982
GMA 2698 A

Untitled*
1982
Tapestry
151 x 241.5
Purchased 1982
GMA 2698 B

Henry Moore

1898–1986

*Drawing for Figure in Metal or Reinforced
Concrete**
1931
Watercolour, pen and ink and black chalk
on paper
27 x 39.2
Bequeathed by Mr H. J. Paterson 1988
GMA 3424

Studies for Sculpture*
c 1939
Watercolour, pen and ink, coloured crayon
and black chalk on paper
26.8 x 18.2
Bequeathed by Mr H. J. Paterson 1988
GMA 3423

The Helmet*
1939–40
Lead
29.1 x 18 x 16.5 (excluding base)
Purchased with assistance from the National
Heritage Memorial Fund, the National Art
Collections Fund (Scottish Fund) and the Henry
Moore Foundation 1992
GMA 3602

Studies for Sculpture*
[verso: *Studies for Sculpture*]
c 1939–42
Watercolour, pen and ink and pencil on paper
22.5 x 17.7
Bequeathed by Mr H. J. Paterson 1988
GMA 3422

Family Group*
d 1944
Watercolour, pen and ink, coloured crayon and
black chalk on paper
52.3 x 44.9
Purchased 1978
GMA 2065

*Reclining Figure**
1951
Bronze
106 x 228.6 x 73.7
Presented by the Arts Council of Great Britain
through the Scottish Arts Council 1969
GMA 1098

*Two-Piece Reclining Figure No. 2**
1960
Bronze (2/7)
128 x 256 x 104
Purchased 1960
GMA 757

Raymond Moore

1920–87

Fletchertown
d 1978
Black and white photograph (gelatin silver print)
22.7 x 22.6 (paper 33.3 x 28.3)
Purchased 1986
GMA 2982

Gigha
d 1985
Black and white photograph (gelatin silver print)
22.8 x 34.1 (paper 29.7 x 39.3)
Purchased 1986
GMA 2983

Giorgio Morandi

1890–1964

*Natura Morta [Still Life]**
1962
Oil on canvas
30.5 x 30.6
Purchased 1965
GMA 906

Gwenda Morgan

1908–91

Summer Flowers
1934
Wood engraving on paper (5/50)
21.4 x 17.6 (paper 22.8 x 18.4)
Presented by Mrs Betty Clark 1993
GMA 3677

Dimple in the Pond
1952
Wood engraving on paper (9/50)
14.5 x 15.6 (paper 19.1 x 19)
Presented by Mrs Betty Clark 1993
GMA 3674

Apple Picking
1952
Wood engraving on paper (34/50)
9.8 x 15.8 (paper 25 x 26.4)
Presented by Mrs Betty Clark 1993
GMA 3676

The Two Houses
1967
Wood engraving on paper (17/75)
10.1 x 15.3 (paper 18 x 26)
Presented by Mrs Betty Clark 1993
GMA 3672

From the Hills to the Sea
1967
Wood engraving on paper (5/50)
15.3 x 9.7 (paper 20.5 x 13.3)
Presented by Mrs Betty Clark 1993
GMA 3675

Moonlight
1970
Wood engraving on paper
6.2 x 6 (paper 13.1 x 9.7)
Presented by Mrs Betty Clark 1993
GMA 3673

William Evan Charles Morgan

1903–

The Visit of the Shepherds
d 1932
Wood engraving on paper (49/100)
16.8 x 23.4 (paper 20.8 x 25.8)
Purchased 1949
GMA 444

Annunciation to the Shepherds
d 1933
Wood engraving on paper (34/100)
16.9 x 23.4 (paper 20.9 x 28.3)
Purchased 1949
GMA 446

Group of Four Figures
c 1935
Wood engraving on paper
14.2 x 9.6 (paper 19.7 x 13.7)
Purchased 1949
GMA 448

Cock Capercailzie in Profile
d 1938
Wood engraving on paper
11.4 x 15.3 (paper 13.7 x 18.6)
Purchased 1949
GMA 445

Cock Capercailzie
d 1938
Wood engraving on paper
11.4 x 15.3 (paper 14.5 x 20.3)
Purchased 1949
GMA 449

A Stoat in Winter
d 1939
Wood engraving on paper
9 x 7.2 (paper 12 x 9.1)
Presented by Mrs Betty Clark 1993
GMA 3694

Vulture
Wood engraving on paper
10.4 x 9.8 (paper 25 x 18.4)
Purchased 1949
GMA 447

Margaret Morris Fergusson

See Margaret Morris FERGUSSON

Alberto Morrocco

1917–

*Methven**
d 1965
Oil on canvas
101.6 x 81.3
Scott Hay Collection: presented 1967
GMA 1050

Leon Morrocco

1942–

Meat Stand
c 1971
Black and coloured chalks on paper
20 x 25.2
Bequeathed by Dr R. A. Lillie 1977
GMA 1930

Bathtime
d 1975
Black and coloured chalks on paper (two sheets joined)
49 x 58.2
Bequeathed by Dr R. A. Lillie 1977
GMA 1929

Alastair Morton

1910–63

*Untitled**
d 1939
Gouache and pencil on paper
51 x 35.7
Purchased 1978
GMA 2001

*Untitled**
d 1940
Pencil on paper
37.3 x 25.8
Purchased 1976
GMA 1527

*Untitled**
d 1940
Gouache, watercolour and pencil on paper
35.5 x 50.8
Purchased 1978
GMA 2002

Robert Motherwell

1915–91

*In Black and White**
d 1960
Gouache and pencil on paper
58.1 x 73.6
Purchased 1968
GMA 1081

Untitled (Black, Red and Orange)
(from 'The Basque Suite')
1970
Screenprint on paper (3/150)
59 x 44.3 (paper 104 x 71)
Purchased 1984
GMA 2884

Otto Mueller

1874–1930

*Ein in Dünen sitzendes, und ein liegendes
Mädchen [Girls in a Sand Dune, One Sitting, One
Lying]**
c 1920–24
Colour lithograph on paper
29.4 x 39 (paper 38.4 x 52.4)
Bequeathed by Dr Kate Silber 1979
GMA 2116

Edvard Munch

1863–1944

*Das kranke Mädchen [The Sick Girl]**
1896
Colour lithograph on paper
42.1 x 56.3 (paper 44.5 x 56.7)
Purchased 1981
GMA 2309

John J. A. Murphy

1888–?

Nativity
exh. 1923
Wood engraving on paper
7.6 x 8.9 (paper 13.4 x 12.7)
Purchased 1949
GMA 450

Adoration of the Holy Child
d 1923
Wood engraving on paper
16.5 x 16.9 (paper 21.2 x 23.2)
Purchased 1949
GMA 451

Charles Murray

1894–1954

View of Florence from San Miniato
c 1922–25
Etching and drypoint on paper
25 x 33.3 (paper 32.3 x 44.1)
Presented by J. Bruce Cameron 1958
GMA 453

San Gimignano
c 1922–25
Etching on paper (6/100)
17.6 x 25.3 (paper 27.5 x 41.9)
Presented by J. Bruce Cameron 1958
GMA 454

Borghese Gardens
1924
Etching on paper
14.5 x 17.1 (paper 23.2 x 29.2)
Purchased 1982
GMA 2560

Rain, Port Bannatyne, Bute
c 1930
Drypoint on paper
17.4 x 25.1 (paper 25.1 x 38.1)
Purchased 1964
GMA 2842

*The Adoration of the Magi**
Etching on paper
25.5 x 16.7 (paper 38.8 x 24.8)
Purchased 1949
GMA 452

Graeme Murray

1946–

Ink Grid on Sycamore
1979
Sycamore wood, ink
26.3 x 44.3 x 36.4
Purchased 1982
GMA 2506

Andrew Mylius

1935–

Massey Ferguson and Cornfields No. 2
1965
Oil on canvas
183 x 152.5
Purchased 1981
GMA 2288

David Nash

1945–

*Ram**
1981
Elmwood (two pieces)
67.5 x 314 x 53.5
Purchased 1983
GMA 2765

Edinburgh Planting: Above the Water of Leith
d 1987
Charcoal and coloured chalk on paper
90 x 64.1
Acquired through the commission of GMA 3430,
1988
GMA 3649

*Edinburgh Planting: Above the Water of Leith**
d 1987
Charcoal on paper
64.1 x 90
Acquired through the commission of GMA 3430,
1988
GMA 3650

Edinburgh Planting: Above the Water of Leith
d 1987
Charcoal and coloured chalk on paper
64.1 x 90
Acquired through the commission of GMA 3430,
1988
GMA 3651

Edinburgh Planting: Above the Water of Leith
d 1987
Charcoal on paper
90 x 64.1
Acquired through the commission of GMA 3430,
1988
GMA 3652

Edinburgh Planting: Above the Water of Leith
1987
Charcoal on paper
64.1 x 90
Acquired through the commission of GMA 3430,
1988
GMA 3653

Edinburgh Planting: Above the Water of Leith
d 1987
Charcoal on paper
64.1 x 90
Acquired through the commission of GMA 3430,
1988
GMA 3654

Edinburgh Planting: Above the Water of Leith
d 1988
Charcoal and pencil on paper
81 x 120
Acquired through the commission of GMA 3430,
1988
GMA 3655

Edinburgh Planting: Above the Water of Leith
Planted 1988
Trees planted in the grounds of the Scottish
National Gallery of Modern Art
Commissioned with funds from the Mushroom
Trust and the Hope Scott Trust 1988
GMA 3430

John Nash

1893–1977

Horned Poppy
(for 'Poisonous Plants' by John Nash and W.
Dallimore)
Published 1927
Wood engraving on paper
15.2 x 11.4 (paper 19.8 x 14)
Purchased 1949
GMA 455

Landscape with Bathers
(from the J. Lyons series 'Lithographs by
Contemporary Artists, vol. I')
Published 1947
Colour lithograph on paper (after watercolour)
74.5 x 99 (paper size)
Presented by J. Lyons & Co. Ltd 1948
GMA 1210

Paul Nash

1889–1946

Berkshire Downs*
d 1922
Oil on canvas
76 x 55.5
Bequeathed by Miss Elizabeth Watt 1989
GMA 3502

Token*
[verso: Tree in a Landscape (unfinished)]
c 1929–30 [verso c 1927–28]
Oil on canvas
51.4 x 61.2
Purchased 1986
GMA 2984

Path (or Path in Savernake Forest)*
d 1932
Watercolour and pencil on paper
55.9 x 38
Bequeathed by Miss Elizabeth Watt 1989
GMA 3503

Avebury*
[verso: Silbury Hill]
c 1936
Watercolour and pencil on paper [verso: pencil]
39.8 x 57.2
Bequeathed by Mr H. J. Paterson 1988
GMA 3426

Landscape of the Brown Fungus*
1943
Oil on canvas
50.8 x 76.4
Bequeathed by Mr H. J. Paterson 1988
GMA 3425

Landscape of the Vernal Equinox (III)*
d 1944
Oil on canvas
63.5 x 76.2
Purchased 1961
GMA 774

The Sunflower Rises*
1945
Watercolour, crayon and pencil on paper
45.2 x 59.8
Purchased 1974
GMA 1317

The Strange Coast (Dymchurch)
1920
Lithograph on brown paper
31 x 40.4 (paper 41.7 x 53)
Purchased 1980
GMA 2200

Genesis (The First Chapter of Genesis in the
Authorised Version)
Published 1924
Book with twelve woodcuts (276/375)
Each woodcut approx 11.3 x 8.8 (paper 27 x 18.5)
Purchased 1979
GMA 2127

Steps in a Field near Swanage
c 1935
Black and white photograph (posthumous print)
17.8 x 30.6
Presented by the Tate Gallery 1974
GMA 1647

Nest of the Skeletons (The Last Defenders of
Maiden Castle)
c 1935
Black and white photograph (posthumous print)
17.8 x 30.7
Presented by the Tate Gallery 1974
GMA 1650

Maiden Castle, Dorset
c 1935–37
Black and white photograph (posthumous print)
17.8 x 30.5
Presented by the Tate Gallery 1974
GMA 1649

Stone Wall, Worth Maltravers, Dorset
c 1935–37
Black and white photograph (posthumous print)
17.8 x 30.5
Presented by the Tate Gallery 1974
GMA 1656

Ploughed Field
c 1937
Black and white photograph (posthumous print)
17.8 x 30.5
Presented by the Tate Gallery 1974
GMA 1648

The White Horse, Uffington, Berkshire
c 1937
Black and white photograph (posthumous print)
17.8 x 30.5
Presented by the Tate Gallery 1974
GMA 1651

The White Horse, Uffington, Berkshire
c 1937
Black and white photograph (posthumous print)
17.8 x 30.5
Presented by the Tate Gallery 1974
GMA 1652

The Park Wall, Ascott Manor, Stadhampton,
Oxfordshire
Probably c 1940
Black and white photograph (posthumous print)
17.8 x 30.6
Presented by the Tate Gallery 1974
GMA 1653

The Box Garden, Beckley Park, Oxfordshire
c 1940–41
Black and white photograph (posthumous print)
17.8 x 30.6
Presented by the Tate Gallery 1974
GMA 1654

Stones at Avebury, Wiltshire
1942
Black and white photograph (posthumous print)
17.8 x 30.5
Presented by the Tate Gallery 1974
GMA 1655

Thomas Nash

1891–1968

The Picnic*
d 1932
Oil and pencil on paper laid on card
35.2 x 25.3
Bequeathed by Miss Elizabeth Watt 1989
GMA 3504

Paul Neagu

1938–

White Cardinal
d 1968 / 1970 / 1972
Mixed-media assemblage
Closed 16.5 x 39.5 x 52.5; open 20 x 81 x 52.5
Purchased 1977
GMA 1666

Platform for Duchamp
d 1970
Mixed-media assemblage
86 x 86 x 12
Purchased 1977
GMA 1667

Self-Portrait
d 1971 and 1972
Pen and ink, watercolour and pencil with paper
additions, on two sheets of paper
31.3 x 47.8
Purchased 1977
GMA 1669

Drawings of Objects Made Between 1969
and 1972
d 1973
Pen and ink on card with mounted photographs
50.3 x 34.4
Purchased 1977
GMA 1671

Generator Gyroscope*
1975
Mixed-media assemblage
81.9 x 41.3 x 139.7
Purchased 1977
GMA 1665

Generator Gyroscope
d 1975
Pen and ink, wash and pencil on paper
25.4 x 33.8
Purchased 1977
GMA 1670

The Flying Horse
d 1974
Lithograph with watercolour and coloured crayon
on paper (7/75)
45.1 x 60.8 (paper 50.8 x 68.7)
Purchased 1978
GMA 2022

Louise Nevelson

1899–1988

Nightscape*
1957–64
Painted wood and formica assemblage
258.5 x 347 x 42
Purchased 1980
GMA 2194

Untitled*
d 1974
Painted card, wood and wire assemblage, on card
103 x 82
Presented by Mme Andrée Stassart 1984
GMA 2827

Christopher R. W. Nevinson

1889–1946

Twilight
1916
Drypoint on paper
20 x 15.1 (paper 34.4 x 23)
Purchased 1949
GMA 459

Building Aircraft: Making the Engine
(from the series 'The Great War: Britain's Efforts and Ideals')
d 1917 (published 1918)
Lithograph on paper
40.1 x 30.3 (paper 47.5 x 38.3)
Presented by the Ministry of Information 1919
GMA 456 A

Building Aircraft: Assembling Parts
(from the series 'The Great War: Britain's Efforts and Ideals')
d 1917 (published 1918)
Lithograph on paper
40.1 x 30 (paper 47 x 38.1)
Presented by the Ministry of Information 1919
GMA 456 B

Building Aircraft: Acetylene Welder
(from the series 'The Great War: Britain's Efforts and Ideals')
d 1917 (published 1918)
Lithograph on paper
40.4 x 30 (paper 47.5 x 37.6)
Presented by the Ministry of Information 1919
GMA 456 C

Building Aircraft: In the Air
(from the series 'The Great War: Britain's Efforts and Ideals')
d 1917 (published 1918)
Lithograph on paper
40.5 x 30 (paper 47.6 x 37.9)
Presented by the Ministry of Information 1919
GMA 456 D

Building Aircraft: Banking at 4,000 feet
(from the series 'The Great War: Britain's Efforts and Ideals')
d 1917 (published 1918)
Lithograph on paper
40.4 x 31.6 (paper 47 x 39.2)
Presented by the Ministry of Information 1919
GMA 456 E

Building Aircraft: Swooping down on a Taube
(from the series 'The Great War: Britain's Efforts and Ideals')*
d 1917 (published 1918)
Lithograph on paper
40 x 30 (paper 47.7 x 38.8)
Presented by the Ministry of Information 1919
GMA 456 F

That Cursed Wood*
d 1918
Etching and drypoint on paper
25.4 x 35.7 (paper 32 x 39.9)
Purchased 1949
GMA 457

Suburbia
c 1924
Etching on paper
17.7 x 12.6 (paper 34.9 x 25.2)
Purchased 1949
GMA 458

Success
Etching and drypoint on paper
20.2 x 15.1 (paper 32 x 23.1)
Purchased 1965
GMA 923

Ben Nicholson

1894–1982

Walton Wood Cottage, No. 1*
d 1928
Oil on canvas
56 x 61
Presented by Miss Helen Sutherland 1965
GMA 930

White Relief*
d 1935
Oil on carved board
54 x 64.3
Purchased 1980
GMA 2149

Painting 1937*
d 1937
Oil on canvas
50.6 x 63.5
Purchased 1979
GMA 2100

Painted Relief (Plover's Egg Blue)*
d 1940
Oil on carved board
47.5 x 48
Presented by Miss Helen Sutherland 1965
GMA 931

*June 1961 (Green Goblet and Blue Square)**
d 1961
Oil and pencil on board
78 x 78
Purchased 1962
GMA 812

*White Relief, Paros**
d 1962
Oil on carved board
62.6 x 64
Purchased 1962
GMA 813

Note: Measurements for the painted reliefs are those of the back-boards

---

*Teapot, Mug, Cups and Saucer**
1930
Linocut on paper
54.5 x 56.1 (paper size)
Purchased 1985
GMA 2962

*Numbers**
c 1933
Linocut on stitched cotton
56 x 76.5 (fabric size)
Presented by Jim Ede 1977
GMA 1684

*Man and Woman: Heads in Profile**
1933
Linocut on paper
25.8 x 18.1 (paper 32 7 x 24.3)
Purchased 1978
GMA 2069

*Five Circles**
1934
Woodcut on paper
15.9 x 20 (paper 23.3 x 33.4)
Purchased 1978
GMA 1999

Still Life
d 1966
Etching with pencil, watercolour and ink additions on paper
20.4 x 21.7 (paper 27.7 x 29.2)
Purchased 1983
GMA 2747

Two and a Half Goblets
c 1967
Etching on paper
26.5 x 24.8 (paper 37.5 x 37.7)
Purchased 1983
GMA 2748

William Nicholson

1872–1949

*The Brig**
d 1906
Oil on canvas-board
27.7 x 34
Purchased 1965
GMA 907

*Poppies in Pewter**
c 1933–34
Oil on wood
41.1 x 32.9
Bequeathed by Dr R. A. Lillie 1977
GMA 1931

Santa Lucia, Malaga
d 1935
Oil on canvas-board
33 x 40.7
Bequeathed by Miss L. P. C. Ranken 1981
GMA 2466

An Alphabet
Published 1897 (d 1898)
Book of 26 colour lithographs and frontispiece (after original woodcuts)
31 x 25 (paper size)
Provenance unrecorded
GMA 1193

Seated Woman
d 1899
Colour lithograph (after original woodcut) on paper
19.5 x 19.5 (paper and image size)
Purchased 1949
GMA 1192

James McNeill Whistler
(*from 'Twelve Portraits'*)
Originally published 1899; lithographic edition
1902
Colour lithograph (after original woodcut) on
paper
25 x 22.6 (paper 26.3 x 24.4)
Purchased 1949
GMA 1191

The End of War
(*from the series 'The Great War: Britain's Efforts
and Ideals'*)
Published 1918
Colour lithograph on paper
43 x 58.2 (paper 55 x 80.4)
Presented by the Ministry of Information 1919
GMA 460

Winifred Nicholson

1893–1981

*Jake and Kate on the Isle of Wight**
1931–32
Oil on canvas
68.5 x 89
Presented by the Trustees of Winifred
Nicholson's estate in accordance with her wishes
1985
GMA 2964

Milivoj Nikolajevic

1912–

Branchages fermés dans l'eau [*Branches Lodged
in Water*]
d 1961
Colour lithograph on paper (A.P.)
28.6 x 36.1 (paper 49 x 67.3)
Presented by the artist 1967
GMA 998

Branchages dispersés dans l'eau I [*Branches
Dispersed in Water I*]
d 1961
Colour lithograph on paper (A.P.)
10.1 x 57.4 (paper 41.1 x 70.5)
Presented by the artist 1967
GMA 999

Ritem Vijevja v Vodi [*Rhythm of Branches in
Water*]
d 1964
Colour lithograph on paper (A.P.)
52.8 x 71.3 (paper size)
Purchased 1967
GMA 997

Sidney Nolan

1917–92

*Leda and the Swan**
d 1958
Polyvinyl acetate on hardboard
121.9 x 152.4
Presented by the Contemporary Art Society 1962
GMA 836

Emil Nolde

1867–1956

Kopf [*Head*]*
1913
Oil on canvas
77.5 x 67.3
Purchased 1968
GMA 1082

Abendhimmel überm Gotteskoog [*Sunset over
Gotteskoog*]*
Watercolour on paper
35 x 46.7
Purchased 1969
GMA 1102

B. J. O. Nordfeldt

1878–1955

Portrait of a Girl
d 1907
Etching on paper
20 x 15 (paper 27.8 x 22.2)
Purchased 1949
GMA 461

Jim Nutt

1938–

"You hoo – little boy"
1977
Etching (brown ink) on paper (42/50)
10 x 11 (paper 36 x 32.5)
Purchased 1980
GMA 2190

"I'm not stopping"
1977
Etching (brown ink) on paper (42/50)
10 x 17.5 (paper 36.2 x 38.5)
Purchased 1980
GMA 2191

"Your so coarse" (tish)
1977
Etching (brown ink) on paper (42/50)
22.5 x 20.1 (paper 49.5 x 41)
Purchased 1980
GMA 2192

"Oh my goodness" (no)
1977
Etching (brown ink) on paper (42/50)
25.1 x 30.1 (paper 51 x 52.5)
Purchased 1980
GMA 2193

Roderic O'Conor

1860–1940

*The Balustrade**
d 1913
Oil on canvas
81.2 x 100.7
Purchased 1971
GMA 1250

Ron O'Donnell

1952–

*The Great Divide**
d 1987
Colour photograph (cibachrome print)
(large version)
183 x 305
Purchased 1987
GMA 3046 A

The Great Divide
1987
Colour photograph (cibachrome print)
(small version)
109.5 x 151.5
Purchased 1987
GMA 3046 B

Elizabeth Ogilvie

1946–

*Sea Paper**
d 1987
Graphite on handmade paper
61 x 244
Purchased 1989
GMA 3470

Glen Onwin

1947–

Salt Room / Crystal
*(from 'The Recovery of Dissolved Substances')**
1977
Salt and wood strips on zinc sheet mounted on
board (three panels)
Each panel 191.8 x 91.3
Purchased 1979
GMA 2114

Roman Opalka

1931–

Metempsychosis
d 1970
Etching on paper (5/50)
62 x 49.5 (paper 75.1 x 61)
Purchased 1970
GMA 1166

William Orpen

1878–1931

*A Bloomsbury Family**
1907
Oil on canvas
86.5 x 91.5
Presented by the Scottish Modern Arts
Association 1964
GMA 881

Christmas and New Year Greetings
d 1930
Pencil and watercolour on paper
29.8 x 20.5
Presented by the Trustees of the 1st Baron Riddell
1935
GMA 2029

James R. Wallace Orr

1907–

Loading a Coal Cart
d 1934
Etching on paper
15.3 x 19 (paper 21.6 x 27.8)
Purchased 1949
GMA 462

Marylebone Goods Yard 1941
d 1946
Etching and drypoint on paper
28.8 x 25.2 (paper 33.5 x 30.8)
Purchased 1982
GMA 2562

A. F. S. Crew Going into Action 1941
d 1946
Etching and drypoint on paper
19.8 x 19.5 (paper 36 x 34.6)
Presented by the artist 1983
GMA 2769

Memory of the Blitz, Upper Thames Street, 1941
d 1946
Etching and drypoint on paper
18.1 x 25.7 (paper 23 x 31.7)
Presented by the artist 1983
GMA 2770

Alfonso Ossorio

1916–90

*The Claw**
1952
Watercolour, ink and wax on paper laid on board
152.4 x 96.5
Presented by Mr Thomas Gibson 1977
GMA 1657

Thérèse Oulton

1953–

Undoings
Published 1989
Portfolio of six lithographs (6/40)
Each image approx. 31 x 29 (paper 75.3 x 56.4)
Purchased 1990
GMA 3554

George Elmslie Owen

1899–1964

Queer Fish
c 1933
Wood engraving on paper (11/30)
14.1 x 17.5 (paper 21 x 24.4)
Purchased 1949
GMA 463

Exotic Fish
c 1933
Wood engraving on paper (30/40)
21 x 16.6 (paper 25 x 20.3)
Purchased 1982
GMA 2561

Mimmo Paladino

1948–

Silenzioso Sangue [*Silent Blood*]*
d 1979 / 1985
Oil, wax and wood on canvas
213.5 x 140
Purchased 1987
GMA 3017

Eduardo Paolozzi

1924–

*Horse's Head**
1946 (d 1947; cast 1974)
Bronze
69 x 35 x 46
Purchased 1993
GMA 3698

*Paris Bird**
1948–49
Bronze (6/6)
33.5 x 34.5 x 15.5
Purchased 1987
GMA 3303

*Two Forms on a Rod**
1948–49
Bronze
51 x 65 x 32.5
Purchased 1988
GMA 3398

Growth (or *Table Sculpture*)*
1949
Bronze (3/6)
83 x 60.5 x 39
Purchased 1988
GMA 3399

Design Exercise
c 1950
Gouache on paper
38.1 x 18.6
Purchased 1978
GMA 2054

Design Exercise
c 1950
Ink on paper
24.2 x 15.7
Purchased 1978
GMA 2055

Design Exercise
[verso: *Five Sketches*]
c 1950
Ink on paper [verso: pencil on paper]
27.3 x 39
Purchased 1978
GMA 2056

Design Exercise
c 1950 ·
Ink on paper
56.3 x 41
Purchased 1978
GMA 2057

Design Exercise
c 1950
Ink on paper
24.2 x 35
Purchased 1978
GMA 2058

Design Exercise
c 1950
Ink on paper
55.8 x 37.8
Purchased 1978
GMA 2063

*Krokodeel**
1956
Bronze
94 x 67 x 23
Purchased 1988
GMA 3400

*Icarus (first version)**
1957
Bronze
134.6 x 72 x 32
Presented by the artist and Messrs Lund
Humphries in memory of the late E. C. Gregory
1962
GMA 824

*Icarus (second version)**
1957
Bronze
144.5 x 60 x 35
Purchased 1993
GMA 3699

*St Sebastian I**
1957
Bronze
214.5 x 72 x 35.5
Purchased 1993
GMA 3700

*Large Frog (new version)**
1958
Bronze (5/6)
72 x 82 x 79
Purchased 1993
GMA 3701

*His Majesty the Wheel**
1958–59
Bronze
183 x 70 x 50
Purchased 1989
GMA 3449

*Tyrannical Tower Crowned with Thorns of
Violence**
1961
Bronze
183.5 x 58 x 41
Purchased 1993
GMA 3702

*Four Towers**
1962
Painted aluminium
203.2 x 77.5 x 78.4
Presented by the artist 1966
GMA 978

*The Bishop of Kuban**
1962
Aluminium
210 x 93 x 60.7
Purchased 1990
GMA 3566

*Chord**
1964
Painted aluminium
180 x 56 x 49
Purchased 1993
GMA 3703

*Domino**
1967–68
Aluminium
9 elements in variable arrangement. Maximum
length of each 310; 217; 163; 135; 127; 102 ; 94;
69; 69
Presented by Mrs Gabrielle Keiller 1984
GMA 2826

*Kreuzberg**
d 1974
Bronze
299 x 11 x 16.5
Purchased 1993
GMA 3704

Kreuzberg
1974
Bronze
59.5 x 108.5 x 11
Purchased 1993
GMA 3705

*Master of the Universe**
d 1989
Bronze
147 x 190.2 x 106.5 (including base)
Purchased 1990
GMA 3580

Marine Composition
d 1950
Colour lithograph on paper
34 x 52.5 (paper 38.1 x 56)
Purchased 1978
GMA 2033

Design Exercise
c 1950
Screenprint on paper
25.9 x 37.7
Purchased 1978
GMA 2059

Design Exercise
c 1950
Screenprint collage with gouache on card
37 x 12.7
Purchased 1978
GMA 2060

Design Exercise
c 1950
Screenprint collage with gouache on card
19.9 x 12.3
Purchased 1978
GMA 2061

Design Exercise
c 1950
Screenprint on paper
27 x 36
Purchased 1978
GMA 2062

Composition
d 1951
Colour lithograph on paper
38.3 x 52.5 (paper 50 x 65)
Purchased 1978
GMA 2034

Man's Head
d 1952
Colour lithograph on paper
51.3 x 39 (paper 65 x 50)
Purchased 1978
GMA 2035

Parrot
(from the portfolio 'As is When')
d 1965
Screenprint on paper
76.8 x 54.6 (paper 96.5 x 66)
Purchased 1966
GMA 992

Moonstrips Empire News
Published 1967
100 photolithographs and screenprints on paper
and acetate in acrylic box (majority marked 489/
500)
Each print 38 x 25.4 or 25.4 x 38 (except one 25.4
x 14.1; one 23.7 x 25.4)
Purchased 1980
GMA 2129

*Cloud Atomic Laboratory: Science and Fantasy
in the Technological World*
Published 1971
Portfolio of eight photogravures (two images on
each sheet), title page and text introduction (A.P.
8)
Each sheet 36 x 53 or 53 x 36
Presented by Mrs Gabrielle Keiller 1980
GMA 2230

Alistair Park

1930–84

*Black Head**
Late 1950s
Oil on chipboard
51 x 43.2
Presented by Mr Robin Spark 1992
GMA 3611

*A Little Woman**
1962
Oil on canvas
76.2 x 101.7
Scott Hay Collection: presented 1967
GMA 1051

*A Field Symbol**
d 1963
Oil on canvas
101.6 x 127
Purchased (Gulbenkian UK Trust Fund) 1963
GMA 832

Agnes Miller Parker

1895–1980

Reed Buck
d 1929
Wood engraving on paper (9/20)
12 x 9.1 (paper 20.4 x 18)
Purchased 1949
GMA 467

Foxe and Raysyns
(for 'The Fables of Esope')
d 1931
Wood engraving on paper (6/12)
10.7 x 12.6 (paper 26.2 x 20)
Purchased 1949
GMA 464

Catte and Chyken
(for 'The Fables of Esope')
d 1931
Wood engraving on paper (6/12)
12 x 12.8 (paper 28.8 x 19.8)
Purchased 1949
GMA 465

Herte and Dogges
(for 'The Fables of Esope')
d 1931
Wood engraving on paper (10/12)
10.8 x 12.6 (paper 26.3 x 20)
Purchased 1949
GMA 466

Carpenter and Mercury
(for 'The Fables of Esope')
d 1931
Wood engraving on paper (2/12)
8.1 x 12.6 (paper 26.2 x 19.8)
Purchased 1949
GMA 470

Ante and Flye
(for 'The Fables of Esope')
d 1931
Wood engraving on paper (2/12)
6.1 x 12.6 (paper 25.4 x 19.9)
Purchased 1949
GMA 471

Yong Man and Comyn Woman
(for 'The Fables of Esope')
d 1931
Wood engraving on paper (4/12)
10.9 x 12.6 (paper 26.3 x 20)
Purchased 1949
GMA 475

Daisy Matthews
(for 'Daisy Matthews and Three Other Tales' by
Rhys Davies)
d 1932
Wood engraving on paper (1/25)
10.7 x 10.6 (paper 28.4 x 22)
Purchased 1949
GMA 469

The Fairy Bride
(for 'XXI Welsh Gypsy Folk-Tales')
d 1933
Wood engraving on paper (6/25)
12 x 12.8 (paper 15 x 16.8)
Purchased 1949
GMA 472

The Leaves that Hung but Never Grew
(for 'XXI Welsh Gypsy Folk-Tales')
d 1933
Wood engraving on paper (6/25)
7 x 12.6 (paper 10.6 x 16.8)
Purchased 1949
GMA 473

The Fiery Dragon
(for 'XXI Welsh Gypsy Folk-Tales')
d 1933
Wood engraving on paper (9/25)
11.9 x 12.6 (paper 15 x 16.8)
Purchased 1949
GMA 474

*The Challenge**
d 1934
Wood engraving on paper (23/35)
14.2 x 16.4 (paper 17.8 x 21)
Purchased 1982
GMA 2563

Iris, Rushes and Burweed
(for 'Down the River' by H. E. Bates)
d 1937
Wood engraving on paper (10/35)
17.7 x 12.4 (paper 26.7 x 21)
Purchased 1949
GMA 468

Two Siamese Cats
c 1939
Wood engraving on paper (folded in two)
8.9 x 10.4 (folded paper 13 x 10.3)
Purchased 1984
GMA 2825

Siamese Cat and Butterfly (Greetings Card)
Printed 1939
Wood engraving on card (folded in two)
13 x 10.4 (folded card 18 x 14)
Purchased 1984
GMA 3057

Stephen Parrish

1846–1938

Hastings
Etching on paper
13.9 x 26.6 (paper 17.6 x 31)
Presented anonymously 1951
GMA 476

Jacki Parry

1941–

Cloud Moving
d 1976
Etching on paper (A.P.)
37.8 x 68.7 (paper 55.8 x 76.1)
Purchased 1976
GMA 1542

Victor Pasmore

1908–

Girl with Bows in her Hair*
Late 1930s
Oil on canvas laid on hardboard
29.2 x 26.3
Bequeathed by Miss Elizabeth Watt 1989
GMA 3505

Spiral Motif (Subjective Landscape) in Black and White*
1951
Oil on wood
80.6 x 22
Purchased (Knapping Fund) 1963
GMA 833

Linear Motif in Black and White*
1960–61
Oil and incised lines on wood relief
124.5 x 124.5 x 5
Purchased (Knapping Fund) 1963
GMA 834

Gardens of Hammersmith 2
d 1948 / 1976
Etching with aquatint on paper (24/55)
27.3 x 37.2 (paper 61.4 x 72)
Purchased 1977
GMA 1693

Abstract 1971
d 1971
Screenprint on paper (72/75)
53.2 x 51 (paper 71.4 x 69.8)
Purchased 1984
GMA 2885

G. W. Lennox Paterson

1915–86

Study of a Head*
1938
Wood engraving on paper
25.4 x 17.7 (paper 36.7 x 26.8)
Purchased 1982
GMA 2564

Boy and Bird
(for the 'Saltire Chapbook')
c 1948
Wood engraving on paper
10.7 x 6.7 (paper 13.1 x 9.9)
Purchased 1980
GMA 2166

Bird Feeding its Young
(for the 'Saltire Chapbook')
c 1948
Wood engraving on paper
2.1 x 5.1 (paper 3.5 x 6.4)
Purchased 1980
GMA 2167

Quill and Scroll
(for the 'Saltire Chapbook')
c 1948
Wood engraving on paper
3.8 x 4 (paper 7.9 x 6.4)
Purchased 1980
GMA 2168

Tailpiece for 'Queen's Own Royal Glasgow
Yeomanry, 1848–1948'
1948
Wood engraving on paper
9.2 x 6 (paper 11 x 8.4)
Purchased 1980
GMA 2185

Menu Design for the Double Crown Club
d 1949
Wood engraving on paper
14.2 x 10.1 (paper 17.8 x 13.8)
Purchased 1980
GMA 2172

Colophon for 'Life Lines'
1950s
Wood engraving on paper
2.9 x 2.9 (paper 5 x 5.4)
Purchased 1980
GMA 2164

Coat of Arms for the Royal Glasgow Institute
of the Fine Arts
1951
Wood engraving on paper
7 x 6.8 (paper 7.8 x 7.3)
Purchased 1980
GMA 2169

Decorated Initial Letters and Tailpieces for
the catalogue 'Templeton Present Carpets of
Distinction'
Published 1952
Wood engravings on paper
From 5.7 x 5.5 to 9.6 x 14.9 (paper from 6.2 x 5.9
to 11 x 15.8)
Purchased 1980
GMA 2174–2179

Book-Plate for Stoke-on-Trent Hospitals Group
Medical Library
c 1953
Wood engraving on paper
9 x 6.7 (paper 10.2 x 7.9)
Purchased 1980
GMA 2170

Book-Plate for Ronald Vincent Singleton
c 1955
Wood engraving on paper
8.2 x 5.7 (paper 8.9 x 6.3)
Purchased 1980
GMA 2165

Book-Plate for Sir Richard Snedden
c 1955
Wood engraving on paper
8.8 x 6.6 (paper 10.3 x 8.2)
Purchased 1980
GMA 2171

Owl
c 1955
Wood engraving on card
3.7 x 2.9 (card 5 x 4.1)
Purchased 1980
GMA 2173

Monach Isles
(for 'Scottish Field')
Published June 1957
Wood engraving on paper
5.1 x 10.1 (paper 8 x 13.6)
Purchased 1980
GMA 2181

Sgurr of Eigg
(for 'Scottish Field')
1957
Wood engraving on paper
5 x 10.2 (paper 8.5 x 13.4)
Purchased 1980
GMA 2182

Acarseid Mhor, South Rona
(for 'Scottish Field')
Published June 1957
Wood engraving on paper
5 x 10.3 (paper 7 x 13.7)
Purchased 1980
GMA 2183

Geese over Summer Isles
(for 'Scottish Field')
Published June 1957
Wood engraving on paper
5 x 10 (paper 7.7 x 13.6)
Purchased 1980
GMA 2184

Twelve Headpieces for 'Dryad Handcrafts
Catalogue'
c 1960
Wood engraving on paper
Each image approx. 7.2 x. 11
Presented by the artist 1980
GMA 2187

Wings: Common Terns
1976
Wood engraving on paper (12/100)
20.5 x 15.7 (paper 24.7 x 19.6)
Purchased 1980
GMA 2188

Marsh Harrier
1976
Wood engraving on paper (2/100)
20.2 x 15.4 (paper 24.3 x 19.4)
Purchased 1982
GMA 2702

Great Black Backed Gulls
1976
Wood engraving on paper (2/100)
20.2 x 15.1 (paper 27.5 x 21.3)
Purchased 1982
GMA 2703

Little Owl and Bindweed
1976
Wood engraving on paper (4/100)
20.6 x 15.3 (paper 24.5 x 19.3)
Purchased 1982
GMA 2704

Blackcaps in an Oak
1976
Wood engraving on paper (5/100)
15.3 x 20.2 (paper 19.3 x 24.1)
Purchased 1982
GMA 2705

Dangerous Moonlight
1976
Wood engraving on paper (6/100)
20.4 x 15.3 (paper 24.5 x 19.5)
Purchased 1982
GMA 2706

Hoopoe and Passion Flower
1976
Wood engraving on paper (31/100)
20.5 x 15.4 (paper 27.4 x 22.4)
Purchased 1982
GMA 2707

Island Evening
1978
Linocut on paper (4/15)
30.5 x 58.3 (paper 43.2 x 66.2)
Purchased 1980
GMA 2163

Crest for Glasgow University
Wood engraving on paper
3.9 x 5.6 (paper 5.3 x 7)
Purchased 1980
GMA 2180

Book-Plate (Heraldic Device)
Wood engraving on paper
10.3 x 5.7 (paper 13.5 x 6.2)
Purchased 1980
GMA 2186

Hamish Paterson

1890–1955

A Cheap Lodging
c 1945
Watercolour on paper
31 x 21
Bequeathed by Dr R. A. Lillie 1977
GMA 1932

James McIntosh Patrick

1907–

The Green Belt
(Design for London Transport Poster: 'Harrow Weald')
c 1938
Watercolour, pen and ink and pencil on card
27 x 36.7
Purchased 1980
GMA 2146

Traquair House*
d 1938
Oil on canvas
35.5 x 45.5
Purchased 1990
GMA 3534

Stobo Kirk
d 1937
Etching on paper
10.7 x 15 (paper 16.5 x 25.3)
Purchased 1982
GMA 2559

Bryan Pearce

1929–

Newlyn Harbour
d 1971
Etching on paper (26/30)
12.4 x 15.3 (paper 23.9 x 28.5)
Presented by Jim Ede 1980
GMA 2216

Harbour Scene
d 1972
Etching on paper (29/30)
19.6 x 14.8 (paper 38.9 x 28.3)
Presented by Jim Ede 1977
GMA 1660

The Stone Boat at Newlyn
d 1972
Etching on paper (A.P.)
11.8 x 14.5 (paper 26 x 29.7)
Presented by Jim Ede 1980
GMA 2215

Charles Pears

1873–1958

Transport by Sea: Maintaining Food Supplies
(from the series 'The Great War: Britain's Efforts and Ideals')
Published 1918
Lithograph on paper
35.6 x 46 (paper 40 x 51.3)
Presented by the Ministry of Information 1919
GMA 477 A

Transport by Sea: Maintaining Export Trade
(from the series 'The Great War: Britain's Efforts and Ideals')
Published 1918
Lithograph on paper
35.5 x 46 (paper 39.2 x 52.5)
Presented by the Ministry of Information 1919
GMA 477 B

Transport by Sea: Supplying the Navy
(from the series 'The Great War: Britain's Efforts and Ideals')
Published 1918
Lithograph on paper
35.8 x 46 (paper 40.5 x 51)
Presented by the Ministry of Information 1919
GMA 477 C

Transport by Sea: Transporting Troops
(from the series 'The Great War: Britain's Efforts and Ideals')
Published 1918
Lithograph on paper
35.7 x 46 (paper 40.2 x 51)
Presented by the Ministry of Information 1919
GMA 477 D

Transport by Sea: Maintaining Forces Overseas
(from the series 'The Great War: Britain's Efforts
and Ideals')
Published 1918
Lithograph on paper
35.7 x 46.3 (paper 39.2 x 53)
Presented by the Ministry of Information 1919
GMA 477 E

Transport by Sea: "The Place of Safety"
(from the series 'The Great War: Britain's Efforts
and Ideals')
Published 1918
Lithograph on paper
35.8 x 46.3 (paper 40 x 51.2)
Presented by the Ministry of Information 1919
GMA 477 F

Claughton Pellew

1890–1966

Rothenburg
d 1928
Etching on paper (2/55)
8.9 x 20.2 (paper 25.7 x 32.8)
Purchased 1982
GMA 2565

Marsh Marigolds
1930
Wood engraving on paper
27.9 x 25.4 (paper 43.7 x 36.8)
Purchased 1949
GMA 478

The Smithy
d 1930
Wood engraving on paper (2/40)
25.3 x 20.2 (paper 38.5 x 29.9)
Purchased 1949
GMA 479

The Entombment
d 1930
Wood engraving on paper (20/30)
37 x 28.2 (paper 53.4 x 36.6)
Purchased 1949
GMA 482

The Squirrel
d 1931
Wood engraving on paper (8/30)
21.7 x 25.4 (paper 27.9 x 38.1)
Purchased 1949
GMA 480

A Gloucestershire Lane
d 1934
Wood engraving on paper (1/50)
25.4 x 20.4 (paper 36.9 x 28.1)
Purchased 1949
GMA 481

The Descent
1937
Wood engraving on paper
30.9 x 21.8 (paper 42.1 x 38.3)
Purchased 1949
GMA 481 A

John Pemberton

1908–60

Since the Bombardment*
c 1948
Oil on canvas
76.6 x 63.7
Bequeathed by Miss Elizabeth Watt 1989
GMA 3506

Joseph Pennell

1860–1926

Coal Breaker on the River
1910
Lithograph on paper
28.7 x 44.6 (paper 31 x 48.2)
Purchased 1949
GMA 3664

Roland Penrose

1900–84

*Ocean Temple**
d 1983
Collage of photographs, watercolour, black chalk
and pencil on paper
45.8 x 60.5
Purchased 1984
GMA 2805

Samuel John Peploe

1871–1935

*Self-Portrait**
c 1900
Oil on wood
50.9 x 30.3
Bequeathed by Dr R. A. Lillie 1977
GMA 1950

*Peonies**
c 1900–05
Oil on wood
24 x 16.3
Bequeathed by Dr R. A. Lillie 1977
GMA 1946

*Man Laughing (Portrait of Tom Morris)**
c 1902
Oil on canvas
71.8 x 51.1
Presented by the Trustees of the late George
Proudfoot 1946
GMA 33

Waves
c 1903
Oil on wood
16 x 24
Bequeathed by Miss Anna G. Blair 1952
GMA 35

*Barra**
1903
Oil on wood
15.5 x 23.9
Bequeathed by Dr R. A. Lillie 1977
GMA 1933

Barra
1903
Oil on wood
16.1 x 23.8
Bequeathed by Dr R. A. Lillie 1977
GMA 1934

Rocks at Barra
1903
Oil on board
16.4 x 24
Bequeathed by Dr R. A. Lillie 1977
GMA 1935

*North Berwick**
d 1903
Oil on board
16 x 23.9
Bequeathed by Dr R. A. Lillie 1977
GMA 1945

*The Green Blouse**
c 1904
Oil on wood
50.8 x 50.2
Purchased 1941
GMA 28

*The Black Bottle**
c 1905
Oil on canvas
50.8 x 61
Presented by Mr J. W. Blyth 1939
GMA 26

*Head of a Girl**
c 1905
Pastel on grey paper
33.4 x 26
Bequeathed by Dr R. A. Lillie 1977
GMA 1940

Etaples
c 1906
Oil on wood
19 x 24.2
Bequeathed by Dr R. A. Lillie 1977
GMA 1937

Game of Tennis, Luxembourg Gardens*
c 1906
Oil on wood
16.1 x 23.8
Bequeathed by Dr R. A. Lillie 1977
GMA 1944

Portrait of the Artist's Wife*
c 1906–08
Oil on canvas
40.9 x 30.8
Bequeathed by Dr R. A. Lillie 1977
GMA 1948

On the French Coast*
c 1907
Oil on wood
15 x 24.3
Bequeathed by Dr R. A. Lillie 1977
GMA 1939

Figures*
c 1910
Gouache and black chalk on paper
17 x 21.6
Bequeathed by Dr R. A. Lillie 1977
GMA 1938

Boats at Royan*
1910
Oil on board
27 x 34.9
Bequeathed by Dr R. A. Lillie 1977
GMA 1949

Veules-les-Roses*
c 1910–11
Oil on board
35.6 x 27
Purchased 1965
GMA 909

Ile de Bréhat*
1911
Oil on canvas-board
32.7 x 40.9
Bequeathed by Dr R. A. Lillie 1977
GMA 1941

Still Life*
c 1913
Oil on canvas
55 x 46
Presented by Mr A. J. McNeill Reid 1946
GMA 32

In Cassis Harbour
1913
Black chalk on paper
14.9 x 22.3
Purchased 1958
GMA 728

Quayside, Cassis
1913
Black chalk on paper
14.8 x 22.2
Bequeathed by Dr R. A. Lillie 1977
GMA 1936

Pink Roses, Chinese Vase*
c 1916–20
Oil on canvas
45.7 x 41
Bequeathed by Dr R. A. Lillie 1977
GMA 1947

Tulips – The Blue Jug
c 1919
Oil on canvas
51 x 61
Purchased 1941
GMA 29

Still Life with Melon*
c 1920
Oil on canvas
45.8 x 40.5
Bequeathed by Dr R. A. Lillie 1977
GMA 1951

Roses*
[verso: Portrait of a Woman]
c 1920–25 [verso c 1908]
Oil on canvas
50.8 x 61
Presented by the Rev. H. G. R. Hay-Boyd 1941
GMA 27

Still Life with Roses and Fan
c 1920–25
Oil on canvas
46 x 41
On permanent loan from the National Museum
of Antiquities of Scotland
GMA L259

Iona Study
1920s
Oil on wood
22.6 x 30.5
Bequeathed by Dr R. A. Lillie 1977
GMA 1943

Landscape at Cassis*
1924
Oil on canvas
55.4 x 45.7
Bequeathed by Mr Gordon Binnie: received 1963
GMA 866

Iona Landscape: Rocks*
c 1925–27
Oil on canvas
40.9 x 46
Bequeathed by Dr R. A. Lillie 1977
GMA 1942

Little Nude
c 1927–30
Oil on canvas
40.5 x 45.8
Purchased 1941
GMA 30

Landscape, South of France*
c 1928
Oil on canvas
50.5 x 55.9
Purchased 1969
GMA 1103

Still Life, Pears and Grapes*
[verso: Flowers (unfinished)]
c 1930
Oil on canvas
30.5 x 38.3
Purchased 1965
GMA 908

Still Life with Plaster Cast*
c 1931
Oil on canvas
55.9 x 51.4
Bequeathed by Mr Kenneth Sanderson 1943
GMA 31

Roses in a Grey Jar
[verso: Iona Landscape]
c 1933
Oil on canvas
50.8 x 40.6
Bequeathed by Miss Anna G. Blair in memory of
Mr R. K. Blair 1952
GMA 34

William Watson Peploe
1869–1933

Orchestral: Study in Radiation*
c 1915
Ink on card
28 x 23.6
Purchased 1990
GMA 3550

Souvenir du triangle rouge [Souvenir of the Red
Triangle]*
1918
Watercolour and ink on postcard
9 x 14.1
Purchased 1973
GMA 1295

Untitled*
1918
Watercolour and ink on postcard
9.1 x 14.1
Purchased 1973
GMA 1296

The Bust in the Garden
Pen and ink on card
11.5 x 9.2
Bequeathed by Mr W. G. Blaikie Murdoch 1940
GMA 729

A Menu Card ('Blessed are they who provide for the Poor')
Pen and ink on card
13.3 x 9.2
Bequeathed by Mr W. G. Blaikie Murdoch 1940
GMA 730

William Perehudoff

1919–

Untitled
(from 'The Commonwealth Print Portfolio')
Published 1978
Screenprint on paper (28/65)
52.2 x 72 (paper 56.5 x 75.3)
Presented by the Canadian High Commission
1979
GMA 2125

Constant Permeke

1886–1952

Hiver en Flandre [Winter in Flanders]*
1930s
Oil on canvas
66 x 80.4
Purchased 1966
GMA 993

Masker [Mask]*
1936
Bronze
23.5 x 17 x 12.5
Purchased 1966
GMA 947

Robin Philipson

1916–92

Rocks at Gardenstown*
d 1953
Watercolour, gouache, ink and gum arabic on paper
50.5 x 63.5
Bequeathed by Dr R. A. Lillie 1977
GMA 1952

Cathedral, Grey*
1960
Watercolour and oil on paper
91.5 x 58.4
Scott Hay Collection: presented 1967
GMA 1055

Fighting Cocks, Grey*
c 1961
Oil on canvas
63 x 75.8
Purchased 1961
GMA 788

Burning at the Sea's Edge*
c 1961
Oil on canvas
63.5 x 76.2
Scott Hay Collection: presented 1967
GMA 1054

Cathedral, Red*
d 1961
Oil on canvas
183 x 101.6
Scott Hay Collection: presented 1967
GMA 1056

Odalisque with Mirror
1962
Oil on board
40.6 x 30.5
Scott Hay Collection: presented 1967
GMA 1052

Odalisque*
1962
Oil on canvas
61 x 61
Scott Hay Collection: presented 1967
GMA 1053

Red Interior
c 1962–65
Watercolour and wax resist on paper laid on board
30.7 x 81.1
George and Isobel Neillands Collection: presented 1988
GMA 3348

*The Burning**
1963
Watercolour, pastel, gouache and black chalk on paper (triptych)
Three panels, each 137.2 x 81.3
Purchased (Gulbenkian UK Trust Fund) 1963
GMA 848

*Church Interior**
1965
Oil, vinyl toluene and paper collage on canvas
91.5 x 121.9
Scott Hay Collection: presented 1967
GMA 1057

*Cathedral Interior, Remembrance**
1965
Oil, vinyl toluene and paper collage on canvas
101.6 x 101.6
Scott Hay Collection: presented 1967
GMA 1058

Shadow in an Eastern Temple
c 1970
Watercolour and gouache on paper laid on board
30.9 x 30.6
George and Isobel Neillands Collection: presented 1988
GMA 3349

*The Covering Sea I**
1982–83
Oil on canvas
183 x 213.5
Purchased 1984
GMA 2802

Peter Phillips

1939–

Custom Print II
(from the portfolio 'Eleven Pop Artists, vol. II')
d 1965
Screenprint on alufoil (no. 24)
60.9 x 76.2 (image and paper size)
Purchased 1975
GMA 1333

Tom Phillips

1937–

22 leaves from 'Humument'
1978
Colour lithographs on paper
Each leaf 19 x 14
Presented by the artist 1978
GMA 2015

Mozart
1980
Screenprint on paper (8/75)
44.6 x 50.5 (paper 69.7 x 72.5)
Purchased 1980
GMA 2227

Francis Picabia

1879–1953

*Fille née sans mère [Girl Born without a Mother]**
1916–17
Gouache and metallic paint on printed paper
50 x 65
Purchased 1990
GMA 3545

Pablo Picasso

1881–1973

*Mère et enfant [Mother and Child]**
1902
Oil on paper laid on canvas
40.5 x 33
Presented by Sir Alexander Maitland in memory of his wife, Rosalind, 1960
GMA 967

*Guitare, bec à gaz, flacon [Guitar, Gas-jet and Bottle]**
1912–13
Oil, charcoal, tinted varnish and grit on canvas
70.4 x 55.3
Purchased 1982
GMA 2501

Les Soles [The Soles]*
d 1940
Oil on canvas
60 x 92
Purchased 1967
GMA 1070

La Main [The Hand or Arm with Sleeve]*
1948
Bronze (3/10)
6.7 x 24 x 9.5
Bequeathed by Hannah Gluck 1978
GMA 1996

Deux figures nues [Two Nude Figures]*
1909
Drypoint on paper
13.1 x 11 (paper 60.7 x 44.2)
Purchased 1986
GMA 3008

Quatre femmes nues et tête sculptée [Four Nude
Women and Sculpted Head]*
(from 'The Vollard Suite', no. 82)
d 1934
Etching and engraving on paper
22.1 x 31.4 (paper 34 x 45)
Purchased 1961
GMA 775

Corrida*
d 1934
Etching on paper
49.4 x 69 (paper 56.8 x 77)
Purchased 1981
GMA 2287

Bacchanale*
d 1959
Colour linocut on paper (25/50)
52.5 x 63.6 (paper 62.1 x 75)
Purchased 1962
GMA 825

John Piper

1903–92

Avebury (or Archaeological Wiltshire)*
d 1936
Collage, gouache and ink on paper
41.2 x 53
Purchased 1964
GMA 893

Black Ground (or Screen for the Sea)*
d 1938
Oil on canvas
121.6 x 182.8
Purchased 1978
GMA 1998

Wheatfield, Oxon.*
d 1941
Watercolour and ink on paper
42 x 54.8
Bequeathed by Miss Elizabeth Watt 1989
GMA 3508

Foliate Heads No. II*
1953
Gouache, watercolour, ink and crayon on paper
laid on board
55.4 x 70.5 (irregular)
Bequeathed by Miss Elizabeth Watt 1989
GMA 3507

Abstract Composition [OL 7]
Published 1936 (d 1937)
Colour lithograph on paper
61 x 46 (paper 67 x 51)
Purchased 1984
GMA 2886

Surgères [OL 112]
1958
Colour lithograph on paper (A.P.)
43 x 64.3 (paper 52.8 x 74.3)
Purchased 1960
GMA 751

Swansea Chapel [OL 175]
1966
Colour lithograph on paper (37/75)
69.5 x 50.8 (paper 81.6 x 59.4)
Purchased 1984
GMA 2887

Jazenne, Charente [OL 196]
1968
Screenprint on paper (49/70)
57.6 x 77.7 (paper 71.5 x 103.5)
Purchased 1984
GMA 2889

St Amand-de-Coly, Dordogne [OL 197]
d 1968
Screenprint on paper (38/70)
58 x 77.4 (paper 70.6 x 100.2)
Purchased 1984
GMA 2888

Welsh Landscape, Tretio [OL 198]
d 1969
Screenprint on paper (26/100)
48 x 70 (paper 59.5 x 82)
Purchased 1984
GMA 2890

[OL refers to the catalogue raisonné of Piper's prints by Orde Levinson (London 1987)]

Lucien Pissarro

1863–1944

The Mill House, Blackpool, Devon*
1913
Oil on canvas
36.3 x 31
Bequeathed by Dr R. A. Lillie 1977
GMA 1954

Near Colchester, Essex*
Coloured crayon on paper
15.2 x 22.3
Bequeathed by Dr R. A. Lillie 1977
GMA 1953

John Platt

1886–1967

The Irish Lady, Land's End
d 1921
Colour woodcut on paper (13/100)
20.3 x 26.5 (paper 23 x 29.7)
Purchased 1949
GMA 484

Pilchard Boats, Cornwall
1923
Colour woodcut on paper (14/100)
16.5 x 31.5 (paper 19.6 x 33.3)
Purchased 1949
GMA 483

Serge Poliakoff

1906–69

Composition rose, rouge et bleue [Composition Rose, Red and Blue]
1958
Colour lithograph on paper (9/60)
32.5 x 25.5 (paper 50.5 x 38.2)
Purchased 1962
GMA 805

Jackson Pollock

1912–56

Untitled*
c 1942–44
Oil, pen and ink, and watercolour on paper
33.5 x 50.7
Purchased 1980
GMA 2198

Untitled*
d 1951
Ink and gouache on paper
63.1 x 99.9
Purchased 1963
GMA 849

Vladimir Polunin

1880–1957

The Salutation (or *The Annunciation*)
d 1926
Oil on canvas
45.9 x 38.2
Bequeathed by Miss Edith Urquhart 1945
GMA 36

François Pompon

1855–1933

*Perdreau [Partridge]**
c 1923
Bronze
25.7 x 22.5 x 11.5
Bequeathed by Miss Edith Urquhart 1945
GMA 973

Monica Poole

1921–

Old Fence
1978
Wood engraving on paper
14 x 23.5 (paper 22.1 x 30.9)
Presented by the artist 1993
GMA 3692

Dry September
1980
Wood engraving on paper (28/75)
20 x 15 (paper 29.5 x 23.6)
Presented by the artist 1993
GMA 3691

Chalk, Flint and Bone
1986
Wood engraving on paper
10.9 x 15.8 (paper 19 x 22.8)
Presented by the artist 1993
GMA 3693

Nicholas Pope

1949–

Stone Stack
1976
Bath stone (6 pieces) on metal base
height 180
Purchased 1982
GMA 2762

Lyubov Popova

1889–1924

*Painterly Architectonic**
1916
Oil on board
59.4 x 39.4
Purchased 1979
GMA 2080

Douglas Portway

1922–93

*Abstract Composition**
1962
Gouache on paper
75.8 x 55.6
Purchased 1963
GMA 857

John Quinton Pringle

1864–1925

Study of a Head (or *Man with a Drinking Mug*)*
d 1904 [?]
Oil on canvas
31 x 25.8
Presented by Mr James Meldrum 1948
GMA 2028

*Poultry Yard, Gartcosh**
1906
Oil on canvas
63.7 x 76.4
Presented by Mr James Meldrum 1948
GMA 37

James Pryde

1866–1941

Moll Cutpurse (or *The Roaring Girl*)*
d 1902
Oil and gouache on paper laid on card
41 x 29.7
Purchased 1991
GMA 3596

*Lumber: A Silhouette**
c 1921
Oil on canvas
151.8 x 131.1
Purchased 1975
GMA 1521

*An Ancient Harbour**
c 1923
Oil on canvas
63.2 x 49.6
Bequeathed by Lady Hutchison of Montrose 1941
GMA 38

Jack Sheppard
(*No. 5 in the series 'The Celebrated Criminals'*)
Published c 1902
Lithograph on paper
36 x 29.7 (paper 46.8 x 38)
Purchased 1991
GMA 3598

Sir Henry Irving as Dubosc in 'The Lyons Mail'
Published 1906
Photographic reproduction on paper laid on card
47.3 x 34.3 (card 57 x 38)
Purchased 1991
GMA 3597

Margaret Pullée

1910–

Scene by the Sea
d 1937
Gouache on paper laid on board
37.4 x 55.3
Bequeathed by Miss Elizabeth Watt 1989
GMA 3509

Houses, Gloucester
d 1938
Gouache and pencil on paper laid on board
38.2 x 56
Bequeathed by Miss Elizabeth Watt 1989
GMA 3510

Charles Pulsford

1913–89

*Untitled**
c 1950–52
Ink and wax resist on paper
38.1 x 42.5
Purchased 1992
GMA 3648

Two Figures in a Landscape
1953
Colour lithograph on paper
40.5 x 28.7 (paper 49.5 x 31.8)
Presented by Mr William Hardie 1992
GMA 3640

Figures in an Urban Landscape
1953
Colour lithograph on paper
26.8 x 40.6 (paper 31.7 x 49.5)
Presented by Mr William Hardie 1992
GMA 3642

Archetypal Figure
1953–54
Colour lithograph on paper
43 x 28.1 (paper 49.8 x 31.9)
Presented by Mr William Hardie 1992
GMA 3639

Demeter
1954
Colour lithograph on paper
43.5 x 29.2 (paper 49.5 x 31.8)
Presented by Mr William Hardie 1992
GMA 3641

Daniel Quintero

1949–

En el Metro (Las Puertas Verdes) [On the Underground (The Green Doors)]*
d 1971 and 1972
Oil and transfer-text on canvas laid on wood
200 x 129.5
Purchased 1976
GMA 1563

Study of an Open Hand (for 'On the Underground')
d 1972
Pencil on paper
13.2 x 11.1
Presented by the artist through Marlborough Fine Art 1976
GMA 1579

Study of a Clenched Fist (for 'On the Underground')*
d 1972
Pencil on paper
14.6 x 11.2
Presented by the artist through Marlborough Fine Art 1976
GMA 1580

Study of a Man (for 'On the Underground')*
d 1972
Pencil on paper
17.9 x 11
Presented by the artist through Marlborough Fine Art 1976
GMA 1581

Study of a Man (for 'On the Underground')
d 1972
Pencil on paper
14.1 x 10.3
Presented by the artist through Marlborough Fine Art 1976
GMA 1582

Barbara Rae

1943–

Floodwater
d 1987
Monotype on paper
75.5 x 105.5 (paper 80.5 x 109.8)
Purchased 1987
GMA 3030

Pebblebank*
d 1984
Lithograph and screenprint on paper (7/10)
60 x 77.2 (paper size)
Purchased 1985
GMA 2948

Mel Ramos

1935–

Tobacco Rose
(from the portfolio 'Eleven Pop Artists, vol. II')
d 1965
Screenprint on paper
71 x 55.6 (paper 76.2 x 60.9)
Purchased 1975
GMA 1342

William Bruce Ellis Ranken

1881–1941

Still Life, Black and White*
d 1925
Oil on canvas
92.5 x 123.4
Purchased 1946
GMA 1006

Gwen Raverat

1885–1957

Clerk Saunders
(*illustration for a Ballad*)
1909
Woodcut on paper
8.8 x 6.3 (paper 9.6 x 6.5)
Purchased 1949
GMA 488

Fair Annie
(*illustration for a Ballad*)
1909
Woodcut on paper
10.5 x 9.3 (paper 11.4 x 9.7)
Purchased 1949
GMA 490

The Quarrel
(*illustration for a Ballad*)
1909
Woodcut on paper
7.7 x 10.3 (paper 8.8 x 10.8)
Purchased 1949
GMA 491

Travellers
1909
Woodcut on paper
8.2 x 10.2 (paper 9 x 10.6)
Purchased 1949
GMA 493

Child Stealers
1909
Woodcut on paper
10.4 x 15.5 (paper 11.4 x 16)
Purchased 1949
GMA 497

Nightmare
1909
Woodcut on paper
10.2 x 6.5 (paper 11.5 x 7)
Purchased 1949
GMA 499

Windy Day
(*tailpiece for a Ballad*)
1909
Woodcut on paper
4.2 x 8.5 (paper 4.9 x 8.8)
Purchased 1949
GMA 500

Despair
(*tailpiece for a Ballad*)
1909
Woodcut on paper
4.8 x 8.7 (paper 5.6 x 9)
Purchased 1949
GMA 501

The Marsh
1909
Woodcut on paper
6.2 x 10.4 (paper 6.8 x 10.6)
Purchased 1949
GMA 503

May Margaret
(*illustration for a Ballad*)
1909
Woodcut on paper
8.4 x 6.2 (paper 8.7 x 6.6)
Purchased 1949
GMA 505

Gypsies
1910
Woodcut on paper
10.4 x 15.5 (paper 11.6 x 15.8)
Purchased 1949
GMA 489

Flying
1910
Woodcut on blue paper
15.7 x 10.5 (paper 16.7 x 11)
Purchased 1949
GMA 492

May Morning
1910
Woodcut on paper
3.6 x 5.6 (paper 4.3 x 5.9)
Purchased 1949
GMA 495

Wood Nymph
1910
Woodcut on paper
6 x 7 (paper 6.9 x 7.5)
Purchased 1949
GMA 496 A

The Dead Knight
(illustration for a Ballad)
1910
Woodcut on paper
4.5 x 9 (paper 5.2 x 9.3)
Purchased 1949
GMA 496 B

A Dream
1911
Woodcut on paper
8.6 x 3.4 (paper 9.4 x 3.7)
Purchased 1949
GMA 502

The Visitation
1912
Woodcut on paper
10.2 x 7.8 (paper 12 x 8.3)
Presented by Sir David Young Cameron through
the National Art Collections Fund 1943
GMA 485

Creation of Light
(after Jacques Raverat)
1912
Woodcut on paper
6.2 x 10.3 (paper 6.6 x 10.6)
Purchased 1949
GMA 498

Dead Christ
(after Jacques Raverat)
1913
Woodcut on paper
10.2 x 4.6 (paper 11 x 5)
Bequeathed by Sir David Young Cameron 1945
GMA 321

Pietà
*(after Jacques Raverat)**
d 1913
Woodcut on paper
10.2 x 15.1 (paper 11.1 x 15.9)
Purchased 1949
GMA 486

Dead Christ
(after Jacques Raverat)
1913
Woodcut on paper
10.2 x 4.6 (paper 11 x 5)
Purchased 1949
GMA 506

The Prodigal Son
(after Jacques Raverat)
1914
Woodcut on paper
6.2 x 6.9 (paper 7 x 7.3)
Bequeathed by Sir David Young Cameron 1945
GMA 320

Spring Morning
1915
Woodcut on paper
8.2 x 8.2 (paper 8.4 x 8.5)
Purchased 1949
GMA 494

The Poacher (Book-Plate for Winifred Cox)
1918
Wood engraving on paper
5.4 x 6.8 (paper 6.2 x 7.2)
Purchased 1949
GMA 487

Sheep
1919
Woodcut on paper
6.3 x 9.4 (paper 7.1 x 9.7)
Purchased 1949
GMA 504

Andersen Cutting out Pictures
1935
Colour wood engraving on paper
11.6 x 10.2 (paper 16.2 x 11.6)
Purchased 1978
GMA 2040

The Reconciliation from the Runaway
1936
Wood engraving on paper
10.2 x 8.1 (paper 12.9 x 10.4)
Purchased 1978
GMA 2042

The Bird Talisman
1939
Colour wood engraving on paper
12.8 x 11.3 (paper 24 x 14.8)
Purchased 1978
GMA 2041

Man Ray

See MAN RAY

June Redfern

1951–

My Baby Moon*
d 1983
Oil on canvas
190.5 x 213.3
Purchased 1983
GMA 2797

Wolf
(from 'The Scottish Bestiary')
Published 1986
Colour lithograph on paper (5/50)
76 x 56.5 (paper size)
Purchased 1987
GMA 3019 E

Lion
(from 'The Scottish Bestiary')
Published 1986
Colour lithograph on paper (5/50)
76 x 56.5 (paper size)
Purchased 1987
GMA 3019 H

Seal
(from 'The Scottish Bestiary')
Published 1986
Colour lithograph and screenprint on paper (5/50)
76 x 56.5 (paper size)
Purchased 1987
GMA 3019 M

Anne Redpath

1895–1965

Girl in a Red Cloak*
c 1920
Oil on plywood
59.7 x 54.2
Purchased 1977
GMA 1646

Houses and Trees (near Denholm)
d 1938
Gouache and black chalk on paper
38.7 x 48.6
Bequeathed by Dr R. A. Lillie 1977
GMA 1959

Near Ashkirk
c 1940
Gouache and black chalk on paper
37.3 x 50.7
Bequeathed by Dr R. A. Lillie 1977
GMA 1955

On the Teviot
c 1940
Gouache and pencil on paper
39.1 x 49.2
Bequeathed by Dr R. A. Lillie 1977
GMA 1967

Farmyard with Cows
c 1940–45
Gouache and black chalk on paper
33.2 x 41
Bequeathed by Dr R. A. Lillie 1977
GMA 1957

The Indian Rug (or Red Slippers)*
[verso: Landscape near Hawick]*
c 1942 [verso c 1942]
Oil on plywood
73.9 x 96.1
Purchased 1965
GMA 932

Broadford, Skye
c 1942
Gouache and pencil on paper
45.1 x 57.2
Bequeathed by Dr R. A. Lillie 1977
GMA 1956

Still Life with Teapot on Round Table*
[verso: Still Life with Milk Bottle]*
c 1945 [verso c 1945]
Oil on hardboard
75 x 75
Bequeathed by Dr R. A. Lillie 1977
GMA 1963

From a Window in Skye
c 1946
Gouache on card
26.3 x 35.3
Bequeathed by Dr R. A. Lillie 1977
GMA 1961

The Worcester Jug*
c 1946
Oil on canvas
86.5 x 111.5
Bequeathed by Dr R. A. Lillie 1977
GMA 1965

The Mantelpiece*
c 1947
Oil on plywood
61 x 59.9
Bequeathed by Dr R. A. Lillie 1977
GMA 1960

Telephone Kiosk, France
c 1948
Gouache, pen and ink and black chalk on paper
25.3 x 20
Bequeathed by Dr R. A. Lillie 1977
GMA 1966

Rain in Spain*
c 1951
Oil on hardboard
61 x 77
Bequeathed by Dr R. A. Lillie 1977
GMA 1962

Two Houses, Concarneau
c 1954
Oil on plywood
35.6 x 45.9
George and Isobel Neillands Collection: presented
1988
GMA 3332

Erbalunga, Corsica*
c 1955
Oil on hardboard
61 x 76.2
Scott Hay Collection: presented 1967
GMA 1059

Old Houses, Corsica
c 1955
Oil on hardboard
51 x 76.2
Bequeathed by Miss Tertia Liebenthal 1970
GMA 1112

Red and White Roses
c 1958
Watercolour, gouache and black chalk on paper
54.5 x 63.7
Bequeathed by Miss Tertia Liebenthal 1970
GMA 1114

Landscape at Kyleakin*
c 1958–60
Oil on board
71.2 x 91.5
Purchased 1962
GMA 814

Playa de San Cristoba
c 1960
Oil on canvas
63.5 x 76.2
Scott Hay Collection: presented 1967
GMA 1065

Lisbon Church*
1961
Oil on hardboard
61 x 76.9
Scott Hay Collection: presented 1967
GMA 1062

Tulips
c 1962
Oil on canvas
63.5 x 76.2
Scott Hay Collection: presented 1967
GMA 1064

In the Church of Madre Deus*
c 1962
Oil on hardboard
61 x 61
Bequeathed by Miss Tertia Liebenthal 1970
GMA 1113

The Golden Teapot
c 1962
Oil on board
51 x 61
Bequeathed by Dr R. A. Lillie 1977
GMA 1958

Madonna from Mexico
c 1963
Oil on canvas
61 x 50.9
Scott Hay Collection: presented 1967
GMA 1061

White Tulips*
c 1963
Oil on hardboard
61 x 91.5
Bequeathed by Dr R. A. Lillie 1977
GMA 1964

In a Venetian Church*
1963 or 1964
Oil on canvas
61 x 50.9
Scott Hay Collection: presented 1967
GMA 1060

The Crypt, St Marks, Venice*
1963 or 1964
Oil on canvas
50.9 x 61
Scott Hay Collection: presented 1967
GMA 1063

Philip Reeves

1931–

Lowland Hill
1958
Colour etching on paper
35 x 39 (paper 45 x 51.4)
Purchased 1963
GMA 874

Barumini, Sardinia*
1960
Colour etching on paper
29.9 x 40 (paper 39 x 57.2)
Purchased 1963
GMA 873

Alghero, Sardinia
1960
Colour etching on paper
29.8 x 39.6 (paper 42.5 x 54)
Purchased 1963
GMA 875

Blea Moor
1969
Colour etching on paper (A.P.)
48.2 x 59.2 (paper 57.4 x 77.7)
Purchased 1980
GMA 2228

Forms on the Shore
1975
Etching on paper (1/10)
45.3 x 55.2 (paper 59.1 x 73.5)
Purchased 1980
GMA 2229

Towards Malvern
1980
Colour etching on paper (6/10)
42.7 x 68.8 (paper 57.2 x 81.8)
Purchased 1981
GMA 2319

Hamish Reid

1929–

*Headland**
d 1961
Watercolour and pen and ink on paper
45 x 67
Bequeathed by Keith Andrews 1990
GMA 3605

Grey Church
d 1963
Watercolour and pen and ink on paper
48.4 x 71.4
Purchased 1963
GMA 871

Church in Trees
d 1964
Watercolour and pen and ink on paper
54.4 x 71.4
Bequeathed by Keith Andrews 1990
GMA 3604

Norman Reid

1915–

*St John's Wood, Behind Alma Square**
d 1947
Oil on canvas
51 x 56
Purchased 1992
GMA 3696

Alan Reynolds

1926–

*Winter Seeding Hillside**
d 1953
Oil on hardboard
76.5 x 101.5
Presented anonymously in memory of William
Johnstone 1984
GMA 2921

Ceri Richards

1903–71

*Relief Construction (Bird and Beast)**
d 1936
Oil on wood relief, raffia and plaster
Relief 42.8 x 60.3; board 60.3 x 78.1
Purchased 1975
GMA 1517

Owl and Skull
d 1953
Monotype on paper
33 x 40.4
Purchased 1978
GMA 2036

*Cycle of Nature, Arabesque I**
d 1964
Oil on canvas
127 x 127
Purchased (Knapping Fund) 1965
GMA 933

Hammerklavier
d 1959
Colour lithograph on paper (40/50)
50 x 75.3 (paper size)
Purchased 1960
GMA 752

La Cathédrale engloutie I
d 1959
Colour lithograph on paper (30/50)
49.8 x 62.3 (paper 57.5 x 80.4)
Purchased 1960
GMA 753

Trafalgar Square
d 1962
Colour lithograph on paper (30/100)
57.3 x 80.8 (paper size)
Purchased with funds given by two anonymous
donors 1963
GMA 850

Clair de lune
d 1967
Screenprint on paper (38/70)
53 x 72.5 (paper 57.5 x 77.5)
Purchased 1984
GMA 2891

Origin of Species
d 1971
Screenprint on paper (74/75)
46 x 62 (paper 65 x 80.7)
Purchased 1984
GMA 2892

Edith Richards

exh. 1909–34

Harbour Scene with Figure
d 1918
Colour woodcut on paper
16.8 x 16.6 (paper 18.8 x 18.3)
Presented by Jim Ede 1977
GMA 1628 A

Harbour Scene with Figure
d 1918
Colour woodcut on paper
16.8 x 16.6 (paper 18.8 x 18.2)
Presented by Jim Ede 1977
GMA 1628 B

Trees by a Lake
Colour woodcut on paper
22.5 x 15.4 (paper 24.2 x 17.7)
Presented by Jim Ede 1977
GMA 1629

Child by a Cottage Door
Colour woodcut on paper
9.3 x 10 (paper 13.3 x 13.2)
Presented by Jim Ede 1977
GMA 1630

Shop Window with Girl
Colour woodcut on paper
22.5 x 11.7 (paper 27.2 x 15.4)
Presented by Jim Ede 1977
GMA 1631

Frances Richardson

1892–1977

Pocra Quay, Aberdeen
d 1957
Oil on hardboard
51 x 61
Bequeathed by Dr R. A. Lillie 1977
GMA 1968

Germaine Richier

1904–59

*Le Courreur [The Runner]**
1955
Bronze (2/6)
120 x 59 x 47
Purchased 1974
GMA 1315

Charles Ricketts

1866–1931

*Don Juan and the Commander**
c 1905
Oil on canvas
43.2 x 33.2
Presented by the Very Rev. Canon J. Gray 1934
GMA 1007

*Costume Design for the Devil in 'Montezuma'**
c 1925–26
Watercolour and pencil on paper (image cut to contour and laid on paper)
30.5 x 19.6 (image size)
Presented by the National Art Collections Fund 1932
GMA 1012

Costume Design for 'The Mikado'
c 1926
Watercolour and pencil on paper (image cut to contour and laid on paper)
40 x 30.3 (image size)
Presented by the National Art Collections Fund 1932
GMA 1013

Costume Design for 'The Mikado'
c 1926
Watercolour and pencil on paper (image cut to
contour and laid on paper)
37.8 x 29 (image size)
Presented by the National Art Collections Fund
1932
GMA 1014

Endymion
(for the Vale Press edition of Plato's 'Symposium')
c 1900–04
Woodcut on paper
12.2 x 8.1 (paper 31.8 x 23.9)
Purchased 1949
GMA 509

The Parable of the Virgins
d 1910
Woodcut on paper (A.P.)
8.3 x 8.2 (paper 15.8 x 11.8)
Purchased 1949
GMA 508

Italia Redenta
*(from the series 'The Great War: Britain's Efforts
and Ideals')*
Published 1918
Colour lithograph on paper
68.3 x 42.8 (paper 80 x 51.5)
Presented by the Ministry of Information 1919
GMA 507

George Rickey
1907–

Two Lines Fixed, Three Moving*
1970
Stainless steel
65.5 x 91.4 x 7.6
Purchased 1970
GMA 1161

Two Lines up Excentric VI*
1977
Stainless steel (3/3)
670.5 height
Purchased 1984
GMA 2844

Bridget Riley
1931–

Over*
1966
Emulsion on board
101.5 x 101.3
Purchased 1974
GMA 1316

Jean-Paul Riopelle
1923–

Ventoux*
d 1958
Oil on canvas
80.7 x 100
Purchased 1964
GMA 883

Derek Roberts
1947–

Blue Rectangle*
1977
Oil, black chalk and oil crayon with paper collage
on canvas
198.3 x 278
Purchased 1979
GMA 2113

Summer Shadows*
1984
Oil on canvas
142 x 121.5
Purchased 1986
GMA 2972

William Roberts

1895–1980

*Sarah**
c 1925
Oil on canvas
61 x 51
Purchased 1976
GMA 1589

*The Rhine Boat**
c 1928
Oil on canvas
50.8 x 40.6
Presented by Miss Elizabeth Watt 1961
GMA 783

*The Ballet**
1932
Oil on canvas
40.8 x 45.6
Bequeathed by Miss Elizabeth Watt 1989
GMA 3511

A Reading of Poetry (or *Woman Reading*)*
1965
Oil on canvas
61 x 50.8
Bequeathed by Miss Elizabeth Watt 1989
GMA 3512

David Robertson

fl. 1900–14

Seascape: Boats in a Rough Sea
c 1901
Oil on wood
8.7 x 13.5
Presented by Mrs Andrew Melvin 1950
GMA 1163

Seascape: Waves Breaking on Rocks
c 1901
Oil on wood
8.7 x 13.5
Presented by Mrs Andrew Melvin 1950
GMA 1164

Eric Robertson

1887–1941

*Terror of War**
d 1914
Pencil on paper
21.3 x 15.5
Purchased 1978
GMA 1715

*Fleet Bay, Kirkcudbrightshire**
c 1923
Oil on canvas
76.4 x 92
Presented by Miss J. M. Robertson 1944
GMA 1008

Thomas Ronaldson

1881–1941

Portrait of Anna Katrina Zinkeisen
c 1924
Oil on canvas
102.5 x 104
Presented by Mrs Dorothy Ronaldson 1942
GMA 1009

Louis Rosenberg

1890–1983

Ingsburg Towers
Etching on paper
22.1 x 12.5 (paper 37.1 x 23.4)
Bequeathed by Mr George Liston-Foulis 1958
GMA 164

James Rosenquist

1933–

Whipped Butter for Eugen Ruchin
(from the portfolio 'Eleven Pop Artists, vol. II')
1965
Screenprint on paper (no. 24)
76.2 x 60.9 (image and paper size)
Purchased 1975
GMA 1334

Mario Rossi

1958–

Phenomenon 1870 (I)*
1986
Bronze
53 x 34.5 x 36.4
Purchased 1987
GMA 3045

Charms, Capillaries and Amulets: Suite no. II*
1987
Indian ink and bleach on paper in iron frames
(suite of nine works)
Each 59.8 x 47.3 (paper size); 61.5 x 48.7 (frame
size)
Purchased 1987
GMA 3044

Medardo Rosso

1858–1928

Ecce Puer [Behold the Boy]*
1906
Plaster, gesso and varnish
46.2 x 43 x 32
Purchased with funds from the estate of Miss
J. L. Rose 1972
GMA 1274

Mimmo Rotella

1918–

The Ghost Car*
1989
Acrylic and black felt-tip pen on poster
59.5 x 69.5
Presented by the artist through the Richard
Demarco Gallery 1990
GMA 3571

William Rothenstein

1872–1945

Portrait of Alphonse Legros
d 1897
Lithograph on paper
37.2 x 24.9 (paper size)
Purchased 1949
GMA 512

Right Hon. John Morley
d 1903
Lithograph on paper
36.6 x 25.6 (paper size)
Purchased 1949
GMA 513

The Triumph of Democracy
(from the series 'The Great War: Britain's Efforts
and Ideals')
d 1917 (published 1918)
Colour lithograph on paper
43.4 x 71 (paper 55.7 x 80.3)
Presented by the Ministry of Information 1919
GMA 510

Work on the Land: Ploughing
(from the series 'The Great War: Britain's Efforts
and Ideals')
d 1917 (published 1918)
Lithograph on paper
35 x 46.2 (paper 41 x 51.7)
Presented by the Ministry of Information 1919
GMA 511 A

Work on the Land: Drilling
(*from the series 'The Great War: Britain's Efforts and Ideals'*)
d 1917 (published 1918)
Lithograph on paper
35.2 x 46.4 (paper 40.8 x 51.6)
Presented by the Ministry of Information 1919
GMA 511 B

Work on the Land: Burning Couch-Grass
(*from the series 'The Great War: Britain's Efforts and Ideals'*)
d 1917 (published 1918)
Lithograph on paper
36 x 46.5 (paper 41 x 52)
Presented by the Ministry of Information 1919
GMA 511 C

Work on the Land: Potato Planting
(*from the series 'The Great War: Britain's Efforts and Ideals'*)
d 1917 (published 1918)
Lithograph on paper
35.8 x 46.3 (paper 41 x 51.6)
Presented by the Ministry of Information 1919
GMA 511 D

Work on the Land: Timber Hauling
(*from the series 'The Great War: Britain's Efforts and Ideals'*)
d 1917 (published 1918)
Lithograph on paper
35.2 x 45.8 (paper 41 x 51.5)
Presented by the Ministry of Information 1919
GMA 511 E

Work on the Land: Threshing
(*from the series 'The Great War: Britain's Efforts and Ideals'*)
d 1917 (published 1918)
Lithograph on paper
34.8 x 47 (paper 41 x 51.8)
Presented by the Ministry of Information 1919
GMA 511 F

Georges Rouault

1871–1958

*Head**
c 1935–40
Oil on paper laid on canvas
61.9 x 48.4
Presented by Sir Alexander Maitland in memory of his wife, Rosalind, 1960
GMA 968

Deux femmes in profil [*Two Women in Profile*]
(*pl. 18 of 'Réincarnations du Père Ubu'*)*
First impressions 1917 (published 1932)
Etching on paper
27.2 x 18.9 (paper 43.8 x 33.1)
Purchased 1966
GMA 970

Solitaire en cette vie d'embuches et de malices
[*Alone in this Life of Pitfalls and Hatred*]
(*pl. 5 of 'Miserere'*)
d 1922 (published 1948)
Etching on paper
58 x 41.7 (paper 65.4 x 50.5)
Purchased 1962
GMA 828

Face à face [*Face to Face*]
(*pl. 40 of 'Miserere'*)
c 1922–27 (published 1948)
Etching on paper
57.5 x 43.7 (paper 65.1 x 51)
Purchased 1962
GMA 826

Obéissant jusqu'à la mort [*Obedient unto Death*]
(*pl. 57 of 'Miserere'*)
d 1926 (published 1948)
Etching on paper
57.6 x 42 (paper 64.9 x 50.5)
Purchased 1962
GMA 827

Le Nègre [The Negro]
(pl. 11 of 'Réincarnations du Père Ubu')
d 1928 (published 1932)
Etching on paper
30.2 x 15.3 (paper 44.5 x 32.7)
Purchased 1966
GMA 969

Paysage avec négresse portant une cruche sur la
tête [Landscape with Negro Woman Carrying a
Pitcher on her Head]
(pl. 13 of 'Réincarnations du Père Ubu')
d 1928 (published 1932)
Etching on paper
29.9 x 18.8 (paper 44.2 x 32.8)
Purchased 1966
GMA 971

Dragon volant [Flying Dragon]
(pl. 16 of 'Réincarnations du Père Ubu')
d 1928 (published 1932)
Etching on paper
21.7 x 31.3 (paper 33.2 x 44.2)
Purchased 1966
GMA 972

Abani Roy

c 1898-c 1975

Fire and Kettle within a Fireplace
Watercolour and pencil on paper
25.3 x 17.8
Presented by Jim Ede 1977
GMA 1635

Fire and Kettle within a Fireplace
Watercolour and pencil on paper
25.3 x 17.8
Presented by Jim Ede 1977
GMA 1636

Indian Round Table Conference
d 1930
Engraving on paper (1/50)
21.7 x 17.6 (paper 29 x 22.7)
Presented by Jim Ede 1977
GMA 1659

Figures at a Table
d 1931
Etching on paper
15.2 x 11.2 (paper 20.3 x 15)
Presented by Jim Ede 1977
GMA 1634

Mabel Royds

1874–1941

Choir Boys
1898
Colour woodcut on paper
7.2 x 8.9 (paper 8.4 x 10)
Purchased 1949
GMA 517 A

Choir Boys (Xmas Greeting 1898)
d 1898
Woodcut on paper
7.2 x 10.7 (paper 8.4 x 11.6)
Purchased 1949
GMA 517 B

Water Carriers, Benares
c 1920
Colour woodcut on paper
19 x 21.8 (paper 24.5 x 24.7)
Bequeathed by Mr Kenneth Sanderson 1943
GMA 515

Goat Herd
c 1920
Colour woodcut on paper
15.1 x 11.7 (paper 16.8 x 13)
Purchased 1949
GMA 533

Bathers, Benares
c 1922
Colour woodcut on paper
11.9 x 11.9 (paper 14.7 x 16.1)
Purchased 1949
GMA 541

Prickly Pear Cactus
c 1924
Colour woodcut on paper
22 x 28.9 (paper 28.6 x 35.7)
Purchased 1949
GMA 530

Housetop
c 1924
Colour woodcut on paper
22.5 x 21.5 (paper 23.8 x 23)
Purchased 1949
GMA 536

Cineraria
exh. 1932 (this example printed 1936)
Colour woodcut on paper
20.6 x 27.5 (paper 24.8 x 32.1)
Provenance unrecorded
GMA 538

Cyclamen
exh. 1933
Colour woodcut on paper
20.5 x 15.8 (paper 24.5 x 18.3)
Provenance unrecorded
GMA 520

The Red Mug
exh. 1934
Colour woodcut on paper
14 x 15.2 (paper 16.1 x 17.5)
Purchased 1949
GMA 527

*Dead Tulips**
c 1934
Colour woodcut on paper
22.5 x 18.7 (paper 26.4 x 21.8)
Purchased 1949
GMA 529

Foxgloves
c 1934
Colour woodcut on paper
16.9 x 20.8 (paper 21.6 x 24.5)
Purchased 1949
GMA 532 A

Foxgloves
c 1934
Colour woodcut on paper
16.9 x 20.8 (paper 20.5 x 24.4)
Purchased 1949
GMA 532 B

Artichoke
c 1935
Colour woodcut on paper
18.5 x 21.3 (paper 20.4 x 23)
Purchased 1949
GMA 525

Snowdrops
c 1935
Colour woodcut on paper
9.3 x 10 (paper 10.5 x 10.5)
Purchased 1949
GMA 526

Columbines
c 1935
Colour woodcut on paper
18.4 x 15.7 (paper 26.6 x 17.6)
Purchased 1949
GMA 539

Magnolia
c 1936
Colour woodcut on paper
19.8 x 23.4 (paper 23.6 x 28.5)
Purchased 1949
GMA 521

Tiger Lilies
exh. 1936
Colour woodcut on paper
22.7 x 19 (paper 28 x 22.1)
Purchased 1949
GMA 524

Red Daisies
c 1936
Colour woodcut on paper
13.4 x 13.8 (paper 16.2 x 17)
Purchased 1949
GMA 528

Grapes
c 1936
Colour woodcut on paper
21.7 x 25.3 (paper 24.5 x 29.7)
Purchased 1949
GMA 534

Honeysuckle
c 1936
Colour woodcut on paper
20.2 x 16.6 (paper 23.5 x 19)
Purchased 1949
GMA 535

White Lilies
exh. 1937
Colour woodcut on paper
21.2 x 24 (paper 23.9 x 28.6)
Bequeathed by Mr Kenneth Sanderson 1943
GMA 514

Water Lilies
exh. 1938
Colour woodcut on paper
16.2 x 17.7 (paper 19.1 x 26.5)
Purchased 1949
GMA 522

The Flight into Egypt
c 1938
Colour woodcut on paper
23.6 x 30.7 (paper 28.5 x 33.7)
Purchased 1949
GMA 531

The Waterfall
c 1938
Colour woodcut on paper
25.4 x 29.4 (paper 28.4 x 33.2)
Purchased 1949
GMA 537 A

The Waterfall
c 1938
Colour woodcut on paper
25.4 x 29.4 (paper 28.6 x 33.8)
Purchased 1949
GMA 537 B

Cactus Rocks, St Abbs
c 1938
Colour woodcut on paper
31.2 x 24 (paper 39.1 x 26.3)
Purchased 1949
GMA 540

Angels Appearing to the Shepherds
c 1938
Colour woodcut on paper
28.8 x 32.8 (paper 32 x 35.7)
Purchased 1949
GMA 542

Cat with T-Square and Shield
Woodcut on paper
14 x 6.7 (paper size)
Purchased 1949
GMA 516

Little Girl with Bowl of Fruit (or *Marjorie*)
Colour woodcut on paper
15.2 x 5 (paper 19.4 x 7.9)
Purchased 1949
GMA 518

Christmas Morning (or *The Stocking*)
Colour woodcut on paper
14 x 6 (paper 15.7 x 7.2)
Purchased 1949
GMA 519

Trees on a Slope
Colour woodcut on paper
26 x 22.7 (paper 31.4 x 24.5)
Purchased 1949
GMA 523 A

Trees on a Slope
Colour woodcut on paper
26 x 22.7 (paper 31.3 x 24.5)
Purchased 1949
GMA 523 B

Henry George Rushbury

1889–1968

Clifford's Inn
d 1912
Drypoint on paper
37.1 x 26.7 (paper 51.3 x 38.7)
Bequeathed by Mr Kenneth Sanderson 1943
GMA 543

Marc Saint-Saëns

1903–

L'Oiseau lyre [Lyre Bird]*
1968
Tapestry
132 x 90
Bequeathed by Miss Elizabeth Watt 1989
GMA 3513

John Salt

1937–

Ironmongers*
d 1981
Oil on canvas
106.8 x 161.3
Purchased 1982
GMA 2474

Giuseppe Santomaso

1907–

Untitled (No. 46)
d 1960
Gouache and black chalk on paper
46.3 x 66.2
Scott Hay Collection: presented 1967
GMA 1066

Eric Schilsky

1898–1974

Gabrielle de Soane*
1920 / 1974
Bronze
53.3 x 40.7 x 17.8
Purchased 1976
GMA 1525

Bather I*
1971
Bronze
23.8 x 7.9 x 12.2
Purchased 1976
GMA 1526

Karl Schmidt-Rottluff

1884–1976

Heiliger Franziskus [St Francis]*
1919
Woodcut on paper
59.7 x 49.4 (paper 78.7 x 62)
Purchased 1982
GMA 2708

Benno Schotz

1891–1984

The Lament*
1943
Wood (lignum vitae)
91.5 x 30.5 x 21.5
Purchased 1971
GMA 1216

Jon R. Schueler

1916–92

The Sound of Sleat (June Night, XI, Romasaig)*
1970
Oil on canvas
102 x 122.5
Purchased 1971
GMA 1217

Bernard Schultze

1915–

Der erste Tag [The First Day]*
1989
Oil on canvas (diptych)
200 x 520 (each canvas 200 x 260)
Presented by Herr Franz Loehr 1990
GMA 3548

Emil Schumacher

1912–

Atischa
1959
Portfolio of nine etchings (32/70)
Each 48 x 35.9 (paper size)
Purchased 1990
GMA 3556

Kurt Schwitters

1887–1948

Ohne Titel (Relief mit roter Pyramide) [*Untitled (Relief with Red Pyramid)*]*
c 1923–25
Oil on wood relief on plywood
60 x 50.2
Purchased 1979
GMA 2077

Gavin Scobie

1940–

Step
d 1974
Aluminium
204.5 x 110.5 x 32
Presented by Mrs Gabrielle Keiller 1985
GMA 2950

*Eve**
1975
Cor-ten steel
206 x 115 x 79
Purchased 1976
GMA 1562

Book: Wittgenstein's Dream
1979
Bronze
Open 5 x 51.7 x 83.8; closed 6.2 x 43.2 x 51.7
Purchased 1980
GMA 2152

*XII: Small Sleep**
d 1982
Bronze
Open 27.4 x 38.3 x 2.9; closed 27.4 x 20.6 x 4.3
Purchased 1982
GMA 2700

Campbell Scott

1930–

Eruption
d 1966
Colour etching on paper (3/30)
49 x 31.8 (paper 57.1 x 39.5)
Purchased 1967
GMA 1000

William Scott

1913–89

*Mackerel**
1947
Oil on canvas
52.1 x 76
Bequeathed by Miss Elizabeth Watt 1989
GMA 3514

*Still Life − Lemons on a Plate**
d 1948
Oil on canvas
50.7 x 61
Purchased 1978
GMA 2066

*Tabletop with Saucepans**
d 1956
Black chalk on paper
48 x 63.2
Purchased 1971
GMA 1248

*Reclining Nude**
1956
Black chalk on paper (two sheets joined)
74.3 x 207
Presented by Miss Erica Brausen 1973
GMA 1278

Blue, Black and White*
1959
Gouache on paper
68 x 69.5
Purchased 1962
GMA 806

Grey Still Life*
1969
Oil on canvas
168 x 172
Purchased 1972
GMA 1262

The Bird Cage
(from the J. Lyons series 'Lithographs by
Contemporary Artists, vol. I')
Published 1947
Colour lithograph on paper (after gouache)
74.5 x 99 (paper size)
Presented by J. Lyons & Co. Ltd 1948
GMA 1211

Barra
d 1962
Colour lithograph on paper (42/75)
49.5 x 59 (paper 57.9 x 73.4)
Purchased with funds given by two anonymous
donors 1963
GMA 851

Benbecula
d 1962
Colour lithograph on paper (53/75)
49.3 x 62.1 (paper 58.1 x 74.7)
Purchased with funds given by two anonymous
donors 1963
GMA 852

The Scottish Bestiary

Published 1986
Unbound book with nineteen poems (by George
Mackay Brown) and twenty prints (woodcuts,
screenprints, etchings and lithograph) by John
Bellany, Steven Campbell, Peter Howson, Jack
Knox, Bruce McLean, June Redfern and Adrian
Wiszniewski
56 x 38 (paper size)
Purchased 1987
GMA 3018

The portfolio edition (GMA 3019) has been
catalogued under the names of the individual
artists. See John BELLANY, Steven CAMPBELL,
Peter HOWSON, Jack KNOX, Bruce McLEAN,
June REDFERN, Adrian WISZNIEWSKI

Elliott Seabrooke

1886–1950

Yachts on the Blackwater
d 1947
Oil on canvas
66.3 x 81.3
Purchased 1976
GMA 1524

Allen William Seaby

1867–1953

Kingfisher (no. I)
by 1908
Colour woodcut on paper
15.3 x 20 (paper 16.6 x 21.3)
Purchased 1949
GMA 547

Seagulls
by 1908
Colour woodcut on paper
23 x 23.5 (paper 26.7 x 24.7)
Purchased 1949
GMA 550

Lapwings
by 1908
Colour woodcut on paper
16.6 x 19.6 (paper 19.4 x 22.5)
Purchased 1949
GMA 551

*Heron (no. I)**
by 1908
Colour woodcut on paper
21.9 x 22 (paper 25.5 x 24.5)
Purchased 1949
GMA 554

Peacock
by 1908 (d 1913)
Colour woodcut on paper
16.3 x 21 (paper 19.6 x 24.5)
Purchased 1949
GMA 545

Vulture
by 1910
Colour woodcut on paper (22/100)
24 x 22 (paper 29.6 x 26.6)
Purchased 1949
GMA 552

Bullfinches
by 1911
Colour woodcut on paper
21.5 x 21.5 (paper 23.6 x 23.6)
Purchased 1949
GMA 549

Crouching Cock
by 1914
Colour woodcut on paper
15.2 x 20 (paper 18 x 22.7)
Purchased 1949
GMA 544

Bittern
by 1918
Colour woodcut on paper (3/100)
14.8 x 20.7 (paper 16.1 x 22.2)
Purchased 1949
GMA 553

Snow and Hare
c 1923
Colour woodcut on paper
12 x 17.5 (paper 14 x 18.9)
Purchased 1949
GMA 548

Blackcock and Greyhen
by 1924
Colour woodcut on paper
12.5 x 17.6 (paper 15.6 x 19.5)
Purchased 1949
GMA 546

Lasar Segall

1891–1957

Lucy with Flower
d 1939–42
Oil on canvas
56.2 x 47.4
Presented by the British Council 1945
GMA 1010

Jozef Sekalski

1904–72

Krakus
(*preparatory tracing for 'Old Polish Legends' by F. C. Anstruther*)
c 1944
Pencil on tracing paper
17.8 x 13
Presented by Mrs R. Sekalska 1981
GMA 2337 E

Studies of Heads
Pencil and red and white chalk on paper
31 x 24
Purchased 1981
GMA 2420

Study of Clouds
Pencil on paper
11.5 x 15
Purchased 1981
GMA 2421 A

Study of Clouds
Pencil on paper
20 x 25.5
Purchased 1981
GMA 2421 B

Sketchbook
Pencil, pen and ink and ball-point pen on paper
25.5 x 20
Purchased 1981
GMA 2422

Sketchbook
Pencil on paper
25.5 x 20
Purchased 1981
GMA 2423

Sketchbook
Pencil and ball-point pen on paper
25.5 x 19
Purchased 1981
GMA 2424

Sketchbook
Pencil on paper
24.7 x 17.5
Purchased 1981
GMA 2425

Sketchbook
Pencil and pen and ink on paper
23 x 18
Purchased 1981
GMA 2426

Sketchbook
Pencil on paper
25.5 x 20.5
Purchased 1981
GMA 2427

Sketchbook
Pencil on paper
24.7 x 17.5
Purchased 1981
GMA 2428

Sketchbook
Pencil and pen and ink on paper
25 x 18
Purchased 1981
GMA 2429

Sketchbook
Pencil on paper
20.5 x 15.5
Purchased 1981
GMA 2430

Sketchbook
Gouache and pencil on paper
23 x 18
Purchased 1981
GMA 2431

Sketchbook
Pencil and ball-point pen on paper
21.5 x 13.5
Purchased 1981
GMA 2432

Sketchbook
Pencil and pen and ink on paper
22.5 x 14
Purchased 1981
GMA 2433

Sketchbook
Pencil on paper
25 x 17.5
Purchased 1981
GMA 2434

Sketchbook
Pencil and pen and ink on paper
20 x 25
Purchased 1981
GMA 2435

Sketchbook
Pencil and pen and ink on paper
25.5 x 20
Purchased 1981
GMA 2436

Folder of drawings
Pencil on paper
26 x 20.7 (folder size)
Purchased 1981
GMA 2437 A

Folder of tracings
Pencil on tracing paper
28 x 19 (folder size)
Purchased 1981
GMA 2437 B

Sketchbook
Pencil and pen and ink on paper
12.5 X 17.5
Purchased 1981
GMA 2438

Sketchbook
Pencil and pen and ink on paper
12.5 X 17.5
Purchased 1981
GMA 2439

Sketchbook
Pencil and pen and ink on paper
11.2 X 18
Purchased 1981
GMA 2440

Sketchbook
Pencil and pen and ink on paper
25 x 36
Purchased 1981
GMA 2441

Sketchbook
Pencil on paper
25.5 X 35.5
Purchased 1981
GMA 2442

Sketchbook
Pencil and ball-point pen on paper
26 x 20
Purchased 1981
GMA 2443

Sketchbook
Pencil on paper
26 x 20.5
Purchased 1981
GMA 2444

Man Reading
Brown chalk on paper
38 x 28
Presented by Mrs R. Sekalska 1981
GMA 2456

Study of Drapery on an Armchair
Pencil on paper
18.6 x 25.2
Presented by Mrs R. Sekalska 1981
GMA 2457 A

Study of Drapery on an Armchair
Pencil and pen and ink on paper
25.6 x 20.4
Presented by Mrs R. Sekalska 1981
GMA 2457 B

Conch Shell
Pencil on paper
20.5 x 25.6
Presented by Mrs R. Sekalska 1981
GMA 2458

Studio Interior
Pencil on paper
25.9 x 19.5
Presented by Mrs R. Sekalska 1981
GMA 2459

Female Nude
Pen and ink on paper
38.2 x 27.9
Presented by Mrs R. Sekalska 1981
GMA 2460

Turnips
[verso: *A Garden*]
Pencil on paper
25.6 x 20.4
Presented by Mrs R. Sekalska 1981
GMA 2461

Flying Shapes
Watercolour, gouache and pencil on paper
48.1 x 36
Presented by Mrs R. Sekalska 1981
GMA 2462

Christmas and New Year Card
1942
Wood engraving on paper (trial proof for GMA
2350 B)
6 x 7.7 (paper 9 x 12)
Presented by Mrs R. Sekalska 1981
GMA 2350 A

Christmas and New Year Card
d 1942
Wood engraving on postcard
10.1 x 7.8 (card 14 x 8.5)
Presented by Mrs R. Sekalska 1981
GMA 2350 B

Cover Design for 'Umarli nie sa Bezbronni'
by Jerzy Pietrkiewicz
Published 1943
Wood engraving on paper
17 x 12 (paper 19.2 x 12.7)
Presented by Mrs R. Sekalska 1981
GMA 2333

The Bishop: Book-Plate for R. D. Caroli Jones
c 1943
Wood engraving on paper
10.3 x 4.3 (paper 14.5 x 9.5)
Presented by Mrs R. Sekalska 1981
GMA 2368

Cover Design for 'A Call from Warsaw'
translated by Albert Mackie
d 1943 (published 1944)
Wood engraving on paper
11.5 x 8.2 (paper 20.2 x 13.5)
Presented by Mrs R. Sekalska 1981
GMA 2334

Lech and Gniezno
(for 'Old Polish Legends' by F. C. Anstruther)
1944 (published 1945)
Wood engraving on paper
18 x 13.5 (paper 26.5 x 17.5)
Presented by Mrs R. Sekalska 1981
GMA 2337 A

Wanda
(for 'Old Polish Legends' by F. C. Anstruther)
d 1944 (published 1945)
Wood engraving on paper
20 x 14.5 (paper 25.5 x 18)
Presented by Mrs R. Sekalska 1981
GMA 2337 B

The Trumpeter of Krakow
*(for 'Old Polish Legends' by F. C. Anstruther)**
1944 (published 1945)
Wood engraving on paper
17.8 x 13 (paper 26.5 x 16.5)
Presented by Mrs R. Sekalska 1981
GMA 2337 C

Krakus
(for 'Old Polish Legends' by F. C. Anstruther)
c 1944 (published 1945)
Wood engraving on paper (trial proof)
16 x 13 (paper 17 x 15.5)
Presented by Mrs R. Sekalska 1981
GMA 2337 D

Wartime Still Life
(early state of back cover design of programme
for Polish Artistes Concert, Farnborough)
1945
Wood engraving on paper
11.5 x 7 (paper 17.5 x 8.7)
Presented by Mrs R. Sekalska 1981
GMA 2335

Letter Designs for 'Trzynaście Godzin Nocy' [The
Thirteen Hours of the Night] by Jan
Rostworowski
c 1946
Fourteen wood engravings on paper (trial proofs)
From 3.3 x 7.3 to 6.1 x 7.3 (paper from 4.9 x 10.3
to 9 x 11.5)
Presented by Mrs R. Sekalska 1981
GMA 2338 A–N

Ars Longa, Vita Brevis
1946
Wood engraving on paper (trial proof
for GMA 2351 B)
9 x 6.5 (paper 11.4 x 9.5)
Presented by Mrs R. Sekalska 1981
GMA 2351 A

Ars Longa, Vita Brevis
(design for a Christmas Card)
d 1946
Wood engraving on paper
9 x 6.5 (paper 13.5 x 9)
Presented by Mrs R. Sekalska 1981
GMA 2351 B

Boogie Woogie
(design for a Christmas Card)
d 1947
Wood engraving on paper
11.6 x 5.5 (paper 17.8 x 9.8)
Presented by Mrs R. Sekalska 1981
GMA 2352

Noli me Tangere
(design for an Easter Card)
1947
Wood engraving on paper
10.1 x 7.5 (paper 13.5 x 10)
Presented by Mrs R. Sekalska 1981
GMA 2353

Letter Heading for Jakymowicz, Kirkcaldy
1947
Wood engraving on paper
5.1 x 5.7 (paper 8 x 9.3)
Presented by Mrs R. Sekalska 1981
GMA 2369

The Sabre Dance
(design for a Christmas Card)
d 1948
Wood engraving on paper
9.5 x 11.6 (paper 14 x 15.5)
Presented by Mrs R. Sekalska 1981
GMA 2354

The Martin: Book-Plate for Gertrude Martin
Hodges
1948
Wood engraving on card
6.5 x 5.2 (card 11 x 10)
Presented by Mrs R. Sekalska 1981
GMA 2370

Canal Bridge, Bath
d 1948
Wood engraving on paper
15.3 x 12.6 (paper 21.3 x 18.4)
Presented by Mrs R. Sekalska 1981
GMA 2455

Serenity 1949
(for 'Twelve Poems' by Alastair Reid)
1949
Wood engraving on paper
12.9 x 5.5 (paper 18 x 9.9)
Presented by Mrs R. Sekalska 1981
GMA 2339

Leaves
(tailpiece for 'Twelve Poems' by Alastair Reid)
1949
Wood engravings on paper (two trial proofs)
Each image 2.8 x 2.8 (paper 5.2 x 15.4)
Presented by Mrs R. Sekalska 1981
GMA 2411

Spade and Palette: Book-Plate for A. Ayton
Young
1949
Wood engraving on paper
7 x 6 (paper 11 x 9)
Presented by Mrs R. Sekalska 1981
GMA 2371

With Watering Can: Book-Plate for A. Ayton
Young
1949
Wood engraving on paper
7.2 x 3.2 (paper 10.9 x 6.1)
Presented by Mrs R. Sekalska 1981
GMA 2372

Wheelbarrow and Palette: Book-Plate for
Stanislaw Przespolewski
1949
Wood engraving on paper
5 x 6.5 (paper 7.5 x 11.5)
Presented by Mrs R. Sekalska 1981
GMA 2374

*The Home-Made Press: Book-Plate for Michael
Oliver*
1949
Wood engraving on paper
3.5 x 4 (paper 9.5 x 9.5)
Presented by Mrs R. Sekalska 1981
GMA 2375

The Shepherds
(*design for a Christmas Card*)
d 1950
Wood engraving on paper
18.5 x 13 (paper 23.5 x 18.7)
Presented by Mrs R. Sekalska 1981
GMA 2355

*The Two Artists: Book-Plate for Winifred and
Alison Mackenzie*
1950
Wood engraving on paper
7.1 x 5.1 (paper 14.1 x 10)
Presented by Mrs R. Sekalska 1981
GMA 2376

*The Monogram: Book-Plate for Margaret
Kidston*
d 1950
Wood engraving on paper
6 x 6.5 (paper 11 x 10)
Presented by Mrs R. Sekalska 1981
GMA 2377

The Open Book: Book-Plate for Robert Dobbie
1950
Wood engraving on paper
7 x 4.5 (paper 12 x 9)
Presented by Mrs R. Sekalska 1981
GMA 2378

Marriage of St Francis
(*theatre programme design; produced for
St Michael's Church, Camden Town*)
d 1950
Wood engraving on paper
15.5 x 11.5 (paper 19.5 x 17.5)
Presented by Mrs R. Sekalska 1981
GMA 2391

'1066 and All That'
c 1950–51
Wood engraving on paper with alterations
in white ink (trial proof for GMA 2393)
18 x 13 (paper 22.5 x 17)
Presented by Mrs R. Sekalska 1981
GMA 2393 A

'1066 and All That'
c 1950–51
Wood engraving on paper (trial proof for GMA
2393)
18 x 13 (paper 22.5 x 18.5)
Presented by Mrs R. Sekalska 1981
GMA 2393 B

'1066 and All That'
(*theatre programme design*)
c 1950–51
Wood engraving on paper
18 x 13 (paper 25 x 17)
Presented by Mrs R. Sekalska 1981
GMA 2393

Harbour and Cathedral, St Andrews
(*cover illustration for 'St Andrews: its Character
and Tradition'*)
1951
Wood engraving on paper
6.3 x 7.5 (paper 11 x 11)
Presented by Mrs R. Sekalska 1981
GMA 2340

Lintel, No. 112 South Street, St Andrews
(*for 'St Andrews: its Character and Tradition'*)
1951
Wood engraving on paper
4.3 x 5.8 (paper 8 x 9.5)
Presented by Mrs R. Sekalska 1981
GMA 2341

Pediment, No. 74 South Street, St Andrews
(*for 'St Andrews: its Character and Tradition'*)
1951
Wood engraving on paper
5.7 x 7 (paper 9 x 9.6)
Presented by Mrs R. Sekalska 1981
GMA 2342

Students' Torchlight Procession
(for 'St Andrews: its Character and Tradition')
1951
Wood engraving on paper
9 x 6.3 (paper 12 x 9.5)
Presented by Mrs R. Sekalska 1981
GMA 2343

Lammas Market
(for 'St Andrews: its Character and Tradition')
1951
Wood engraving on paper
8.8 x 6.3 (paper 13.3 x 9.5)
Presented by Mrs R. Sekalska 1981
GMA 2344

Georgian Portico, St Andrews
1951
Wood engraving on paper
7.2 x 4.6 (paper 9.7 x 8.4)
Presented by Mrs R. Sekalska 1981
GMA 2345

The Cathedral in Winter
1951
Wood engraving on paper
6.3 x 10 (paper 15 x 19.2)
Presented by Mrs R. Sekalska 1981
GMA 2346

Wood Carving in St Andrews Town Hall:
the Crucified St Andrew and a Boar
1951
Wood engraving on card
6.1 x 5 (card 9.3 x 7.5)
Presented by Mrs R. Sekalska 1981
GMA 2348

'I Saw Three Ships'
(design for a Christmas Card)
1951
Wood engraving on paper
10.6 x 15.7 (paper 18.8 x 24)
Presented by Mrs R. Sekalska 1981
GMA 2356

St Monance
(design for a Christmas Card)
1951
Wood engraving on paper
14.1 x 19.4 (paper 21.3 x 26.6)
Presented by Mrs R. Sekalska 1981
GMA 2357

Christmas Card for New Park School,
St Andrews
1951
Wood engraving on card
10.7 x 7 (card 13 x 20.2)
Presented by Mrs R. Sekalska 1981
GMA 2358

An Angel
(design for a Christmas Card)
1951
Wood engraving on paper
15.6 x 10.7 (paper 18.7 x 15.5)
Presented by Mrs R. Sekalska 1981
GMA 2359

The Guitar: Book-Plate for Victoria Kingsley
1951
Wood engraving on paper
6.5 x 4 (paper 13 x 9)
Presented by Mrs R. Sekalska 1981
GMA 2379 A

The Guitar: Book-Plate for Victoria Kingsley
1951
Wood engraving on paper (intermediary proof)
7.8 x 5.1 (paper 12.2 x 7.3)
Presented by Mrs R. Sekalska 1981
GMA 2379 B

Adam and Eve: Book-Plate for Norman Gash
1951
Wood engraving on paper
9.5 x 4.5 (paper 14 x 10)
Presented by Mrs R. Sekalska 1981
GMA 2380

Tree of Knowledge: Book-Plate for Norman Gash
1951
Wood engraving on paper
8.5 x 4 (paper 12.5 x 8.5)
Presented by Mrs R. Sekalska 1981
GMA 2381

St Andrews from the Sea: Book-Plate for Three
Students
1951
Wood engraving on paper
3.5 x 8 (paper 8 x 13)
Presented by Mrs R. Sekalska 1981
GMA 2382

R. and J.: Book-Plate for Roberta and Jozef
Sekalski
1951
Wood engraving on paper
9.7 x 5 (paper 17.4 x 10.5)
Presented by Mrs R. Sekalska 1981
GMA 2383

The King Comes into his Own
(theatre programme design)
d 1951
Wood engraving on paper (7/15)
15.5 x 11 (paper 22.5 x 18)
Presented by Mrs R. Sekalska 1981
GMA 2392

Star (first version)
1952
Wood engraving on paper
17.6 x 12.4 (paper 19.1 x 13.2)
Presented by Mrs R. Sekalska 1981
GMA 2360 A

Star (second version)
1952
Wood engraving on paper
17.6 x 11.8 (paper 20.4 x 14.5)
Presented by Mrs R. Sekalska 1981
GMA 2360 B

Book-Plate for Thomas Lindsay
1952
Wood engraving on paper
5.5 x 4.2 (paper 8.7 x 7.3)
Presented by Mrs R. Sekalska 1981
GMA 2388

The Fourth Day of Christmas
1953
Wood engraving on card
15.1 x 11.2 (card 19.3 x 13.1)
Presented by Mrs R. Sekalska 1981
GMA 2361

Bees and Thistles: Book-Plate for Rev. Wilfred
Hulbert
1953
Wood engraving on paper
5.7 x 5.7 (paper 9.4 x 7.4)
Presented by Mrs R. Sekalska 1981
GMA 2385

The Byre Theatre
(theatre programme design)
1953
Wood engraving on paper
14.5 x 10.7 (paper 26.5 x 18.5)
Presented by Mrs R. Sekalska 1981
GMA 2394

Figure under a Tree
1953
Wood engraving (green ink) on paper
4.2 x 3.7 (paper 8.5 x 7)
Presented by Mrs R. Sekalska 1981
GMA 2409

Diamond Shape: Book-Plate for Anne Dow
c 1953–56
Wood engraving on paper
4.5 x 3.1 (paper 6.5 x 4.7)
Presented by Mrs R. Sekalska 1981
GMA 2384

The Towers of St Andrews
(design for a Christmas Card)
1955 or 1960
Wood engraving on card
14 x 9 (card 20.2 x 12.5)
Presented by Mrs R. Sekalska 1981
GMA 2362

E. M. 1956: Book-Plate for Edward Morenko
1956
Wood engraving on paper
4 x 5.6 (paper 7.5 x 8.4)
Presented by Mrs R. Sekalska 1981
GMA 2386

E. M. 1956: Book-Plate for Edward Morenko
(design with lettering only)
d 1956
Wood engraving on paper
2.7 x 3.8 (paper 6.2 x 6.7)
Presented by Mrs R. Sekalska 1981
GMA 2387

St Leonard's and St Katherine's Schools Appeal
1958
Wood engraving on paper
18 x 14 (paper 26.5 x 24)
Presented by Mrs R. Sekalska 1981
GMA 2397

Christmas and New Year Card
1961
Wood engraving on paper in two halves
Each half-image 17.5 x 10.5
Presented by Mrs R. Sekalska 1981
GMA 2363 A

Christmas and New Year Card
1961
Wood engraving on card
17.5 x 21 (image and card size)
Presented by Mrs R. Sekalska 1981
GMA 2363 B

The Byre Theatre
(theatre programme design)
c 1962
Wood engraving on paper
17 x 10.5 (paper 24 x 14.5)
Presented by Mrs R. Sekalska 1981
GMA 2395

Studio Still Life
1963
Colour linocut on paper (trial proof)
30.4 x 48.5 (paper 47.5 x 58.2)
Presented by Mrs R. Sekalska 1981
GMA 2415

Papers on a Table
d 1963
Colour linocut on paper (8/12)
25.5 x 32 (paper 38 x 42.5)
Presented by Mrs R. Sekalska 1981
GMA 2416

The Quarry
1963
Colour linocut on paper
Presented by Mrs R. Sekalska 1981
GMA 2418

Flying Shapes
d 1964
Colour linocut on paper (6/12)
36.1 x 48.3 (paper 47.7 x 57.7)
Presented by Mrs R. Sekalska 1981
GMA 2417 A

Flying Shapes
d 1964
Colour linocut on paper (10/12)
36.2 x 48.4 (paper 47.5 x 61)
Presented by Mrs R. Sekalska 1981
GMA 2417 B

Flying Shapes
1964
Colour linocut on paper
36.2 x 48.4 (paper 50 x 62)
Presented by Mrs R. Sekalska 1981
GMA 2417 C

Flying Shapes
1964
Colour linocut on paper (12/12)
36.2 x 48.4 (paper 49 x 59.5)
Presented by Mrs R. Sekalska 1981
GMA 2417 D

Beech Hotel, Leven (Dinner Dance)
1965
Wood engraving on paper
6.6 x 8.6 (paper 10 x 10.5)
Presented by Mrs R. Sekalska 1981
GMA 2400

Studio Still Life
Wood engraving on paper
12.5 x 7 (paper 19 x 10)
Presented by Mrs R. Sekalska 1981
GMA 2336

Gregory Place, St Andrews
Wood engraving on paper
10 x 7.2 (paper 22.5 x 16.8)
Presented by Mrs R. Sekalska 1981
GMA 2347

Celtic Stone Carving in St Andrews Cathedral Museum
Wood engraving on paper
9.8 x 4 (paper 12.5 x 9.5)
Presented by Mrs R. Sekalska 1981
GMA 2349

Polish Church and Pine Cones
(design for a Christmas Card)
Wood engraving on paper
12.5 x 10 (paper 14 x 14)
Presented by Mrs R. Sekalska 1981
GMA 2364

View of a Square in Cracow
(*design for a Christmas Card*)
Wood engraving on paper
6.2 x 10 (paper 10.5 x 12.5)
Presented by Mrs R. Sekalska 1981
GMA 2365

Mermaid and Merman in St Andrews Harbour
Wood engraving on paper
10 x 10 (paper 15.5 x 13)
Presented by Mrs R. Sekalska 1981
GMA 2366

St Andrews Harbour Week Card
Wood engraving on card
7 x 8 (card 8 x 12.5)
Presented by Mrs R. Sekalska 1981
GMA 2367

Letter Heading for A. Ayton Young, St Andrews
Wood engraving on paper
3.6 x 3.3 (paper 7.7 x 7.6)
Presented by Mrs R. Sekalska 1981
GMA 2373

Letter Heading: 17 Holly Hill, Hampstead
Wood engraving on paper
3.6 x 4.9 (paper 8 x 10.4)
Presented by Mrs R. Sekalska 1981
GMA 2389

Letter Heading: 13 Hopetoun Grange, Bucksburn
Wood engraving (black ink) on card (trial proof)
6 x 6 (card 12.5 x 8.5)
Presented by Mrs R. Sekalska 1981
GMA 2390 A

Letter Heading: 13 Hopetoun Grange, Bucksburn
Wood engraving (red ink) on card
6 x 6 (card 12.5 x 8.5)
Presented by Mrs R. Sekalska 1981
GMA 2390 B

Dame Alice Owen's Girls' School: Prize Certificate
Wood engraving on paper
16 x 10.5 (paper 23 x 15.5)
Presented by Mrs R. Sekalska 1981
GMA 2396

Pitmilly House Hotel Menu
Wood engraving on paper
10.5 x 8 (paper 11.5 x 10)
Presented by Mrs R. Sekalska 1981
GMA 2398

Pitmilly House Hotel: 'Dine and Wine by Candlelight'
Wood engraving on paper (verso of Christmas card)
5 x 15 (paper 9.9 x 20.3)
Presented by Mrs R. Sekalska 1981
GMA 2399

Civil Defence Corps Insignia (Fife)
Wood engraving on paper
6.6 x 5 (paper 11.5 x 8)
Presented by Mrs R. Sekalska 1981
GMA 2401

St Andrews Boating Club
Wood engraving on card
4.5 x 14 (card 5.5 x 16.5)
Presented by Mrs R. Sekalska 1981
GMA 2402

Vignette: House with Lake
Wood engraving on paper
2.1 x 3.5 (paper 3.9 x 6)
Presented by Mrs R. Sekalska 1981
GMA 2403

Flowerways
Wood engraving on paper
8.5 x 6.5 (paper 12.5 x 9.5)
Presented by Mrs R. Sekalska 1981
GMA 2404

Still Life: Flowers in a Vase
Wood engraving (red ink) on paper
6.2 x 5 (paper 11.5 x 8.5)
Presented by Mrs R. Sekalska 1981
GMA 2405

Still Life: Flowers in a Vase (II)
Wood engraving (brown ink) on paper
3 x 3 (paper 7 x 7)
Presented by Mrs R. Sekalska 1981
GMA 2406

Equestrian Monument
Wood engraving on paper
3.5 x 4 (paper 7 x 7)
Presented by Mrs R. Sekalska 1981
GMA 2407

Curling
Wood engraving on paper
5.1 x 7.7 (paper 7.5 x 9.5)
Presented by Mrs R. Sekalska 1981
GMA 2408 A

Curling
Wood engraving on paper
5.1 x 7.7 (paper 6 x 9.4)
Presented by Mrs R. Sekalska 1981
GMA 2408 B

Stairs with Curtain and Picture
Wood engraving on paper
4 x 3.3 (paper 8.6 x 8)
Presented by Mrs R. Sekalska 1981
GMA 2410

Scarecrow
Wood engraving on paper
9.4 x 7 (paper 14.8 x 10.5)
Presented by Mrs R. Sekalska 1981
GMA 2412

Conch Shell with Figures
Wood engraving on paper (trial proof)
11.5 x 15.2 (paper 14.5 x 20)
Presented by Mrs R. Sekalska 1981
GMA 2413

St Andrews Harbour Week Poster
Linocut (blue ink) on paper
58.9 x 45.5 (paper 84.6 x 61.7)
Presented by Mrs R. Sekalska 1981
GMA 2414 A

St Andrews Harbour Week Poster
Linocut (black ink) on paper
58.9 x 45.5 (paper 84.6 x 61.7)
Presented by Mrs R. Sekalska 1981
GMA 2414 B

Untitled
Etching on paper
12.2 x 22.5 (paper 28 x 38)
Presented by Mrs R. Sekalska 1981
GMA 2419

Terry Setch

1936–

Beach Car Wreck
(from 'The London Suite')
1982
Screenprint on paper (11/75)
60.8 x 83.7 (image and paper size)
Purchased 1983
GMA 2755

Charles Haslewood Shannon

1863–1937

Caresses
1894
Lithograph (sanguine ink) on paper
21.3 x 15.8 (paper 36.4 x 28)
Purchased 1949
GMA 556

The Little Venus
1895
Lithograph on paper
15.7 x 11.5 (paper 24 x 14.4)
Presented by Mr and Mrs Alexander Maitland
1953
GMA 557

Alphonse Legros
d 1896
Lithograph on paper
32 x 27.4 (paper 33.5 x 28.3)
Bequeathed by Sir David Young Cameron 1945
GMA 1023

The Rebirth of the Arts
(from the series 'The Great War: Britain's Efforts
and Ideals')
d 1917 (published 1918)
Colour lithograph on paper
74.4 x 49 (paper 80.5 x 51)
Presented by the Ministry of Information 1919
GMA 555

Babe Shapiro

1937–

*Swallow the Call Note**
d 1973
Acrylic on canvas
244.5 x 137.2
Purchased 1975
GMA 1522

David Sharpe

1944–

Nude with Still Life
d 1980
Oil on canvas
168 x 183.5
Purchased 1980
GMA 2221

James Shaw

The Clyde
Colour etching and aquatint on paper
30.4 x 40.3 (paper 36.5 x 49.2)
Purchased 1982
GMA 2566

Claude Shepperson

1867–1921

Tending the Wounded: Advanced Dressing Station in France
(from the series 'The Great War: Britain's Efforts and Ideals')
Published 1918
Lithograph on paper
34.7 x 46 (paper 38 x 50.7)
Presented by the Ministry of Information 1919
GMA 558 A

Tending the Wounded: Casualty Clearing Station in France
(from the series 'The Great War: Britain's Efforts and Ideals')
Published 1918
Lithograph on paper
35.7 x 45.6 (paper 39.2 x 50.7)
Presented by the Ministry of Information 1919
GMA 558 B

Tending the Wounded: On Board a Hospital Transport
(from the series 'The Great War: Britain's Efforts and Ideals')
Published 1918
Lithograph on paper
35.9 x 46.7 (paper 40 x 50.7)
Presented by the Ministry of Information 1919
GMA 558 C

Tending the Wounded: Detraining in England
(from the series 'The Great War: Britain's Efforts and Ideals')
Published 1918
Lithograph on paper
34.6 x 46 (paper 38.1 x 50.5)
Presented by the Ministry of Information 1919
GMA 558 D

Tending the Wounded: In Hospital in England
(from the series 'The Great War: Britain's Efforts and Ideals')
Published 1918
Lithograph on paper
34.5 x 46 (paper 39.2 x 50.7)
Presented by the Ministry of Information 1919
GMA 558 E

Tending the Wounded: Convalescence in England
(from the series 'The Great War: Britain's Efforts and Ideals')
Published 1918
Lithograph on paper
35.7 x 46 (paper 39.3 x 50.7)
Presented by the Ministry of Information 1919
GMA 558 F

Walter Richard Sickert

1860–1942

Seascape
c 1885–87
Oil on wood
23.7 x 14.3
Bequeathed by Dr Dorothea Walpole and Mr
R. H. Walpole 1963
GMA 864

*Portrait of Israel Zangwill**
c 1897–98
Oil on canvas laid on board
61 x 50.8
Purchased 1959
GMA 740

Dieppe
c 1900
Oil on canvas
33 x 41
Bequeathed by Dr R. A. Lillie 1977
GMA 1969

*Corner of St Mark's, Venice**
c 1901
Oil on canvas
45.7 x 38.1
Purchased 1965
GMA 910

*La Rue Pecquet, Dieppe**
c 1906–08
Oil on canvas
32.4 x 24.5
Bequeathed by Dr Dorothea Walpole and Mr
R. H. Walpole 1963
GMA 863

Envermeu
c 1924
Oil on canvas
33 x 41.1
Bequeathed by Dr R. A. Lillie 1977
GMA 1970

*The Rural Dean**
c 1932
Oil on canvas
61.1 x 41.8
Bequeathed by Dr R. A. Lillie 1977
GMA 1972

*High-Steppers**
c 1938
Oil on canvas
132 x 122.5
Purchased 1979
GMA 2099

Noctes Ambrosianae
1906
Etching and aquatint on brown paper (second
state, 37/50)
22.1 x 25.8 (paper 32 x 45.82)
Bequeathed by Mr Kenneth Sanderson 1943
GMA 562

Cicely Hey
c 1922–24
Etching and drypoint on paper
19 x 16.2 (paper 27.2 x 21)
Bequeathed by Dr R. A. Lillie 1977
GMA 1971

Mario Sironi

1885–1961

*Mountain Landscape**
c 1936
Oil (and tempera ?) with grit on paper laid on
board
35.9 x 66
Purchased 1964
GMA 884

Moltiplicazione (8) [Multiplication (8)]
c 1938
Watercolour on paper
52 x 53.3
Purchased 1964
GMA 885

Aaron Siskind

1903–91

Gloucester 28
d 1944
Black and white photograph (gelatin silver print)
32.4 x 24 (paper 35.5 x 27.9)
Purchased 1980
GMA 2139

New York 2
d 1951
Black and white photograph (gelatin silver print)
30.4 x 24 (paper 35.4 x 27.8)
Purchased 1980
GMA 2140

Seaweed 4
d 1952
Black and white photograph (gelatin silver print)
13.8 x 22.5 (paper 20.4 x 25.1)
Purchased 1980
GMA 2138

John Skeaping

1901–80

*Nude Study**
d 1926
Chalk and pencil on brown paper
37.6 x 27.1
Presented by the National Art Collections Fund
from the Sir Edward Marsh Collection 1953
GMA 731

Alan Smith

1941–

Untitled
(*from the 'Roots' series*)
1975 / 1978
Wood, steel and beeswax
46 x 71.5 x 25.7
Purchased 1978
GMA 2020

Ian McKenzie Smith

1935–

*Summer (Canna)**
1963
Oil on canvas
67 x 82.3
Purchased 1963
GMA 868

Bu' Series III
d 1980
Etching and chine collé on paper (A.P.)
53 x 35 (paper 76.1 x 56.3)
Purchased 1981
GMA 2320

Jack Smith

1928–

*The Natural and the Geometric (Summer) II**
d 1970
Oil on canvas
183 x 183
Purchased 1979
GMA 2101

Matthew Smith

1879–1959

*Femme de cirque [Circus Woman]**
d 1925
Oil on canvas
116.8 x 81.3
Purchased 1960
GMA 758

*Portrait of Augustus John**
1944
Oil on canvas
102.3 x 77
Purchased 1981
GMA 2324

Percy Smith

1882–1948

The Dance of Death, 1914–18
1) *Death Forbids*
2) *Death Marches*
3) *Death Awed*
4) *Death Refuses*
5) *Death Waits*
6) *Death Ponders*
7) *Death Intoxicated*
d 1919
Portfolio of seven etchings with drypoint on
paper (32/100)
Each 20 x 25 (paper 27.2 x 33.2)
Purchased 1949
GMA 563

Richard Smith

1931–

*Ceiling III**
1959
Oil on canvas
183 x 182.3
Purchased 1984
GMA 2829

Robert N. Snodgrass

The Engravers
1929
Etching and drypoint on paper
16.9 x 21.8 (paper 25.3 x 31.7)
Bequeathed by Mr Kenneth Sanderson 1943
GMA 564

Pierre Soulages

1919–

*Peinture, 3 novembre 1958 [Painting, 3
November 1958]**
1958
Oil on canvas
161 x 113.3
Purchased 1984
GMA 2828

Lithographie no. 6 [Lithograph No. 6]
1957
Colour lithograph on paper (A.P.)
56.2 x 44.3 (paper 65.5 x 50.5)
Purchased 1989
GMA 3466

Chaïm Soutine

1893–1943

*Les Gorges du Loup**
c 1921–23
Oil on canvas
62.8 x 86.3
Purchased 1981
GMA 2312

Ruskin Spear

1911–90

Billiards Saloon
(*from the J. Lyons series 'Lithographs by
Contemporary Artists, vol. I'*)
Published 1947
Colour lithograph on paper (after oil)
74.5 x 99 (paper size)
Presented by J. Lyons & Co. Ltd 1948
GMA 1212

Hilda Spencer

1889–1950

*Stanley Spencer**
d 1931
Pencil on paper
50.8 x 35.3
Purchased 1978
GMA 2068

Stanley Spencer

1891–1959

*Hilda Spencer**
1931
Pencil on paper
50.8 x 35.2
Purchased 1978
GMA 2067

*Fire Alight**
1936
Oil on canvas
76.2 x 50.8
Bequeathed by Miss Elizabeth Watt 1989
GMA 3515

*Christ Delivered to the People**
1950
Oil on canvas
68.8 x 149
Purchased 1983
GMA 2759

Klaus Staeck

1938-

Collection of 33 Satirical Postcards
1969–80
Postcards
Each 14.9 x 10.5 or 10.5 x 14.9
Purchased 1980
GMA 2233

Collection of 18 Satirical Posters
1971–80
Posters
Each 84 x 59 or 59 x 84
Purchased 1980
GMA 2232

Nicolas de Staël

1914–55

*L'Eclair [Flash of Lightning]**
d 1946
Oil on canvas
115.5 x 89
Purchased 1983
GMA 2795

*Le Bateau [The Boat]**
1954
Oil on canvas
46.3 x 61
Purchased 1962
GMA 817

Philip Wilson Steer

1860–1942

Hayling Island
c 1894
Oil on wood
21.1 x 27
Presented by Miss Dorothea Hamilton 1970
GMA 1125

Knaresborough, Yorkshire
c 1897–1900
Pencil and wash on paper
28 x 38.7
Presented by Miss Dorothea Hamilton 1970
GMA 1155

Ludlow
d 1899
Pencil, pen and ink and wash on paper
27.9 x 38.2
Presented by Miss Dorothea Hamilton 1970
GMA 1159

The Blue Dress*
c 1900
Oil on canvas
50.8 x 40.6
Presented by Miss Dorothea Hamilton 1970
GMA 1122

Stroud
d 1902
Pencil on paper
28 x 37.8
Presented by Miss Dorothea Hamilton 1970
GMA 1152

Flying Kites
(Sketch for Bourton House Decorations)
c 1902–03
Oil on wood
25 x 27
Presented by Mr J. A. F. H. Hamilton 1967
GMA 1071

Two Studies of a Woman
c 1903
Pencil and wash on paper
25.4 x 38
Presented by Miss Dorothea Hamilton 1970
GMA 1139

Richmond, Yorkshire
c 1903
Watercolour and black chalk on paper
28.5 x 38
Presented by Miss Dorothea Hamilton 1970
GMA 1153

Richmond, Yorkshire
1903
Watercolour and pencil on paper
24.8 x 36.8
Bequeathed by Dr R. A. Lillie 1977
GMA 1980

Richmond, Yorkshire
1903
Pencil over watercolour on paper
24.5 x 36.6
Bequeathed by Dr R. A. Lillie 1977
GMA 1981

Hawes
[verso: Fishing Boat or Sailing Coaster]
1904
Watercolour and pencil on paper [verso: pencil]
28 x 39.1
Presented by Miss Dorothea Hamilton 1970
GMA 1146

Hawes
[verso: Trees in a Landscape]
1904
Watercolour and black chalk on paper [verso:
pencil]
28 x 39.1
Presented by Miss Dorothea Hamilton 1970
GMA 1149

Two Studies of Chepstow Castle
[verso: Two Sketches of River Bends]
d 1905
Pencil on paper
39.2 x 28
Presented by Miss Dorothea Hamilton 1970
GMA 1150

Chepstow Castle
c 1905
Watercolour and black chalk on paper
24.8 x 37
Bequeathed by Dr R. A. Lillie 1977
GMA 1974

Montreuil-sur-Mer
1907
Watercolour and black chalk on paper
28 x 38
Presented by Miss Dorothea Hamilton 1970
GMA 1154

Montreuil-sur-Mer
1907
Watercolour, gouache and pencil on paper
28.3 x 38.2
Bequeathed by Dr R. A. Lillie 1977
GMA 1976

Landscape (The Horseshoe Bend of The Severn)
d 1909
Watercolour and pencil on paper
20.7 x 34.9
Bequeathed by Miss Anna G. Blair 1952
GMA 1017

Ironbridge, Shropshire
c 1910
Pencil on paper
28.3 x 40
Presented by Miss Dorothea Hamilton 1970
GMA 1151

*Three Girls Bathing, Thame**
c 1911
Oil on canvas
71.1 x 91.5
Presented by Miss Dorothea Hamilton 1970
GMA 1124

A Quiet Evening
d 1912
Watercolour on paper
24.4 x 34.9
Bequeathed by Sir James and Lady Caw 1951
GMA 1016

Porchester
d 1912
Watercolour and black chalk on paper
19.5 x 28.1
Presented by Miss Dorothea Hamilton 1970
GMA 1141

The Old Hulk
d 1913
Watercolour on paper
20.3 x 34.5
Bequeathed by Dr R. A. Lillie 1977
GMA 1979

Haresfoot
d 1915
Watercolour on paper
28.2 x 39.1
Presented by Miss Dorothea Hamilton 1970
GMA 1130

Chirk Castle
d 1916
Watercolour on paper
28 x 39.1
Presented by Miss Dorothea Hamilton 1970
GMA 1137

Rosyth
d 1917
Watercolour and pencil on paper
28.2 x 39.1
Presented by Miss Dorothea Hamilton 1970
GMA 1138

The Needles
d 1919
Watercolour and pencil on paper
26.6 x 38.6
Presented by Miss Dorothea Hamilton 1970
GMA 1157

Hythe, Southampton
1921
Watercolour and pencil on paper
24.2 x 33.1
Presented by Miss Dorothea Hamilton 1970
GMA 1147

Brill, Buckinghamshire
d 1923
Watercolour on paper
24.6 x 34.3
Presented by Mr A. E. Anderson 1931
GMA 1019

Long Crendon
d 1924
Oil on canvas
50.8 x 61.2
Presented by Miss Dorothea Hamilton 1970
GMA 1123

Bridgenorth
d 1925
Watercolour on paper
23.1 x 31.1
Presented by Miss Dorothea Hamilton 1970
GMA 1135

Jetty and Sailing Ship
d 1926
Watercolour on paper
22.5 x 33.2
Presented by Miss Dorothea Hamilton 1970
GMA 1126

Shoreham (A Creek with a Grounded Sailing Boat)
d 1926
Watercolour on paper
18.8 x 26
Presented by Miss Dorothea Hamilton 1970
GMA 1133

Landscape
d 1928
Watercolour on paper
22.1 x 30.8
Presented by Mr A. E. Anderson 1931
GMA 1018

Framlingham Castle and Church
d 1928
Pen and ink and ink wash on paper
22.1 x 34.4
Presented by Miss Dorothea Hamilton 1970
GMA 1145

Framlingham Castle, Suffolk
d 1928
Watercolour on paper
23.8 x 33.5
Presented by Miss Dorothea Hamilton 1970
GMA 1156

Barges near Harwich
d 1929
Watercolour on paper
19.3 x 27.8
Bequeathed by Dr R. A. Lillie 1977
GMA 1973

Sailing Ships in a Harbour
c 1930
Watercolour on paper
23.9 x 34
Presented by Miss Dorothea Hamilton 1970
GMA 1131

The Harbour, Dover
d 1930
Watercolour on paper
24 x 31.2
Bequeathed by Dr R. A. Lillie 1977
GMA 1977

Off Dover
d 1930
Watercolour on paper
22.8 x 31.4
Bequeathed by Dr R. A. Lillie 1977
GMA 1978

The Sands, Whitstable
d 1931
Watercolour on paper
22.5 x 28.2
Bequeathed by Dr R. A. Lillie 1977
GMA 1982

Near Totland, Isle of Wight
d 1932
Watercolour on paper
18 x 28
Presented by Miss Dorothea Hamilton 1970
GMA 1134

Derelict Building, North Fleet
d 1932
Watercolour on paper
24.3 x 31.7
Presented by Miss Dorothea Hamilton 1970
GMA 1136

Greenhithe
d 1932
Watercolour on paper
24.2 x 34.2
Presented by Miss Dorothea Hamilton 1970
GMA 1142

Greenhithe
d 1932
Watercolour on paper
24.5 x 31.8
Presented by Miss Dorothea Hamilton 1970
GMA 1148

Fishermen's Cottages, Greenhithe
d 1932
Watercolour on paper
22.8 x 31
Bequeathed by Dr R. A. Lillie 1977
GMA 1975

A Sailing Boat
d 1933
Watercolour on paper
23 x 30.7
Presented by Miss Dorothea Hamilton 1970
GMA 1132

Near Maldon
d 1933
Watercolour on paper
22.7 x 31
Presented by Miss Dorothea Hamilton 1970
GMA 1144

Walmer
d 1934
Watercolour on paper
24.1 x 31.7
Presented by Miss Dorothea Hamilton 1970
GMA 1143

Bosham
c 1935–39
Watercolour and pencil on paper
24 x 33.9
Presented by Miss Dorothea Hamilton 1970
GMA 1127

A Woodland Scene
Pencil and brush and ink on paper
25 x 36.8
Presented by Miss Dorothea Hamilton 1970
GMA 1128

A Wooded Landscape with Pool or River
Watercolour and black chalk on paper
23.3 x 35.3
Presented by Miss Dorothea Hamilton 1970
GMA 1129

Study of a Girl in a Long White Dress
Watercolour and pencil on paper
37.7 x 26.8
Presented by Miss Dorothea Hamilton 1970
GMA 1140

Landscape with Trees
Watercolour on paper
21 x 27.5
Presented by Miss Dorothea Hamilton 1970
GMA 1158

Sunny Landscape
Watercolour on paper
13.3 x 30.6
Bequeathed by Dr R. A. Lillie 1977
GMA 1984

Fred Stiven

1929-

Small Box 11
d 1983
Wood construction (stained, painted and glazed)
29.4 x 15.6 x 8
Purchased 1984
GMA 2806

Alexander Stoddart

1959-

Heroic Bust; Henry Moore*
1990 (cast 1992)
Bronze
261 x 51 x 49
Purchased 1992
GMA 3669

See also WILD HAWTHORN PRESS

Reynolds Stone

1909–79

Girl on a Gate
Wood engraving on paper
10 x 8.3 (paper 17.5 x 13.7)
Purchased 1978
GMA 2039

Edmund Sullivan

1869–1933

The Reign of Justice
(from the series 'The Great War: Britain's Efforts
and Ideals')
d 1917 (published 1918)
Colour lithograph on paper
69.2 x 44.5 (paper 77.7 x 51)
Presented by the Ministry of Information 1919
GMA 3636

Carol Summers

1925-

Palm Tree
Woodcut on paper (50/50)
94 x 91.5
Purchased (Knapping Fund) 1967
GMA 1001

Graham Sutherland

1903–80

Western Hills*
1938 / 1941
Oil on canvas
55.5 x 90.5
Purchased 1967
GMA 1072

Landscape with Rocks (Wolf's Castle)*
d 1939
Gouache, ink and pencil on paper
50 x 68.3
Purchased 1964
GMA 894

Entrance to a Lane*
d 1939
Watercolour, ink and pencil on paper
13.5 x 21.6
Bequeathed by Mr H. J. Paterson 1988
GMA 3427

Association of Oaks*
d 1939–40
Gouache, watercolour and pencil on paper
68.6 x 48.6
Purchased 1980
GMA 2219

Thistles and Sun*
d 1945
Gouache and black and coloured crayon on paper
45 x 40.4
Presented by Mr and Mrs J. H. Macdonell 1960
GMA 763

Thorn Head*
d 1949
Oil on canvas
60.7 x 46
Purchased 1978
GMA 1711

Number Forty-Nine
1924
Etching on paper (12/60)
17.8 x 25 (paper 23 x 29.7)
Presented by Mr and Mrs J. H. Macdonell 1960
GMA 764

Pecken Wood
d 1925
Etching on paper
13.6 x 18.8 (paper 21.6 x 24.6)
Presented by Mr and Mrs J. H. Macdonell 1960
GMA 765

Village
d 1925
Etching on paper
17.6 x 22.5 (paper 22.4 x 27.8)
Presented by Mr and Mrs J. H. Macdonell 1960
GMA 766

Hatching II
1977
Colour etching and aquatint on paper (35/40)
40 x 31 (paper 66.9 x 48.7)
Purchased 1980
GMA 2225

Helen Sveinbjörnsson

Pedro
d 1913
Colour woodcut on paper
14.9 x 19.7 (paper 16.3 x 21.5)
Provenance unrecorded
GMA 566

Antoni Tàpies

1923-

*Croix sur gris [Cross on Grey]**
d 1959
Mixed media on canvas laid on board
60.8 x 74.3
Purchased 1963
GMA 858

*Gris violacé aux rides [Violet Grey with Wrinkles]**
d 1961
Mixed media on canvas
200 x 176
Purchased 1983
GMA 2760

John Taylor

1936-

Discovery
1986
Watercolour and gouache on paper
51.5 x 69.5
Purchased 1987
GMA 3027

Furrow
1980
Screenprint on paper (9/20)
56.5 x 44.7 (paper 72.6 x 57.4)
Purchased 1981
GMA 2318

Linda Taylor

1959-

Pine
1986–88
Sixteen watermarked sheets of paper, each in glazed lead frames; sixteen pine shelves; boxed set of 64 watermarked sheets of paper; three colour photographs
28.4 x 18.5 (paper size); 35.6 x 26.8 (frame size)
Purchased 1989
GMA 3457

*Drawing for Tap No. 2 of 'Unseen Currents'**
1988
Watercolour and pencil on paper
41.8 x 29.6
Purchased 1990
GMA 3558

*Drawing for Tap No. 3 of 'Unseen Currents'**
1988
Watercolour and pencil on paper
41.8 x 29.6
Purchased 1989
GMA 3462

Drawing for Tap No. 5 of 'Unseen Currents'
1988
Watercolour and pencil on paper
41.8 x 29.6
Purchased 1990
GMA 3576

Drawing for Tap No. 6 of 'Unseen Currents'
1988
Watercolour and pencil on paper
41.8 x 29.6
Purchased 1990
GMA 3559

Drawing for Tap No. 7 of 'Unseen Currents'
1988
Watercolour and pencil on paper
41.8 x 29.6
Purchased 1990
GMA 3577

Drawing for Tap No. 9 of 'Unseen Currents'
1988
Watercolour and pencil on paper
41.8 x 29.6
Purchased 1989
GMA 3581

Drawing for Tap No. 10 of 'Unseen Currents'
1988
Watercolour and pencil on paper
41.8 x 29.6
Purchased 1990
GMA 3560

Drawing for Tap No. 11 of 'Unseen Currents'
1988
Watercolour and pencil on paper
41.8 x 29.6
Purchased 1989
GMA 3582

Drawing for Tap No. 12 of 'Unseen Currents'
1988
Watercolour and pencil on paper
41.8 x 29.6
Purchased 1990
GMA 3578

Margaret Thomas

1916-

Postcards and Flowers
d 1949
Oil on canvas
51.3 x 51
Bequeathed by Dr R. A. Lillie 1977
GMA 1986

Cyclamen
d 1953
Oil on cheesecloth laid on hardboard
51.1 x 61.2
Bequeathed by Dr R. A. Lillie 1977
GMA 1985

Richard Thompson

1945-

*In the Midst of the Flood**
d 1980
Oil on canvas
151 x 244
Purchased 1980
GMA 2220

Leslie Thornton

1925-

*Figure in Coat**
1961
Bronze (unique)
89 x 34.5 x 30.5
Purchased 1963
GMA 859

Harry Thubron

1915–85

Untitled
(from 'The London Suite')
d 1982
Screenprint on paper (11/75)
37.2 x 39.2 (paper 83.5 x 61.2)
Purchased 1983
GMA 2756

Geoffrey Tibble

1909–52

*The Print Room**
d 1950
Oil on canvas
61.2 x 45.8
Presented anonymously in memory of Hugh
'Binkie' Beaumont 1984
GMA 2914

Joe Tilson
1928-

Nine Elements*
d 1963
Mixed media on wood relief
259 x 182.8
Purchased 1983
GMA 2761

Lufbery and Rickenbacker
d 1963
Screenprint on paper (A.P.)
69 x 49 (paper 91.3 x 58.4)
Purchased 1984
GMA 2893

21st
d 1964
Screenprint with collage on card (A.P.)
82.5 x 61 (card 101.2 x 76)
Purchased 1984
GMA 2894

Geometry ?
d 1965
Screenprint on paper (17/70)
55.1 x 54.8 (paper 68.8 x 99.2)
Purchased 1984
GMA 2895

Rainbow Grill
d 1965
Screenprint and mixed media on card (7/10)
61 x 61 (card 80 x 80)
Purchased 1984
GMA 2896

New Coloured Fire from the Vast Strange
Country
d 1968
Screenprint with collage on paper (A.P.)
100.5 x 60.2 (paper 101.6 x 68.7)
Purchased 1984
GMA 2897

Is this Che Guevara?
1969
Screenprint with collage, paper clips and metal
pins on paper
101.5 x 68.7 (paper size with extending image
size)
Purchased 1984
GMA 2898

Transparency Clip-o-matic Lips 2
d 1969
Screenprint on paper (A.P.)
88 x 65.7 (paper 92.2 x 68.2)
Purchased 1984
GMA 2899

Jan Palach
d 1970
Screenprint with collage and paper clips on paper
(A.P.)
100.5 x 60.4 (paper 102.2 x 70.2)
Purchased 1984
GMA 2900

Snow White and the Black Dwarf
d 1970
Etching on paper (A.P.)
78.1 x 50.2 (paper 91 x 64)
Purchased 1984
GMA 2901

Sun Mantra
d 1979
Etching and aquatint on paper, with string, metal
clip and hand painted stencil plate (2/75)
74.5 x 83.6 (paper 87 x 96.8)
Purchased 1980
GMA 2159

Two Untitled Etchings (for 'Circhi e Cene'
['Circuses and Suppers'] by Andrea Zanzotto)
Published 1979
Book containing two colour etchings
38.7 x 25.5 (book size)
Purchased 1982
GMA 2478

Jean Tinguely

1925–91

La Jalousie II [Blind Jealousy II]*
1961
Painted bead curtain, metal rod and electric motor
217.5 x 91.5 x 35.5
Purchased 1984
GMA 2832

Murray Macpherson Tod

1909–74

The Pond
1933
Etching on paper
17.1 x 22.8 (paper 21.4 x 27.8)
Purchased 1949
GMA 567

Arthur R. Middleton Todd

1891–1966

Old Soldier
Wood engraving on paper
12.2 x 7.9 (paper 16.8 x 12.1)
Provenance unrecorded
GMA 568

Feliks Topolski

1907–89

Edinburgh
c 1942–43
Chalk and watercolour on paper
76.4 x 57.1
Presented by Count Jan Tarnowski 1960
GMA 767

Julian Trevelyan

1910–88

During the Night...
1935 (printed 1971)
Etching on paper (A.P.)
10.5 x 14.9 (paper 28.2 x 39.6)
Purchased 1978
GMA 2044

Dream Scaffold
1936 (printed 1971)
Etching with gouache on paper (9/20)
20.3 x 35 (paper 28.5 x 39.7)
Purchased 1984
GMA 2903

Little Fool...
1937 (printed 1971)
Etching with gouache on paper (10/20)
25 x 20.1 (paper 39.6 x 28.5)
Purchased 1984
GMA 2902

Quarries
c 1959
Colour etching with aquatint on paper (11/50)
38 x 49.7 (paper 55.4 x 73)
Purchased 1960
GMA 754

Ernest Trova

1927-

Aluminium Shadow (FM 135)*
d 1969
Aluminium
3.2 x 63.5 x 23.5
Presented by Mr Alan Roger 1977
GMA 1692

William Tucker

1935-

D (Brown)
d 1969
Screenprint on two pieces of card laid on card
(47/75)
76 x 97.5 (card size)
Purchased 1972
GMA 1271

John Tunnard

1900–71

Untitled*
d 1939
Gouache, watercolour, pencil and coloured crayon
on paper
38.3 x 56
Bequeathed by Miss Elizabeth Watt 1989
GMA 3517

Composition*
d 1942
Gouache, watercolour and black chalk on paper
37.5 x 56
Bequeathed by Miss Elizabeth Watt 1989
GMA 3518

Sanctuary*
d 1943
Gouache, watercolour and black chalk on paper
38.1 x 55.7
Bequeathed by Miss Elizabeth Watt 1989
GMA 3519

Ascent*
1944
Oil over gesso on board
53.4 x 43.2
Bequeathed by Miss Elizabeth Watt 1989
GMA 3520

Attack*
d 1957
Gouache and black chalk on paper laid on board
27.9 x 37.8
Bequeathed by Miss Elizabeth Watt 1989
GMA 3521

Abacus for Astronauts*
d 1964
Gouache and coloured crayon on paper laid
on board
38 x 56
Bequeathed by Miss Elizabeth Watt 1989
GMA 3516

William Turnbull

1922-

Untitled*
d 1950
Oil and ink on paper
73.6 x 54.5
Purchased 1989
GMA 3452

Untitled*
d 1953
Monotype on paper
46.2 x 35.4
Purchased 1992
GMA 3647

Untitled*
1954
Monotype on newspaper
19 x 51.5
Purchased 1992
GMA 3646

15–1959 (Red Saturation)*
d 1959
Oil on canvas
178 x 178
Purchased 1984
GMA 2830

Night*
1962–63
Bronze and rosewood
161.4 x 124.5 x 43
Purchased 1984
GMA 2831

Gate II*
1962–63
Bronze, rosewood and stone
209 x 187 x 45
Purchased 1986
GMA 3601

*Gate**
1972
Stainless steel
217.2 x 292 x 91.4
Purchased 1974
GMA 1310

Fragments
d 1971
Portfolio of four etchings and title page
Plate 1 25.3 x 20; plates 2, 3 and 4 35 x 27.2
(paper 61 x 47.4)
Purchased 1980
GMA 2158

Helen Monro Turner

1901–77

*Study for Glass Engraving: Presidential Badge of
the Institution of Agricultural Engineers*
d 1961
White gouache on blue card
20.2 x 12.6
Purchased 1981
GMA 2297 A

*Study for Glass Engraving: Presidential Badge of
the Institution of Agricultural Engineers*
d 1961
White gouache on blue card
20.4 x 12.7
Purchased 1981
GMA 2297 B

*Four Designs for Engraved Glass Souvenir
Tumblers*
c 1961
White gouache on brown card
25.6 x 19.5
Purchased 1981
GMA 2298

*Design for a Diamond-point Engraved Glass
Goblet for Mrs Pheysey*
d 1961
White gouache on black card
26.6 x 30.3
Purchased 1981
GMA 2299

Smelthouses
c 1941
Wood engraving on paper
14.8 x 22.5 (paper 18.3 x 24.6)
Purchased 1981
GMA 2300

The Pool
c 1941
Linocut on paper (1/12)
15.7 x 22.9 (paper 22.4 x 34.2)
Purchased 1981
GMA 2302

*Bald Mingie
(for 'The Path by the Water' by A. R. B.
Haldane)*
1943
Wood engraving on paper
15.3 x 10.2 (paper 26.3 x 18.4)
Purchased 1981
GMA 2301

Jerry Uelsman

1934-

Untitled
d 1970
Black and white photograph (gelatin silver print)
34 x 25
Presented by the artist 1984
GMA 2926

Béla Uitz

1887–1972

Mountain Landscape
c 1920
Drypoint and aquatint on paper
42.6 x 31.9 (paper 67.5 x 49)
Purchased 1982
GMA 2721

Self-Portrait
d 1920
Drypoint and aquatint on paper
30.5 x 21.5 (paper 68 x 49)
Purchased 1982
GMA 2722

Woman and Man
1920
Drypoint on paper
42.2 x 32.5
Purchased 1982
GMA 2723

Woman with Hands Crossed and Eyes Closed
d 1920
Drypoint and aquatint on paper
42.3 x 32.4 (paper 60 x 43.5)
Purchased 1982
GMA 2724

Woman in a Head Shawl
d 1920
Drypoint and aquatint on paper
18 x 13.7 (paper 33 x 24.4)
Purchased 1982
GMA 2725

Woman in a Head Shawl
c 1920
Drypoint and aquatint on paper
30.4 x 21.5 (paper 49 x 34)
Purchased 1982
GMA 2726

Woman Holding up a Vase of Flowers
d 1920
Drypoint and aquatint on paper
42.5 x 32 (paper 60 x 43.5)
Purchased 1982
GMA 2727

Woman in Profile Contemplating Flowers
c 1920
Drypoint and aquatint on paper
40.8 x 32.5 (paper 67.2 x 49)
Purchased 1982
GMA 2728

Four Female Heads with a Flower
c 1920
Drypoint and aquatint on paper
42.5 x 33 (paper 67.7 x 49.1)
Purchased 1982
GMA 2729

Woman in Profile Holding Flowers
c 1920
Drypoint and aquatint on paper
40.6 x 32.5 (paper 67.7 x 49)
Purchased 1982
GMA 2730

*Five Women**
1920
Drypoint and aquatint on paper
32.5 x 43.2 (paper 49 x 67.8)
Purchased 1982
GMA 2731

Four Women
c 1920
Drypoint and aquatint on paper
43 x 33 (paper 67.8 x 49.1)
Purchased 1982
GMA 2732

Two Heads
c 1920
Drypoint and aquatint on paper
25 x 21 (paper 42 x 30.4)
Purchased 1982
GMA 2733

Woman Holding Branches
c 1920
Drypoint and aquatint on paper
42.5 x 32.1 (paper 60.5 x 43)
Purchased 1982
GMA 2734

Head of a Girl
c 1920
Drypoint and aquatint on paper
18 x 14 (paper 42 x 30.5)
Purchased 1982
GMA 2735

Head of a Boy
c 1920
Drypoint and aquatint on paper
17.5 x 14 (paper 42 x 30.5)
Purchased 1982
GMA 2736

Crouching Woman in a Shawl
1920
Drypoint and aquatint on paper
41.2 x 32.5 (paper 68 x 49)
Purchased 1982
GMA 2737

Female Nude Seated on the Ground
c 1920
Drypoint and aquatint on paper
37 x 33 (paper 67.9 x 49)
Purchased 1982
GMA 2738

Seated Figure with Drapery
c 1920
Drypoint and aquatint on paper
42.5 x 33 (paper 67.9 x 49)
Purchased 1982
GMA 2739

Russian Baroque Building
c 1921
Etching, drypoint and aquatint on paper
43 x 33 (paper 65.5 x 50.7)
Purchased 1982
GMA 2715

A Russian Church with Trees in the Foreground
c 1921
Etching, drypoint and aquatint on paper
43 x 33 (paper 65.5 x 50)
Purchased 1982
GMA 2716

Russian Baroque
c 1921
Drypoint and aquatint on paper
42.7 x 32.7 (paper 65.5 x 51)
Purchased 1982
GMA 2717

Cathedral of St Basil the Blessed, Red Square, Moscow
c 1921
Drypoint and aquatint on paper
42.9 x 32.7 (paper 65 x 50.5)
Purchased 1982
GMA 2718

Cathedral of St Basil the Blessed, Red Square, Moscow
c 1921
Drypoint and aquatint on paper
42.9 x 32.7 (paper 65 x 50.5)
Purchased 1982
GMA 2719

The Kremlin
c 1921
Drypoint and aquatint on paper
33 x 42.5 (paper 50.8 x 65.7)
Purchased 1982
GMA 2720

Analizis*
d 1921 (published 1922)
Portfolio of 37 linocuts with hand-coloured cover
Print sizes variable (each cut out and laid on paper
33 x 42.5 or 42.5 x 33)
Purchased 1982
GMA 2713 (1–37)

General Ludd
d 1923
Portfolio of thirteen etchings
From 32.9 x 28.7 to 33.3 x 42.5 (paper 67.4 x 49.5
or 49.5 x 67.4)
Purchased 1982
GMA 2714 (1–13)

Rick Ulman

1940-

Veronica Cloth
d 1965
Monotype on paper (1/1)
82.5 x 69.8 (paper size)
Purchased 1965
GMA 935

Ruin Stone
d 1964
Etching on paper (second state, 4/4)
24.3 x 34.3 (paper 33.2 x 50)
Purchased 1965
GMA 934

Leon Underwood

1890–1975

*The Sower**
1948 (cast and d 1953)
Bronze (5/7)
46.5 x 31.5 x 15
Bequeathed by Miss Elizabeth Watt 1989
GMA 3522

The Diver
1923
Wood engraving on paper
17 x 5 (paper 22.8 x 15.7)
Purchased 1978
GMA 2047

Persephone
1924
Wood engraving on paper
16.7 x 5 (paper 24.2 x 16.2)
Purchased 1978
GMA 2049

Canyon
1924
Wood engraving on paper
14.6 x 9.5 (paper 27.7 x 19.2)
Purchased 1978
GMA 2051

Love
(for 'Human Proclivities')
d 1925
Lino engraving on paper (25/30)
17.7 x 26.6 (paper 22.7 x 35.2)
Purchased 1978
GMA 2045

Masquerade
d 1926 and 1927
Wood engraving on paper (11/40)
28.3 x 21.2 (paper 39.5 x 25.2)
Purchased 1978
GMA 2052

Bird and Fish
d 1927
Lino engraving on paper (2/50)
13 x 21.6 (paper 19 x 26.2)
Purchased 1978
GMA 2050

Yucatecas
1929
Wood engraving on paper (second state)
18.7 x 14.6 (paper 29.6 x 23.1)
Purchased 1978
GMA 2053

Dogma and Law
(for 'Art for Heaven's Sake')
1934
Wood engraving on paper
5.2 x 6.4 (paper 14 x 17)
Purchased 1978
GMA 2046

Volcano
(for 'Art for Heaven's Sake')
1934
Wood engraving on paper
12.7 x 7.8 (paper 21.7 x 16.7)
Purchased 1978
GMA 2048

Unknown

Figures Descending a Flight of Steps
Pen and ink and wash on paper
18.5 x 25.2 (paper 20.2 x 20.8)
Presented by the National Art Collections Fund
from the Sir Edward Marsh Collection 1953
GMA 739

Maurice Utrillo

1883–1955

*La Place du Tertre**
c 1910
Oil on canvas
49.5 x 72.4
Presented by Mr A. J. McNeill Reid in memory
of his father, Alexander Reid: received 1972
GMA 1083

Italo Valenti

1912-

Postcard
d 1970
Collage and ball-point pen on postcard
10.2 x 14.6
Presented by Jim Ede 1977
GMA 1604

*La Lune [The Moon]**
d 1978
Paper collage with white chalk, laid on hardboard
104 x 99
Presented by the artist and Jim Ede 1981
GMA 2303

Victor Vasarely

1908-

*Taïmyr**
d 1958
Oil on canvas
162 x 130
Purchased 1973
GMA 1279

Sian
d 1961
Screenprint on paper (48/85)
24.9 x 47 (paper 60 x 70)
Purchased 1965
GMA 914

Maandra
1961
Screenprint on paper (26/60)
52.7 x 35.1 (paper 75.8 x 63.3)
Purchased 1965
GMA 915

See also WILD HAWTHORN PRESS

Keith Vaughan

1912–77

*Dancer Resting**
d 1950
Gouache and ink on paper
14.5 x 17.8
Presented anonymously in memory of the artist
1984
GMA 2916

Landscape with Two Bathers (or *The Diver*)*
d 1954
Oil on hardboard
121.7 x 152.1
Purchased 1984
GMA 2804

*Winter Tide**
d 1962
Oil on hardboard
91.5 x 101.6
Purchased 1962
GMA 829

*Assembly of Figures VIII**
d 1964
Oil on canvas
122.2 x 137.2
Purchased 1976
GMA 1534

Jacques Villon

1875–1963

*Yvonne D. de face [Portrait of Yvonne D.]**
1913
Drypoint and etching on paper (6/28)
55.2 x 41.4 (paper 64.4 x 45)
Purchased 1981
GMA 2286

Maurice Vlaminck

1876–1958

*Portrait de femme [Portrait of a Woman]**
1924
Lithograph on paper (first state)
22.7 x 15.2 (paper 48.2 x 32.1)
Purchased 1962
GMA 807

Friedrich Vordemberge-Gildewart

1899–1962

*Komposition 14 [Composition 14]**
1925
Oil on canvas
104.8 x 104.8
Purchased 1980
GMA 2148

Edouard Vuillard

1868–1940

*Le Petit manteau [The Little Cape]**
c 1891
Black chalk on paper
13.1 x 7.9
Presented anonymously in memory of Vivien
Leigh 1984
GMA 2917

*La Causette [The Chat]**
c 1892
Oil on canvas
32.4 x 41.3
Presented by Sir Alexander Maitland in memory
of his wife, Rosalind, 1960
GMA 2934

*Deux ouvrières dans l'atelier de couture [Two
Seamstresses in the Workroom]**
d 1893
Oil on millboard
13.3 x 19.4
Purchased with assistance from the National Art
Collections Fund (Scottish Fund) and the National
Heritage Memorial Fund, 1990
GMA 3583

*La Fenêtre ouverte [The Open Window]**
c 1899
Oil on millboard
56.9 x 45
Presented by Sir Alexander Maitland in memory
of his wife, Rosalind, 1960
GMA 2933

*Nature morte au bougeoir [The Candlestick]**
c 1900
Oil on millboard
43.6 x 75.8
Presented by Mrs Isabel M. Traill 1979
GMA 2935

*La Chambre rose [The Pink Room]**
c 1903
Oil on canvas
64 x 53
Presented by Mrs Isabel M. Traill 1979
GMA 2936

*Le Pot de fleurs [Pot of Flowers or Corner of the
Studio]**
c 1904
Oil on millboard
48.5 x 62
Presented by Mrs Isabel M. Traill 1979
GMA 2937

Edward Wadsworth

1889–1949

*Composition, Crank and Chain**
d 1932
Tempera on board
35 x 40
Presented by Mr and Mrs J. H. Macdonell 1960
GMA 768

A Black Country Village (or *Northern Roofscape*)
1920
Woodcut on paper
15.3 x 10.2 (paper 28.3 x 17)
Purchased 1978
GMA 2043

William Walcot

1874–1943

Queen's College, Oxford
by 1919
Etching and aquatint on paper
29.2 x 39 (paper 40.6 x 55)
Bequeathed by Mr Kenneth Sanderson 1943
GMA 569

Anthony in Egypt
by 1919
Etching on paper
55 x 46.1 (paper 84.8 x 67.4)
Presented by Mr D. Muir Wood 1965
GMA 920

Ethel Walker

1861–1951

*The Spanish Shawl**
c 1921–26
Oil on canvas
61.5 x 51.3
Bequeathed by Dr R. A. Lillie 1977
GMA 1989

*Portrait of Lucien Pissarro**
Oil on canvas
61 x 50.8
Purchased 1975
GMA 1498

Amroth Bay
Oil on plywood
25.5 x 35.8
Bequeathed by Dr R. A. Lillie 1977
GMA 1987

Stormy Weather
Oil on canvas
51 x 61
Bequeathed by Dr R. A. Lillie 1977
GMA 1988

Vase of Roses
Oil on canvas
51.3 x 41
Bequeathed by Dr R. A. Lillie 1977
GMA 1990

Sea at Weymouth
Watercolour and black chalk on paper
25.1 x 36.1 (paper 28.1 x 39.1)
Bequeathed by Dr R. A. Lillie 1977
GMA 1991

Wind and Rain
Oil on canvas
63.5 x 89.2
Bequeathed by Dr R. A. Lillie 1977
GMA 1992

Frances Walker

1930-

Finnish Interior
1979
Screenprint on paper (19/40)
47 x 58.5 (paper 56.3 x 75.5)
Purchased 1981
GMA 2321

John Walker

1939-

Labyrinth II*
d 1979
Oil and encaustic on canvas
244 x 289.5
Purchased 1980
GMA 2137

Alba Study 6*
d 1981
Charcoal on paper
122 x 80.5
Purchased 1982
GMA 2509

Untitled
(*from 'The London Suite'*)
1982
Screenprint on paper (11/75)
80.5 x 60.9 (image and paper size)
Purchased 1983
GMA 2757

Armyne Ware

exh. 1931–42

Burn and Fallen Tree
d 1934
Etching on paper
21.7 x 21.7 (paper 26.3 x 24.8)
Purchased 1949
GMA 570 A

Burn and Fallen Tree
d 1934
Etching on paper
21.7 x 21.7 (paper 27.6 x 25.6)
Purchased 1949
GMA 570 B

The Pine Wood
d 1934
Etching on paper
26.4 x 25.5 (paper 29.3 x 29)
Purchased 1949
GMA 571

Harry Fabian Ware

exh. 1928–42

Fallen Tree and Rocks
d 1934
Drypoint and etching on paper
22.2 x 31.8 (paper 26.3 x 46.6)
Purchased 1949
GMA 574

Rocks by the Sea
d 1935
Drypoint and etching on paper
23.9 x 37.4 (paper 28.7 x 47)
Purchased 1949
GMA 573

Tree Trunks
d 1938
Etching on paper
26.1 x 32.5 (paper 30.6 x 41.9)
Purchased 1949
GMA 572

Andy Warhol

1928–87

Jacqueline Kennedy II
(*from the portfolio 'Eleven Pop Artists, vol. II'*)*
1965
Screenprint on paper (no. 24)
60.9 x 76.2 (image and paper size)
Purchased 1975
GMA 1336

David Waterson

1870–1954

The Market Day
d 1900
Pencil on card
22.9 x 15.3
Presented by Mrs D. Waterson through the
Hon. Mrs Helen Lubbock 1968
GMA 1073 A

The Market Day
1900
Pencil on tracing paper
20.5 x 13.6
Presented by Mrs D. Waterson through the
Hon. Mrs Helen Lubbock 1968
GMA 1073 B

*Sketchbook of Landscapes, Environs of Brechin
in Angus*
d 1920–27
Pencil and ink on paper
17.8 x 23.5
Presented by Mrs D. Waterson through the
Hon. Mrs Helen Lubbock 1968
GMA 1074

Landscape
d 1927
Mezzotint on paper
40.2 x 52.1 (paper 48.4 x 62.5)
Presented by Mrs D. Waterson through the
Hon. Mrs Helen Lubbock 1968
GMA 1075

Barrington Watson

The Athlete's Nightmare
(from 'The Commonwealth Print Portfolio')
d 1978
Lithograph on paper (15/65)
69.2 x 50.4 (paper 76.3 x 56.7)
Presented by the Canadian High Commission
1979
GMA 2126

Alonso C. Webb

1888–1975

Empire State Building, New York*
c 1931
Coloured chalk and gouache on paper laid on
board
53.4 x 33.8
Presented by Mr Alan Roger 1981
GMA 2471

Chrysler Building, New York
c 1931
Coloured chalk and gouache on paper laid on
board
51.6 x 34
Presented by Mr Alan Roger 1981
GMA 2472

Carel Weight

1908-

Sinister Encounter*
1984
Oil on hardboard
106.8 x 76.1
Purchased 1985
GMA 2952

Albert Bridge
*(from the J. Lyons series 'Lithographs by
Contemporary Artists, vol. I')*
Published 1947
Lithograph on paper
72.5 x 97.5 (paper 74.5 x 98.6)
Presented by J. Lyons & Co. Ltd 1948
GMA 1213

John Wesley

1928-

Bird Lady
(from the portfolio 'Eleven Pop Artists, vol. II')
d 1965
Screenprint on paper (no. XXIV)
60.9 x 76.2 (image and paper size)
Purchased 1975
GMA 1340

Tom Wesselmann

1931-

Nude
(*from the portfolio 'Eleven Pop Artists, vol. II'*)
1965
Screenprint on paper (no. XXIV)
60.9 x 76.2 (image and paper size)
Purchased 1975
GMA 1341

John Wheatley

1892–1955

Old Rogers
Etching and drypoint on paper
26.1 x 17.3 (paper 38.2 x 25.8)
Purchased 1949
GMA 575

Ethelbert White

1891–1972

*The Lake**
c 1930
Watercolour and pencil on paper
28.5 x 35.5 (paper 31.1 x 41.4)
Bequeathed by Miss Elizabeth Watt 1989
GMA 3532

The Wood's Edge
c 1932
Wood engraving on paper (7/50)
15 x 19.7 (paper 26.4 x 31.2)
Purchased 1949
GMA 576

Kate Whiteford

1952-

*Symbol Stones: The Peacock**
d 1983
Acrylic on paper
151.1 x 114.2
Purchased 1989
GMA 3442

*Symbol Stones: The Arc**
d 1983
Acrylic on paper
151.2 x 114.3
Purchased 1989
GMA 3443

*Symbol Stones: The Snake**
d 1983
Acrylic on paper
151.5 x 114.3
Purchased 1989
GMA 3444

*Red Spiral**
1986
Acrylic on paper in painted frame
150.5 x 113.5 (frame 157.5 x 120.6)
Purchased 1989
GMA 3459

Traces, Shadows, Contours, Logos
Published 1988
Book of sixteen screenprints (6/500), with loose
screenprint (6/50)
27 x 21.7 (page size)
Purchased 1989
GMA 3445

Herbert Whone

1925-

Tramcar in Fog*
d 1962
Oil on canvas
106.7 x 96.5
Bequeathed by Mr and Mrs G. D. Robinson
through the National Art Collections Fund 1988
GMA 3353

Franz Widerberg

1934-

Untitled
1986
Colour lithograph on two sheets of paper (52/60)
Top sheet 60 x 80.5 (paper 64.4 x 91.5) bottom
sheet 60.4 x 80.2 (paper 65 x 91.5)
Presented by the artist 1987
GMA 3035

Janusz Wiktorowski

1939-

*Art Work for 'Atelier 72' Poster (Demarco
Gallery, Edinburgh International Festival)*
1972
Paper collage with inks on paper laid on board
70 x 49.7
Purchased 1980
GMA 2239

Gerald Wilde

1905–86

Untitled
Screenprint on paper (2/30)
80.9 x 104.8 (paper 87.4 x 113.8)
Provenance unrecorded
GMA 3579

Wild Hawthorn Press

Established by Iam Hamilton Finlay and Jessie
McGuffie, 1961

My Friend Tree
(by Lorine Niedecker with introduction by Ed
Dorn with Walter Miller) [IHF 1.1]
1961
Book, 40 pp
13 x 19
Purchased 1991
GMA A4.522

Fish-sheet One
(by Finlay, Morgan, Brown, Hawkins, etc.) [IHF
1.3]
1963
Letterpress on paper
20.7 x 33
Purchased 1991
GMA A4.533

A Very Particular Hill
(by Gael Turnbull with Alexander McNeish) [IHF
1.4]
Published 1963
Book, 20 pp
15 x 20
Presented anonymously 1965
GMA A4.523

Cidade / City / Cité
(by Augusto de Campos) [IHF 1.5]
1964
Folded screenprint on paper
20.1 x 24.5
Purchased 1991
GMA A4.524

Fleece
(by Stephen Bann with Alister Cant) [IHF 1.6]
1964
Screenprint on paper
58 x 46
Purchased 1975
GMA A4.130

Epitaph für Konrad Bayer
(by Franz Mon) [IHF 1.7]
1964
Screenprint on paper
50.5 X 43
Purchased 1975
GMA A4.109

Paradis (Poster Poem)
(by Pierre-Albert Birot) [IHF 1.8]
1964
Screenprint on paper
44.3 X 57.4
Presented anonymously 1965
GMA A4.314

Poem / Print
(by Ferdinand Kriwet) [IHF 1.9]
1964
Screenprint on paper
56.9 X 44.2
Purchased 1975
GMA A4.328

Polar
(by John Furnival) [IHF 1.10]
1965
Screenprint on paper
44.2 X 55.7
Presented anonymously 1965
GMA A4.334

Sports et Divertissements
(by Ronald Johnston and Erik Satie with John
Furnival) [IHF 1.11]
1965
Book, 24 pp
24 X 12
Purchased 1975
GMA A4.415

Sea Poem
(by Robert Lax with Emil Antonucci) [IHF 1.12]
1966
Folder with plastic spine, 4 pp
28 X 43.3
Purchased 1975
GMA A4.391

Drawing
(by Victor Vasarely) [IHF 1.13]
1966
Screenprint on paper
53.2 X 42 (paper 57 X 44.3)
Purchased 1975
GMA A4.638

Terror is the Piety of the Revolution
(by Alexander Stoddart) [IHF 1.14]
1986
Booklet, 16 pp
11 X 7.7
Purchased 1986
GMA A4.437

[IHF refers to the catalogue raisonné of the printed
works of Ian Hamilton Finlay and the Wild
Hawthorn Press, published by the Graeme
Murray Gallery (Edinburgh 1990)]

See also Ian Hamilton FINLAY and APPENDIX

Alison Wilding

1948-

*Hand to Mouth**
1986
Leaded steel, brass; wood, lead, beeswax
200 X 54 X 55; 29 X 47.5 X 32
Presented by the Contemporary Art Society
(Henry Moore Foundation Grant) 1992
GMA 3661

Stephen Willats

1943-

The Edinburgh Social Model Construction Project
1973
Mixed-media documentary material including
texts, photographs, recording tape, plans and
drawings
Purchased 1981
GMA 2296

*What is the Difference between the Inside and
the Outside?*
1) *Conception*
2) *Realisation*
3) *Presentation*
d 1982
Collage and mixed media on paper laid on
cardboard (three panels)
Each panel 135 x 95
Purchased 1983
GMA 2766

Andrew Williams

1954-

Leaping Basketball Player
1986
Oil on canvas
198 x 228.7
Purchased 1986
GMA 2986

Dordogne Landscape I*
1988
Oil on canvas
66.4 x 81.5
Purchased 1989
GMA 3475

Cyril Wilson

1911-

Seedhead Landscape – The Mourners
d 1963
Oil on canvas
86.1 x 74.4
Purchased 1963
GMA 872

Scottie Wilson

1889–1972

Grotesque Design with Birds and Fish*
c 1940
Coloured crayon and pen and ink on paper
27.8 x 18.3
Presented by Mr and Mrs Robert Lewin 1977
GMA 1676

Untitled*
c 1950
Watercolour, coloured crayon and pen and ink on
paper
56.5 x 38
Purchased 1966
GMA 979

Design with Fish*
c 1950s
Coloured crayon and pen and ink on paper
38 x 28.7
Purchased 1964
GMA 895

A Whispering Paradise (or Earth and Heaven)*
1951
Coloured crayon and pen and ink on black paper
90.2 x 154.4
Presented by Mr and Mrs Robert Lewin 1978
GMA 1997

Peaceful Village*
1963
Porcelain
49 x 40 (oval)
Presented by Mr and Mrs Robert Lewin 1977
GMA 1677

Oval Plate with Bird Motifs
c 1963
Ceramic
36 x 28.3 (oval)
Purchased 1981
GMA 2291

Circular Plate with 'Bird Tree' Motif
c 1963
Ceramic
31 (diameter)
Purchased 1981
GMA 2292

William Wilson

1905–72

Provins, France
(study for an etching)
d 1926
Pencil on paper
25 x 33.8
Purchased 1980
GMA 2514

Road with Farm
(study for an etching)
c 1930
Pencil on paper
27.9 x 38.5
Purchased 1980
GMA 2511

Farm near Edinburgh
(study for an etching [GMA 2252])
c 1930
Pencil on paper
24.9 x 30.3
Purchased 1980
GMA 2512

Hill Town
(study for an etching)
c 1930
Pencil on paper
25.3 x 34.3
Purchased 1980
GMA 2515

On the Road to Gubbio
c 1930–32
Pencil on paper
36 x 50.2
Purchased 1980
GMA 2513

Soave: Castle of the Scaligeri
d 1931
Pencil on paper
25.1 x 33
Purchased 1980
GMA 2510

*Toledo**
1932
Pen and ink, ink wash, pencil and black chalk
on paper
40.6 x 53.8
Purchased 1980
GMA 2281

Granada
1932
Ink, ink wash, pencil and red chalk on paper
41.8 x 53.1
Purchased 1980
GMA 2516

Elgol, Skye
d 1934
Ink, ink wash, pencil and black chalk on paper
32.4 x 47.2
Purchased 1980
GMA 2280

Girl with Guitar (or *The Guitar*)*
c 1937
Pencil over engraving on paper
30.3 x 25.1 (paper 39.7 x 31.1)
Purchased 1980
GMA 2271

Women in a Garden
c 1940
Stained glass panel
58.4 x 27.3
Presented anonymously 1961
GMA 789

Design for a Stained Glass Window in a Music Room
c 1943
Watercolour, gouache, ink and black chalk on
paper
81.6 x 57.7
Purchased 1982
GMA 2538

*Design for a War Memorial Stained Glass
Window, St Mary's, Biggar*
c 1947
Watercolour and black chalk on paper
21.5 x 14.4
Purchased 1982
GMA 2529

*Design for a Stained Glass Window: Baptistry
Window for St David's Church, Bathgate*
c 1948
Watercolour, ink and pencil on paper laid on card
53.6 x 6.3
Purchased 1982
GMA 2531

The Stackyard
d 1948
Ink and chalk on paper
31 x 57
George and Isobel Neillands Collection: presented
1987
GMA 3328

*The Irish Jig**
1948
Stained glass panel
91 x 76.5
Purchased 1992
GMA 3660

*Design for a Stained Glass Window for St
Salvator's Chapel, St Andrews (Three Lights:
Christ and St Paul; Dante and Virgil; St Francis
and Plato)*
c 1950
Watercolour, ink and pencil on board
54 x 30.7
Purchased 1982
GMA 2528

*Design for a Stained Glass Window for the North
Aisle of Brechin Cathedral (Three Lights:
Abraham, Adam and Isaac)**
c 1952
Watercolour and chalk on paper
32.1 x 22.7
Purchased 1980
GMA 2527

St Séverin, Paris
c 1957
Watercolour, gouache and ink on paper
50 x 65.2
Presented by the artist 1972
GMA 1256

*Design for a Memorial Stained Glass Window
dedicated to Christina Steele Mack or Carlyle for
Fairmilehead Parish Church*
1957
Watercolour and black chalk on paper
36.8 x 13.5
Purchased 1982
GMA 2530

*Design for a Stained Glass Window for the
Clerestory of Brechin Cathedral (St Mungo)**
1959
Watercolour, gouache, ink and black chalk on
paper
90 x 52.5
Purchased 1982
GMA 2537

*Design for a Stained Glass Window for the
Convent Chapel of Marie Reparatrice, Elie*
c 1959–60
Watercolour and black chalk on paper
9.2 x 10.7
Purchased 1982
GMA 2535 A

*Design for a Stained Glass Window for the
Convent Chapel of Marie Reparatrice, Elie*
c 1959–60
Watercolour and black chalk on paper
9.6 x 10.8
Purchased 1982
GMA 2535 B

*Design for a Stained Glass Window for the
Convent Chapel of Marie Reparatrice, Elie*
c 1959–60
Watercolour and black chalk on paper
9.7 x 11.5
Purchased 1982
GMA 2535 C

Design for a Stained Glass Window dedicated to
Ross of Pitcalnie for St Andrew's Scottish
Episcopal Church, Tain (Three Lights: St Miriam,
St David, St Cecilia)
c 1961
Watercolour, ink and pencil on paper
36.5 x 35.4
Purchased 1982
GMA 2533

Gethsemane
Stained glass panel
98.5 x 35
Purchased with funds given by the Rev. Ian
Forrester in memory of his parents 1970
GMA 1162

St Monance
Black chalk and ink on paper
26.6 x 23
Purchased 1980
GMA 2279

Design for a Stained Glass Window
Watercolour, gouache, ink and pencil on paper,
with two pieces of paper stuck on
53.8 x 33
Purchased 1980
GMA 2526

Design for a Pair of Stained Glass Windows
Watercolour, gouache, ink and pencil on paper
17 x 16.3
Purchased 1982
GMA 2532 A

Design for a Pair of Stained Glass Windows
Watercolour, gouache, ink and pencil on paper
17.6 x 13.9
Purchased 1982
GMA 2532 B

Design for a Pair of Stained Glass Windows
Watercolour, ink, pencil and gouache on paper
17.8 x 14.3
Purchased 1982
GMA 2532 C

Design for a Stained Glass Window (St David of
Scotland)
Watercolour, ink and black chalk on paper
21.3 x 8
Purchased 1982
GMA 2534 A

Design for a Stained Glass Window (St
Margaret)
Watercolour, ink and black chalk on paper
21.4 x 8.7
Purchased 1982
GMA 2534 B

Design for a Stained Glass Window: Nec Tamen
Consumebatur (Burning Bush and Fishermen)
Watercolour and ink on paper
77.8 x 17.8
Purchased 1982
GMA 2536

San Simone Piccolo
Watercolour, gouache, pen and ink and pencil
on paper
50 x 65
Bequeathed by Mr Alan Stark 1983
GMA 2774

Le Pont Neuf, Paris
d 1925
Etching on green paper
18.1 x 22.6 (paper 22.5 x 30)
Purchased 1980
GMA 2264

Dunfermline
d 1928
Engraving on paper (4/25)
13.8 x 19 (paper 20.2 x 26)
Provenance unrecorded
GMA 600

Edinburgh
c 1928–29
Engraving on paper (7/30)
14 x 17.5 (paper 24 x 30)
Purchased 1949
GMA 584

Sheds at Station
c 1928–29
Engraving on paper
12.9 x 16.2 (paper 22.2 x 26.6)
Purchased 1980
GMA 2255

St Monance
d 1929
Engraving on paper (first state, 2/10)
15.2 x 19 (paper 18.4 x 29.1)
Purchased 1949
GMA 582

Rothenburg ob der Tauber
d 1929
Engraving on paper (6/30)
15.5 x 20.8 (paper 21.2 x 27.4)
Purchased 1949
GMA 583

The Walls, Rothenburg
d 1929
Engraving on paper (9/30)
21.6 x 20.3 (paper 29.9 x 24.1)
Purchased 1949
GMA 585

Farm near Edinburgh
d 1930
Engraving on paper
17.2 x 22.5 (paper 22.8 x 32.3)
Purchased 1980
GMA 2252

A Bavarian Gate
d 1930
Engraving on paper
20.3 x 15.2 (paper 31.6 x 21.3)
Purchased 1982
GMA 2520

San Gimignano
c 1930
Engraving on paper
20.2 x 26.4 (paper 30 x 37)
Purchased 1980
GMA 2249

San Gimignano
c 1930–32
Engraving on paper
22.6 x 25.8 (paper 28.1 x 37.6)
Purchased 1980
GMA 2254

Siena
1931
Engraving with pencil on paper (early state of
GMA 578)
24.5 x 20.2 (paper 36.7 x 25)
Purchased 1980
GMA 2273

Siena
d 1931
Engraving on paper
24.5 x 20.3 (paper 27.2 x 22.1)
Bequeathed by Mr Kenneth Sanderson 1943
GMA 578

Siena
1931 (printed c 1971)
Engraving on paper
24.5 x 20.1 (paper 51.6 x 39.7)
Purchased 1981
GMA 2468

Flemish Gate, Bruges
d 1931
Engraving on paper (trial proof)
23 x 29.9 (paper 26.4 x 33.8)
Purchased 1980
GMA 2266

View of Ghent
d 1931
Engraving on paper (4/30)
21.8 x 22.2 (paper 34.8 x 23.9)
Purchased 1982
GMA 2522

A Castle near Verona*
d 1932
Engraving on paper (1/20)
23.6 x 29.1 (paper 26.7 x 31.4)
Purchased 1949
GMA 581

Santa Maria della Salute, Venice
d 1932
Engraving on paper
24.1 x 28.5 (paper 28 x 30)
Purchased 1949
GMA 586

Santa Maria della Salute, Venice
1932 (printed c 1971)
Engraving on paper
24 x 28.4 (paper 38.5 x 51)
Purchased 1981
GMA 2469

Bridge of the Scaligers, Verona
c 1932
Engraving on paper
26.4 x 20.3 (paper 31 x 22.8)
Purchased 1980
GMA 2253

Adam and Eve
1932
Engraving on paper
27.7 x 21.6 (paper 32.6 x 23.1)
Purchased 1980
GMA 2261

Ronda
c 1932–33
Etching on paper (30/30)
32.7 x 44 (paper 40.9 x 48)
Purchased 1980
GMA 2250

Spain
c 1932–33
Etching with black chalk on paper (early state)
26.4 x 32 (paper 32.9 x 41.4)
Purchased 1980
GMA 2269

St Martin's Bridge, Toledo
d 1933
Etching and engraving on paper (5/30)
35.2 x 42.9 (paper 41.5 x 49.5)
Purchased 1949
GMA 594

Church Gate, Colinton
c 1933
Etching on paper (early state of GMA 580)
18.4 x 22.6 (paper 24.5 x 30.5)
Purchased 1980
GMA 2278

Church Gate, Colinton
c 1933
Etching and engraving on paper (2/20)
18.5 x 22.7 (paper 21.8 x 27.5)
Purchased 1949
GMA 580

Avila
c 1933–35
Engraving on paper (early state of GMA 595)
29 x 36.6 (paper 35 x 41.9)
Purchased 1982
GMA 2524

Avila
d 1933–35 in plate (d 1935 in margin)
Engraving on paper (4/30)
29 x 36.4 (paper 40.3 x 49.3)
Purchased 1949
GMA 595

North Highland Landscape
d 1934
Etching on paper (16/35)
35.6 x 38.8 (paper 39.9 x 51.5)
Purchased 1949
GMA 596

Sutherland
1934
Etching with chalk on paper (early state of GMA 599)
30.5 x 40.2 (paper 38.8 x 42.9)
Purchased 1980
GMA 2275

Sutherland
d 1934
Etching on paper (7/30)
30.4 x 40.2 (paper 38.4 x 49.4)
Purchased 1949
GMA 599

Railway Siding, Colinton
1934
Engraving on paper
20.8 x 25.3 (paper 26 x 35.8)
Purchased 1980
GMA 2248

The Bridge, Colinton
1934
Etching with white and black chalk on paper
(early state of GMA 2282)
22.2 x 27.3 (paper 25.5 x 38)
Purchased 1980
GMA 2270

The Bridge, Colinton
d 1934
Etching on paper (2/30)
22.2 x 27.3 (paper 25.3 x 36.1)
Provenance unrecorded
GMA 2282

The House on the Rock
d 1935
Etching on paper
17.7 x 16.2 (paper 31 x 19.5)
Purchased 1949
GMA 587

The Hen Farm
d 1935
Engraving on paper
17.6 x 23.4 (paper 21.9 x 27)
Purchased 1949
GMA 589

The Hunter's Tryst
d 1935
Etching on paper (7/30)
17.1 x 24.1 (paper 21.1 x 30.2)
Purchased 1949
GMA 593

Loch Scavaig, Skye
d 1935
Etching on paper (8/35)
29.6 x 37.8 (paper 38.6 x 45.9)
Purchased 1949
GMA 597

Loch Scavaig, Skye
1935 (printed c 1971)
Etching on paper
29.5 x 37.2 (paper 46 x 57.8)
Purchased 1981
GMA 2467

Old Street, Edinburgh
d 1935
Etching on paper
25.1 x 19.8 (paper 36.7 x 25.3)
Purchased 1980
GMA 2258

Tenements
1935
Etching with pencil and chalk on paper (early
state of GMA 588)
21.7 x 21.4 (paper 34.1 x 26.5)
Purchased 1980
GMA 2274

Tenements
1935
Etching on paper
21.7 x 21.4 (paper 32 x 25)
Purchased 1949
GMA 588

'From my Window 23 Dec 1935'
(Christmas Card)
d 1935
Etching on paper (folded in two)
10.4 x 11.6 (paper 14.8 x 34.3)
Purchased 1984
GMA 2819

The Harrow
c 1935–36
Etching on paper (15/16)
20.4 x 33.1 (paper 42 x 52.2)
Purchased 1980
GMA 2247

The Black Barn
d 1936
Etching on paper
18.2 x 28.3 (paper 25.3 x 36.3)
Purchased 1949
GMA 579

Sea Wall
(*Christmas Card*)
d 1936
Etching on paper (folded in two)
13.8 x 16.3 (paper 17 x 40.3)
Purchased 1949
GMA 590

Duck Pond, Netteswell, Essex
1936
Engraving with pencil and ink additions on paper
(early state of GMA 592)
12.5 x 13.8 (paper 22.5 x 28)
Purchased 1982
GMA 2525

Duck Pond, Netteswell, Essex
1936
Engraving on paper
12.7 x 14 (paper 18.8 x 19)
Purchased 1949
GMA 592

Ruined Sheiling, Skye
c 1936
Etching on paper
20.2 x 25.3 (paper 23.4 x 27.8)
Purchased 1980
GMA 2256

The Cuillins, Skye
1936
Etching on paper (early state of GMA 2283)
26.4 x 31.9 (paper 32.9 x 43.5)
Purchased 1980
GMA 2267

The Cuillins, Skye
d 1936
Etching on paper
26.3 x 31.9 (paper 29.7 x 41.3)
Purchased 1949
GMA 2283

Derelict Boats
1936
Etching with black chalk on paper (early state)
18.9 x 30 (paper 28.4 x 45)
Purchased 1980
GMA 2272

Latton Priory
d 1936
Etching on paper
14.8 x 17.5 (paper 20.6 x 26.5)
Purchased 1982
GMA 2517

Sea Wall
(*Christmas Card*)
d 1936
Etching on paper (folded in two)
13.8 x 16.3 (paper 15.8 x 38.8)
Purchased 1984
GMA 2820

Swanston Farm (*under Snow*)
d 1937
Engraving on paper
10.2 x 14.7 (paper 16.2 x 25.3)
Bequeathed by Mr Kenneth Sanderson 1943
GMA 577

Swanston Farm (*under Snow*)
(*Christmas Card*)
1937
Engraving on paper (folded in two)
10.3 x 14.8 (paper 13.4 x 38.4)
Purchased 1984
GMA 2821

Fishers' Haven
d 1937
Engraving on paper
17.1 x 17.1 (paper 25.3 x 20.3)
Purchased 1949
GMA 591

The Threshing Machine
d 1937
Etching on paper
24.5 x 33.3 (paper 30 x 38.4)
Purchased 1949
GMA 598

St Monance
1937
Etching on paper (13/15)
23.4 x 28.1 (paper 42 x 53)
Purchased 1980
GMA 2244

Self-Portrait
1937
Etching on paper
29.8 x 23 (paper 36.2 x 25.5)
Purchased 1980
GMA 2263

Edinburgh Castle
(*Christmas Card*)
1938
Etching on paper
12.6 x 10 (paper 15 x 11)
Purchased 1984
GMA 2818

Lowland Farm
1938
Etching on paper (early state of GMA 2257)
13.8 x 18.9 (paper 20.5 x 25.4)
Purchased 1980
GMA 2277

Lowland Farm
d 1938
Etching on paper
13.9 x 19.1 (paper 24.6 x 33)
Purchased 1980
GMA 2257

'In this Year of our Lord – 1939'
d 1939
Etching on paper
9 x 11.6 (paper 13.9 x 13.2)
Purchased 1984
GMA 2817

A Welsh Castle
d 1940
Etching on paper
30 x 33 (paper 38.6 x 43.9)
Purchased 1980
GMA 2259

On Walmersley Moor
d 1940
Etching on paper
17.5 x 25.2 (paper 26.9 x 40.1)
Purchased 1980
GMA 2260

Welsh Village
d 1940
Etching on paper
23.3 x 28.9 (paper 28.5 x 35.5)
Purchased 1980
GMA 2265

The Harbour Wall
c 1940
Etching on paper (early state)
31.4 x 38.2 (paper 41.3 x 45.6)
Purchased 1980
GMA 2276

York Minster
c 1940
Etching with pencil and chalk on paper (trial proof
– early state of GMA 2246 and GMA 2518)
27.7 x 24.3 (paper 32.3 x 25.4)
Purchased 1982
GMA 2519

York Minster
c 1940
Etching with pencil on paper (early state of GMA
2246)
27.5 x 24.3 (paper 38.6 x 28)
Purchased 1982
GMA 2518

York Minster
c 1940
Etching on paper (14/15)
27.5 x 24.2 (paper 51.7 x 39.8)
Purchased 1980
GMA 2246

Ronda
c 1946
Drypoint with black chalk on paper (early state)
22.7 x 25.2 (paper 28.6 x 36.7)
Purchased 1980
GMA 2268

Canongate
Etching on paper (15/15)
20.2 x 26.4 (paper 40.2 x 51.8)
Purchased 1980
GMA 2243

Holyrood in Snow
Etching on paper (13/15)
23.6 x 30 (paper 39.8 x 51.6)
Purchased 1980
GMA 2245

Le Pont Neuf, Paris
Engraving on paper
17.5 x 25.1 (paper 22.8 x 28.4)
Purchased 1980
GMA 2251

A Scottish Port
Etching on paper
21.1 x 30.1 (paper 28.5 x 38)
Purchased 1980
GMA 2262

Canal and Bridge
Etching with white chalk on paper
12.2 x 18.2 (paper 25.3 x 32.3)
Purchased 1982
GMA 2521

Gothic Barn
Etching, drypoint and aquatint on paper
20.2 x 22.8 (paper 26.1 x 35.3)
Purchased 1982
GMA 2523

Fettes College
(*Christmas Card*)
Etching on paper (folded in two)
11.3 x 14.7 (paper 13.8 x 32.7)
Purchased 1984
GMA 2816

A Country Church
Etching on paper
13.2 x 10.5 (paper 15.7 x 12.6)
Purchased 1984
GMA 2822

A Village in Winter
(*Christmas Card*)
Etching on paper (folded in two)
5.4 x 11 (paper 9.1 x 26.6)
Purchased 1984
GMA 2823

A Tower House
(*Christmas Card*)
Etching on paper (folded in two)
12.3 x 6.2 (paper 17.8 x 19)
Purchased 1984
GMA 2824

Gerd Winner

1936-

Dockland III
1972
Screenprint on paper (A.P.)
62.7 x 85 (paper 70 x 101.5)
Purchased 1980
GMA 2161

Stahlwand
c 1972
Screenprint on paper (A.P.)
60 x 94.7 (paper 69 x 104)
Purchased 1980
GMA 2162

Adrian Wiszniewski

1958-

Bound to Love and Cherish*
1984
Charcoal on paper
201 x 287
Purchased 1987
GMA 3043

Kingfisher*
d 1987
Acrylic and felt-tip pen on canvas
213.5 x 213.5
Purchased 1987
GMA 3042

Raven
(*from 'The Scottish Bestiary'*)
Published 1986
Screenprint on paper (5/50)
53.5 x 35.5 (paper 76 x 56.5)
Purchased 1987
GMA 3019 B

Dragon
(*from 'The Scottish Bestiary'*)
Published 1986
Lithograph on paper (5/50)
53.2 x 34.2 (paper 76 x 56.5)
Purchased 1987
GMA 3019 J

Unicorn
(*from 'The Scottish Bestiary'*)
Published 1986
Etching on paper (5/50)
51.5 x 33.7 (paper 76 x 56.5)
Purchased 1987
GMA 3019 O

Unicorn
(*unused proof for 'The Scottish Bestiary'*)
1986
Lithograph on paper (A.P.)
52 x 34.2 (paper, folded 56:8 x 76)
Presented by the artist 1992
GMA 3599

Salmon
(*unused proof for 'The Scottish Bestiary'*)
1986
Lithograph on paper (A.P.)
52.2 x 34 (paper, folded 56.4 x 76.2)
Presented by the artist 1992
GMA 3600

The Sculptor's Nightmare
d 1986
Etching and aquatint on paper (16/70)
60.5 x 91 (paper 74.7 x 104)
Purchased 1987
GMA 3028

Chez Nous
1987
Colour woodcut on paper (four sheets joined
together) (2/25)
Each sheet 121 x 91.4 (total size 242 x 182.8)
Purchased 1987
GMA 3304

For Max
Published 1988
Book of 25 colour linocuts and frontispiece (58/
100)
26.6 x 21.5 (paper size)
Purchased 1988
GMA 3409

Untitled
(*from 'The Haymarket Print Suite'*)
Published 1990
Screenprint on paper (A.P.)
152 x 101 (paper 157 x 107)
Purchased 1990
GMA 3570

Harlequin Series
d 1991
Portfolio of ten etchings with aquatint (19/30)
57.1 x 54.1 (paper size)
Presented by Mr Charles Booth-Clibborn 1992
GMA 3624

Edward Wolfe

1897–1982

*The Model**
1923
Oil on canvas
25.5 x 20.7
Presented anonymously in memory of Margaret
Leighton and Michael Wilding 1984
GMA 2918

Man Wearing a Fez
Drypoint and etching on paper
11.8 x 11.5 (paper 17.2 x 14.6)
Presented by Jim Ede 1977
GMA 1632

Man Wearing a Fez
Drypoint and etching on paper
11.8 x 11.5 (paper 18.9 x 17.8)
Presented by Jim Ede 1977
GMA 1633

Christopher Wood

1901–30

*Portrait of Jeanne Bourgoint**
c 1925–26
Pencil on paper
53.9 x 42.1
Presented by Jim Ede 1977
GMA 1638

The Steps, Chelsea*
1927
Oil on plywood
32.8 x 40.7
Bequeathed by Miss Elizabeth Watt 1989
GMA 3523

Bridge over the Seine*
1927
Oil on wood
37.8 x 45.9
Bequeathed by Miss Elizabeth Watt 1989
GMA 3524

Cumberland Landscape*
1928
Pencil on paper
25.4 x 35.7
Presented by Jim Ede 1977
GMA 1637

Nude Boy in a Bedroom*
1930
Oil on hardboard laid on plywood
53.8 x 65
Purchased 1978
GMA 1712

Study of a Male Nude from Behind*
Pencil on paper
41.9 x 29.3
Presented by Jim Ede 1977
GMA 1639

Studies of a Female Nude
Pencil on paper
41.9 x 29.3
Presented by Jim Ede 1977
GMA 1640

Standing Female Nude*
Black chalk on paper
47 x 25
Bequeathed by Miss Elizabeth Watt 1989
GMA 3525

Francis Derwent Wood
1871–1926

Boy with Chanticleer*
d 1925
Bronze
40 x 24 x 19.5
Bequeathed by Sir David Young Cameron 1945
GMA 1011

Frank Watson Wood
1862–1953

Berwick-on-Tweed
Etching on paper
19 x 34.3 (paper 24.3 x 39)
Purchased 1940
GMA 601

Roy Wood
1937-

Levenshall
d 1980
Hand-coloured photo-etching on paper (A.P. II)
30.1 x 20 (paper 75.1 x 56.4)
Purchased 1981
GMA 2322

Bill Woodrow
1948-

Clamp*
1986
Metal ventilation ducting, enamel paint
248.5 x 67 x 51
Purchased 1986
GMA 3007

Gary Wragg

1946-

Discarded Talisman
(from 'The London Suite')
d 1982
Screenprint on paper
61 x 85 (image and paper size)
Purchased 1983
GMA 2758

John Wragg

1937–

Untitled*
1964
Aluminium over wood
50.1 x 33.3 x 25.7
Presented by Sir Norman and Lady Reid in
memory of their parents, 1992
GMA 3695

John Buckland Wright

1897–1954

Café dansant No. II
d 1930
Wood engraving on paper (23/30)
21.5 x 27.8 (paper 29.3 x 35.3)
Purchased 1984
GMA 2837

Ligeia
d 1930
Wood engraving on paper (A.P. 3/5)
13.8 x 10.7 (paper 18.1 x 12.3)
Purchased 1984
GMA 2839

The Island of the Fay
1930
Wood engraving on paper
16 x 10.8 (paper 25.5 x 17.3)
Purchased 1984
GMA 2841 A

The Island of the Fay
d 1930
Wood engraving on paper (3/5)
16 x 10.8 (paper 18.1 x 12.4)
Purchased 1984
GMA 2841 B

Baigneuses Balinaises*
d 1931
Wood engraving on paper (11/30)
27.9 x 21.5 (paper 50.4 x 32.8)
Purchased 1984
GMA 2838

Baigneuse et satyre No. I
d 1934
Engraving and soft-ground etching on paper
(29/30)
23.8 x 17.6 (paper 40.5 x 30)
Purchased 1984
GMA 2840

Bryan Wynter

1915–75

Still Life*
c 1947
Watercolour, gouache and ink on paper laid on
board
25.3 x 37.7
Bequeathed by Miss Elizabeth Watt 1989
GMA 3526

Cyclamen*
d 1948
Gouache on paper
50.5 x 37.4 (irregular)
Bequeathed by Miss Elizabeth Watt 1989
GMA 3527

Hostile Tribe*
1956
Oil on canvas
112.1 x 142.5
Purchased 1982
GMA 2479

Sandspoor XI*
d 1963
Oil on canvas
142.5 x 111.8
Presented by the Peter Stuyvesant Foundation
1977
GMA 1687

Jack Butler Yeats

1871–1957

Queen Maeve Walked upon this Strand*
1950
Oil on canvas
91.5 x 122
Purchased 1971
GMA 1245

Ainslie Yule

1941-

Proposition for a Floor Piece*
1977
Charcoal, chalk, gouache, ink and felt-tip pen on
paper
96.4 x 110
Purchased 1978
GMA 2070

Three Related Objects on Sand
d 1977
Paper collage, pencil, watercolour, crayon and
plaster on paper
56.3 x 94.7
Purchased 1978
GMA 2071

Ossip Zadkine

1890–1967

La Danse [The Dance]*
1927
Bronze (2/3)
57.8 x 19 x 19.3
Presented by Miss Elizabeth Watt 1960
GMA 769

Torse de femme [Torso of a Woman]*
1943
Stone (diorite)
45 x 28.5 x 15
Presented by Miss Elizabeth Watt 1985
GMA 2965

Le Combat antique [Antique Combat]
d 1964
Etching on paper
27.5 x 83.6 (paper 37.4 x 96.3)
Bequeathed by Miss Elizabeth Watt 1989
GMA 3528

Aleksander Zyw

1905-

Untitled [z 87]
1947
Watercolour, gouache and ink on paper
40.2 x 32.6
Purchased 1976
GMA 1549

Untitled [z 306]
1948–49
Watercolour and pen and ink on paper
30.1 x 23.4
Purchased 1976
GMA 1550

Untitled [z 317]
1949
Watercolour, pen and coloured ink on paper
25.3 x 36.7
Purchased 1976
GMA 1551

Journey Woven in Imagination*
1950
Oil on canvas
102 x 127
Purchased 1975
GMA 1518

Untitled [z 401]
1950
Watercolour and pen and ink on paper
27.9 x 37.9
Purchased 1976
GMA 1553

Untitled [z 455]
c 1950
Pen and ink on paper
19.3 x 27.3
Purchased 1976
GMA 1554

Untitled [z 392]
1950–51
Watercolour, pen and ink and ink wash on paper
25.3 x 37.5
Purchased 1976
GMA 1552

Untitled [z 728]
1951–52
Watercolour and pen and ink on paper
49.9 x 39.8
Purchased 1976
GMA 1556

Movement*
1953
Oil on canvas
98 x 131
Purchased 1972
GMA 1272

Untitled [z 699]
c 1953–54
Pen and ink on paper
31.9 x 26
Purchased 1976
GMA 1555

Untitled [z 900]
1956–57
Watercolour on paper
56 x 38.2
Purchased 1976
GMA 1557

Sea Pebbles II (No. 3)
1963
Oil on canvas
142.3 x 111.7
Purchased 1975
GMA 1519

Flower of Life
c 1958
Colour lithograph on paper (15/50)
73.5 x 54 (paper size)
Purchased 1960
GMA 755

[z refers to the artist's unpublished list of his own drawings and watercolours]

Ian Hamilton Finlay

1925–

For an explanation of terms and catalogue order, see p. 18. For Finlay's non-printed work, and for the prints published by the Wild Hawthorn Press (which Finlay co-established), see the main catalogue section.

'2'
[IHF 5.162]; 1991; folding card; 14.4 x 11.9; purchased 1992; GMA A4.683

3/3 's
[IHF 3.29]; 1969; booklet, 12 pp; 21.2 x 18; purchased 1975; GMA A4.2

3 Columns
(with Catherine Lovegrove)
[IHF 5.179]; 1991; lithograph; 37.5 x 26.1; purchased 1992; GMA A4.711

3 Developments
[IHF 3.91]; 1982; booklet, 28 pp; 9.9 x 11.1; purchased 1982; GMA A4.3

3 Names of Barges
(with Margot Sandeman)
[IHF 4.18]; 1969; card; 16.6 x 12.2; purchased 1975; GMA A4.4

3 Spaces
[IHF 5.171]; 1991; concertina; 9.8 x 7.8; purchased 1992; GMA A4.680

3 Stitches
(with Kathleen Lindsley)
[IHF 3.124]; 1991; booklet, 16 pp; 10.8 x 7.9; purchased 1992; GMA A4.662

3 Texts
(with Stephen Raw)
[IHF 3.110]; 1989; booklet, 16 pp; 13.5 x 13; purchased 1991; GMA A4.599

4 Baskets
(with Kathleen Lindsley)
[IHF 3.122]; 1990; booklet, 16 pp; 9.8 x 9.3; purchased 1992; GMA A4.664

4 Blades
(with Gary Hincks)
[IHF 3.101]; 1986; 6 cards and folded card in folder; 7.6 x 8; purchased 1987; GMA A4.5

4 Colonnes, 8 Affiches pour l'Abbaye Cistercienne de l'Epau
[IHF 6.20]; 1986; eight lithographic texts in folder; 42.2 x 64.5; purchased 1987; GMA A4.6

4 Sails
(with Ed Wright and photograph by J. W. Lucas)
[IHF 4.20]; 1969; card; 16.5 x 13.7; purchased 1975; GMA A4.7

4 Sails
(with Ed Wright)
[IHF 5.3]; 1966; folding letterpress sheet; 16.6 x 13.8; purchase date unrecorded; GMA A4.8

5 Proverbs for Jacobins
(with Kathleen Lindsley)
[IHF 3.116]; 1989; booklet, 20 pp; 11.6 x 7; purchased 1991; GMA A4.588

5 Signposts
(with Kathleen Lindsley)
[IHF 6.38]; 1989; folding card; 21 x 15; purchased 1991; GMA A4.534

5 Words
[IHF 4.207]; 1986; folding card; 8.5 x 5.9; purchased 1987; GMA A4.9

10. Counter-Argument
[IHF 4.136]; 1978; card; 9.4 x 13.8; purchased 1978; GMA A4.10

30 Signatures to Silver Catches
(with Margot Sandeman)
[IHF 3.38]; 1971; booklet, 80 pp; 7.6 x 21.6; purchased 1975; GMA A4.11

35 One-Word Poems
See Curfew/Curlew; Deep-V-Hull/ Geese; Drip-Dry/May; Moorland/ Marquetry; Osiris/Osiers

1794
[IHF 5.152]; 1990; folder with 4 pp insert; 17.6 x 11; purchased 1992; GMA A4.686

1930 / 1980
[IHF 4.269]; 1988; card; 10.1 x 12.7; purchased 1991; GMA A4.619

1989 Belongs to the Public . . .
See Sandwich Board: 1989 Belongs . . .

According to the National Trust . . .
[IHF 4.230]; 1987; card; 11 x 8; purchased 1987; GMA A4.13

Achtung: Minen
(with Michael Harvey)
[IHF 4:123]; 1977; card; 15 x 10.4; purchased 1977; GMA A4.14

Acrobats
[IHF 5.5]; 1966; screenprint; 53.4 x 38; purchased 1975; GMA A4.16

'Adventurer' – Bath
(with Laurie Clark)
[IHF 4.117]; 1976; card; 15 x 10; purchased 1991; GMA A4.605

Advertising Fascism
[IHF 4.247]; 1987; card; 9.6 x 15.2; purchased 1987; GMA A4.17

After
(with Grahame Jones)
[IHF 3.112]; 1989; booklet, 8 pp; 13.5 x 13; purchased 1991; GMA A4.594

After Basho
[IHF 4.282]; 1988; card; 13.4 x 8.3; purchased 1991; GMA A4.624

After Bernini
(with Gary Hincks)
[IHF 5.101]; 1987; screenprint; 70.9 x 45.7; purchased 1987; GMA A4.18

After John Flaxman R. A.
(with Gary Hincks)
[IHF 4.152]; 1980; card; 13.6 x 11.8; purchased 1980; GMA A4.19

After Piranesi
(with Gary Hincks)
[IHF 5.176]; 1991; lithograph; 47.2 x 37; purchased 1992; GMA A4.709

After Thomas Hearn
See Paladian Picturesque: After Thomas Hearn

Against the Hébertists and the Dantonists
[IHF 4.173]; 1983; card; 17.8 x 12.8; purchased 1983; GMA A4.21

Air Letters
(with Robert Frame)
[IHF 3.27]; 1968; booklet, 20 pp; 25.6 x 10.4; purchased 1991; GMA A4.563

Airs, Waters, Graces
(with Ron Costley)
[IHF 3.60]; 1975; booklet, 16 pp; 26 x 17.5; purchased 1976; GMA A4.71

Ajar
[IHF 5.9]; 1967; screenprint; 57.4 x 40.6; purchased 1975; GMA A4.24

All that Glitters . . .
See Picabia Series (I)

Amaryllis BCK 55 (from set of three tiles)
(with Michael Harvey)
[IHF 7.51]; c 1976–78; ceramic tile; 15.3 x 15.3; purchased c 1976–78; GMA A4.25

L'Ami du peuple
[IHF 5.134]; 1989; lithograph; 42 x 30; purchased 1991; GMA A4.560

The Anaximander Fragment
(with Harvey Dwight)
[IHF 3.87]; 1981; booklet, 40 pp; 11.5 x 11.6; purchased 1981; GMA A4.26

And Even as She Fled . . . (1)
(with John R. Nash)
[IHF 5.99]; 1987; printed text; 43 x 56; purchased 1987; GMA A4.27

'And How Many Divisions Has Arcady ?'
(with John Borg Manduca)
[IHF 4.146]; 1979; card; 10.4 x 14.9; purchased 1981; GMA A4.29

Angélique et Medor
(with Nicholas Sloan)
[IHF 5.72]; 1981; screenprint in folder; 23 x 16.5; purchased 1981; GMA A4.30

Anticipations
[IHF 3.94]; 1982; booklet, 12 pp; 11.4 x 10.4; purchased 1982; GMA A4.31

Apollo and Daphne, after Bernini
(with Ron Costley)
[IHF 5.60]; 1977; screenprint; 49.7 x 36; purchased 1977; GMA A4.32

Apollo in Strathclyde
(photograph by Marius Alexander)
[IHF 4.220]; 1986; card; 14 x 18.4; purchased 1986; GMA A4.33

Arbre (Tree)
[IHF 4.150]; 1979; bookmark; 15.8 x 3.6; purchased 1981; GMA A4.35

Arbre de la liberté
[IHF 4.243]; 1987; folding card; 14.2 x 12; purchased 1987; GMA A4.34

Arcadia
(with George Oliver)
[IHF 5.45]; 1973; screenprint; 35.5 x 43.8; purchased 1975; GMA A4.36

Arcadian Gliders
(with Steve Wheatley)
[IHF 7.21]; 1981; boxed models with instructions and rubber bands to make nine gliders; 22 x 15.5 x 1.2; purchased 1981; GMA A4.37

Arcadian Sundials
(with Margot Sandeman)
[IHF 4.25]; 1970; folding card; 11.3 x 15.8 (folded); purchased 1975; GMA A4.39

The Archangel of Archangel (A Full Rigged Ship in the Manner of Fuseli)
(with Sydney McK. Glen)
[IHF 5.28]; 1971; print in folder; 25.4 x 19.6; purchased 1975; GMA A4.20

Are Aircraft Carriers Urban or Rural?
(with John Borg Manduca)
[IHF 5.56]; 1976; lithograph; 34.3 x 48.2; purchased 1976; GMA A4.40

Arrosoir
(with Gary Hincks)
[IHF 5.83]; 1984; print; 29.5 x 23; purchased 1992; GMA A4.724

Arrosoir: A Regeneration
(with Gary Hincks)
[IHF 4.183]; 1984; folding card; 23 x 18; purchased 1992; GMA A4.734

Arrow
(with Ron Costley)
[IHF 4.195]; 1985; folding card; 20.5 x 10.5; purchased 1986; GMA A4.41

Art Press is Part Cress . . .
See Picabia Series (I)

Art Press, Paris Announces
[IHF 4.245]; 1987; card; 16.8 x 13.1; purchased 1987; GMA A4.42

Attack Letter Dart
See Beat the Reds with the White Wedge. Correspond

'Auch ich war in Arkadien'
[IHF 4.137]; 1978; card; 9.6 x 14; purchased 1978; GMA A4.43

Autumn
[IHF 5.180]; 1991; folder with 4 pp insert; 17.8 x 14; purchased 1992; GMA A4.687

The Axis
(with Alexander Finlay)
[IHF 3.63]; 1975; booklet, 12 pp; 11.2 x 11.2; purchased 1976; GMA A4.44

Bal des victimes
[IHF 5.132]; 1989; screenprint; 62 x 81.5; purchased 1991; GMA A4.655

Barges
See 3 Names of Barges

Bark / Barque / Baroque
(with John R. Nash)
[IHF 4.281]; 1988; card; 13.1 x 20.3; purchased 1988; GMA A4.45

Barque: Homage to Jonathan Williams
(with Michael Harvey)
[IHF 4.65]; 1972; card; 18 x 13.8; purchased 1975; GMA A4.46

Basta
See I Saw a Work . . . (Basta)

Bath Roundels
(photograph by George Oliver)
[IHF 4.76]; 1973; card; 10.5 x 15.2; purchased 1975; GMA A4.47

Battle of Little Sparta (Anniversary Cards)
See March 15 1987 . . .; February 4 Nothing . . .; Third Anniversary . . .

Battle of Midway. 4 June 1942 (I)
(with Ron Costley)
[IHF 5.58]; 1977; screenprint; 64 x 97; purchased 1977; GMA A4.48

Battle of Midway. 4 June 1942
[IHF 7.53]; c 1977; ceramic tile; 15.3 x 15.3; purchased c 1977; GMA A4.49

Battle of Midway. 4 June 1942 (II)
(with Ron Costley)
[IHF 5.59]; 1977; screenprint; 64.1 x 97.1; purchased 1977; GMA A4.50

Battle of the Atlantic, Livingston
[IHF 4.126]; 1977; card; 26.7 x 11.1; purchased 1977; GMA A4.51

Beat the Reds with the White Wedge: Correspond
[IHF 4.160]; 1983; triangular folding card; 22.9 x 19; purchased 1983; GMA A4.52

La Belle hollandaise
(with Herbert Rosenthal)
[IHF 5.10]; 1967; screenprint; 56.5 x 43.3; purchased 1975; GMA A4.236

Betula Pendula
(with Gary Hincks)
[IHF 4.125]; 1977; card; 11.5 x 13.5; purchased 1977; GMA A4.53

Bicentenary Texts
[IHF 3.115]; 1989; booklet, 20 pp; 22
x 17.3; purchased 1991; GMA A4.575

Bicentenary Tricolour
(with Gary Hincks)
[IHF 5.133]; 1989; print; 40.5 x 52;
purchased 1991; GMA A4.558

Birch-Bark
(with Diane Tammes)
[IHF 4.46]; 1971; card; 16.7 x 10.3;
purchased 1975; GMA A4.54

Birds Fly, Waterfowl Ply
(with Gary Hincks)
[IHF 4.289]; 1989; folding card; 11.5
x 8.9; purchased 1991; GMA A4.600

The Blade Stained . . .
See Sandwich Board: The Blade . . .

Blades
[IHF 3.114]; 1989; booklet, 16 pp; 15.3
x 20.6; purchased 1991; GMA A4.574

Blades
(with Gary Hincks)
[IHF 4.273]; 1988; concertina; 8.8 x 8;
purchased 1991; GMA A4.627

The Blue and the Brown Poems
See Jargon: The Blue and the Brown
Poems

Blue Water's Bark
(with Ron Costley)
[IHF 4.148]; 1979; folding card; 7.8
x 24; purchased 1981; GMA A4.57

Blue Water's Bark
(with Diane Tammes)
[IHF 4.66]; 1972; folding card; 5.4
x 7.6; purchased 1975; GMA A4.188

A Boatyard
[IHF 3.31]; 1969; folding card-booklet;
12.5 x 10.2; purchased 1975; GMA
A4.58

Bobbin
(with Karl Torok)
[IHF 4.89]; 1974; folding card; 8.8
x 11.7; purchased 1975; GMA A4.62

Bois d'amour – Homage to Sérusier
[IHF 5.65]; 1978; card in folder; 20
x 16.5; purchased 1978; GMA A4.59

Book-Flag
(with Ron Costley)
[IHF 4.48]; 1971; screenprint; 4.9
x 14.9; purchased 1975; GMA A4.60

Both the Garden Style . . .
(with Gary Hincks)
[IHF 5.104]; 1987; print; 47.5 x 30.5;
purchased 1987; GMA A4.144

Bouleau / Birch
(with Caroline Webb)
[IHF 4.319]; 1991; card; 3.1 x 14.6;
purchased 1992; GMA A4.658

'Brailed'
(with Grahame Jones)
[IHF 5.128]; 1988; print in folder; 25.1
x 21.5; purchased 1991; GMA A4.648

Broken / Bent
[IHF 5.175]; 1991; folder with 4 pp
insert; 13.4 x 11; purchased 1992;
GMA A4.695

Brount
[IHF 4.250]; 1987; card; 16.8 x 11.5;
purchased 1987; GMA A4.64

'But Pleasures are like Poppies
Spread'
[IHF 4.283]; 1988; folding card; 8.5
x 12.7; purchased 1991; GMA A4.618

Butterfly
See A Red Admiral or A. B.

Butterfly Garden
(with George L. Thomson)
[IHF 7.13]; 1979; envelope with 12
tags and ties; envelope 13 x 19; tags
3.7 x 11.3; purchased 1979; GMA
A4.65

Calendar
(with Laurie Clark)
[IHF 4.113]; 1975; folding card; 22.2
x 14.6; purchased 1991; GMA A4.585

Callimachus (Kilkenny Castle
Exhibition poster)
(with Gary Hincks)
[IHF 5.143]; 1989; poster; 60.1 x 46.7;
purchased 1991; GMA A4.642

A Calm in a Tea-cup (after Kate
Greenaway)
(with Richard Demarco)
[IHF 4.82]; 1973; folding card; 16.5
x 13.6; purchased 1975; GMA A4.66

Canal Stripe Series 3
[IHF 3.6]; 1964; booklet, 32 pp; 15
x 20; purchased 1991; GMA A4.562

Canal Stripe Series 4
[IHF 3.7]; 1964; booklet, 16 pp; 17.5
x 28; purchased 1991; GMA A4.577

Capital
(with Michael Harvey)
[IHF 5.166]; 1991; screenprint; 30.2
x 81; purchased 1992; GMA A4.717

Capital, n. A Republican Crown
(with Lucius Burckhardt)
[IHF 4.156]; 1981; folding card; 5 x 7;
purchased 1981; GMA A4.67

Card for the Third Anniversary of
Strathclyde Region's Assault on the
Garden Temple, Little Sparta, March
15, 1983
[IHF 4.201]; 1986; card; 12.5 x 8.2;
purchased 1991; GMA A4.589

Carnation
[IHF 5.107]; 1987; text cut in two in
envelope; 22.5 x 15.5; purchased
1987; GMA A4.69

Carnation
[IHF 7.29]; 1987; cut card in envelope;
23 x 16.3; purchased 1991; GMA
A4.571

The Case of the Intellectual Terrorist
See Committee of General Security

Catameringue
(with Peter Grant)
[IHF 5.19]; 1970; screenprint; 35.5
x 43.8; purchased 1975; GMA A4.70

Catches
(with Margot Sandeman)
[IHF 4.52]; 1971; folding card; 11.4
x 11.4; purchased 1975; GMA A4.72

Ceci n'est pas une pipe (after
Magritte)
(with Gary Hincks)
[IHF 5.168]; 1991; print; 62.2 x 80.9;
purchased 1992; GMA A4.722

A Celebration of the Grove: a
Proposal for the Improvement of the
Olive Grove at Celle
(with Nicholas Sloan)
[IHF 6.3]; 1984; book, 30 pp; 21.9
x 14.5; purchased 1984; GMA A4.73

Ceolfrith 5: 'Ian Hamilton Finlay
with photographs by Diane Tammes'
[IHF 3.36]; 1970; book with loose
photographs and texts; 25 x 20;
purchase date unrecorded; GMA A4.74

Chanson d'automne
[IHF 5.93]; 1986; 2 cards in folder; 22
x 16.5; purchased 1987; GMA A4.76

A Chant for a Regional Occasion:
2000 Voices
[IHF 5.79]; 1983; folding card; 14.2
x 15; purchased 1983; GMA A4.77

Charm
(with Laurie Clark)
[IHF 4.187]; 1984; card; 15.3 x 11.8;
purchased 1986; GMA A4.495

Cherry Stones
(photograph by Dave Paterson)
[IHF 4.99]; 1975; card; 10.2 x 14.7;
purchased 1975; GMA A4.78

Christmas 1990: Les petites nativités
(with Ron Costley)
[ex IHF]; 1990; card in wrapper; 21
x 29.7; purchased 1990; GMA A4.79

Christmas Card
[IHF 4.318]; 1991; folding card; 10
x 7.2; purchased 1992; GMA A4.679

Christmas Card (Month of the Pocket
Battleship)
[IHF 4.193]; 1984; folding card; 10.2
x 9; purchased 1986; GMA A4.282

Les Cimetières des naufrages
[IHF 5.69]; 1981; card in folder; 19
x 16; purchased 1981; GMA A4.244

Le Circus (Poster-poem)
[IHF 5.4]; 1964; screenprint; 44.3
x 57.7; presented anonymously 1965;
GMA A4.347

Classical / Neoclassical
(with Gary Hincks)
[IHF 5.112]; 1987; print; 63.5 x 24.5;
purchased 1991; GMA A4.651

A Classic Landscape
(with Ian Gardner)
[IHF 5.70]; 1981; print, 43 x 35.5;
purchased 1981; GMA A4.80

Clay the Life
(with Alexander Stoddart)
[IHF 5.123]; 1987; folding print; 35
x 26.5; purchased 1991; GMA A4.547

Closed
[IHF 4.181]; 1983; card; 20.5 x 15.5;
purchased 1983; GMA A4.81

Column – Drum to Drum
(with Gary Hincks)
[IHF 5.178]; 1991; lithograph; 23.7
x 57.3; purchased 1992; GMA A4.708

Committee of General Security
[IHF 4.270]; 1988; card; 10.1 x 14.8;
purchased 1991; GMA A4.622

Concilium Artium . . .
See Posters Against the S. A. C.

A Concise Classical Dictionary
[IHF 3.107]; 1988; book, 52 pp; 31.4
x 22; purchased 1991; GMA A4.579

Copyright
(with Ron Costley)
[IHF 5.41]; 1973; folding card; 11.2
x 11.2 (folded); purchased 1975; GMA
A4.85

Corinthian Capital
(with Nicholas Sloan)
[IHF 5.85]; 1985; paper cut-out; 42.5
x 32; purchased 1985; GMA A4.86

Counter-Argument
See 10. Counter-Argument

Countercomposition
(with Gary Hincks)
[IHF 5.142]; 1989; screenprint; 79
x 62; purchased 1991; GMA A4.656

A Country Lane (A Proposal for the
Glasgow Garden Festival)
(with Laurie Clark)
[IHF 6.30]; 1988; booklet, 24 pp; 15.4
x 10.8; purchased 1991; GMA A4.592

Le Couperet n'est pas . . .
See Sandwich Board: Le Couperet . . .

Cruel and Ingenious Sophists . . .
[IHF 4.266]; 1987; card; 10.3 x 14.2;
purchased 1991; GMA A4.625

Curfew / Curlew (from '35 One-
Word Poems')
(with Ian Gardner)
[IHF 4.158]; 1982; card; 14.8 x 10.5;
purchased 1982; GMA A4.506

'Cythera'
(with Peter Lyle)
[IHF 4.145]; 1979; card; 19 x 9.3;
purchased 1981; GMA A4.88

D 1 (The Haystack's Wisp)
(with Michael Harvey)
[IHF 5.38]; 1972; two prints in folder;
16.2 x 16.2; purchased 1975; GMA
A4.90

'Daddy, What Did You Do in the
Little Spartan War ?'
[IHF 4.190]; 1984; card; 18.3 x 12.4;
purchased 1986; GMA A4.91

Daisies
(with Ian Gardner)
[IHF 4.47]; 1971; card; 15.3 x 10.2;
purchased 1975; GMA A4.89

Decal Sheet 62
(with Gary Hincks)
[IHF 5.154]; 1990; lithograph; 59.5
x 42; purchased 1992; GMA A4.719

Deep-V-Hull / Geese (from '35 One-
Word Poems')
(with Ian Gardner)
[IHF 4.158]; 1982; card; 14.8 x 10.5;
purchased 1991; GMA A4.630 B

A Definition for Michael Blum.
Ambiguous, n.
[IHF 4.284]; 1988; folding card; 5.2
x 9.6; purchased 1991; GMA A4.620

Definitions of Lawns 2
(with Michael Harvey)
[IHF 4.87]; 1974; folding card; 6.6
x 11.9; purchased 1975; GMA A4.92

Delegation without Response
[IHF 5.121]; 1987; printed text; 30
x 21; purchased 1991; GMA A4.543

De Man
[IHF 4.301]; 1989; card; 12.8 x 20.3;
purchased 1991; GMA A4.570

The Desmoulins Connection
[IHF 4.285]; 1988; set of five folding
cards; 4.5 x 10; purchased 1988; GMA
A4.95

Detached Sentences on Weather
(with Jo Hincks)
[IHF 3.104]; 1986; booklet, 20 pp; 18.2
x 12; purchased 1987; GMA A4.96

Detached Sentences on Friendship
(with Kathleen Lindsley)
[IHF 3.130]; 1991; booklet, 20 pp; 9.8
x 6.8; purchased 1992; GMA A4.702

Dialogue
[IHF 4.227]; 1987; card; 11.4 x 14.1;
purchased 1987; GMA A4.97

Diamond-Studded Fish-Net
(with Julie Farthing)
[IHF 5.165]; 1991; screenprint; 26.2
x 90; purchased 1992; GMA A4.715

The Difference between a House . . .
(with Mark Stewart)
[IHF 4.241]; 1987; card; 12.8 x 10;
purchased 1987; GMA A4.98

Dim Wim: The Wee Wimp's in his Crazy Windmill
[IHF 4.234]; 1987; card; 13.5 x 10.1; purchased 1987; GMA A4.99

The Divided Meadows of Aphrodite
(with Ron Costley)
[IHF 4.101]; 1975; card; 14.9 x 10.5; purchase date unrecorded; GMA A4.100

Don't Cast Your Revolutions . . .
See Picabia Series (II)

Don't Put All Your Heads . . .
See Picabia Series (II)

Dove, Dead in its Snows
(with Julie Farthing)
[IHF 5.164]; 1991; screenprint; 20.1 x 101.5; purchased 1992; GMA A4.738

Drip-Dry / May (from '35 One-Word Poems')
(with Ian Gardner)
[IHF 4.158]; 1982; card; 14.8 x 10.5; purchased 1991; GMA A4.630 C

A Dryad Discovered
(with Grahame Jones)
[IHF 4.164]; 1983; folding card; 20 x 8.8; purchased 1983; GMA A4.101

Dzaezl
(with John Borg Manduca)
[IHF 3.75]; 1979; booklet, 20 pp; 15 x 21; purchased 1979; GMA A4.102

Eastertide
(with Laurie Clark)
[IHF 4.105]; 1975; folding card; 7.7 x 8; purchased 1975; GMA A4.103

'Elegiac Inscription' (Stonypath Garden and Gallery Series)
(with John Andrew, photograph by Michael McQueen)
[IHF 4.112]; 1975; card; 22 x 15.2; purchased 1991; GMA A4.572

The End
(with Ian Gardner)
[IHF 4.60]; 1972; folding card; 7.5 x 8.6; purchased 1972; GMA A4.104

The Enlightenment
[IHF 4.235]; 1987; card; 7.1 x 22.6; purchased 1987; GMA A4.105

Enterprise (A Celebration of Earth, Air, Fire and Water)
(with Ron Costley)
[IHF 7.55]; c 1976–78; ceramic tile; 15.3 x 15.3; purchased c 1976–78; GMA A4.106

Epictetus Discourse ('The External Impressions . . .')
(with Grahame Jones)
[IHF 5.76]; 1982; watercolour in folder; watercolour 7.5 x 10.4 (paper 42 x 29.4cm); purchased 1982; GMA A4.108

Epicurus at Châtou
(with Ron Costley)
[IHF 3.100]; 1985; booklet, 24 pp; 8.9 x 31.7; purchased 1987; GMA A4.107

Equality Does not Consist . . . (Ian Hamilton Finlay Poster)
[IHF 5.82]; 1983; poster; 21 x 30; purchased 1983; GMA A4.201 C

Errata
(with David Button)
[IHF 5.18]; 1970; two prints in folder; 25.4 x 50.8; purchased 1975; GMA A4.111

The Errata of Ovid
[IHF 3.96]; 1983; 8 cards in folder; 7.8 x 8.2; purchased 1986; GMA A4.110

Estuary Cupboards
(with Michael Harvey)
[IHF 4.71]; 1973; folding card; 14.1 x 12.1; purchased 1975; GMA A4.113

Evening / Sail
[IHF 5.17]; 1970; screenprint; 80.5 x 28; purchased 1975; GMA A4.220

Evening / Sail 2
(with Michael Harvey)
[IHF 3.44]; 1971; booklet, 12 pp; 8.3 x 13; purchased 1975; GMA A4.114

Evening / Sail
[IHF 7.61]; 1991; enamelled metal brooch; 5.1 x 1.2; purchased 1992; GMA A4.703

Evening / Sail*
[IHF 5.173]; 1991; screenprint; 84 x 28; purchased 1992; GMA A4.716

Even the Oatmeal Drink . . .
[IHF 4.210]; 1986; folding card; 5.5 x 4; purchased 1987; GMA A4.115

'Every Effect . . .'
(with Jo Hincks)
[IHF 5.129]; 1988; folding print; 15.5 x 24.5; purchased 1991; GMA A4.556

Every Goal Negates . . .
[IHF 4.194]; 1985; triangular folded card; 21 x 17.3; purchased 1985; GMA A4.116

Exercise X
(with George L. Thomson)
[IHF 3.53]; 1973; booklet, 24 pp; 13.9 x 9.5; purchased 1975; GMA A4.117

Ex Libris, RH 202 Lyre
[IHF 7.36]; 1989; card; 11.8 x 8.9; purchased 1991; GMA A4.626

F 1
(photograph by John Roberts)
[IHF 4.59]; 1972; folding card; 6.7 x 18.6; purchased 1975; GMA A4.118

A Family
[IHF 3.50]; 1973; booklet, 16 pp, with bookmark; 15.4 x 11.7; purchased 1975; GMA A4.119

Family Group
(with Karl Torok)
[IHF 5.43]; 1973; print in folder; 16.1 x 26.2; purchased 1975; GMA A4.120

Family. A Homage to Simon Cutts
(photograph by Dave Paterson)
[IHF 4.104]; 1975; folding card; 11.8 x 13.6; purchased 1975; GMA A4.184

February 4 Nothing: Fourth Anniversary of the Battle of Little Sparta
[IHF 4.222]; 1987; card; 14 x 12.6; purchased 1987; GMA A4.121

Fewer Sculptures . . .
[IHF 4.196]; 1985; card; 10.5 x 24.6; purchased 1986; GMA A4.122

Filiger (from the Nabis Series)
[IHF 5.108]; 1987; card in folder; 22.8 x 22.2; purchased 1987; GMA A4.123

Fill in the Flowers . . .
(with Jim Downie, after Laurie and Tom Clark)
[IHF 5.62]; 1977; print in folder; 23 x 28; purchase date unrecorded; GMA A4.132

The First Battle of Little Sparta (Medal of the Little Spartan War)
[IHF 7.34]; 1984; bronze medal; 2.9 x 5.4 x 0.2; purchased 1984; GMA A4.124

First Suprematist Standing Poem
[IHF 4.5]; 1965; folding card; 22.8 x 9.5; presented by Mr Edward Lucie-Smith through the Victoria and Albert Museum 1976; GMA A4.125

Fishing News News
(with Margot Sandeman)
[IHF 3.35]; 1970; concertina; 7.3 x 10.3; purchased 1975; GMA A4.126

Five . . .
See also 5

Five Fore-and-Afters
(with George L. Thomson)
[IHF 7.41]; c 1976–78; ceramic tile;
15.4 x 15.4; purchased c 1976–78;
GMA A4.127

The Flageolet's Surname
(with Kathleen Lindsley)
[IHF 4.296]; 1989; card; 6.4 x 8.9;
purchased 1991; GMA A4.614

Flags
(with acknowledgements to Simon
Cutts)
[IHF 4.38]; 1971; card; 12.1 x 16.7;
purchased 1975; GMA A4.128

Flakes
(with Gary Hincks)
[IHF 3.123]; 1990; booklet, 32 pp; 7.5
x 7.5; purchased 1992; GMA A4.667

Flotte de pêche
(with Ron Costley)
[IHF 4.94]; 1974; card; 10.4 x 14.7;
purchased 1975; GMA A4.131

Flowers
See Fill in the Flowers . . .

A Flute for Saint-Just
[IHF 4.171]; 1983; card; 20.6 x 12.4;
purchased 1983; GMA A4.133

Follies – A Little Spartan Guide to
the National Trust
[IHF 5.95]; 1987; paper; 30 x 21;
purchased 1987; GMA A4.134

Forget-me-not
(with Stephanie Kedik)
[IHF 4.205]; 1986; folding card; 9.1
x 6; purchased 1987; GMA A4.288

For Klaus Werner. Proposal for a
Postscript to 'The Present Order'
[IHF 6.50]; 1991; pamphlet, 4 pp; 18 ?
x 11; purchased 1992; GMA A4.672

For Simon Cutts
[IHF 4.290]; 1989; folding card; 14
x 9.5; purchased 1991; GMA A4.623

Four . . .
See also 4

Four Monostichs
[IHF 3.132]; 1991; booklet, 12 pp with
4 fold-outs; 10.7 x 16.1; purchased
1992; GMA A4.669

The Four Seas-ons as Fore and Afters
[exc. IHF]; c 1976–78; ceramic tile;
10.9 x 10.9; purchase date
unrecorded; GMA A4.135

The French Attaché . . .
See Picabia Series (I)

From 'An Inland Garden'
(with Ian Gardner)
[IHF 3.43]; 1971; booklet, 12 pp; 14.9
x 11; purchased 1975; GMA A4.138

From 'Clerihews for Liberals'
[IHF 4.255]; 1987; card; 13.5 x 14.2;
purchased 1987; GMA A4.136

From "The Metamorphoses of
'Fishing News'"
[IHF 4.26]; 1970; card; 12.6 x 16.9;
purchased 1975; GMA A4.139

From the Nabis Series
See Filiger . . .; Der Untergang . . .;
Poire / Loire

Futura 7: Five Poems
[IHF 3.9]; 1966; folded sheet; 24 x 16;
presented by Mr Edward Lucie-Smith
through the Victoria and Albert
Museum 1976; GMA A4.141

The Garden is Open
[IIII 4.256]; 1987; card; 9 x 12.7;
purchased 1987; GMA A4.142

Gateway to a Grove
(with Michael Harvey)
[IHF 6.14]; 1985; two prints in folder;
25 x 29.5; purchased 1986; GMA
A4.145

Le Geste Girondin . . .
See Sandwich Board: Le Geste . . .

Girondism is Not a Faith . .
See Sandwich Board: Girondism . . .

The Girondist Perceives . . .
See Sandwich Board: The
Girondist . . .

Glossary
(with Richard Demarco)
[IHF 5.29]; 1971; screenprint with
folded screenprint; 22.9 x 41.3;
purchased 1975; GMA A4.146

Golden Age
(with Gary Hincks)
[IHF 5.160]; 1990; folder with 4 pp
insert; 19.5 x 11.8; purchased 1992;
GMA A4.685

Gourd
(with Ron Costley)
[IHF 5.47]; 1974; screenprint in
folder; 27.9 x 20.9; purchased 1975;
GMA A4.147

The Great Piece of Turf: Stoneypath
Garden and Gallery Series
(photograph by Michael McQueen)
[IHF 4.110]; 1975; card; 15.3 x 22;
purchased 1975; GMA A4.148

Grove, n.
(with Gary Hincks)
[IHF 5.120]; 1987; print in folder; 38.5
x 45; purchased 1991; GMA A4.650

Gulfs and Wars
[IHF 5.169]; 1991; screenprint; 59.5
x 40.2; purchased 1992; GMA A4.718

Handley Page Heyford
(with Gary Hincks)
[IHF 4.140]; 1978; card; 16.7 x 12.8;
purchased 1978; GMA A4.150

The Harbour
(with Michael Harvey)
[IHF 7.43]; c 1976–78; ceramic tile;
15.4 x 15.4; purchased c 1976–78;
GMA A4.151

The Harbour at Gravelines
(with Gary Hincks)
[IHF 5.64]; 1978; screenprint; 51
x 61; purchased 1978; GMA A4.152

Harlequin
(with Karl Torok)
[IHF 4.85]; 1974; folding card; 10.1
x 10.1; purchased 1975; GMA A4.153

Head of Gwyn Headley
[IIII 4.251]; 1987; card; 16.9 x 10.4;
purchased 1987; GMA A4.156

Head of the Dead Marat
(with Gary Hincks)
[IHF 5.96]; 1987; lithograph; 77
x 62.5; purchased 1987; GMA A4.155

Head of Waldemar Januszczak
[IHF 4.252]; 1987; card; 16.9 x 10.4;
purchased 1987; GMA A4.157

A Heart-Shape
(with Ron Costley)
[IHF 4.45]; 1971; card; 14.9 x 10.6;
purchased 1975; GMA A4.159

Hedgehog Garden Hint
[IHF 4.277]; 1988; card; 10 x 14;
purchased 1991; GMA A4.610

Heraclitean Variations
[IHF 3.102]; 1986; booklet, 20 pp; 11
x 9; purchased 1987; GMA A4.160

Heroic Anagrams: Saint-Just
(with Alexander Stoddart)
[IHF 4.182]; 1983; folding card; 22.5
x 9.5; purchased 1983; GMA A4.164

He Spoke Like an Axe
(with Richard Healy)
[IHF 4.184]; 1984; folding card; 6.5
x 21; purchased 1986; GMA A4.163

He was the First Schoolmaster . . .
[IHF 4.240]; 1987; card; 9.5 x 14;
purchased 1987; GMA A4.165

Les Hirondelles
(with Ron Costley)
[IHF 4.29]; 1970; card; 14.9 x 10.4;
purchased 1991; GMA A4.640

H. M. S. Illustrious
(with Richard England)
[IHF 5.36]; 1972; screenprint; 49.7
x 76.3; purchased 1975; GMA A4.166

Homage to Agam (Transformable Line Segments)
(with David Button)
[IHF 5.54]; 1976; two prints in folder;
38.5 x 26.6; purchased 1976; GMA A4.167

Homage to Donald McGill
[IHF 4.37]; 1971; card; 14.6 x 9.5;
purchased 1991; GMA A4.621

Homage to E. A. Hornel
[IHF 4.58]; 1972; card; 10.6 x 15.3;
purchased 1975; GMA A4.176

Homage to J. M. Synge
(with John Borg Manduca)
[IHF 4.129]; 1977; card; 11.8 x 15;
purchased 1977; GMA A4.170

Homage to Jonathan Williams
See Barque: Homage to Jonathan
Williams

Homage to Kahnweiler
(with Stuart Barrie)
[IHF 4.68]; 1972; card; 12.1 x 16.7;
purchased 1975; GMA A4.171

Homage to Kandinsky
(with Ron Costley)
[IHF 4.67]; 1971; card; 14.8 x 10.6;
purchased 1975; GMA A4.177

Homage to the L. A. Doust Art Manuals
[IHF 4.103]; 1975; folding card; 4.8
x 11.1; purchased 1975; GMA A4.178

Homage to Malevich
(with Michael Harvey)
[IHF 5.46]; 1974; lithograph in folder;
27.7 x 27.7; purchased 1975; GMA A4.172

Homage to Max Bill (Wild Hawthorn Weapons Series No. 2)
[IHF 4.91]; 1974; card; 15.3 x 10.2;
purchased 1975; GMA A4.173

Homage to Modern Art*
(with Jim Nicholson)
[IHF 5.35]; 1972; screenprint; 76.2
x 53.9; purchased 1975; GMA A4.179

Homage to "Mozart"
(with Ron Costley)
[IHF 5.22]; 1970; screenprint; 38.1
x 50.8; purchased 1975; GMA A4.181

Homage to Pop Art
(with Sydney McK. Glen)
[IHF 4.77]; 1973; card; 10.6 x 14.9;
purchased 1975; GMA A4.182

Homage to Poussin
(with John Borg Manduca)
[IHF 3.69]; 1977; booklet, 24 pp; 13
x 13; purchase date unrecorded; GMA A4.183

Homage to Robert Lax
[IHF 3.54]; 1974; booklet, 12 pp; 25.6
x 10.1; purchased 1975; GMA A4.369

A Homage to Simon Cutts
See Family. A Homage to Simon
Cutts

Homage to Victor Sylvester
(with Michael Harvey)
[IHF 4.79]; 1973; card; 11.5 x 13.8;
purchased 1975; GMA A4.185

Homage to Walter Reekie's Ring Netters
(with Ron Costley)
[IHF 4.62]; 1972; card; 10.6 x 14.9;
purchased 1975; GMA A4.186

Homage to Watteau: L'embarquement pour l'île de Cythère
[IHF 5.51]; 1975; print in folder; 35.4
x 24; purchase date unrecorded; GMA A4.243

Homage to Watteau: L'embarquement pour l'île de Cythère
[IHF 4.119]; 1976; card; 12 x 17.7;
purchased 1991; GMA A4.636

Hommage à David (1)
(with Ron Costley and Gary Hincks)
[IHF 4.166]; 1983; folding card; 8.4
x 7; purchased 1983; GMA A4.174

Hommage à David (2)
(with Ron Costley)
[IHF 4.167]; 1983; card; 27.2 x 10;
purchased 1983; GMA A4.175

Horloge de flore
(with Laurie Clark)
[IHF 4.106]; 1975; folding card; 15.6
x 17.6; purchased 1975; GMA A4.189

H) our Lady
(with Ron Costley)
[IHF 7.42]; c 1976–78; ceramic tile;
15.3 x 15.3; purchased c 1976–78;
GMA A4.190

How Will One Hide . . .
[IHF 4.209]; 1986; folding card; 4
x 5.5; purchased 1987; GMA A4.191

Idylle
(with Gary Hincks)
[IHF 5.181]; 1991; folder with 4 pp
insert; 16 x 6.1; purchased 1992; GMA A4.689

L'Idylle des cerises
(with Michael Harvey)
[IHF 6.17]; 1986; booklet, 8 pp; 14.8
x 21; purchased 1987; GMA A4.208

The Illustrated Esoteric Dictionary
See The Temple of Fame . . .

Imitations, Variations, Reflections, Copies
(with John Andrew, photographs by
Norman Dixon)
[IHF 3.66]; 1976; booklet, 28 pp; 11.7
x 12; purchased 1991; GMA A4.590

Imprisoned in Every Italian Battleship . . .
(with Mark Stewart)
[IHF 4.242]; 1987; card; 16.1 x 11;
purchased 1987; GMA A4.211

An Improved Classical Dictionary
[IHF 3.88]; 1981; booklet, 28 pp; 11.4
x 9.3; purchased 1981; GMA A4.212

Improvisation No. 1
(with Carl Heideken)
[IHF 4.128]; 1977; card; 6.6 x 21;
purchased 1977; GMA A4.213

In Memoriam (The Roberts)
[IHF 4.122]; 1977; card; 11.9 x 9;
purchased 1977; GMA A4.214

Interior (Intérieur): Homage to Vuillard
(with Michael Harvey)
[IHF 5.32]; 1971; screenprint; 27.9 x 27.9; purchased 1975; GMA A4.216

Interpolations in Hegel
[IHF 3.98]; 1984; booklet, 20 pp; 14 x 9.7; purchased 1986; GMA A4.217

'In the Back of Every Dying Civilisation . . .'
[IHF 4.154]; 1981; card; 11.5 x 16.5; purchased 1981; GMA A4.218

Into the Forest
(with Andrew Townsend)
[IHF 6.37]; 1989; folding card; 10 x 12.4; purchased 1991; GMA A4.539

In World War I, Many Ships were Sunk . . .
[IHF 4.131]; 1977; folding card; 10.5 x 14.9; purchased 1991; GMA A4.595

I Only Know what is Just
(with Ian Calder Stewart)
[exc. IHF]; cut-out sundial in folder; 21 x 14.9; purchased 1992; GMA A4.735

Iron Ship
(with Ian Gardner)
[IHF 4.64]; 1972; card; 13.6 x 16; purchased 1975; GMA A4.219

I Saw a Work . . . (Bastu)
[IHF 4.278]; 1988; card; 16.5 x 14; purchased 1991; GMA A4.598

Is There a Ship Named the Wave Sheaf ?
(with Michael Harvey)
[IHF 4.57]; 1972; card; 10.6 x 14.9; purchased 1975; GMA A4.222

'I was a Member of the National Trust'
[IHF 4.212]; 1906; card; 18.2 x 14.1; purchased 1987; GMA A4.493

'I was Published by Jonathan Cape'
[IHF 4.213]; 1986; card; 18.2 x 14.1; purchased 1987; GMA A4.223

Jacobin Definitions
(with Kathleen Lindsley)
[IHF 3.125]; 1991; booklet, 24 pp; 10 x 10.4; purchased 1992; GMA A4.666

The Jacobin Vasarely
(with Gary Hincks)
[IHF 5.153]; 1990; two prints in folder; 21 x 21; purchased 1992; GMA A4.704

Jam-Pot Covers (Sundials: Lux Umbra Dei)
[IHF 7.9]; 1977; printed sheet; 16 x 30; purchased 1977; GMA A4.224

Jam-Pot Covers (Sundials)
[IHF 7.9]; 1977; printed sheet; 16 x 30; purchased 1977; GMA A4.261 A

Jam-Pot Covers (Sundials: Ferrea Virga Est / Stay-Sail)
[IHF 7.9]; 1977; printed sheet; 16 x 30; purchased 1977; GMA A4.261 B

Januszczak (Within this Thicket . . .)
[IHF 4.276]; 1988; card; 8.4 x 13; purchased 1991; GMA A4.608

Jargon: The Blue and Brown Poems
(with Atlantic Richfield and Stephen Bann)
[IHF 3.28]; 1968; calendar (12 poem-prints with commentaries); 51 x 38; purchased 1975; GMA A4.225

Jeunesse dorée of the Counter Revolution
[IHF 4.233]; 1987; card; 12.5 x 14.9; purchased 1987; GMA A4.226

Jibs
(photographs by Diane Tammes)
[IHF 3.47]; 1972; booklet, 26 pp; 10.8 x 11.6; purchased 1975; GMA A4.227

Join the Saint-Just Vigilantes (1) drums
[IHF 4.188]; 1983; card; 19.3 x 6.6; purchased 1986; GMA A4.229

Join the Saint-Just Vigilantes (2)
[IHF 4.189]; 1983; card; 16.4 x 12.6; purchased 1987; GMA A4.228

Joseph Bara, after Gris
(with Gary Hincks)
[IHF 5.98]; 1987; screenprint; 77 x 62.5; purchased 1987; GMA A4.230

Joseph Bara / Agricol Viala
[IHF 4.316]; 1991; card; 11.7 x 14.6; purchased 1992; GMA A4.731

Justice for the Fat Stupid Kids . . .
[IHF 4.238]; 1987; card; 9.5 x 14; purchased 1987; GMA A4.231

Kamikaze Butterflies
[IHF 3.48]; 1973; pamphlet; 21 x 13 (folded); purchased 1975; GMA A4.232

King
[IHF 5.150]; 1990; folder with 4 pp insert; 18.4 x 11.1; purchased 1992; GMA A4.674

Klassische Landschaft
(with Gary Hincks)
[IHF 6.13]; 1985; print in folder; 48.5 x 32.4; purchased 1986; GMA A4.233

Knitting was a Reserved Occupation
[IHF 5.105]; 1987; printed text; 21 x 29.5; purchased 1987; GMA A4.234

Laconic
(with Gary Hincks)
[IHF 5.118]; 1987; screenprint; 76 x 58.5; purchased 1991; GMA A4.646

Landscape / Interior
(with Karl Torok)
[IHF 4.81]; 1973; card; 9 x 19.5; purchased 1975; GMA A4.237

Landscape with Woods and a Pillar Box . . .
(with Ian Gardner)
[IHF 4.151]; 1980; card; 13.8 x 9; purchased 1981; GMA A4.238

The Land's Shadows
(with Ann Stevenson)
[IHF 4.12]; 1968; card; 9.6 x 25.4; purchased 1975; GMA A4.239

Lanes
(with Margot Sandeman)
[IHF 3.32]; 1969; book, 30 pp; 21.2 x 9.1; purchased 1975; GMA A4.240

Lasciate Ogni Speranza
[IHF 5.122]; 1987; print in black; 38 x 50.5; purchased 1991; GMA A4.554

The Last Cruise of the Emden
(with Ron Costley)
[IHF 7.54]; c 1976–78; ceramic tile; 7.6 x 15.4; purchased c 1976–78; GMA A4.210

The Last Norfolk Wherry
See Norfolk Woods: The Last Norfolk Wherry

The Laws of Liberty . . . (Ian Hamilton Finlay Poster)
[IHF 5.82]; 1983; poster; 21 x 30; purchased 1983; GMA A4.201 D

Leaf / Bark
[IHF 4.139]; 1978; bookmark; 15.8 x 3.9; purchased 1978; GMA A4.241

The League of Rights . . .
See Picabia Series (I)

Lettre de cachet
(with Gary Hincks)
[IHF 5.71]; 1981; print; 59 x 41.5; purchased 1981; GMA A4.247

Let us Invite Nature
[exc. IHF]; c 1977; white jam-pot
cover; 14.9 x 14.9; purchase date
unrecorded; GMA A4.637 A

Let us Invite Nature
[exc. IHF]; c 1977; blue jam-pot cover;
14.9 x 14.9; purchase date
unrecorded; GMA A4.637 B

Let us Invite Nature
[exc. IHF]; c 1977; red jam-pot cover;
14.9 x 14.9; purchase date
unrecorded; GMA A4.637 C

Lexical Diversions
(with Mark Stewart)
[IHF 4.175]; 1983; card; 15.2 x 15.4;
purchased 1983; GMA A4.248

Liberal Democracy . . .
[IHF 4.239]; 1987; card; 9.5 x 14;
purchased 1987; GMA A4.249

The Life of Saint-Just . . .
See Sandwich Board: The Life . . .

Ligue
[IHF 4.272]; 1988; card; 12 x 9.7;
purchased 1991; GMA A4.616

Ligue des droits
[IHF 4.271]; 1988; card; 13.2 x 10.8;
purchased 1991; GMA A4.615

Ligues des droits de l'homme
[IHF 5.119]; 1987; print; 29.7 x 42;
purchased 1991; GMA A4.559 A

Ligues des droits de l'homme
[IHF 5.119]; 1987; print; 42 x 29.7;
purchased 1991; GMA A4.559 B

A Litany, a Requiem
[IHF 3.85]; 1981; booklet, 12 pp; 9.7
x 5.7; purchased 1981; GMA A4.250

Little Fountain in Three Colours
[IHF 5.111]; 1987; print in folder; 22.5
x 17; purchased 1987; GMA A4.251

The Little Seamstress
(with Richard Demarco)
[IHF 5.21]; 1970; screenprint; 50.9
x 64.1; purchased 1975; GMA A4.252

Little Sermons Series: Cherries
(with Ian Gardner)
[IHF 3.89]; 1982; booklet, 12 pp; 7.6
x 9; purchased 1982; GMA A4.253

Little Sermons Series: Volume Makes
Beauty
(with Ian Gardner)
[IHF 3.90]; 1982; booklet, 12 pp; 7.6
x 9; purchased 1982; GMA A4.255

Little Sparta
[IHF 4.294]; 1989; card; 17.3 x 14.7;
purchased 1991; GMA A4.601

Little Sparta's Christmas Card:
Invitation to Football Match
[IHF 4.179]; 1983; card; 11 x 15;
purchased 1983; GMA A4.254

Loaves
(with Howard Eaglestone and Antonia
Reeve)
[IHF 3.105]; 1987; booklet, 8 pp; 7.1
x 10.5; purchased 1987; GMA A4.256

The Lone Sail
(with Laurie Clark)
[IHF 4.88]; 1974; bookmark; 12.7
x 4.6; purchased 1975; GMA A4.61

Long Laws are Public Calamities (Ian
Hamilton Finlay Poster)
[IHF 5.82]; 1983; poster; 21 x 30;
purchased 1983; GMA A4.201 B

Louis Treize
[IHF 4.248]; 1987; card; 9.6 x 15.2;
purchased 1987; GMA A4.257

Luftwaffe – after Mondrian
(with Jud Fine)
[IHF 5.53]; 1976; lithograph; 41.6
x 52.9; purchased 1976; GMA A4.258

Lullaby
(with John Andrew)
[IHF 5.52]; 1975; screenprint; 58.8
x 41.8; purchased 1975; GMA A4.259

Lullaby
(with John Andrew)
[IHF 4.96]; 1975; card; 14.9 x 10.6;
purchased 1975; GMA A4.260

Lyres 1
(photograph by Carl Heideken)
[IHF 4.115]; 1976; card; 15.3 x 10.2;
purchased 1991; GMA A4.593

Lyres 2
(photograph by Carl Heideken)
[IHF 4.121]; 1977; card; 10.5 x 15.6;
purchased 1977; GMA A4.262

The Mailed Pinkie
(with Gary Hincks)
[IHF 3.92]; 1982; booklet, 20 pp; 11.4
x 11.1; purchased 1982; GMA A4.263

Marat / Aplan
[IHF 4.216]; 1986; folding card; 3.1
x 13.3; purchased 1987; GMA A4.264

Marat assassiné
(with Gary Hincks)
[IHF 5.90]; 1986; lithograph; 76.8
x 62.7; purchased 1992; GMA A4.732

The Marble Arrow
[IHF 4.186]; 1984; triangular folding
card; 21 x 17.4; purchased 1984; GMA
A4.265

March 15 1987: Fourth Anniversary
of Strathclyde Region's Assault on
the Garden Temple, Little Sparta
[IHF 4.223]; 1987; card; 11.1 x 14.6;
sent by the artist 1987; GMA A4.266 A

March 15 1987: Fourth Anniversary
of Strathclyde Region's Assault on
the Garden Temple, Little Sparta
[IHF 4.223]; 1987; card; 11.1 x 14.6;
purchased 1987; GMA A4.266 B

Marine
(with Patrick Caulfield)
[IHF 5.12]; 1968; screenprint; 50.9
x 64.3; purchased 1975; GMA A4.267

Marine Prototypes
(photograph by Vic Smeed)
[IHF 4.100]; 1975; card; 15.1 x 10.7;
purchased 1976; GMA A4.268

Marionette 1
(photograph by Dave Paterson)
[IHF 4.132]; 1978; card; 10.3 x 15.3;
purchased 1978; GMA A4.269

Marionette 2
(photograph by Dave Paterson)
[IHF 4.133]; 1978; card; 15.3 x 10.3;
purchased 1978; GMA A4.270

Martin Waters
[IHF 4.298]; 1989; folding card; 5.5
x 9.9; purchased 1991; GMA A4.586

A Mast of Hankies
(photographs by Dave Paterson)
[IHF 3.62]; 1975; nine cards in folder;
14.6 x 10.1; purchased 1975; GMA
A4.271

Matisse chez Duplay
(with Julie Farthing)
[IHF 5.139]; 1989; screenprint; 59.5
x 42; purchased 1991; GMA A4.653

Matisse chez Duplay
(with Julie Farthing)
[IHF 7.38]; 1989; ceramic mug; 10.6
x 12.8 x 9.1; purchased 1989; GMA
A4.737

The Medium is the Message
[IHF 5.117]; 1987; screenprint; 76
x 58.5; purchased 1991; GMA A4.645

Memory
(with Ron Costley)
[IHF 4.259]; 1987; folding card; 7.5
x 7.5; purchased 1992; GMA A4.729

A Memory of Summer
(with Jim Nicholson)
[IHF 3.42]; 1971; folding card; 15.2
x 17.6; purchase date unrecorded;
GMA A4.272

A Memory of the '90s
[IHF 3.108]; 1989; folding card; 10.5
x 8.2; purchased 1991; GMA A4.591

Menu à la carte
[IHF 4.229]; 1987; card; 13.6 x 8.2;
purchased 1987; GMA A4.273

The Mexican Navy
(with Martin Fidler)
[IHF 4.84]; 1974; card; 10.2 x 15.3;
purchased 1975; GMA A4.275

Mid-Pacific Elements
[IHF 4.74]; 1973; concertina; 8 x 11.5
(folded); purchased 1975; GMA A4.276

Midway 3
(with Grahame Jones)
[IHF 3.93]; 1982; booklet, 8 pp; 13
x 25.2; purchased 1982; GMA
A4.278 A

Millet: Pseudo-Moralist
[IHF 5.115]; 1987; print; 42 x 30;
purchased 1991; GMA A4.544

A Mixed Exhibition
[IHF 3.95]; 1983; 2 booklets and folder
containing 11 cards in slipcase; 10.5
x 8; purchased 1983; GMA A4.280

A Model of Order . . .
(with Gary Hincks)
[IHF 4.311]; 1991; card; 18.6 x 8.6;
purchased 1992; GMA A4.661

A Modest Hero
(with Gary Hincks)
[IHF 4.215]; 1986; card; 19 x 11.8;
purchased 1987; GMA A4.281

Monostich for the French Election
[IHF 4.268]; 1988; card; 10.3 x 15;
purchased 1991; GMA A4.617

The Months
(with Nicholas Sloan)
[IHF 5.75]; 1982; print; 61 x 30.5;
purchased 1982; GMA A4.283

*Moorland / Marquetry (from '35
One-Word Poems')*
(with Ian Gardner)
[IHF 4.158]; 1982; card; 14.8 x 10.5;
purchased 1991; GMA A4.630 D

Morning and Evening
(with Gary Hincks)
[IHF 5.182]; 1991; pamphlet, 4 pp;
15.3 x 11; purchased 1992; GMA
A4.688

Mors Concilio . . .
See Posters Against the S. A. C.

Motoring Chocolate Soldier
(with Carl Heideken)
[IHF 4.116]; 1976; folding card; 11.3
x 16.6; sent by Sue Finlay 1976; GMA
A4.284

Mower is Less
[IHF 4.78]; 1973; card; 10.5 x 14.8;
purchased 1975; GMA A4.285

Mr Greene and the White Brigands
[IHF 4.228]; 1987; card; 15.5 x 11.7;
purchased 1987; GMA A4.286

Myriam Salomon Owns . . .
[IHF 4.249]; 1987; card; 9.6 x 15.3;
purchased 1987; GMA A4.287

The Name of the Bow . . .
[IHF 4.208]; 1986; folding card; 5.5
x 4; purchased 1987; GMA A4.289

Names on Trees
See Paris and Oenone . . .

National Flags Series: Arcadia
(with Ron Costley)
[IHF 4.92]; 1974; card; 10.4 x 14.7;
purchased 1975; GMA A4.293

National Flags Series: Cythera
(with Karl Torok)
[IHF 4.93]; 1974; card; 10.6 x 14.9;
purchased 1975; GMA A4.292

National Flags Series: Utopia
(with Michael Harvey)
[IHF 4.109]; 1975; card; 10.6 x 14.9;
purchased 1975; GMA A4.291

National Flags Series: Valhalla
(with Michael Harvey)
[IHF 4.108]; 1975; card; 10.6 x 14.9;
purchased 1975; GMA A4.290

The National Trust Follifies . . .
[IHF 4.225]; 1987; card; 10.2 x 15.3;
purchased 1987; GMA A4.294

Nature is the Devil . . .
[IHF 4.265]; 1987; card; 12.1 x 15.2;
purchased 1991; GMA A4.597

Necktank (1918)
(with Michael Harvey)
[IHF 5.44]; 1973; screenprint; 35.5
x 43.8; purchased 1975; GMA A4.296

'Neoclassicism Needs You'
[IHF 4.191]; 1984; card; 16.3 x 13.9;
purchased 1986; GMA A4.297

Néoclassicisme révolutionnaire
(with Gary Hincks)
[IHF 4.279]; 1988; card; 17.4 x 10.1;
purchased 1988; GMA A4.298

Néoclassicisme révolutionnaire
(with Gary Hincks)
[IHF 5.124]; 1988; screenprint; 82
x 54.5; purchased 1991; GMA A4.657

Nettles . . .
See The Pears and Frets of Nettles

Nineteen-Thirty . . .
See 1930 . . .

*Norfolk Woods: The Last Norfolk
Wherry*
(with Michael Harvey)
[IHF 4.86]; 1974; folding card; 9.5 x 5
(folded); purchased 1975; GMA A4.301

Nous regarderons la révolution . . .
See Sandwich Board: Nous
regarderons . . .

*Now the Names of the Twelve are
these . . .*
(with John R. Nash)
[IHF 5.102]; 1987; printed text; 64
x 32; purchased 1987; GMA A4.302

Nude / Draped Nude
(with Gary Hincks)
[IHF 5.6/]; 1980; print; 24.9 x 63.7;
purchased 1980; GMA A4.303

Ocean Stripe Series 2
[IHF 3.10]; 1965; booklet, 16 pp; 12.7
x 10.3; purchased 1991; GMA A4.607

Ocean Stripe Series 4
(with Emil Antonucci)
[IHF 3.20]; 1966; booklet, 16 pp; 9.7
x 13.8; purchased 1991; GMA A4.582

'Of Famous Arcady Ye Are'
(with Michael Harvey)
[IHF 5.63]; 1977; screenprint; 32.7
x 40.5; purchased 1977; GMA A4.304

Oh Nature . . . .
(with Gary Hincks)
[IHF 5.103]; 1987; print; 32.3 x 63.9;
purchased 1987; GMA A4.305

The Old Stonypath, Hoy
(with Gary Hincks)
[IHF 3.131]; 1991; book, 36 pp; 21
x 15; purchased 1992; GMA A4.690

The Olsen Excerpts
(photographs by Diane Tammes)
[IHF 3.41]; 1971; booklet, 20 pp; 15.6
x 15.7; purchased 1975; GMA A4.306

*A One Word Poem for the Ladies of
Art Press*
[IHF 4.246]; 1987; card; 8 x 19;
purchased 1987; GMA A4.307

Order is Repetition
[IHF 4.300]; 1989; folding card; 7.2
x 8.4; purchased 1989; GMA A4.308

*Osiris / Osiers (from '35 One-Word
Poems')*
(with Ian Gardner)
[IHF 4.158]; 1982; card; 14.8 x 10.5;
purchased 1991; GMA A4.630 E

Other and Still Other Waters Flow
[IHF 4.206]; 1986; folding card; 7.6
x 6.5; purchased 1987; GMA A4.309

*Pacific (Board War-Game for Two
Players)*
[IHF 7.8]; 1975; board, playing pieces
and instructions in plastic wallet; 20
x 30; purchased 1975; GMA A4.310

*Palladian / Picturesque: after Thomas
Hearne*
(with Gary Hincks)
[IHF 4.124]; 1977; card; 15 x 10.7;
purchased 1977; GMA A4.311

Panzer am Waldrande
(with Jim Nicholson)
[IHF 4.98]; 1975; card; 13.3 x 10.2;
purchased 1975; GMA A4.312

A Panzer Selection
(with David Button)
[IHF 5.50]; 1975; lithograph; 35.6
x 44; purchased 1975; GMA A4.313

*Paris and Oenone (after Jacques
Blanchard) or Names on Trees*
(with Mark Stewart)
[IHF 4.192]; 1984; card; 21.7 x 11.4;
purchased 1987; GMA A4.494

Parisians Spoil the French
See Picabia Series (I)

Partisan Gallery Handout
[IHF 7.1]; 1963; printed text; 23.7
x 36; purchased 1991; GMA A4.537

A Patch for a Rip-Tide: Sail
(with Margot Sandeman)
[IHF 4.30]; 1970; card; 11.7 x 16.5;
purchased 1975; GMA A4.317

Pax Tuguriis . . .
See Posters against the S. A. C.

Pear
(with Stephanie Kedik)
[IHF 4.203]; 1986; folding card; 9
x 10.5; purchased 1987; GMA A4.318

The Pears and Frets of Nettles
(with Stephanie Kedik)
[IHF 4.204]; 1986; folding card; 5.1
x 5.1; purchased 1987; GMA A4.319

Penny Browns
(with Ian Gardner)
[IHF 5.74]; 1982; print; 30.5 x 53;
purchased 1982; GMA A4.320

Pereant Tyranni . . .
See Posters Against the S. A. C.

The Perfect Sentence
(with Kathleen Lindsley)
[IHF 4.288]; 1989; concertina; 5.1
x 9.3; purchased 1991; GMA A4.602

Persevere
[IHF 4.135]; 1978; card; 9.4 x 13.8;
purchased 1978; GMA A4.321

Personnes intéressées
[IHF 5.125]; 1988; screenprint; 55
x 44; purchased 1991; GMA A4.654

Peterhead Fragments
(with Margot Sandeman)
[IHF 3.74]; 1979; booklet, 12 pp; 15.4
x 20.6; purchased 1979; GMA A4.322

Peterhead Power Station Projects
(with Ian Appleton)
[IHF 3.70]; 1978; book, 32 pp; 21
x 30; purchased 1978; GMA A4.323

*Picabia Series (I): 'The French
Attaché is Papier Maché'*
[IHF 5. 126]; 1988; poster in black; 42
x 29.6; purchased 1988; GMA
A4.324 A

*Picabia Series (I): 'Art Press is Part
Cress'*
[IHF 5. 126]; 1988; poster in black; 42
x 29.6; purchased 1988; GMA
A4.324 B

*Picabia Series (I): 'All that Glitters is
not Aryan'*
[IHF 5. 126]; 1988; poster in black; 42
x 29.6; purchased 1988; GMA
A4.324 C

*Picabia Series (I): 'Parisians Spoil the
French'*
[IHF 5. 126]; 1988; poster in black; 42
x 29.6; purchased 1988; GMA
A4.324 D

*Picabia Series (I): 'The League of
Rights Intrigues in Tights'*
[IHF 5. 126]; 1988; poster in black; 42
x 29.6; purchased 1988; GMA
A4.324 E

*Picabia Series (I): 'The French
Attaché is Papier Maché'*
[IHF 5. 126]; 1988; poster in red; 42
x 29.6; purchased 1991; GMA
A4.580 A

*Picabia Series (I): 'Art Press is Part
Cress'*
[IHF 5. 126]; 1988; poster in red; 42
x 29.6; purchased 1991; GMA
A4.580 B

*Picabia Series (I): 'All that Glitters is
not Aryan'*
[IHF 5. 126]; 1988; poster in red; 42
x 29.6; purchased 1991; GMA
A4.580 C

*Picabia Series (I): 'Parisians Spoil the
French'*
[IHF 5. 126]; 1988; poster in red; 42
x 29.6; purchased 1991; GMA
A4.580 D

*Picabia Series (I): 'The League of
Rights Intrigues in Tights'*
[IHF 5. 126]; 1988; poster in red; 42
x 29.6; purchased 1991; GMA
A4.580 E

*Picabia Series (II): 'Spare the Blade
and Spoil the Factions'*
[IHF 4.286]; 1988; card; 10.5 x 14.8;
purchased 1991; GMA A4.611 A

*Picabia Series (II): 'Don't Cast Your
Revolutions before Swine'*
[IHF 4.286]; 1988; card; 10.5 x 14.8;
purchased 1991; GMA A4.611 B

*Picabia Series (II): 'Don't Put All
Your Heads in One Basket'*
[IHF 5.126 A]; 1988; poster in black;
29.6 x 41.8; purchased 1992; GMA
A4.726 A

Picabia Series (II): 'Spare the Blade and Spoil the Factions'
[IHF 5.126 B]; 1988; poster in black; 29.6 x 41.8; purchased 1992; GMA A4.726 B

Picabia Series (II): 'Don't Cast Your Revolutions before Swine'
[IHF 5.126 C]; 1988; poster in black; 29.6 x 41.8; purchased 1992; GMA A4.726 C

Pierrot. Hommage à Gris
(photographs by Dave Paterson)
[IHF 4.102]; 1975; folding card; 16.7 x 13.6; purchased 1975; GMA A4.325

'Pink Melon Joy' – and More
[IHF 4.172]; 1983; card; 18 x 13.6; purchased 1983; GMA A4.326

A Pittenweem Fancy (Diamond Studded Fishnet)
[IHF 4.56]; 1972; folding card; 8 x 31.5; purchased 1991; GMA A4.565

A Placement
(photograph by Andrew Griffiths)
[IHF 4.177]; 1983; folding card; 11.6 x 7.6; purchased 1983; GMA A4.327

Plaint of the Barge Sails
[exc. IHF]; c 1976–78; ceramic tile; 9.9 x 20; purchase date unrecorded; GMA A4.277

Poem / Print No. 11
(with John Furnival)
[IHF 5.15]; 1969; screenprint; 50.9 x 71.3; purchased 1975; GMA A4.329

Poem / Print No. 14
(with John Furnival)
[IHF 5.20]; 1970; screenprint; 50.9 x 71.3; purchased 1975; GMA A4.330

Poems to Hear and See
[IHF 3.39]; 1971; book, 48 pp; 20.8 x 18.4; purchase date unrecorded; GMA A4.331

Point-to-Point
(with Jim Nicholson)
[IHF 4.19]; 1969; card; 16.5 x 12.1; purchased 1975; GMA A4.332

Poire / Loire (from the Nabis Series)
[IHF 5.110]; 1987; two cards in folder; 26.5 x 12; purchased 1987; GMA A4.333

The Poor Fisherman, After Puvis
(with Gary Hincks)
[IHF 5.116]; 1987; print; 42.5 x 40.5; purchased 1991; GMA A4.641

Poppy, n. The Phrygian Flower
[IHF 4.257]; 1987; folding card; 10 x 10; purchased 1987; GMA A4.345

Porphyry
(with Ron Costley)
[IHF 5.61]; 1977; print in folder; 26.6 x 26.6; purchased 1977; GMA A4.346

Port Distinguishing Letters of Scottish Fishing Vessels
(with George L. Thompson)
[IHF 7.44]; c 1976–78; ceramic tile; 15.3 x 15.3; purchased c 1976–78; GMA A4.385

'Posters Against the S. A. C.': Concilium Artium Delendum Est
(with Nicholas Sloan)
[IHF 5.78]; 1982; linocut in red; 38.4 x 50.5; purchased 1982; GMA A4.515

'Posters Against the S. A. C.': Mors Concilio Artium
(with Nicholas Sloan)
[IHF 5.78]; 1982; linocut in black; 38.4 x 50.5; purchased 1982; GMA A4.514

'Posters Against the S. A. C.': Pax Tuguriis Bellum Conc Artium
(with Nicholas Sloan)
[IHF 5.78]; 1982; linocut in red; 38.4 x 50.5; purchased 1982; GMA A4.513

'Posters Against the S. A. C.': Pereant Tyranni Nummari
(with Nicholas Sloan)
[IHF 5.78]; 1982; linocut in black; 38.4 x 50.5; purchased 1982; GMA A4.516

Poverty
(with Julie Farthing)
[IHF 5.170]; 1991; screenprint; 20.2 x 102; purchased 1992; GMA A4.720

'The Present Order . . .'
(with Nicholas Sloan)
[IHF 4.169]; 1983; card; 18.5 x 20.3; purchased 1983; GMA A4.349

A Pretty Kettle of Fish
(photographs by Diane Tammes)
[IHF 3.55]; 1974; booklet, 24 pp; 11.7 x 12; purchased 1975; GMA A4.350

Prinz Eugen
(with Gary Hincks)
[IHF 5.161]; 1990; folder with 4 pp insert; 8 x 20.8; purchased 1992; GMA A4.694

Prinz Eugen: Homage to Gomringer
(with Ron Costley)
[IHF 5.33]; 1972; screenprint; 38.1 x 50.8; purchased 1975; GMA A4.351

Proclamation
[IHF 5.87]; 1985; print in blue; 42 x 29.5; purchased 1991; GMA A4.552

Project for a Monument to Saint-Just
(with Nicholas Sloan)
[IHF 6.10]; 1985; card cut-out; 27.5 x 27.5; purchased 1986; GMA A4.353 A

Project for a Monument to Saint-Just
(with Nicholas Sloan)
[IHF 6.10]; 1985; card cut-out; 27.5 x 27.5; purchased 1986; GMA A4.353 B

A Project for a Promontory
(with Kathleen Lindsley and Malcolm Fraser)
[IHF 6.45]; 1990; booklet, 24 pp; 10 x 7.7; purchased 1992; GMA A4.670

Proposal for a Monument to Jean-Jacques Rousseau
(with Gary Hincks)
[IHF 6.21]; 1986; lithographic print in folder; 27.5 x 50.5; purchased 1987; GMA A4.354

A Proposal for Arne
(with Gary Hincks)
[IHF 6.39]; 1989; booklet, 8 pp; 21 x 14.8; purchased 1991; GMA A4.538

Proposal for the Camouflaging of a Type 22 Pillbox in a Classical Park
(with Grahame Jones)
[IHF 6.32]; 1988; lithograph; 33.5 x 42; purchased 1991; GMA A4.520

A Proposal for the Celebration of the Bicentenary
[IHF 4.299]; 1989; folding card; 10.7 x 11.2; purchased 1989; GMA A4.355

A Proposal for the Forest of Dean
(with Gary Hincks)
[IHF 6.31]; 1988; lithograph in folder; 33.3 x 27; purchased 1991; GMA A4.519

A Proposal for the Furka Pass
(with Wouter Weijers and Kathleen Lindsley)
[IHF 6.23]; 1987; folding print; 35 x 27; purchased 1987; GMA A4.356

Proposal for the Glasgow Garden Festival
See A Country Lane: A Proposal for . . .

Proposal for the Improvement of Stockwood Park . . .
See Six Proposals for the Improvement . . .

Proposal for a Monument to Ludwig Feuerbach ('Every Goal Negates')
(with Gary Hincks)
[IHF 6.22]; 1986; lithograph; 25 x 64; purchased 1987; GMA A4.352

Proposal for a Pair of Gate Finials
(with Andrew Townsend)
[IHF 6.46]; 1990; folding lithograph; 42.2 x 14.7; purchased 1992; GMA A4.707

A Proposal for Pauline Karpidas
(with Andrew Townsend)
[IHF 6.41]; 1989; folding print; 30 x 21; purchased 1991; GMA A4.540

A Proposal for a Private Garden in Germany for Dr M. Hanstein
(with Robert Johnston)
[IHF 6.42]; 1989; folding print; 20.3 x 31.5; purchased 1991; GMA A4.541

A Proposal for the Robert Louis Stevenson Club
(with Michael Harvey)
[IHF 6.27]; 1987; print in folder; 39 x 38.8; purchased 1987; GMA A4.357

Proposal for a Sundial to be placed on Jean-Paul Marat's House in Paris
(with Eric Marland)
[IHF 6.33]; 1988; lithograph; 60.6 x 42; purchased 1991; GMA A4.521

Proposal for a Tree-Plaque
(with Michael Harvey)
[IHF 6.47]; 1991; print in folder; 31 x 27.1; purchased 1992; GMA A4.713

Proposal for a Wall . . .
See Spitfire Segments . . .

Qui croit au compromis . . .
See Sandwich Board: Qui croit . . .

Rapel
[IHF 3.5]; 1963; cover containing four of the set of ten 'Fauve' and 'Suprematist' poems; 26 x 21; purchased 1991; GMA A4.578

Reap the S. A. C. Faction
[IHF 5.86]; 1985; poster; 28 x 18.5; purchased 1986; GMA A4.358

A Red Admiral or A. B.
(with Ivy Sky Rutzky)
[IHF 4.144]; 1979; folding card; 4.4 x 3.4; purchased 1979; GMA A4.359

Red Boat Red
[exc. IHF]; 1963; printed text; 30.5 x 40.6; purchased 1992; GMA A4.725

Reed-Pipe
[IHF 4.221]; 1986; card; 5.8 x 20.5; sent by the artist 1986; GMA A4.360

Reed-Pipe
[IHF 4.221]; 1986; card; 5.8 x 20.5; purchased 1986; GMA A4.361

A Reflection on the French Revolution
[IHF 4.315]; 1991; folding card; 14.6 x 10.5; purchased 1992; GMA A4.681

A Remembrance of Annette (1)
(with Gary Hincks)
[IHF 6.28]; 1987; concertina in cover; 13.7 x 15; purchased 1987; GMA A4.363 A

A Remembrance of Annette (2)
(with Gary Hincks)
[IHF 6.29]; 1987; concertina in cover; 13.7 x 15; purchased 1987; GMA A4.363 B

A Remembrance of R. L. S.
(with Kathleen Lindsley)
[IHF 6.26]; 1987; booklet, 28 pp; 20.5 x 15.5; purchased 1987; GMA A4.365

Reply Card ('Thank you for your Communication')
(with John Borg Manduca)
[IHF 4.142]; 1978; folding card; 8.8 x 14; purchased 1978; GMA A4.445

Reuse Trees
[IHF 7.23]; 1981; self-adhesive postal label; 13 x 14.2; purchased 1981; GMA A4.366

The Revolution
[IHF 5.151]; 1990; folder with 4 pp insert; 21.4 x 13.7; purchased 1992; GMA A4.673

Une Révolution qui employait . . .
See Sandwich Board: Une Révolution . . .

Rhymes for Lemons
(with Margot Sandeman and Gordon Huntly)
[IHF 3.34]; 1970; concertina; 11.7 x 20.9; purchased 1975; GMA A4.368

Ripple
[IHF 4.155]; 1981; folding card; 11.5 x 21.5; purchased 1981; GMA A4.370

A Rock Rose
(with Richard Demarco)
[IHF 5.27]; 1971; screenprint; 44.3 x 62.2; purchased 1975; GMA A4.371

Romances, Emblems, Enigmas
[IHF 3.80]; 1980; booklet, 36 pp; 14.2 x 8.5; purchased 1980; GMA A4.372

Rose Pettigrew
(with Kathleen Lindsley)
[IHF 5.149]; 1989; folder with 4 pp insert; 13.4 x 9.2; purchased 1992; GMA A4.659

Rotkehlchen
[IHF 4.95]; 1975; card; 10.2 x 15.3; purchased 1975; GMA A4.373

Rowan
[IHF 5.113]; 1987; print; 48 x 22; purchased 1991; GMA A4.545

Rowan
[IHF 4.263]; 1987; card; 20 x 10; purchased 1991; GMA A4.604

S. A. C. / A. C. G. B. / K. G. B.
[IHF 7.11]; 1978; metal badge; diameter 6.4; purchased 1991; GMA A4.581

Sackcloth
[IHF 5.174]; 1991; folder with 4 pp insert; 13.6 x 8.9; purchased 1992; GMA A4.699

The Sacramento Proposal (Sculpture for the 1201 K Street Office Tower)
(with Neil McLeish)
[IHF 6.44]; 1990; folding print; 29.7 x 41.5 (unfolded); purchased 1991; GMA A4.535

Sailing Barge Redwing
(with Ian Gardner)
[IHF 5.26]; 1971; screenprint in folder; 33 x 30.7; purchased 1975; GMA A4.374

Sailors, Revolutionaries
(with Gary Hincks)
[IHF 5.97]; 1987; print; 54.5 x 50; purchased 1987; GMA A4.375

Sail / Stamp
[IHF 4.97]; 1975; card in envelope; 10.2 x 15.3; purchased 1975; GMA A4.376

Sail / Sundial
[IHF 3.46]; 1972; booklet, 12 pp; 7.7 x 7.6; purchased 1975; GMA A4.377

Sails / Waves 1
(with Ron Costley)
[IHF 4.42]; 1971; card; 14.9 x 10.6; purchased 1975; GMA A4.378

Sails / Waves 2
(with Ron Costley)
[IHF 4.43]; 1971; card; 14.9 x 10.6;
purchased 1975; GMA A4.379

Sail Wholemeal
(with Jim Nicholson)
[IHF 5.34]; 1972; screenprint; 76.2
x 53.7; purchased 1975; GMA A4.380

Saint-Just Cube
(with Nicholas Sloan)
[IHF 5.88]; 1986; paper cut-out; 34
x 40.5; purchased 1986; GMA A4.381

Saint-Just Posters (Death to
Strathclyde Region): Terror is the
Piety . . .
[IHF 5.81 A]; 1983; print; 21 x 29.8;
purchased 1983; GMA A4.382 A

Saint-Just Posters (Death to
Strathclyde Region): To be a Hero . . .
[IHF 5.81 B]; 1983; print; 21 x 29.8;
purchased 1983; GMA A4.382 B

Saint-Just Posters (Death to
Strathclyde Region): To Cease to
Believe . . .
[IHF 5.81 C]; 1983; print; 21 x 29.8;
purchased 1983; GMA A4.382 C

Saint-Just Posters (Death to
Strathclyde Region): Freedom of
Speech . . .
[IHF 5.81 D]; 1983; print; 21 x 29.8;
purchased 1983; GMA A4.382 D

Saint-Just Pyramid
See Project for a Monument to Saint
Just

Sandwich Board: Girondism is Not a
Faith . . .
[IHF 5.145 A]; 1989; printed text; 90
x 50.7; purchased 1992; GMA
A4.733 A

Sandwich Board: 1989 Belongs to the
Public and to the Politicians . . .
[IHF 5.145 B]; 1989; printed text; 90
x 50.7; purchased 1992; GMA A4.733 B

Sandwich Board: Nous regarderons la
révolution française . . .
[IHF 5.145 C]; 1989; printed text; 90
x 50.7; purchased 1992; GMA
A4.733 C

Sandwich Board: Le Geste
Girondin . . .
[IHF 5.145 D]; 1989; printed text; 90
x 50.7; purchased 1992; GMA
A4.733 D

Sandwich Board: The Life of Saint-
Just . . .
[IHF 5.145 E]; 1989; printed text; 90
x 50.7; purchased 1992; GMA
A4.733 E

Sandwich Board: Qui croit au
compromis est compromis . . .
[IHF 5.145 F]; 1989; printed text; 90
x 50.7; purchased 1992; GMA A4.733 F

Sandwich Board: The Girondist
Perceives the Blade . . .
[IHF 5.145 G]; 1989; printed text; 90
x 50.7; purchased 1992; GMA
A4.733 G

Sandwich Board: Une Révolution qui
employait . . .
[IHF 5.145 H]; 1989; printed text; 90
x 50.7; purchased 1992; GMA
A4.733 H

Sandwich Board: Le Couperet n'est
pas un icone . . .
[IHF 5.145 I]; 1989; printed text; 90
x 50.7; purchased 1992; GMA
A4.733 I

Sandwich Board: The Blade Stained
with Blood . . .
[IHF 5.145 J]; 1989; printed text, 90
x 50.7; purchased 1992; GMA
A4.733 J

Les Sansculottes
(with Laurie Clark)
[IHF 4.244]; 1987; folding card; 9
x 13.4; purchased 1987; GMA A4.245

Saved by Helicopter
[IHF 7.49]; c 1976–78; ceramic tile;
10.9 x 10.9; purchased c 1976–78;
GMA A4.383

Schiff
(with Ron Costley)
[IHF 4.83]; 1974; folding card; 12
x 7.8; purchased 1975; GMA A4.384

Scottish Zulu
(with David Button)
[IHF 5.24]; 1970; screenprint; 35.7
x 43.4; purchased 1975; GMA A4.386

Scud
[IHF 3.127]; 1991; booklet, 8 pp; 11.1
x 7.6; purchased 1992; GMA A4.684

Scythe / Lightning Flash
(with Gary Hincks)
[IHF 5.158]; 1990; lithograph; 28.6
x 51.5; purchased 1992; GMA A4.710

Sea Coast, after Claude Lorrain
(with Gary Hincks)
[IHF 6.11]; 1985; lithograph; 48.8
x 53; purchased 1986; GMA A4.388

Sea / Land
(with Herbert Rosenthal)
[IHF 5.11]; 1967; screenprint; 43.3
x 56.1; purchased 1975; GMA A4.390

Seams
[IHF 5.16]; 1969; screenprint; 43.4
x 56.2; purchased 1975; GMA A4.389

Sea Poppy 1
(with Alistair Cant)
[IHF 4.10]; 1968; card; 15.8 x 15.8;
purchased 1975; GMA A4.392

Sea Poppy 1 (Star)
(with Alistair Cant)
[IHF 5.7]; 1966; screenprint; 56.1
x 42.9; purchased 1975; GMA A4.393

Sea Poppy 2
(with Peter Grant)
[IHF 4.11]; 1968; card; 15.8 x 15.8;
purchased 1975; GMA A4.394

Sea Poppy 2
[IHF 5.13]; 1968; screenprint; 55.8
x 43.1; purchased 1975; GMA A4.395

Seashells
(with Ian Proctor and Ron Costley)
[IHF 5.30]; 1971; screenprint; 30.5
x 26.8; purchased 1975; GMA A4.396

A Sea Street Anthology
(photograph by Gloria Wilson)
[IHF 4.36]; 1971; card; 11.8 x 16.6;
purchased 1975; GMA A4.397

The Sea's Waves
(with Stuart Barrie)
[IHF 4.72]; 1973; folding card in
folder; 11.4 x 18.8; purchased 1975;
GMA A4.498

The Sea's Waves' Sheaves
(with Stuart Barrie)
[exc. IHF]; 1973; folding card in
folder; 15.1 x 15.3; purchase date
unrecorded; GMA A4.497

Seven Definitions Pertaining to Ideal
Landscape
(with John Nash)
[IHF 5.135]; 1989; 7 prints in folder;
35 x 49.5; purchased 1991; GMA
A4.647

Seven Definitions
(with John Nash)
[IHF 8.41]; 1991; booklet, 20 pp; 10.9
x 14.9; purchased 1992; GMA A4.671

Seven Seed Packets
(with Gary Hincks)
[exc. IHF]; 1987; lithograph; 63
x 40.5; purchased 1992; GMA A4.723

Seventeen-Ninety-Four
See 1794

SF
(with George L. Thomson)
[IHF 3.73]; 1978; booklet, 16 pp; 19.8
x 16.6; purchased 1978; GMA A4.364

A Shaded Path (1)
[IHF 6.24]; 1987; folding print in
folder; 11 x 48; purchased 1987; GMA
A4.400

A Shaded Path (2)
[IHF 6.40]; 1989; folding print in
folder; 11 x 36; purchased 1991; GMA
A4.536

Sheaves
[IHF 4.31]; 1970; folding card; 15.1
x 45.3; purchased 1992; GMA A4.728

Shepherd Lad KY 216 (from set of
three tiles)
(with Michael Harvey)
[IHF 7.51]; c 1976–78; ceramic tile;
15.3 x 15.3; purchased c 1976–78;
GMA A4.401

Shock Tropes
(with Nicholas Sloan)
[IHF 4.161]; 1983; folding card; 19.7
x 12.6; purchased 1983; GMA A4.402

Sickle / Lightning Flash
(with Gary Hincks)
[IHF 5.156]; 1990; concertina; 46.9
x 29.8; purchased 1992; GMA A4.677

The Sign of the Nudge
(with Michael Harvey)
[IHF 4.39]; 1971; card; 9 x 14.2;
purchased 1975; GMA A4.403

Le Silence éternel de Checkpoint
Sandy
(photograph by Antonia Reeve)
[IHF 4.219]; 1986; card; 17.4 x 18.3;
purchased 1986; GMA A4.404

Silhouettes
(with Laurie Clark)
[IHF 3.56]; 1974; booklet, 4 pp; 29.7
x 13; purchased 1975; GMA A4.405

Six Mile Stones: a Proposal for
Floriade, The Hague, Holland 1992
(with Michael Harvey)
[IHF 6.48]; 1991; booklet, 24 pp; 17.7
x 20.4; purchased 1992; GMA A4.692

Six Proposals for the Improvement of
Stockwood Park Nurseries in the
Borough of Luton
(with Gary Hincks)
[IHF 6.18]; 1986; six prints with
individual folders in folder; 27 x 34;
purchased 1987; GMA A4.406

Six Tree-Column Bases
(with Iain Stewart)
[IHF 6.35]; 1988; 4 prints in folder;
29.3 x 38.2; purchased 1991; GMA
A4.542

A Small Classical Dictionary
[IHF 3.81]; 1980; booklet, 12 pp; 8.9
x 10.8; purchased 1980; GMA A4.407

Small is Quite Beautiful
[exc. IHF]; 1976 / 1991; card; 10.5
x 14.7; purchased 1992; GMA A4.675

Snow . . .
(with Gary Hincks)
[IHF 4.302]; 1989; folding card; 12
x 15; purchased 1991; GMA A4.573

Snow / Bark
(with Ron Costley)
[IHF 4.149]; 1979; card; 5.5 x 13.5;
purchased 1981; GMA A4.408

Snow Sail Drop Flake
[IHF 3.57]; 1974; booklet, 4 pp, in
envelope; 10 x 5.7; purchased 1991;
GMA A4.639

Socle
[IHF 4.258]; 1987; card; 16.4 x 6.9;
purchased 1987; GMA A4.409

Someone, Somewhere Wants a Cable
from You*
(with Jim Nicholson)
[IHF 5.57]; 1977; screenprint; 56.8
x 76.6; purchased 1977; GMA A4.410

Some Versions of Pastoral
(with Gary Hincks)
[IHF 4.138]; 1978; card; 14.8 x 12.2;
purchased 1978; GMA A4.188

Somewhere in the Wood . . .
[IHF 4.211]; 1986; folding Christmas
card; 12.4 x 18.6; purchased 1986;
GMA A4.411

The Sound of Running Water
(with Nicholas Sloan)
[IHF 5.144]; 1989; screenprint; 17
x 116.5; purchased 1991; GMA A4.649

So You Want to be a Panzer Leader
(with Laurie Clark)
[IHF 3.59]; 1975; booklet, 16 pp; 12.8
x 10.1; purchased 1975; GMA A4.412

Spare the Blade . . .
See Picabia Series (II)

Special K
[exc. IHF]; 1975; typed booklet, 12 pp
(2/3); 15.2 x 14.8; presented by Mr
Philip Wright 1975; GMA A4.180

Spiral Binding
(with Ron Costley)
[IHF 5.37]; 1972; shaped card with
spiral binding; 45.7 x 18.7; purchased
1975; GMA A4.413

Spitfire Segments / Messerschmitt
Mottle (Proposal for a Wall)
(with Gary Hincks)
[IHF 6.12]; 1985; lithograph; 24.7
x 64; purchased 1986; GMA A4.414

Stamps: Kingdom of Fife; Arcadia;
Strathclyde Region
[IHF 7.26]; 1982; adhesive stamps; 3.3
x 5.3; 3.5 x 3; 3.1 x 2; purchased
1991; GMA A4.525

Standing Poem 2 (Apple / Heart)
[IHF 4.3]; 1965; folding card; 25 x 25;
purchased 1992; GMA A4.727

Standing Poem 3 (Hearts Standing
Poem)
[IHF 4.4]; 1965; card in folding card;
22.7 x 11.4; presented by Mr Edward
Lucie–Smith through the Victoria and
Albert Museum 1976; GMA A4.416

Star / Steer
[IHF 5.6]; 1966; screenprint; 57
x 44.3; purchased 1975; GMA A4.417

Stationery
(with Ron Costley and David Button)
[IHF 5.42]; 1973; card in folder; 29.8
x 21; purchased 1975; GMA A4.418

Stem and Stern
(with Julie Farthing)
[IHF 5.167]; 1991; screenprint; 37
x 40; purchased 1992; GMA A4.712

Sticker for Victory
[IHF 4.224]; 1987; card; 17.1 x 13;
purchased 1987; GMA A4.419 A

Sticker for Victory
[IHF 4.224]; 1987; card; 17.1 x 13;
purchased 1987; GMA A4.419 B

Still Life
(with Carlo Rossi)
[IHF 3.111]; 1989; booklet, 4 pp; 10.4
x 14.1; purchased 1991; GMA A4.609

Still Life with Lemon
[IHF 4.28]; 1970; card; 12.4 x 17;
purchased 1975; GMA A4.420

Stonypath Garden and Gallery Series
See 'The Great Piece of Turf';
'U. S. S. Nautilus'; 'Elegiac
Inscription'

Straiks
(with Simon Cutts and Sydney McK.
Glen)
[IHF 3.51]; 1973; booklet, 12 pp; 9.1
x 7.6; purchased 1975; GMA A4.421

Strawberry Hill
[IHF 4.214]; 1986; printed text; 36.2
x 17.8; purchased 1991; GMA A4.548

Sub Specie Aeternitatis
(with John Borg Manduca)
[IHF 5.68]; 1980; lithograph; 66
x 93.5; purchased 1980; GMA A4.424

Summer Poem
(with Jim Nicholson)
[IHF 5.8]; 1967; screenprint; 58.6
x 45.1; purchased 1975; GMA A4.425

Summer Poem
[IHF 4.280]; 1988; booklet, 4 pp; 3.1
x 7.1; purchased 1991; GMA A4.628

Sundial
(with Kathleen Lindsley)
[IHF 3.109]; 1989; booklet, 4 pp; 13
x 9.1; purchased 1991; GMA A4.603

Swallows Little Matelots
(with Michael Harvey)
[IHF 5.138]; 1989; screenprint; 59
x 59; purchased 1991; GMA A4.643

Swans
(with Ron Costley)
[IHF 4.90]; 1974; folding card; 6.2
x 24.1; purchased 1975; GMA A4.427

Swastika, n.
[IHF 3.106]; 1988; booklet, 8 pp; 10.1
x 12.4; purchased 1991; GMA A4.576

Table-Talk of Ian Hamilton Finlay
[IHF 3.99]; 1985; book, 12 pp; 31.7
x 20.8; purchased 1986; GMA A4.428

Der Tag
(with Ron Costley)
[IHF 4.70]; 1972; card; 10.3 x 10.3;
purchased 1975; GMA A4.93

*Tea-Card: A. F. V. T. (Armoured
Fighting Vehicle Tea)*
(with Simon Cutts)
[IHF 4.75]; 1973; card; 10.2 x 15.3;
purchased 1975; GMA A4.431

*Tea-Card: M. F. V. T. (Motor
Fishing Vessel Tea)*
(with Simon Cutts)
[IHF 4.75]; 1973; card; 10.2 x 15.3;
purchased 1975; GMA A4.432

*Tea-Card: O. A. P. T. (Old Age
Pensioners' Tea)*
(with Simon Cutts)
[IHF 4.75]; 1973; card; 10.2 x 15.3;
purchased 1975; GMA A4.430

Tea-Leaves and Fishes
[IHF 3.19]; 1966; booklet, 28 pp; 10.2
x 25.6; presented by Mr Edward
Lucie-Smith through the Victoria and
Albert Museum 1976; GMA A4.433

Temple, n. (after Claude)
(with Mark Stewart)
[IHF 5.80]; 1983; folding print; 31.4
x 21.6; purchased 1991; GMA A4.546

Temple of Apollo, Façade
(with Nicholas Sloan)
[IHF 4.159]; 1983; card; 15.4 x 16.2;
purchased 1983; GMA A4.435

Temple of Bara
(with Mark Stewart)
[IHF 6.15]; 1986; lithograph; 42 x 24;
purchased 1986; GMA A4.436

*The Temple of Fame, Sudley Royal
(From an Illustrated Esoteric
Dictionary)*
(with Ian Gardner)
[IHF 5.77]; 1982; folding card; 24
x 18.5; purchased 1982; GMA A4.496

Ten . . .
See 10

*Terror and Virtue: a Corner of the
Garden Temple*
(photographs by John Stathatos)
[IHF 4.174]; 1983; card; 13.3 x 15.6;
purchased 1983; GMA A4.87

*Terror / Virtue (Medal of the Little
Spartan War)*
[IHF 7.35]; 1984; bronze medal; 5.3
x 5.3 x 0.6; purchased 1984; GMA
A4.438

Textbooklet 1
[IHF 3.65]; 1975; concertina; 10.2
x 5.3; purchased 1975; GMA A4.439

Textbooklet 2
[IHF 3.76]; 1979; concertina; 10 x 5.2;
purchased 1991; GMA A4.606

Textbooklet 3
[IHF 3.77]; 1979; concertina; 10 x 5.2;
purchased 1991; GMA A4.587

Thermidor
(with Laurie Clark)
[IHF 3.113]; 1989; booklet, 32 pp; 21.5
x 14.5; purchased 1991; GMA A4.566

*They Returned Home Tired but
Happy*
[IHF 7.52]; c 1976–78; ceramic tile; 9.9
x 19.8; purchased c 1976–78; GMA
A4.440

*Third Anniversary of the Battle of
Little Sparta, February 4, 1983*
[IHF 4.200]; 1986; card; 11.5 x 17.8;
purchased 1986; GMA A4.68

Thirty Signatures . . .
See 30 Signatures . . .

Thoughts on Waldemar
[IHF 3.103]; 1986; sixteen cards in
folder; 5.5 x 8.5; purchased 1987;
GMA A4.441

Three . . .
See also 3 . . .

Three Kings for the Republic
(with Gary Hincks)
[IHF 5.84]; 1984; print; 20.5 x 42;
purchased 1991; GMA A4.549

Three Norfolk Dishes
(with Michael Harvey)
[IHF 7.40]; c 1976–78; ceramic tile;
15.3 x 15.3; purchased c 1976–78;
GMA A4.442

Three Sundials
[IHF 3.58]; 1974; booklet, 16 pp; 27.5
x 19.7; purchased 1975; GMA A4.443

Through a Dark Wood / Midway
[IHF 7.47]; c 1976–78; ceramic tile;
15.3 x 15.3; purchased c 1976–78;
GMA A4.444

Tombeau de Rousseau au Panthéon
(with Gary Hincks)
[IHF 5.131]; 1989; print; 52 x 37;
purchased 1991; GMA A4.555

Topiary Aircraft Carrier
(with Ian Gardner)
[IHF 5.40]; 1972; screenprint; 34.3
x 47.6; purchased 1975; GMA A4.447

Tower of the Nets
(with Mark Stewart)
[exc. IIHF]; 1984; booklet, 28 pp, 21.4
x 15.2; purchased 1984; GMA A4.140

Trailblazers
(with C. Tissiman)
[IHF 3.71]; 1978; booklet, 28 pp; 7
x 9.5; purchased 1978; GMA A4.449

Tree Column-Base 'Saint-Just'
(with Andrew Townsend)
[IHF 4.170]; 1983; card; 12.4 x 15.2;
purchased 1983; GMA A4.450

Tree-Shells
(with Bernard Lassus)
[IHF 4.127]; 1977; folding card; 11.5
x 7; purchase date unrecorded; GMA
A4.451

Tree-Shells
(with Jim Downie)
[IHF 7.45]; c 1977; ceramic tile; 15.3
x 15.3; purchased c 1977; GMA A4.452

Le Tricot était une occupation réservé
[IHF 5.106]; 1987; printed text; 21
x 29.5; purchased 1987; GMA A4.246

La Tricoteuse
[IHF 4.253]; 1987; card; 12 x 8.5;
purchased 1987; GMA A4.453

Trim Here
(with Michael Harvey)
[IHF 4.73]; 1973; folding card; 9
x 10.4; purchased 1975; GMA A4.56

Trombone Carrier
[IHF 3.64]; 1975; card with paperclips
in folder; 10.7 x 14.8; purchased
1976; GMA A4.454

Twilight
[IHF 5.92]; 1986; card in folder; 20
x 17.2; purchased 1987; GMA A4.455

Two
See '2'

Two Adaptations
[IHF 3.126]; 1991; booklet, 8 pp; 12.8
x 8.8; purchased 1992; GMA A4.665

Two Billows
[IHF 3.78]; 1980; booklet, 4 pp; 14.1
x 8.1; purchased 1980; GMA A4.456

Two Epicurean Poems and an
Epicurean Paradox
[IHF 3.86]; 1981; 3 cards in folder; 18
x 14; purchased 1981; GMA A4.457

Two Examples
[IHF 5.163]; 1991; pamphlet, 4 pp; 17
x 12; purchased 1992; GMA A4.682

Two Landscapes of the Sublime
(with Gary Hincks)
[IHF 5.136]; 1989; lithograph; 29.6
x 21; purchased 1991; GMA A4.557

Two Landscapes, Viewed through the
Vision Slit of a Tank
(with Ian Gardner and John Robert
Cozens)
[IHF 4.317]; 1991; concertina; 9.1
x 10.4; purchased 1992; GMA A4.691

Two Poems
[IHF 3.119]; 1990; booklet, 4 pp; 18.4
x 11.2; purchased 1991; GMA A4.564

Two Prospects
(with Ian Gardner)
[IHF 4.163]; 1983; folding card; 8.2
x 10.8; purchase date unrecorded;
GMA A4.458

Two Scythes
(with Gary Hincks)
[IHF 5.157]; 1990; lithograph; 28.2
x 51.5; purchased 1992; GMA A4.706

Two Still Lives
[IHF 5.130]; 1989; folding print; 28.6
x 34.6; purchased 1991; GMA A4.551

Two Translations
[IHF 4.180]; 1983; card; 20.5 x 15.5;
purchased 1983; GMA A4.459

Two Trees ('Arbor Felice' and 'The
Birch Tree')
(with Richard Healy)
[IHF 4.157]; 1982; two folding cards;
9.7 x 11.7; 13.8 x 11.6; purchased
1992; GMA A4.730

Two Visions
[IHF 5.94]; 1987; card; 29.5 x 21;
purchased 1987; GMA A4.460

Tye Cringle
[IHF 4.69]; 1972; christmas card; 26
x 11.5; purchased 1975; GMA A4.461

Ulysses was Here
(with Ron Costley)
[IHF 5.66]; 1979; print; 29 x 21;
purchased 1979; GMA A4.462

Umbra Solis (Sundial)
(with Michael Harvey)
[IHF 5.49]; 1975; screenprint; 37.4
x 75.4; purchased 1975; GMA A4.423

Unicorn
(with Diane Tammes)
[IHF 4.53]; 1971; folding card; 10.8
x 13.2; purchased 1975; GMA A4.464

Unnatural Pebbles
(with Richard Grasby)
[IHF 3.82]; 1981; book with three
fold-outs, 56 pp; 16 x 16; purchased
1981; GMA A4.465

Der Untergang des Abendlandes
(from the Nabis Series)
[IHF 5.109]; 1987; card in folder; 21
x 19.5; purchased 1987; GMA A4.467

Urn (Garden Poem)
[IHF 5.89]; 1986; folding print; 81
x 21.6; purchased 1986; GMA A4.468

'U.S.S. Nautilus' (Stonypath Garden
and Gallery Series)
(with John Andrew, photograph by
Michael McQueen)
[IHF 4.111]; 1975; card; 20 x 15.2;
purchased 1991; GMA A4.635

Valses pour piano (Water Music)
[IHF 4.23]; 1970; letterpress visiting
card in envelope; 6.1 x 9.3; purchased
1975; GMA A4.469

A Variation on Lines by Pope
[IHF 6.19]; 1986; 7 sheets in folder;
38.4 x 33.2; purchased 1987; GMA
A4.470

Ventose
(with Gary Hincks)
[IHF 5.177]; 1991; lithograph; 50.9
x 38.4; purchased 1992; GMA A4.714

Venus of the Hours
(with Ron Costley)
[IHF 5.48]; 1975; screenprint; 76
x 38; purchased 1991; GMA A4.644

A View on the Hedgehog Garden
(with Norman Lockhart)
[IHF 4.176]; 1983; card; 17.8 x 12.8;
purchased 1983; GMA A4.466

Voysey Stile
(with Mark Stewart)
[IHF 4.291]; 1989; card; 15.3 x 11.4;
purchased 1991; GMA A4.612

Waldemar is the Venom . . .
[IHF 4.236]; 1987; card; 8 x 14;
purchased 1987; GMA A4.472

The Wartime Garden
(with Ron Costley)
[exc. IHF]; c 1989–90; booklet, 12 pp;
22 x 15.4; purchased 1990; GMA
A4.473

Water-Cooled Watercress
[exc. IHF]; screenprint; 49.4 x 101.4;
purchased 1991; GMA A4.652

A Waterlily Pool
(with Ian Gardner)
[IHF 4.27]; 1970; letterpress card; 14.7
x 10.6; purchased 1975; GMA A4.474

Wave
[IHF 4.147]; 1979; card; 9.3 x 13.8;
purchased 1975; GMA A4.475

The Weed Boat Masters Ticket,
Preliminary Test (Part Two)
(with Ian Gardner)
[IHF 3.45]; 1971; booklet, 16 pp; 12.8
x 10.3; purchased 1975; GMA A4.476

When Man Obeys . . . (Ian Hamilton
Finlay Poster)
[IHF 5.82]; 1983; poster; 21 x 30;
purchased 1983; GMA A4.201 A

When the World Took to
Tolerance . . .
[IHF 4.237]; 1987; card; 11.2 x 20.2;
sent by the artist 1987; GMA A4.477 A

When the World Took to
Tolerance . . .
[IHF 4.237]; 1987; card; 11.2 x 20.2;
purchased 1987; GMA A4.477 B

'Whimbrel' and 'Petrel'
(with Ron Costley)
[IHF 7.58]; c 1976–78; ceramic tile;
15.3 x 15.3; purchased c 1976–78;
GMA A4.478

Wildflower
[IIIF 4.165]; 1983; pressed flower in
folding card; 14 x 10; purchased
1983; GMA A4.479

The Wild Hawthorn Art Test
(with Martin Fidler)
[IHF 3.68]; 1977; booklet, 16 pp; 12.8
x 10.2; purchased 1977; GMA A4.480

The Wild Hawthorn Press, New
Publications
[IHF 7.6]; 1971; booklet, 8 pp; 17.8
x 12.1; purchased 1991; GMA A4.526

Wild Hawthorn Weapon Series No. 1
(O'Erlikon)
(with Susan Goodricke)
[IHF 4.80]; 1973; card; 14 x 10.2;
purchased 1991; GMA A4.634

Wild Hawthorn Weapon Series:
Saint-Just Vigilantes Celebrate . . .
[IHF 4.231]; 1987; card; 12.5 x 15;
purchased 1987; GMA A4.481 A

Wild Hawthorn Weapon Series:
Saint-Just Vigilantes Celebrate . . .
[IHF 4.231]; 1987; card; 12.5 x 15;
purchased 1987; GMA A4.481 B

The Wild Hawthorn Wonder Book of
Boats
(with Martin Fidler)
[IHF 3.61]; 1975; booklet, 36 pp; 15.3
x 10.2; purchased 1976; GMA A4.483

Willow
[IHF 5.114]; 1987; print; 41.5 x 21;
purchased 1991; GMA A4.561

Willow
[IHF 4.264]; 1987; card; 20 x 10;
purchased 1991; GMA A4.613

Windmills Winding Waters
[IHF 4.197]; 1985; concertina; 5.3
x 7.3; purchased 1986; GMA A4.484

'Within the System . . .'
(with Mark Stewart)
[IIIF 4.178]; 1983; card; 15.3 x 13;
purchased 1983; GMA A4.492

Within this Thicket . . .
See Januszczak (Within this
Thicket . . .)

A Woodland Flute
(with Ron Costley)
[IIIF 4.141]; 1978; card; 15.3 x 10.1;
purchased 1978; GMA A4.485

Woodpaths
(decorated by Solveig Hill)
[IHF 3.121]; 1990; booklet, 16 pp; 8.7
x 14.4; purchased 1992; GMA A4.668

Woods and Seas
[IIIF 3.79]; 1980; booklet, 8 pp; 6
x 9.2; purchased 1980; GMA A4.486

Woods and Seas: a Selection
[IIIF 7.20]; 1980; three booklets, two
cards, one folding card, two stamps
and one bookmark in an envelope; 18
x 24.5; purchased 1991; GMA A4.550

Wordsworth / Wadsworth
(with Jim Downie)
[IHF 4.130]; 1977; card; 8 x 16.6;
purchased 1977; GMA A4.487

Xmas Morn 1965
(with Michael Harvey)
[IHF 4.55]; 1971; folding card; 12.4
x 16.4; purchased 1991; GMA A4.596

Yamato
(with Jim Downie)
[IHF 7.57]; c 1976–78; ceramic tile; 7.7
x 15.4; purchased c 1976–78; GMA
A4.209

The Young Blade
[IHF 4.254]; 1987; card; 12 x 8.5;
purchased 1987; GMA A4.489

Zephyr Ins 6 (from set of three tiles)
(with Michael Harvey)
[IHF 7.51]; c 1976–78; ceramic tile;
15.3 x 15.3; purchased c 1976–78;
GMA A4.490

Zulu 'Chieftain'
(with A. Doyle Moore)
[IHF 4.35]; 1971; card; 10.5 x 14.9;
purchased 1975; GMA A4.491

ADAMS, Norman
Bathers in a Bright Light
d 1975
GMA 2094

ADAMS, Robert
Climbing Forms, Opus 166
1962
GMA 2979

ADLER, Jankel
*Hommage à Naum Gabo [Homage
to Naum Gabo]*
d 1946
GMA 1710

AGAR, Eileen
The Lotus Eater
d 1939
GMA 2079

AGAR, Eileen
Slow Movement
d 1970
GMA 1514

AINSLEY, Sam
Warrior Woman V: The Artist
1986
GMA 3026

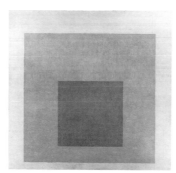

AITCHISON, Craigie
Still Life No. 4
1974
GMA 1501

ALBERS, Josef
Homage to the Square: R–NW IV
d 1966
GMA 2030

ANDREA, John de
Model in Repose
1981
GMA 2314

ANDREWS, Michael
Edinburgh (Old Town)
d 1990–93
GMA 3697

APPEL, Karel
Head over Landscape
d 1958
GMA 808

APPEL, Karel
Danse d'espace avant la tempête
[Dance in Space before the Storm]
d 1959
GMA 815

ARIKHA, Avigdor
Self-Portrait in Foreshortening
d 1973
GMA 3384

ARMAN (Armand Fernandez)
Violoncelle dans l'espace [Cello in Space]
1967–68
GMA 2793

ARMSTRONG, John
Battle of the Rocking Horse
d 1953
GMA 3481

ARP, Jean
S'élèvant [Rising up]
1962
GMA 1253

AUERBACH, Frank
Primrose Hill: High Summer
1959
GMA 1302

AUERBACH, Frank
Head of E.O.W. IV
1961
GMA 1537

AUERBACH, Frank
Primrose Hill: Spring Sunshine
1961–62 / 1964
GMA 2847

AUERBACH, Frank
Tree at Tretire
1975
GMA 2848

AUSTIN, Robert Sargent
Woman Milking a Goat
d 1925
GMA 47

BABOULÈNE, Eugène
Nature morte [Still Life]
1957
GMA 2141

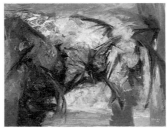

BAILLIE, William
Cocos Palms
d 1964
GMA 1024

BAIN, Donald
The Children of Llyr
d 1945
GMA 1587

BAIRD, Edward
Still Life
d 1940
GMA 3535

BALTHUS (Balthasar Klossowski
de Rola)
Le Lever [Getting up]
1955
GMA 2311

BARLACH, Ernst
Schreitende Frau (or *Schreitende
Nonne*) [*Walking Woman* or
Walking Nun]
1909
GMA 1664

BARLACH, Ernst
Das Schlimme Jahr 1937 [The Terrible Year 1937]
d 1936
GMA 3036

BARNS-GRAHAM, Wilhelmina
White Rocks, St Mary's, Scilly Isles
d 1953
GMA 1697

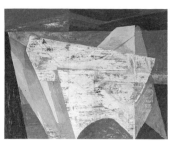

BARNS-GRAHAM, Wilhelmina
Zennor Rock – Rose II
d 1953
GMA 3482

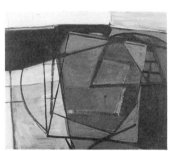

BARNS-GRAHAM, Wilhelmina
March 1957 (Starbotton)
d 1957
GMA 2778

BASELITZ, Georg
Ohne Titel [Untitled (Figure with Raised Arm)]
1982–84
GMA 3530

BASELITZ, Georg
Kopfkissen [Pillow]
d 1987
GMA 3372

BAWDEN, Edward
The Queen's Beasts (The White Greyhound of Richmond)
1953
GMA 2572 A

BAYES, Gilbert
Knight on Horseback
d 1913
GMA 1

BECKMANN, Max
Tegeler Freibad [Swimming at Lake Tegel]
d 1911
GMA 2925

BECKMANN, Max
*Der Nachhausweg [The Way
Home] (from the portfolio 'Die
Hölle' ['Hell'])*
1919
GMA 2465 (1)

BECKMANN, Max
*Die Nacht [The Night] (from the
portfolio 'Die Hölle' ['Hell'])*
1919
GMA 2465 (6)

BELLANY, John
Allegory
d 1964
GMA 3359

BELLANY, John
My Father
1966
GMA 2987

BELLANY, John
Kinlochbervie
1966
GMA 2988

BELLANY, John
The Bereaved One
1968
GMA 2989

BELLANY, John
Lap Dog
c 1973
GMA 2990

BELLANY, John
Mizpah
d 1978
GMA 2197

BELLANY, John
The Ventriloquist
1983
GMA 2803

BELLANY, John
Cockenzie
1985
GMA 3361

BELLANY, John
Bel Ami
d 1985
GMA 3362

BELLANY, John
Self-Portrait (from 'The Addenbrookes Hospital Series')
d 14 April 1988
GMA 3536

BELLANY, John
Self-Portrait (from 'The Addenbrookes Hospital Series')
d 12 May 1988
GMA 3537

BEUYS, Joseph
Three Pots for the Poorhouse – Action Object
d 1974
GMA 1318

BEVAN, Robert
The Well at Mydlow, Poland
c 1907
GMA 1255

BEVAN, Robert
The Well at Mydlow, Poland (No. 2)
1922
GMA 1244

BISSIER, Julius
A.15 April 64
d 1964
GMA 1106

BLACKADDER, Elizabeth
Housesteads, Hadrian's Wall
c 1960–61
GMA 1888

BLACKADDER, Elizabeth
Houses and Fields, Mykonos
1962
GMA 839

BLACKADDER, Elizabeth
Flowers on an Indian Cloth
d 1965
GMA 1026

BLACKADDER, Elizabeth
Untitled
1967–68
GMA 1105

BLISS, Douglas Percy
Lovers Sheltering from a Storm
1926
GMA 2081

BLYTH, Robert Henderson
Holland (Troops on the Dutch Frontier)
d 1945
GMA 3025

BOMBERG, David
Bargees
c 1919
GMA 3055

BOMBERG, David
Three Figures
c 1919
GMA 3056

BOMBERG, David
Self-Portrait
d 1937
GMA 994

BOMBERG, David
Vigilante
d 1955
GMA 2944

BOMBERG, David
Ronda, Evening
d 1956
GMA 2945

BONE, Muirhead
The National Gallery and Bank of Scotland
d 1910
GMA 682

BONE, Muirhead
Archway at Fonte
GMA 936

BONE, Muirhead
Todi from the Rocca
GMA 937

BONE, Phyllis Mary
Red Deer – Mother and Son
c 1942
GMA 1275 B

BONNARD, Pierre
Ruelle à Vernonnet [Lane at Vernonnet]
c 1912–14
GMA 2932

BONNARD, Pierre
Echappée sur la rivière, Vernon [View of the River, Vernon]
1923
GMA 2931

BORÈS, Francisco
Le Déjeuner [The Lunch]
d 1935
GMA 3483

BOSHIER, Derek
Plaza
d 1965
GMA 1539

BOURDELLE, Emile-Antoine
Petite bacchante aux jambes croisées [Small Bacchante with Crossed Legs]
c 1906–10
GMA 941

BOURDELLE, Emile-Antoine
La Vierge d'Alsace [The Virgin of Alsace]
1919–21
GMA 2

BOYLE, Mark
Addison Crescent Study (London Series)
1969
GMA 1304

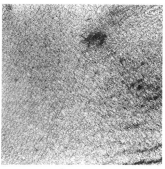

BOYLE, Mark
Skin Series No. 8
1973
GMA 1305

BOYLE FAMILY
Study from the Broken Path Series with Border Edging
1986
GMA 3016

BRANGWYN, Frank
Assisi Woodland
GMA 2776

BRAQUE, Georges
Le Bougeoir [The Candlestick]
1911
GMA 1561

BRAQUE, Georges
Pal [Pale Ale]
1911
GMA 835

BREININ, Raymond
In the Forest
d 1942
GMA 1002

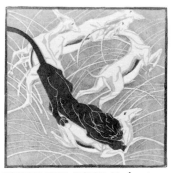

BRESSLERN-ROTH, Norbertine
Tigers
c 1925
GMA 109 A

BROCKHURST, Gerald Leslie
James McBey
d 1931
GMA 113

BRODZKY, Horace
The Wash Basin
1919
GMA 3005

BROODTHAERS, Marcel
La Tour visuelle [The Visual Tower]
1966
GMA 2794

BROWN, Helen Paxton
Portrait of Jessie M. King
GMA 1698

BROWN, Roger
Misty Morning
1975
GMA 2313

BRUS, Günter
Ohne Titel [Untitled]
1965
GMA 3054

BUCKELS, Alec
The Merry Men
d 1932
GMA 116

BUGATTI, Rembrandt
Le Faön [The Fawn]
c 1909–10
GMA 1264

BURRA, Edward
The Watcher
c 1937
GMA 1115

BURRA, Edward
Soldiers Resting in a Field
1947
GMA 2904

BURRA, Edward
Izzy Orts
1955
GMA 2147

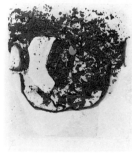

BURRI, Alberto
Combustione No. 3
1965
GMA 986

BUTLER, Reg
Personage
1949
GMA 1661

BUTLER, Reg
Girl
1957–58
GMA 809

CADELL, F. C. B.
The Model
c 1912
GMA 3

CADELL, F. C. B.
Peggy in Blue and White
d 1912
GMA 865

CADELL, F. C. B.
Still Life (The Grey Fan)
c 1920–25
GMA 1311

CADELL, F. C. B.
Portrait of a Lady in Black
c 1921
GMA 3350

CADELL, F. C. B.
Orange and Blue, Iona
c 1925–30
GMA 1892

CADELL, F. C. B.
Iona Croft
c 1925–30
GMA 1893

CADELL, F. C. B.
Aspidistra and Bottle on Table
c 1930
GMA 3351

CADELL, F. C. B.
Melancholy Portrait of a Poet
c 1934
GMA 1891

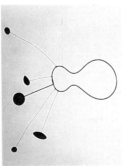

CALDER, Alexander
The Spider
c 1935–37
GMA 1586

CALLENDER, Robert
Abandoned Red Rudder
1983
GMA 2953

CAMPBELL, Steven
A Man Perceived by a Flea
1985
GMA 3049

CAMPBELL, Steven
Elegant Gestures of the Drowned after Max Ernst
1986
GMA 3296

CARLISLE, Fionna
Theresa's Place
1984
GMA 2985

CARO, Anthony
Table Piece CCCLXXXVIII
1977
GMA 2464

CASTILLO, Jorge
Maria Elena and Olga (2)
d 1963
GMA 995

CAULFIELD, Patrick
Parish Church
d 1967
GMA 1536

CÉSAR (César Baldaccini)
La Pacholette
1966
GMA 1107

CÉSAR (César Baldaccini)
Compression
d 1966
GMA 2505

CHADWICK, Lynn
Winged Figures
1955
GMA 761

CHADWICK, Lynn
Maquette for 'Moon of Alabama' II
1957–58
GMA 2764

CHAPPELL, William
Two Figures
d 1925
GMA 2922

CHEYNE, Ian
Hell's Glen
1928
GMA 199

CHIA, Sandro
Courageous Boys at Work
d 1981
GMA 2503

CINA, Colin
MH/37
d 1973
GMA 1298

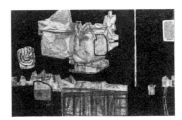

CLOUGH, Prunella
Yard at Night
1959
GMA 1502

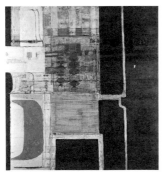

CLOUGH, Prunella
Electrical Landscape
1960
GMA 1535

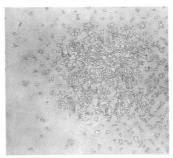

CLOUGH, Prunella
Mesh II
1981
GMA 2744

COHEN, Harold
Conclave
d 1963
GMA 1515

COKER, Peter
Forest VIII
1959
GMA 3417

COLQUHOUN, Robert
The Dubliners
1946
GMA 842

COLQUHOUN, Robert
The Spectators
d 1947
GMA 2746

COLQUHOUN, Robert
Figures in a Farmyard
d 1953
GMA 1306

COLQUHOUN, Robert
Edgar in Battle Dress (Costume Design for 'King Lear')
1953
GMA 3573

COLVIN, Calum
Narcissus
1987
GMA 3047

CONROY, Stephen
Healing of a Lunatic Boy
1986
GMA 3039

CONROY, Stephen
The Enthusiasts
1987
GMA 3040

COPLEY, John
Le Monde où l'on s'amuse
1914
GMA 211 A

CORINTH, Lovis
Der Ritter [The Knight]
1914
GMA 1197

COWIE, James
Male Student (Study for 'A Portrait Group')
c 1932–33
GMA 1326

COWIE, James
Student and Plaster Cast
c 1933
GMA 1328

COWIE, James
Head of a Girl (Study for 'Falling Leaves')
c 1933–34
GMA 2815

COWIE, James
A Portrait Group
1933 / c 1940
GMA 1325

COWIE, James
Playground, Bellshill
c 1934
GMA 1331

COWIE, James
Still Life with Jug
1940s
GMA 1329

COWIE, James
Composition
1947
GMA 1167

CRAIG, Edward Gordon
Waiting for 'The Marchioness'
1899
GMA 254

CRAXTON, John
Man in a Garden
d 1942
GMA 3307

CRAXTON, John
Welsh Estuary Foreshore
1943
GMA 1257

CRAXTON, John
*Landscape with the Elements
(Cartoon for 'The Four Seasons'
Tapestry)*
1973–75
GMA 2956

CROSBIE, William
Heart Knife
d 1934
GMA 1714

CROSBIE, William
Recapitulation
c 1940
GMA 3448

CROSBIE, William
In Memoriam
c 1948–50
GMA 2218

CROZIER, William
Italian Landscape
c 1927
GMA 3473

CROZIER, William
*Study for 'Edinburgh (from
Salisbury Crags)'*
c 1927
GMA 1592

CROZIER, William
Edinburgh (from Salisbury Crags)
c 1927
GMA 7

CROZIER, William
Edinburgh in Snow
c 1928
GMA 8

CROZIER, William
Burning Field, Essex
d 1960
GMA 816

CROZIER, William
Trees by the Sea
1985
GMA 2959

CUMMING, James M.
The Lewis Poacher
d 1960
GMA 1031

CURRIE, Ken
Glasgow Triptych: Template of the Future
1986
GMA 3012 A

CURRIE, Ken
Glasgow Triptych: The Apprentices
1986
GMA 3012 B

CURRIE, Ken
Glasgow Triptych: Young Glasgow Communists
1986
GMA 3012 C

CURSITER, Stanley
The Regatta
1913
GMA 3034

CURSITER, Stanley
The Kame of Hoy
d 1950
GMA 2711

DAVIE, Alan
Seascape Venice No. I
d 1948
GMA 3708

DAVIE, Alan
Jingling Space
d 1950
GMA 3308

DAVIE, Alan
Seascape Erotic
d 1955
GMA 1084

DAVIE, Alan
*Woman Bewitched by the Moon
No. 2*
d 1956
GMA 3309

DAVIE, Alan
*The Horse that has Visions of
Immortality No. 2*
d 1963
GMA 882

DAVIE, Alan
*Hallucination with a Red Headed
Parrot*
d 1984
GMA 3416

DAVIES, John
For the Last Time
1970–72
GMA 3450

DELAUNAY, Robert
*L'Equipe de Cardiff [The Cardiff
Team]*
1922–23
GMA 2942

DENNY, Robyn
Glass 2 (From There)
1971
GMA 1516

DERAIN, André
Collioure
1905
GMA 1280

DELAUNAY, Sonia with
CENDRARS, Blaise
La Prose du transsibérien et de la petite Jehanne de France [Trans-Siberian Prose]
d 1913
GMA 2199

DINGWALL, Kenneth
Grey Surface
d 1979
GMA 2135

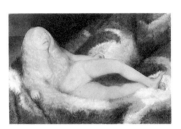

DIX, Otto
Mädchen auf Fell [Nude Girl on a Fur]
d 1932
GMA 2195

DIX, Otto
Kartenspieler [Cardplayers]
1920
GMA 2960

DIX, Otto
Gastote (Templeux-la-Fosse, August 1916) [Soldiers Killed by Gas (Templeux-la-Fosse, August 1916)]
Published 1924
GMA 2032

DOCHERTY, Michael
An Object Fixed in Time
d 1977
GMA 2013

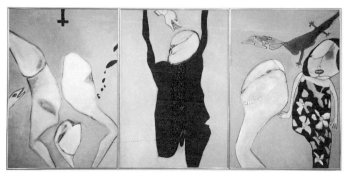

DOUTHWAITE, Pat
The End of the World
1970
GMA 1117

DOUTHWAITE, Pat
Death of Amy Johnson
d 1976
GMA 1645

DUBUFFET, Jean
Villa sur la route [Villa by the Road]
d 1957
GMA 830

DUBUFFET, Jean
Dispositif aux vaisselles [Dishwasher]
d 1965
GMA 2151

DUCHAMP, Marcel
La Boîte-en-valise [Box in a Suitcase]
1935–41
GMA 3472

DUFRESNE, Charles
L'Enlèvement d'Europe [The Rape of Europa]
1924
GMA 745

DURWARD, Graham
The Incurable Romantic
d 1983
GMA 2796

EARDLEY, Joan
Seine Boat
c 1949
GMA 3322

EARDLEY, Joan
Street Kids
c 1949–51
GMA 887

EARDLEY, Joan
Sleeping Nude
1955
GMA 897

EARDLEY, Joan
A Stove
c 1955
GMA 2801

EARDLEY, Joan
Seeded Grasses and Daisies, September
1960
GMA 889

EARDLEY, Joan
The Wave
1961
GMA 791

EARDLEY, Joan
Children and Chalked Wall 3
1962–63
GMA 853

EARDLEY, Joan
Catterline in Winter
c 1963
GMA 888

EARDLEY, Joan
Boats on the Shore
c 1963
GMA 1036

EHRLICH, Georg
Age and Youth
c 1961
GMA 1273

EHRLICH, Georg
Horse's Head
1963–64
GMA 1246

ELK, Ger van
The Missing Persons: Lunch II
d 1976
GMA 2508

ENSOR, James
L'Entrée du Christ à Bruxelles [The Entry of Christ into Brussels]
d 1896
GMA 2285

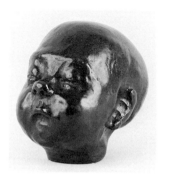

EPSTEIN, Jacob
Baby Asleep
c 1904
GMA 12

EPSTEIN, Jacob
The Risen Christ
1917–19
GMA 1092

EPSTEIN, Jacob
Albert Einstein
1933
GMA 13

EPSTEIN, Jacob
Consummatum Est
1936–37
GMA 2304

EPSTEIN, Jacob
Betty Cecil
1938
GMA 943

EPSTEIN, Jacob
Head of Marie Tracey
1938
GMA 3484

ERNST, Max
Mer et soleil [Sea and Sun]
d 1925
GMA 1119

ERNST, Max
Le Grand amoureux I [The Great Lover I]
1926
GMA 2134

ERNST, Max
La Forêt [The Forest]
c 1928
GMA 2217

EWART, David Shanks
The Return
d 1927
GMA 2222

FEININGER, Lyonel
Gelmeroda III
1913
GMA 2951

FERGUSSON, John Duncan
Nude
c 1898–1904
GMA 2920

FERGUSSON, John Duncan
The Toreador
c 1901–03
GMA 793

FERGUSSON, John Duncan
Dieppe, 14 July 1905: Night
d 1905
GMA 1713

FERGUSSON, John Duncan
Portrait of Anne Estelle Rice
d 1908
GMA 1247

FERGUSSON, John Duncan
Twilight, Royan
d 1910
GMA 1897

FERGUSSON, John Duncan
Tin Openers
c 1918
GMA 1350

FERGUSSON, John Duncan
Eástre (Hymn to the Sun)
1924 (cast 1971)
GMA 1263

FERGUSSON, John Duncan
The Log Cabin Houseboat
d 1925
GMA 974

FERGUSSON, John Duncan
In the Patio: Margaret Morris Fergusson
1925
GMA 3352

FERGUSSON, Margaret Morris
Red Roofs (Dieppe)
1922
GMA 2846

FINLAY, Ian Hamilton
(with Michael Harvey)
Beware of the Lark
1974
GMA 3706

FINLAY, Ian Hamilton
(with Michael Harvey)
Sundial: Umbra Solis non Aeris
1975
GMA 1520

FINLAY, Ian Hamilton
(with John Andrew)
Et in Arcadia Ego
1976
GMA 1583

FINLAY, Ian Hamilton
(with Susan Goodricke)
Conning Tower Draughts
1976
GMA 1584

FINLAY, Ian Hamilton
(with Peter Grant)
Coastal Boy (Fishing Boat: A534)
1977
GMA 3603

FINLAY, Ian Hamilton
(with Sue Finlay, Nicholas Sloan,
David Paterson, Wilma Paterson)
*Fragonard (from 'Nature over again
after Poussin')*
1979–80
GMA 2293

FINLAY, Ian Hamilton
(with Jim Nicholson)
Homage to Modern Art
1972
GMA A4.179

FINLAY, Ian Hamilton
(with Jim Nicholson)
*Someone, Somewhere Wants a
Cable from You*
1977
GMA A4.410

FINLAY, Ian Hamilton
Evening / Sail
1991
GMA A4.716

FISHER, Beth
*Fear for My Children (from the
'Canopy' series)*
d 1987
GMA 3584

FLAVIN, Dan
Monument to V. Tatlin
1975
GMA 2799

FLEMING, Ian
Gethsemane
1931
GMA 2545

FLEMING, Ian
Spanish Village
c 1934
GMA 2543

FLETCHER, Frank Morley
Girl Reading (or *The Bookworm*)
by 1904
GMA 266

FLINT, William Russell
Provençal Landscape
GMA 2143

FRANKENTHALER, Helen
Saturn
d 1963
GMA 1258

FRENCH, Annie
*Title Page Design for 'Goblin
Market' by Christina Rossetti*
c 1912–13
GMA 710

FRENCH, Annie
Cinderella and the Ugly Sisters
GMA 708

FREUD, Lucian
Two Men
1987–88
GMA 3410

FRINK, Elisabeth
Bird
1959
GMA 1108

FROST, Terry
*Black and White Movement
on Blue and Green II*
d 1951–52
GMA 1299

FROST, Terry
Grey Figure
d 1957
GMA 794

FRY, Roger
White Road with Farm
c 1912
GMA 1500

FULTON, Hamish
*A Four Day Walk across the Border
Country of England and Scotland,
West Coast to East Coast from the
Solway Firth to Holy Island, Early
Spring 1977*
GMA 2201

FULTON, Hamish
*Lightning over Liathach: A Five
Day Hill Walk in June, Wester
Ross, Scotland, 1980*
1980
GMA 2306

GABO, Naum
Spiral Theme
1941
GMA 2978

GAGE, Edward
Self-Portrait
d 1951
GMA 3363

GAUDIER-BRZESKA, Henri
Head of an Idiot
c 1912 (posthumous cast)
GMA 1668

GAUDIER-BRZESKA, Henri
Woman in a Long Dress
c 1913
GMA 960

GAUDIER-BRZESKA, Henri
Figure
c 1914
GMA 961

GAUDIER-BRZESKA, Henri
Bird Swallowing a Fish
1914 (posthumous cast)
GMA 2150

GEAR, William
Fantôme blanc
d January 1948
GMA 3300

GEAR, William
Landscape
d March 1949
GMA 1300

GEAR, William
Interior
d August 1949
GMA 3297

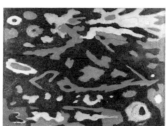

GEAR, William
Coucher de soleil
d January – February 1950
GMA 3298

GEAR, William
Autumn Landscape
d September 1950
GMA 1301

GEAR, William
White Interior
d December 1954
GMA 890

GEAR, William
Broken Yellow
d 1967
GMA 1307

GIACOMETTI, Alberto
Objet désagréable, à jeter
[Disagreeable Object, to be Disposed
of]
1931
GMA 3547

GIACOMETTI, Alberto
Femme egorgée [Woman with her Throat Cut]
1932
GMA 1109

GIBBINGS, Robert
Clear Waters
1920
GMA 1603

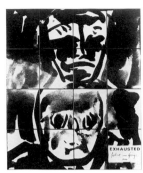

GILBERT and GEORGE
Exhausted
d 1980
GMA 2507

GILES, William
The Passing of the Crescent, Umbria
1910
GMA 282

GILL, Eric
Talitha Cumi (Maiden I say unto Thee, Arise)
c 1909
GMA 2021

GILL, Eric
Christ on the Cross
c 1913
GMA 14

GILL, Eric
Spirit and Flesh
1917
GMA 317

GILL, Eric
Hair Combing
1922
GMA 351

GILLIES, William
Sunshine, Cramond
c 1916–21
GMA 1717

GILLIES, William
Skye Hills from near Morar
c 1931
GMA 1833

GILLIES, William
Near Durisdeer
c 1932
GMA 1747

GILLIES, William
The Harbour
c 1934–37
GMA 1766

GILLIES, William
In Ardnamurchan
c 1936
GMA 1723

GILLIES, William
Poppies and Cretonne Cloth
c 1937–40
GMA 1820

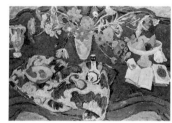

GILLIES, William
Flowers on a Sideboard
c 1941
GMA 1759

GILLIES, William
Fishing Boats, Anstruther Harbour
c 1945
GMA 1722

GILLIES, William
St Monance
c 1949
GMA 1829

GILLIES, William
The Peebles Train
c 1950
GMA 1811

GILLIES, William
Still Life, Lamplight
c 1953
GMA 1845

GILLIES, William
Double Still Life
c 1954
GMA 1040

GILLIES, William
Still Life with Black Fishes
1965
GMA 1039

GONCHAROVA, Natalya
Rabbi with Cat
c 1912
GMA 796

GONCHAROVA, Natalya
Backdrop Design for 'Le Coq d'or'
Act II
d 1913 (possibly executed 1914)
GMA 797

GONCHAROVA, Natalya
The Forest
c 1913
GMA 1674

GONCHAROVA, Natalya
Costume Design for One of the
Three Kings in 'La Liturgie'
1915
GMA 798

GONCHAROVA, Natalya
Two Figures
c 1916–20
GMA 1642

GONZÁLEZ, Julio
L'Arlequin [Harlequin]
c 1929–30 (posthumous cast)
GMA 1259

GORMLEY, Antony
Present Time
1986–88
GMA 3561

GOTLIB, Henryk
Nude by Garden Door
1942
GMA 1120

GOTLIB, Henryk
Nude
1964–65
GMA 1121

GRANT, Duncan
Vanessa Bell Painting
1915 (incorrectly dated 1913)
GMA 900

GRANT, Duncan
Farmhouse among Trees
d 1928
GMA 2144

GRAY, Eileen
Untitled
c 1940–42
GMA 1662

GRECO, Emilio
Anna
d 1954
GMA 3486

GRECO, Emilio
Danzatrice [Dancer]
c 1955
GMA 3485

GREG, Barbara
Europa
GMA 371

GRIGGS, Frederick
Lanterns of Sarras
1932
GMA 379

GROSSMAN, Rudolf
*Portrait of Hubert Renfro
Knickerbocker*
c 1923–24
GMA 3032

GROSZ, George
*Die Besitzkröten [Toads of
Property]*
1920
GMA 2102

HAIG, The Earl
The Tweed at Mertoun
1968
GMA 1293

HAMBLING, Maggi
The Holyrood
d 1987
GMA 3397

HAMILTON, Richard
Desk
d 1964
GMA 2155

HANSON, Duane
Tourists
1970
GMA 2132

HARDIE, Gwen
Head I
d 1985
GMA 3718

HARDIE, Gwen
Fist I
d 1986
GMA 3038

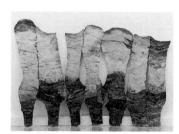

HARDIE, Gwen
Dance
1989
GMA 3551

HASIOR, Wládysláw
Nailed to the Stars
1972
GMA 1267

HATWELL, Anthony
King and Queen
1962
GMA 3354

HATWELL, Anthony
Seated Girl
d 1967
GMA 3357

HATWELL, Anthony
Girl in a Long Dress Tying her Hair
d 1967
GMA 3358

HAYTER, Stanley William
Tropic of Cancer
d 1949
GMA 771

HÉLION, Jean
Nu accoudé [Nude Leaning on her Elbows]
d 1948
GMA 3305

HEPWORTH, Barbara
Dyad
1949
GMA 854

HEPWORTH, Barbara
Conversation with Magic Stones
1973
GMA 2000

HERMAN, Josef
Outside the Fish and Chip Shop
1946
GMA 913

HERMAN, Josef
*Miners (Study for Festival
of Britain Mural)*
d 1951
GMA 1269

HERON, Patrick
Red Painting, July 25, 1963
d 1963
GMA 1675

HILL, Anthony
Relief Construction (F 4)
1966
GMA 1686

HILLIER, Tristram
La Confiserie
c 1931
GMA 3487

HILLIER, Tristram
Pylons
1933
GMA 3488

HILLIER, Tristram
Quantoxhead
d 1946
GMA 3489

HILTON, Roger
June 1953
d 1953
GMA 831

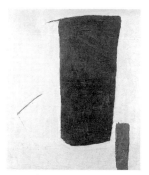

HILTON, Roger
January 1954
d 1954
GMA 2289

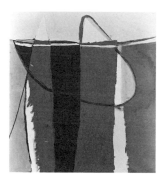

HILTON, Roger
Palisade
d 1959
GMA 1312

HILTON, Roger
Dancing Woman
d 1963
GMA 2463

HITCHENS, Ivon
The Verandah
1943
GMA 3491

HITCHENS, Ivon
Tangled Pool, No. 10
1946
GMA 975

HITCHENS, Ivon
Sunflowers and Blue Jar
c 1947
GMA 3490

HITCHENS, Ivon
River Rother, Dark Evening
1951
GMA 1688

HOCKNEY, David
Rocky Mountains and Tired Indians
1965
GMA 1538

HODGKIN, Eliot
Quinces
d 1969
GMA 3492

HODGKIN, Eliot
Leaves
d 1970
GMA 3493

HODGKIN, Howard
Portrait of Mrs Rhoda Cohen
1962
GMA 2131

HODGKINS, Frances
Chairs and Pots
c 1939
GMA 3494

HODGKINS, Frances
Lilies and Still Life
c 1940
GMA 3495

HODLER, Ferdinand
Thunersee mit Stockhornkette [Lake Thun and the Stockhorn Mountains]
d 1910
GMA 1523

HOLLOWAY, Edgar
Alec Buckels
d 1934
GMA 3003

HOUSTON, John
Flowers in a Landscape
d 1960
GMA 1042

HOUSTON, John
Bathers
d 1965 / 1966
GMA 976

HOWIE, James
City Painting
d 1964
GMA 892

HOWSON, Peter
Heroic Dosser
1986
GMA 3013

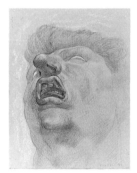

HOWSON, Peter
Head of Saint Anthony
d 1986
GMA 3014

HOWSON, Peter
Just Another Bloody Saturday
1987
GMA 3041

HOWSON, Peter
Heroic Dosser
1987
GMA 3460

HUBBARD, John
After the Snow, 4
d 1963
GMA 856

HUBBUCH, Karl
Zwei Modelle [Two Models]
c 1926
GMA 2957

HUGHES, Ian
Apperception (I)
d 1987
GMA 3048

HUGHES-STANTON, Blair
Flowers (for 'Birds, Beasts and Flowers' by D.H. Lawrence)
d 1930
GMA 393

HUNTER, Alexis
*Approach to Fear III: Taboo
Demystify (1–4)*
d 1976
GMA 2202

HUNTER, George Leslie
Still Life
c 1920–25
GMA 19

HUNTER, George Leslie
Figures on a Quay, Largo
c 1920–25
GMA 1905

HUNTER, George Leslie
Cottages, Fife
c 1923–24
GMA 1903

HUNTER, George Leslie
Stubble Field
c 1923–24
GMA 1911

HUNTER, George Leslie
Still Life with Flowers and Fruit
c 1923–26
GMA 1906

HUNTER, George Leslie
Juan-les-Pins
c 1927–29
GMA 1907

HUNTER, George Leslie
Still Life with Gladioli
c 1927–30
GMA 1348

HUNTER, George Leslie
Reflections, Balloch
c 1929–30
GMA 18

HUNTER, George Leslie
Still Life
c 1930
GMA 20

HUNTER, George Leslie
Still Life, Stocks
c 1930
GMA 1910

HUNTER, George Leslie
Still Life of Apples, Plate and Knife
GMA 717

HUNTER, Margaret
Whisper . . .
1988
GMA 3418

HUNTER, Margaret
Precious Belonging
1988
GMA 3419

HURD, Peter
Anselmo's House
d 1941
GMA 1003

HURRY, Leslie
Death Mask of Mary Queen of Scots
d 1946
GMA 3006

HUTCHISON, William Oliphant
Oak Tree and Windmill
GMA 1214

INLANDER, Henry
Yellow Landscape
d 1965
GMA 945

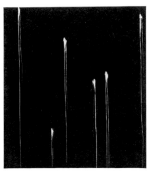

INNES, Callum
Six Identified Forms
d 1992
GMA 3670

JAWLENSKY, Alexei
Frauenkopf [Head of a Woman]
c 1911
GMA 896

JOHN, Augustus
Grace Westry
c 1897
GMA 860

JOHN, Augustus
Head of a Girl
d 1906
GMA 719

JOHN, Augustus
Woman Standing
c 1907–08
GMA 861

JOHN, Augustus
Woman in a Landscape
c 1911–12
GMA 862

JOHN, Gwen
A Sleeping Nun
c 1914–18
GMA 1530

JOHN, Gwen
A Young Nun
c 1915–20
GMA 1116

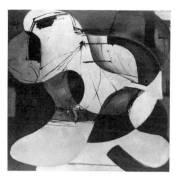

JOHNSTONE, William
Summer, Selkirk
c 1927 / c 1938 / c 1951 (d 1927)
GMA 1100

JOHNSTONE, William
Study for 'A Point in Time'
c 1928
GMA 3562

JOHNSTON, Alan
Untitled (from the suite 'From the Mountain to the Plain')
1978
GMA 2009

JOHNSTONE, William
A Point in Time
c 1929 / 1937
GMA 1254

JOHNSTONE, William
Portrait of Mrs J. E. Winand
c 1945
GMA 2712

JOHNSTONE, William
Embryonic
1972–73
GMA 3563

JOHNSTONE, William
Celebration of Earth, Air, Fire and Water
d 1974
GMA 1313

JONES, David
View from No. 1 Elm Row, Hampstead
c 1927
GMA 1641

JONES, David
Northumberland Fields
c 1930
GMA 1165

JONES, David
Princess with Longboats
c 1948–49
GMA 1533

JONES, David
Glass Chalice with Flowers and Mug
c 1950
GMA 1532

JONES, David
In Principio Erat Verbum ...
c 1951
GMA 1531

JUDD, Donald
Progression
d 1978
GMA 2504

KANDINSKY, Wassily
Improvisation 19
1911
GMA 2710

KANDINSKY, Wassily
Kleine Welten III [Small Worlds III]
d 1922
GMA 2779

KAPOOR, Anish
Untitled
1983
GMA 2954

KENNINGTON, Eric
Making Soldiers: Into the Trenches (from the series 'The Great War: Britain's Efforts and Ideals')
Published 1918
GMA 394 D

KING, Jessie Marion
The Fisherman Watched over by Mermaids
c 1913
GMA 1672

KING, Jessie Marion
Design for One Wall of a Child's Nursery
1913
GMA 1673

KING, Jessie Marion
Princess Melilot
c 1916–17
GMA 720

KING, Philip
Small Wall Sculpture
d 1974
GMA 1314

KIRCHNER, Ernst Ludwig
Japanisches Theater [Japanese Theatre]
c 1909
GMA 911, RECTO

KIRCHNER, Ernst Ludwig
Interior with Nude Woman and Man
c 1924
GMA 911, VERSO

KIRCHNER, Ernst Ludwig
Weisse Tänzerin in Kleinen Variété [White Dancer in a Cabaret]
1914
GMA 2924

KITAJ, R. B.
If Not, Not
1975–76
GMA 1585

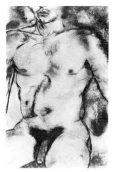

KITAJ, R. B.
Actor (Richard)
1979
GMA 3373

KLEE, Paul
Gespenst eines Genies [Ghost of a Genius]
d 1922
GMA 2106

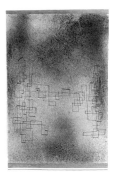

KLEE, Paul
Drohender Schneesturm [Threatening Snowstorm]
d 1927
GMA 1015

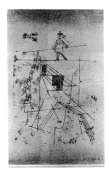

KLEE, Paul
Seiltänzer [Tightrope Walker]
d 1923
GMA 762

KLEE, Paul
Rechnender Greis [Old Man Calculating]
1929
GMA 2095

KLIMT, Gustav
Stehende Frau mit durchsichtigem Gewand [Standing Woman with Transparent Drapery]
c 1902
GMA 1249

KLIMT, Gustav
Schwangere mit Mann nach links: Studie zu 'Hoffnung I' [Pregnant Woman with Man: Study for 'Hoffnung I']
c 1903–04
GMA 2946

KLINGER, Max
Handlung [Action] (from the portfolio 'Paraphrase über den Fund eines Handschuhes' ['On the Finding of a Glove'])
1881/1924
GMA 2980 (2)

KLINGER, Max
Ein Mord [A Murder] (from the portfolio 'Dramen' ['Dramas'])
1883/1922
GMA 2768 (7)

KNIGHT, Laura
Spanish Dancer No. 1
1923
GMA 397

KNOX, Jack
Aftermath
c 1960
GMA 1168

KNOX, Jack
Bajazet Encag'd
c 1962
GMA 867

KNOX, Jack
How It Is
d 1968
GMA 3010

KNOX, Jack
Three Piles of Cherries
c 1978
GMA 2/73

KNOX, Jack
West Highland Way
1982
GMA 3009

KOKOSCHKA, Oskar
Alma Muhler
c 1913
GMA 3037

KOKOSCHKA, Oskar
Zrání (Summer)
1938–40
GMA 21

KOKOSCHKA, Oskar
Kathleen, Countess of Drogheda
d 1940
GMA 3451

KOKOSCHKA, Oskar
The Crucified Christ Helping the
Hungry Children
d 1945
GMA 811

KOKOSCHKA, Oskar
Die träumenden Knaben [The Dreaming Boys]
1908 (published 1917)
GMA 3552

KOKOSCHKA, Oskar
Selbstbildnis von zwei Seiten als Maler [Self-Portrait as a Painter from Two Aspects]
1923
GMA 3557

KOKOSCHKA, Oskar
The Crucified Christ Helping the Hungry Children ('En Memoria de los Niños de Viena')
1945–46
GMA 3549

KOLLWITZ, Käthe
Gesenkter Frauenkopf [Woman with Bowed Head]
1905
GMA 2096

KOLLWITZ, Käthe
Bewaffnung in einem Gewölbe [Arming in a Cellar]
1906 (published 1921)
GMA 2097

KOSSOFF, Leon
Portrait of Father
1978
GMA 2105

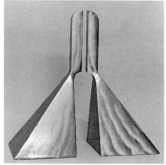

LAING, Gerald
Pyramid
1971
GMA 1503

LAING, Gerald
Galina 3
1974
GMA 1504

LAING, Gerald
Just Another Pretty Face
d 1968
GMA 1511

LAMB, William
An Old Man Reading a Newspaper
(or *'The Daily News'*)
c 1930s
GMA 1104

LANYON, Peter
Solo Flight
d 1960
GMA 2742

LANYON, Peter
Ginger Hill
d 1961
GMA 2290

LARIONOV, Mikhail
Soldier in a Wood
c 1911
GMA 799

LARIONOV, Mikhail
*Costume Design for 'Les Contes
Russes'*
d 1915
GMA 800

L'ARRIVÉ, Jean-Baptiste
Vierge et enfant [Virgin and Child]
c 1910
GMA 1005

LASCAUX, Elie
*L'Eglise de Puteaux [The Church at
Puteaux]*
1927
GMA 3496

LAURENS, Henri
*Femme debout à la draperie au bras
levé [Standing Woman with
Drapery, Arm Raised]*
1928
GMA 1101

LAWRENCE, Alfred Kingsley
Portrait of a Woman
d 1925
GMA 721

LAWRENCE, Eileen
Naples, Serpent, Fascine
d 1983–84
GMA 2958

LAWRENCE, Eileen
The Blood of the Peacock
1986
GMA 3011

LE BRUN, Christopher
Sir Bedivere
d 1982–83
GMA 2833

LÉGER, Fernand
Femme et nature morte [*Woman and Still Life*]
d 1921
GMA 962

LÉGER, Fernand
Le Tronc d'arbre sur fond jaune [*Tree Trunk on Yellow Ground*]
d 1945
GMA 2310

LÉGER, Fernand
Etude pour 'Les Constructeurs': l'équipe au repos [*Study for 'The Constructors': The Team at Rest*]
d 1950
GMA 2845

LÉGER, Fernand
Le Profil à la corde: étude pour 'Les Constructeurs' [*Man in Profile with Rope: Study for 'The Constructors'*]
1950 or 1951
GMA 2955

LEHMBRUCK, Wilhelm
Mädchenkopf, sich umwendend [*Head of a Girl Looking over her Shoulder*]
1913–14 (posthumous cast)
GMA 3731

LEWIS, Percy Wyndham
A Reading of Ovid (Tyros)
1920–21
GMA 1685

LEWIS, Percy Wyndham
Seated Figure
c 1921
GMA 3428

LEWIS, Percy Wyndham
Portrait of Edwin Evans
1922–23
GMA 1079

LEWITT, Sol
*Five Modular Structures
(Sequential Permutations on the
Number Five)*
1972
GMA 1308

LICHTENSTEIN, Roy
In the Car
d 1963
GMA 2133

LIPCHITZ, Jacques
Figure assise [Seated Figure]
c 1916–17
GMA 1091

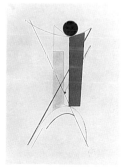

LISSITSKY, El
*Untitled (Print No. 1) (from '1°
Kestnermappe Proun [Proun 1st
Kestner Portfolio'])*
Published 1923
GMA 2767(1)

LISSITSKY, El
*Untitled (Print No. 3) (from '1°
Kestnermappe Proun [Proun 1st
Kestner Portfolio'])*
Published 1923
GMA 2767(3)

LITTLEJOHN, William
Still Life, Harbour and Bird
1964–66
GMA 991

LONG, Richard
Stone Line
1980
GMA 2196

LOWRY, L. S.
Canal and Factories
d 1955
GMA 1349

LUMSDEN, Ernest S.
James McBey
1920
GMA 407

MCBEY, James
New York, March 1930 (East River Sunset)
d 1934
GMA 416

MACBRYDE, Robert
Still Life
c 1947
GMA 3497

MACBRYDE, Robert
The Chess Player
c 1947–50
GMA 2772

MACBRYDE, Robert
Two Women Sewing
c 1948
GMA 1588

MACBRYDE, Robert
Still Life with Cucumber
1948
GMA 3306

MACBRYDE, Robert
Still Life – Fish on a Pedestal Table
c 1950
GMA 946

MCCALL, Charles
William McCall
d 1935
GMA 3592

MCCANCE, William
*Heavy Structures in a Landscape
Setting*
c 1922
GMA 3432

MCCANCE, William
*Heavy Structures in a Landscape
Setting*
d 1922
GMA 3612

MCCANCE, William
Abstract Cat
c 1922–24
GMA 3620

MCCANCE, William
Agnes Miller Parker
d 1925
GMA 3433

MCCANCE, William
Portrait of Joseph Brewer
d 1925
GMA 3446

MCCANCE, William
Joseph Brewer
d 1925
GMA 3471

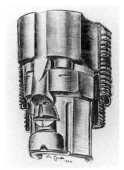

MCCANCE, William
Study for a Colossal Steel Head
d 1926
GMA 3439

MCCANCE, William
Hiroshima (or *Atom Horizon*)
d 1947
GMA 3613

MCCLURE, David
Figure and Flowers
d 1963
GMA 869

MACDONALD, Tom
Clown before the Mirror
d 1963
GMA 880

MCEWEN, Rory
Untitled (Grey Plate Glass, Series 1968, No. 4)
1968
GMA 1086

MCEWEN, Rory
Datchet Road, Eton
d 1979
GMA 2136

MACH, David
Matchead
1986
GMA 3468

MACH, David
Dying for It
1989
GMA 3469

MCINTYRE, Keith
Lochwood Oaks
d 1985
GMA 3015

MACKENNA, Tracy
Objects 8,9,10
1989
GMA 3461

MACKENNA, Tracy
Sinners (Unexplored Routes)
1990
GMA 3585

MACKENNA, Tracy
Sinners (Unexplored Routes)
1990
GMA 3586

MACKINTOSH, Charles Rennie
*Revolving Bookcase for Hous'hill,
Nitshill, Glasgow*
1904
GMA 3447

MACKINTOSH, Charles Rennie
Mont Alba
c 1924–27
GMA 3533

MACLAURIN, Robert
Amongst the Turkish Wilderness
d 1988
GMA 3420

MACLAURIN, Robert
Under the Armenian Bridge
d 1988
GMA 3421

MCLEAN, Bruce
Landscape Painting
d 1968
GMA 3572

MCLEAN, Bruce
*People Who Make Art in Glass
Houses, Work (panel B)*
1969 / 1970
GMA 2223 B

MCLEAN, Bruce
Untitled Blue
c 1980
GMA 2777

MCLEAN, John
Escalator
d 1988
GMA 3476

MCLEAN, Talbert
Ochre
1973
GMA 1294

MACLEAN, Will
Bard McIntyre's Box
d 1984
GMA 2973

MACNAB, Iain
The Waterfront, Calvi, Corsica
1930
GMA 2084

MCNAIRN, Caroline
Looking Outside
d 1987
GMA 3474

MACTAGGART, William
Snow, near Lasswade
c 1928
GMA 1087

MACTAGGART, William
The Old Mill, East Linton
c 1942
GMA 1922

MACTAGGART, William
Poppies against the Night Sky
c 1962
GMA 1046

MACTAGGART, William
Nocturne
1963
GMA 847

MACTAGGART, William
The Wigtown Coast
d 1968
GMA 2740

MAGRITTE, René
Le Drapeau noir [The Black Flag]
1937
GMA 1261

MAGRITTE, René
La Représentation [Representation]
1937
GMA 3546

MAILLOL, Aristide
Eve à la pomme [Eve with the Apple]
1899
GMA 2941

MAISTRE, Roy de
The Lacemaker's Lamp
c 1953
GMA 1099

MAN RAY
Involute
d 1917
GMA 2064

MARC, Franz
Geburt der Pferde [Birth of Horses]
1913
GMA 2949

MARCHAND, Jean
Le Lac [The Lake]
c 1910
GMA 1097

MARIL, Herman
Going to the Blacksmith
d 1936
GMA 3498

MARINI, Marino
Pomona
1949
GMA 2027

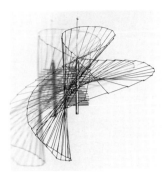

MARTIN, Kenneth
Screw Mobile
1959
GMA 1590

MASCHERINI, Marcello
Danzatrice [Dancer]
c 1958
GMA 3499

MASSON, André
La Rivière en hiver [The River in Winter]
1951
GMA 1068

MATISSE, Henri
Jeannette II
1910
GMA 1995

MATISSE, Henri
La Séance de peinture (or La Leçon de peinture) [The Painting Session or The Painting Lesson]
1919
GMA 929

MATISSE, Henri
Nu assis (or 'Le Grand bois') [Seated Nude (or 'The Large Woodcut')]
1906
GMA 787

MATISSE, Henri
Icarus (Plate VIII from 'Jazz')
Published 1947
GMA 2284

MAVOR, Osborne Henry (BRIDIE, James)
The Angel and the Vice
d 1942
GMA 776

MAXWELL, John
View from a Tent
d 1933
GMA 977

MAXWELL, John
Fish Market
d 1934
GMA 1926

MAXWELL, John
Harbour with Three Boats
d 1934
GMA 3342

MAXWELL, John
The Pleasures of the Snow
c 1936
GMA 3338

MAXWELL, John
Requiem for a Decayed Affection
d 1937
GMA 1324

MAXWELL, John
Self-Portrait
c 1937–39
GMA 3346

MAXWELL, John
The Circus
d 1941
GMA 3335

MAXWELL, John
Ventriloquist
d 1952
GMA 3347

MAXWELL, John
Nudes and Flowers
d 1953
GMA 3341

MAYER-MARTON, George
Remembering the Danube
d 1952
GMA 1277

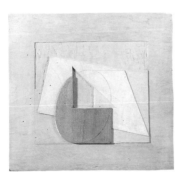

MELLIS, Margaret
Relief Construction in Wood
1941
GMA 2745

MELLIS, Margaret
White Painting (with Red, Blue, Violet and Ochre)
1964
GMA 1499

MENINSKY, Bernard
Girl with a Book
d 1924
GMA 3501

MENINSKY, Bernard
Fish with Lemons
c 1948
GMA 3500

METZINGER, Jean
Paysage [Landscape]
c 1921
GMA 1111

MICHIE, Alastair
The Far Side of the Field
d 1964
GMA 1047

MICHIE, David
Houses in a Fife Village
1961
GMA 1928

MICHIE, David
Houses on a Hill, Lisbon
1963
GMA 1048

MILNE, John MacLaughlin
Landscape, Sutherland
c 1930–35
GMA 1069

MILOW, Keith
Cross No. 88
1978
GMA 2763

MIRÓ, Joan
Maternité [Maternity]
d 1924
GMA 3589

MIRÓ, Joan
Peinture [Painting]
d 1925
GMA 2078

MOFFAT, Alexander
Ian Hamilton Finlay
d 1975
GMA 1591

MOFFAT, Alexander
Gwen Hardie (2)
d 1987
GMA 3454

MOHOLY-NAGY, László
Sil I
d 1933
GMA 1663

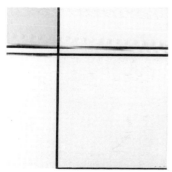

MONDRIAN, Piet
Composition
d 1932
GMA 2502

MONNINGTON, Walter Thomas
*Sketch for Mural in St Stephen's
Hall, Westminster (The English and
Scottish Commissioners Present the
Articles of Agreement for the Union
to Queen Anne, 1707)*
c 1924
GMA 24

MOON, Jeremy
7/73
d 1973
GMA 1309

MOONEY, John
Untitled
1982
GMA 2698 B

MOORE, Henry
*Drawing for Figure in Metal or
Reinforced Concrete*
1931
GMA 3424

MOORE, Henry
Studies for Sculpture
c 1939
GMA 3423

MOORE, Henry
The Helmet
1939–40
GMA 3602

MOORE, Henry
Studies for Sculpture
c 1939–42
GMA 3422

MOORE, Henry
Family Group
d 1944
GMA 2065

MOORE, Henry
Reclining Figure
1951
GMA 1098

MOORE, Henry
Two-Piece Reclining Figure No. 2
1960
GMA 757

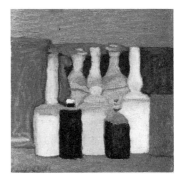

MORANDI, Giorgio
Natura Morta [Still Life]
1962
GMA 906

MORROCCO, Alberto
Methven
d 1965
GMA 1050

MORTON, Alastair
Untitled
d 1939
GMA 2001

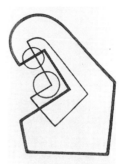

MORTON, Alastair
Untitled
d 1940
GMA 1527

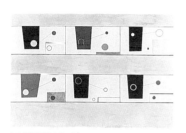

MORTON, Alastair
Untitled
d 1940
GMA 2002

MOTHERWELL, Robert
In Black and White
d 1960
GMA 1081

MUELLER, Otto
*Ein in Dünen sitzendes, und ein
liegendes Mädchen [Girls in a Sand
Dune, One Sitting, One Lying]*
c 1920−24
GMA 2116

MUNCH, Edvard
*Das kranke Mädchen [The Sick
Girl]*
1896
GMA 2309

MURRAY, Charles
The Adoration of the Magi
GMA 452

NASH, David
Ram
1981
GMA 2765

NASH, David
*Edinburgh Planting: Above the
Water of Leith*
d 1987
GMA 3650

NASH, Paul
Berkshire Downs
d 1922
GMA 3502

NASH, Paul
Token
c 1929–30
GMA 2984

NASH, Paul
Path (or *Path in Savernake Forest*)
d 1932
GMA 3503

NASH, Paul
Avebury
c 1936
GMA 3426

NASH, Paul
Landscape of the Brown Fungus
1943
GMA 3425

NASH, Paul
*Landscape of the Vernal
Equinox (III)*
d 1944
GMA 774

NASH, Paul
The Sunflower Rises
1945
GMA 1317

NASH, Thomas
The Picnic
d 1932
GMA 3504

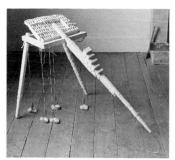

NEAGU, Paul
Generator-Gyroscope
1975
GMA 1665

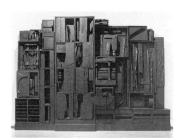

NEVELSON, Louise
Nightscape
1957–64
GMA 2194

NEVELSON, Louise
Untitled
d 1974
GMA 2827

NEVINSON, Christopher R. W.
*Building Aircraft: Swooping down
on a Taube (from the series
'The Great War: Britain's Efforts
and Ideals')*
d 1917 (published 1918)
GMA 456 F

NEVINSON, Christopher R. W.
That Cursed Wood
d 1918
GMA 457

NICHOLSON, Ben
Walton Wood Cottage, No. 1
d 1928
GMA 930

NICHOLSON, Ben
White Relief
d 1935
GMA 2149

NICHOLSON, Ben
Painting 1937
d 1937
GMA 2100

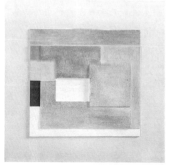

NICHOLSON, Ben
Painted Relief (Plover's Egg Blue)
d 1940
GMA 931

NICHOLSON, Ben
June 1961 (Green Goblet and Blue Square)
d 1961
GMA 812

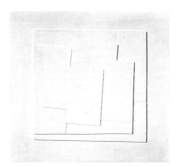

NICHOLSON, Ben
White Relief, Paros
d 1962
GMA 813

NICHOLSON, Ben
Teapot, Mug, Cups and Saucer
1930
GMA 2962

NICHOLSON, Ben
Numbers
c 1933
GMA 1684

NICHOLSON, Ben
Man and Woman: Heads in Profile
1933
GMA 2069

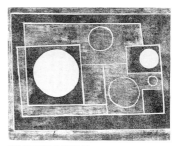

NICHOLSON, Ben
Five Circles
1934
GMA 1999

NICHOLSON, William
The Brig
d 1906
GMA 907

NICHOLSON, William
Poppies in Pewter
c 1933–34
GMA 1931

NICHOLSON, Winifred
Jake and Kate on the Isle of Wight
1931–32
GMA 2964

NOLAN, Sidney
Leda and the Swan
d 1958
GMA 836

NOLDE, Emil
Kopf [Head]
1913
GMA 1082

NOLDE, Emil
Abendhimmel überm Gotteskoog
[Sunset over Gotteskoog]
GMA 1102

O'CONOR, Roderic
The Balustrade
d 1913
GMA 1250

O'DONNELL, Ron
The Great Divide
d 1987
GMA 3046 A

OGILVIE, Elizabeth
Sea Paper
d 1987
GMA 3470

ONWIN, Glen
Salt Room / Crystal (from 'The
Recovery of Dissolved Substances')
1977
GMA 2114

ORPEN, William
A Bloomsbury Family
1907
GMA 881

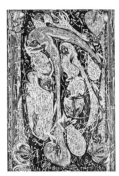

OSSORIO, Alfonso
The Claw
1952
GMA 1657

PALADINO, Mimmo
Silenzioso Sangue [Silent Blood]
d 1979 / 1985
GMA 3017

PAOLOZZI, Eduardo
Horse's Head
1946
GMA 3698

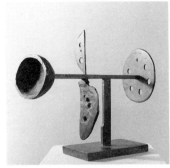

PAOLOZZI, Eduardo
Paris Bird
1948–49
GMA 3303

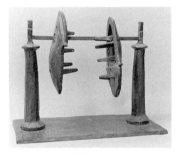

PAOLOZZI, Eduardo
Two Forms on a Rod
1948–49
GMA 3398

PAOLOZZI, Eduardo
Growth (or Table Sculpture)
1949
GMA 3399

PAOLOZZI, Eduardo
Krokodeel
1956
GMA 3400

PAOLOZZI, Eduardo
Icarus (first version)
1957
GMA 824

PAOLOZZI, Eduardo
Icarus (second version)
1957
GMA 3699

PAOLOZZI, Eduardo
St Sebastian I
1957
GMA 3700

PAOLOZZI, Eduardo
Large Frog (new version)
1958
GMA 3701

PAOLOZZI, Eduardo
His Majesty the Wheel
1958–59
GMA 3449

PAOLOZZI, Eduardo
Tyrannical Tower Crowned with Thorns of Violence
1961
GMA 3702

PAOLOZZI, Eduardo
Four Towers
1962
GMA 978

PAOLOZZI, Eduardo
The Bishop of Kuban
1962
GMA 3566

PAOLOZZI, Eduardo
Chord
1964
GMA 3703

PAOLOZZI, Eduardo
Domino
1967–68
GMA 2826

PAOLOZZI, Eduardo
Kreuzberg
d 1974
GMA 3704

PAOLOZZI, Eduardo
Master of the Universe
d 1989
GMA 3580

PARK, Alistair
Black Head
Late 1950s
GMA 3611

PARK, Alistair
A Little Woman
1962
GMA 1051

PARK, Alistair
A Field Symbol
d 1963
GMA 832

PARKER, Agnes Miller
The Challenge
d 1934
GMA 2563

PASMORE, Victor
Girl with Bows in her Hair
Late 1930s
GMA 3505

PASMORE, Victor
*Spiral Motif (Subjective Landscape)
in Black and White*
1951
GMA 833

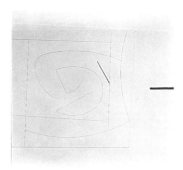

PASMORE, Victor
Linear Motif in Black and White
1960–61
GMA 834

PATERSON, G. W. Lennox
Study of a Head
1938
GMA 2564

PATRICK, James McIntosh
Traquair House
d 1938
GMA 3534

PEMBERTON, John
Since the Bombardment
c 1948
GMA 3506

PENROSE, Roland
Ocean Temple
d 1983
GMA 2805

PEPLOE, Samuel John
Self-Portrait
c 1900
GMA 1950

PEPLOE, Samuel John
Peonies
c 1900–05
GMA 1946

PEPLOE, Samuel John
Man Laughing (Portrait of Tom Morris)
c 1902
GMA 33

PEPLOE, Samuel John
Barra
1903
GMA 1933

PEPLOE, Samuel John
North Berwick
d 1903
GMA 1945

PEPLOE, Samuel John
The Green Blouse
c 1904
GMA 28

PEPLOE, Samuel John
The Black Bottle
c 1905
GMA 26

PEPLOE, Samuel John
Head of a Girl
c 1905
GMA 1940

PEPLOE, Samuel John
Game of Tennis, Luxembourg Gardens
c 1906
GMA 1944

PEPLOE, Samuel John
Portrait of the Artist's Wife
c 1906–08
GMA 1948

PEPLOE, Samuel John
On the French Coast
c 1907
GMA 1939

PEPLOE, Samuel John
Figures
c 1910
GMA 1938

PEPLOE, Samuel John
Boats at Royan
1910
GMA 1949

PEPLOE, Samuel John
Veules-les-Roses
c 1910–11
GMA 909

PEPLOE, Samuel John
Ile de Bréhat
1911
GMA 1941

PEPLOE, Samuel John
Still Life
c 1913
GMA 32

PEPLOE, Samuel John
Pink Roses, Chinese Vase
c 1916–20
GMA 1947

PEPLOE, Samuel John
Still Life with Melon
c 1920
GMA 1951

PEPLOE, Samuel John
Roses
c 1920–25
GMA 27

PEPLOE, Samuel John
Landscape at Cassis
1924
GMA 866

PEPLOE, Samuel John
Iona Landscape: Rocks
c 1925–27
GMA 1942

PEPLOE, Samuel John
Landscape, South of France
c 1928
GMA 1103

PEPLOE, Samuel John
Still Life, Pears and Grapes
c 1930
GMA 908

PEPLOE, Samuel John
Still Life with Plaster Cast
c 1931
GMA 31

PEPLOE, William Watson
Orchestral: Study in Radiation
c 1915
GMA 3550

PEPLOE, William Watson
Souvenir du triangle rouge
[*Souvenir of the Red Triangle*]
1918
GMA 1295

PEPLOE, William Watson
Untitled
1918
GMA 1296

PERMEKE, Constant
Hiver en Flandre [*Winter in
Flanders*]
1930s
GMA 993

PERMEKE, Constant
Masker [*Mask*]
1936
GMA 947

PHILIPSON, Robin
Rocks at Gardenstown
d 1953
GMA 1952

PHILIPSON, Robin
Cathedral, Grey
1960
GMA 1055

PHILIPSON, Robin
Fighting Cocks, Grey
c 1961
GMA 788

PHILIPSON, Robin
Burning at the Sea's Edge
c 1961
GMA 1054

PHILIPSON, Robin
Cathedral, Red
d 1961
GMA 1056

PHILIPSON, Robin
Odalisque
1962
GMA 1053

PHILIPSON, Robin
The Burning
1963
GMA 848

PHILIPSON, Robin
Church Interior
1965
GMA 1057

PHILIPSON, Robin
Cathedral Interior, Remembrance
1965
GMA 1058

PHILIPSON, Robin
The Covering Sea I
1982–83
GMA 2802

PICABIA, Francis
*Fille née sans mère [Girl Born
without a Mother]*
1916–17
GMA 3545

PICASSO, Pablo
Mère et enfant [*Mother and Child*]
1902
GMA 967

PICASSO, Pablo
Guitare, bec à gaz, flacon [*Guitar, Gas-jet and Bottle*]
1912–13
GMA 2501

PICASSO, Pablo
Les Soles [*The Soles*]
d 1940
GMA 1070

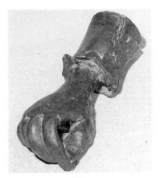

PICASSO, Pablo
La Main [*The Hand* or *Arm with Sleeve*]
1948
GMA 1996

PICASSO, Pablo
Deux figures nues [*Two Nude Figures*]
1909
GMA 3008

PICASSO, Pablo
Quatre femmes nues et tête sculptée [*Four Nude Women and Sculpted Head*]
d 1934
GMA 775

PICASSO, Pablo
Corrida
d 1934
GMA 2287

PICASSO, Pablo
Bacchanale
d 1959
GMA 825

PIPER, John
Avebury (or *Archaeological Wiltshire*)
d 1936
GMA 893

PIPER, John
Black Ground (or *Screen for the Sea*)
d 1938
GMA 1998

PIPER, John
Wheatfield, Oxon.
d 1941
GMA 3508

PIPER, John
Foliate Heads No. II
1953
GMA 3507

PISSARRO, Lucien
The Mill House, Blackpool, Devon
1913
GMA 1954

PISSARRO, Lucien
Near Colchester, Essex
GMA 1953

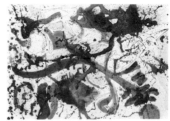

POLLOCK, Jackson
Untitled
c 1942–44
GMA 2198

POLLOCK, Jackson
Untitled
d 1951
GMA 849

POMPON, François
Perdreau [Partridge]
c 1923
GMA 973

POPOVA, Lyubov
Painterly Architectonic
1916
GMA 2080

PORTWAY, Douglas
Abstract Composition
1962
GMA 857

PRINGLE, John Quinton
Study of a Head (or *Man with a Drinking Mug*)
d 1904 [?]
GMA 2028

PRINGLE, John Quinton
Poultry Yard, Gartcosh
1906
GMA 37

PRYDE, James
Moll Cutpurse (or *The Roaring Girl*)
d 1902
GMA 3596

PRYDE, James
Lumber: A Silhouette
c 1921
GMA 1521

PRYDE, James
An Ancient Harbour
c 1923
GMA 38

PULSFORD, Charles
Untitled
c 1950–52
GMA 3648

QUINTERO, Daniel
En el Metro (Las Puertas Verdes)
[*On the Underground (The Green Doors)*]
d 1971 and 1972
GMA 1563

QUINTERO, Daniel
Study of a Clenched Fist (for 'On the Underground')
d 1972
GMA 1580

QUINTERO, Daniel
Study of a Man (for 'On the Underground')
d 1972
GMA 1581

RAE, Barbara
Pebblebank
d 1984
GMA 2948

RANKEN, William Bruce Ellis
Still Life, Black and White
d 1925
GMA 1006

RAVERAT, Gwen
Pietà (after Jacques Raverat)
d 1913
GMA 486

REDFERN, June
My Baby Moon
d 1983
GMA 2797

REDPATH, Anne
Girl in a Red Cloak
c 1920
GMA 1646

REDPATH, Anne
The Indian Rug (or Red Slippers)
c 1942
GMA 932, RECTO

REDPATH, Anne
Landscape near Hawick
c 1942
GMA 932, VERSO

REDPATH, Anne
Still Life with Teapot on Round Table
c 1945
GMA 1963, RECTO

REDPATH, Anne
Still Life with Milk Bottle
c 1945
GMA 1963, VERSO

REDPATH, Anne
The Worcester Jug
c 1946
GMA 1965

REDPATH, Anne
The Mantelpiece
c 1947
GMA 1960

REDPATH, Anne
Rain in Spain
c 1951
GMA 1962

REDPATH, Anne
Erbalunga, Corsica
c 1955
GMA 1059

REDPATH, Anne
Landscape at Kyleakin
c 1958–60
GMA 814

REDPATH, Anne
Lisbon Church
1961
GMA 1062

REDPATH, Anne
In the Church of Madre Deus
c 1962
GMA 1113

REDPATH, Anne
White Tulips
c 1963
GMA 1964

REDPATH, Anne
In a Venetian Church
1963 or 1964
GMA 1060

REDPATH, Anne
The Crypt, St Marks, Venice
1963 or 1964
GMA 1063

REEVES, Philip
Barumini, Sardinia
1960
GMA 873

REID, Hamish
Headland
d 1961
GMA 3605

REID, Norman
St John's Wood, Behind Alma Square
1947
GMA 3696

REYNOLDS, Alan
Winter Seeding Hillside
d 1953
GMA 2921

RICHARDS, Ceri
Relief Construction (Bird and Beast)
d 1936
GMA 1517

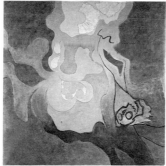

RICHARDS, Ceri
Cycle of Nature, Arabesque I
d 1964
GMA 933

RICHIER, Germaine
Le Courreur [The Runner]
1955
GMA 1315

RICKETTS, Charles
Don Juan and the Commander
c 1905
GMA 1007

RICKETTS, Charles
*Costume Design for the Devil
in 'Montezuma'*
c 1925–26
GMA 1012

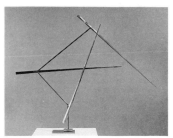

RICKEY, George
Two Lines Fixed, Three Moving
1970
GMA 1161

RICKEY, George
Two Lines up Excentric VI
1977
GMA 2844

RILEY, Bridget
Over
1966
GMA 1316

RIOPELLE, Jean-Paul
Ventoux
d 1958
GMA 883

ROBERTS, Derek
Blue Rectangle
1977
GMA 2113

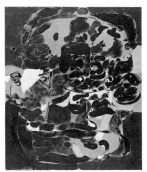

ROBERTS, Derek
Summer Shadows
1984
GMA 2972

ROBERTS, William
Sarah
c 1925
GMA 1589

ROBERTS, William
The Rhine Boat
c 1928
GMA 783

ROBERTS, William
The Ballet
1932
GMA 3511

ROBERTS, William
A Reading of Poetry (or *Woman Reading*)
1965
GMA 3512

ROBERTSON, Eric
Terror of War
d 1914
GMA 1715

ROBERTSON, Eric
Fleet Bay, Kirkcudbrightshire
c 1923
GMA 1008

ROSSI, Mario
Phenomenon 1870 (I)
1986
GMA 3045

ROSSI, Mario
Untitled (from 'Charms, Capillaries and Amulets: Suite no. II')
1987
GMA 3044

ROSSO, Medardo
Ecce Puer [*Behold the Boy*]
1906
GMA 1274

ROTELLA, Mimmo
The Ghost Car
1989
GMA 3571

ROUAULT, Georges
Head
c 1935–40
GMA 968

ROUAULT, Georges
Deux femmes in profil [Two Women in Profile] (pl. 18 of 'Réincarnations du Père Ubu')
1917 (published 1932)
GMA 970

ROYDS, Mabel
Dead Tulips
c 1934
GMA 529

SAINT-SAËNS, Marc
L'Oiseau lyre [Lyre Bird]
1968
GMA 3513

SALT, John
Ironmongers
d 1981
GMA 2474

SCHILSKY, Eric
Gabrielle de Soane
1920 / 1974
GMA 1525

SCHILSKY, Eric
Bather I
1971
GMA 1526

SCHMIDT-ROTTLUFF, Karl
Heiliger Franziskus [St Francis]
1919
GMA 2708

SCHOTZ, Benno
The Lament
1943
GMA 1216

SCHUELER, Jon R.
The Sound of Sleat (June Night, XI, Romasaig)
1970
GMA 1217

SCHULTZE, Bernard
Der erste Tag [*The First Day*]
1989
GMA 3548

SCHWITTERS, Kurt
Ohne Titel (Relief mit roter Pyramide) [*Untitled (Relief with Red Pyramide)*]
c 1923−25
GMA 2077

SCOBIE, Gavin
Eve
1975
GMA 1562

SCOBIE, Gavin
XII: Small Sleep
d 1982
GMA 2700

SCOTT, William
Mackerel
1947
GMA 3514

SCOTT, William
Still Life − Lemons on a Plate
d 1948
GMA 2066

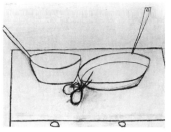

SCOTT, William
Tabletop with Saucepans
d 1956
GMA 1248

SCOTT, William
Reclining Nude
1956
GMA 1278

SCOTT, William
Blue, Black and White
1959
GMA 806

SCOTT, William
Grey Still Life
1969
GMA 1262

SEABY, Allen William
Heron (no. I)
by 1908
GMA 554

SEKALSKI, Jozef
The Trumpeter of Krakow
1944 (published 1945)
GMA 2337 C

SHAPIRO, Babe
Swallow the Call Note
d 1973
GMA 1522

SICKERT, Walter Richard
Portrait of Israel Zangwill
c 1897–98
GMA 740

SICKERT, Walter Richard
Corner of St Mark's, Venice
c 1901
GMA 910

SICKERT, Walter Richard
La Rue Pecquet, Dieppe
c 1906–08
GMA 863

SICKERT, Walter Richard
The Rural Dean
c 1932
GMA 1972

SICKERT, Walter Richard
High-Steppers
c 1938
GMA 2099

SIRONI, Mario
Mountain Landscape
c 1936
GMA 884

SKEAPING, John
Nude Study
d 1926
GMA 731

SMITH, Ian Mackenzie
Summer (Canna)
1963
GMA 868

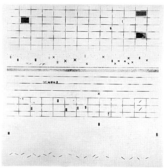

SMITH, Jack
*The Natural and the Geometric
(Summer) II*
d 1970
GMA 2101

SMITH, Matthew
Femme de cirque [Circus Woman]
d 1925
GMA 758

SMITH, Matthew
Portrait of Augustus John
1944
GMA 2324

SMITH, Richard
Ceiling III
1959
GMA 2829

SOULAGES, Pierre
Peinture, 3 novembre 1958
[Painting, 3 November 1958]
1958
GMA 2828

SOUTINE, Chaïm
Les Gorges du Loup
c 1921–23
GMA 2312

SPENCER, Hilda
Stanley Spencer
d 1931
GMA 2068

SPENCER, Stanley
Hilda Spencer
1931
GMA 2067

SPENCER, Stanley
Fire Alight
1936
GMA 3515

SPENCER, Stanley
Christ Delivered to the People
1950
GMA 2759

STAËL, Nicolas de
L'Eclair [Flash of Lightning]
d 1946
GMA 2795

STAËL, Nicolas de
Le Bateau [The Boat]
1954
GMA 817

STEER, Philip Wilson
The Blue Dress
c 1900
GMA 1122

STEER, Philip Wilson
Three Girls Bathing, Thame
c 1911
GMA 1124

STODDART, Alexander
Heroic Bust; Henry Moore
1990 (cast 1992)
GMA 3669

SUTHERLAND, Graham
Western Hills
1938 / 1941
GMA 1072

SUTHERLAND, Graham
Landscape with Rocks (Wolf's Castle)
d 1939
GMA 894

SUTHERLAND, Graham
Entrance to a Lane
d 1939
GMA 3427

SUTHERLAND, Graham
Association of Oaks
d 1939–40
GMA 2219

SUTHERLAND, Graham
Thistles and Sun
d 1945
GMA 763

SUTHERLAND, Graham
Thorn Head
d 1949
GMA 1711

TÀPIES, Antoni
Croix sur gris [Cross on Grey]
d 1959
GMA 858

TÀPIES, Antoni
*Gris violacé aux rides [Violet Grey
with Wrinkles]*
d 1961
GMA 2760

TAYLOR, Linda
*Drawing for Tap No. 2 of 'Unseen
Currents'*
1988
GMA 3558

TAYLOR, Linda
*Drawing for Tap No. 3 of 'Unseen
Currents'*
1988
GMA 3462

THOMPSON, Richard
In the Midst of the Flood
d 1980
GMA 2220

THORNTON, Leslie
Figure in Coat
1961
GMA 859

TIBBLE, Geoffrey
The Print Room
d 1950
GMA 2914

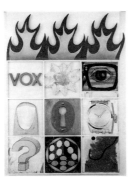

TILSON, Joe
Nine Elements
d 1963
GMA 2761

TINGUELY, Jean
La Jalousie II [Blind Jealousy II]
1961
GMA 2832

TROVA, Ernest
Aluminium Shadow (FM 135)
d 1969
GMA 1692

TUNNARD, John
Untitled
d 1939
GMA 3517

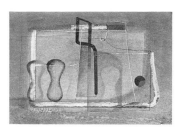

TUNNARD, John
Composition
d 1942
GMA 3518

TUNNARD, John
Sanctuary
d 1943
GMA 3519

TUNNARD, John
Ascent
1944
GMA 3520

TUNNARD, John
Attack
d 1957
GMA 3521

TUNNARD, John
Abacus for Astronauts
d 1964
GMA 3516

TURNBULL, William
Untitled
d 1950
GMA 3452

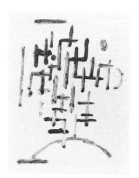

TURNBULL, William
Untitled
d 1953
GMA 3647

TURNBULL, William
Untitled
1954
GMA 3646

TURNBULL, William
15–1959 (Red Saturation)
d 1959
GMA 2830

TURNBULL, William
Night
1962–63
GMA 2831

TURNBULL, William
Gate II
1962–63
GMA 3601

TURNBULL, William
Gate
1972
GMA 1310

UITZ, Béla
Five Women
1920
GMA 2731

UITZ, Béla
Untitled (No. IX from the portfolio 'Analyzis')
d 1921 (published 1922)
GMA 2713 (9)

UNDERWOOD, Leon
The Sower
1948
GMA 3522

UTRILLO, Maurice
La Place du Tertre
c 1910
GMA 1083

VALENTI, Italo
La Lune [The Moon]
d 1978
GMA 2303

VASARELY, Victor
Taïmyr
d 1958
GMA 1279

VAUGHAN, Keith
Dancer Resting
d 1950
GMA 2916

VAUGHAN, Keith
Landscape with Two Bathers (or
The Diver)
d 1954
GMA 2804

VAUGHAN, Keith
Winter Tide
d 1962
GMA 829

VAUGHAN, Keith
Assembly of Figures VIII
d 1964
GMA 1534

VILLON, Jacques
Yvonne D. de face [Portrait of
Yvonne D.]
1913
GMA 2286

VLAMINCK, Maurice
Portrait de femme [Portrait of a
Woman]
1924
GMA 807

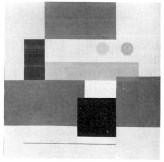

VORDEMBERGE-
GILDEWART, Friedrich
Komposition 14 [Composition 14]
1925
GMA 2148

VUILLARD, Edouard
Le Petit manteau [The Little Cape]
c 1891
GMA 2917

VUILLARD, Edouard
La Causette [The Chat]
c 1892
GMA 2934

VUILLARD, Edouard
*Deux ouvrières dans l'atelier
de couture [Two Seamstresses
in the Workroom]*
d 1893
GMA 3583

VUILLARD, Edouard
*La Fenêtre ouverte [The Open
Window]*
c 1899
GMA 2933

VUILLARD, Edouard
*Nature morte au bougeoir [The
Candlestick]*
c 1900
GMA 2935

VUILLARD, Edouard
La Chambre rose [The Pink Room]
c 1903
GMA 2936

VUILLARD, Edouard
*Le Pot de fleurs [Pot of Flowers
or Corner of the Studio]*
c 1904
GMA 2937

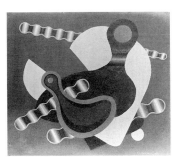

WADSWORTH, Edward
Composition, Crank and Chain
d 1932
GMA 768

WALKER, Ethel
The Spanish Shawl
c 1921–26
GMA 1989

WALKER, Ethel
Portrait of Lucien Pissarro
GMA 1498

WALKER, John
Labyrinth II
d 1979
GMA 2137

WALKER, John
Alba Study 6
d 1981
GMA 2509

WARHOL, Andy
*Jacqueline Kennedy II (from
the portfolio 'Eleven Pop Artists,
vol. II')*
1965
GMA 1336

WEBB, Alonso C.
Empire State Building, New York
c 1931
GMA 2471

WEIGHT, Carel
Sinister Encounter
1984
GMA 2952

WHITE, Ethelbert
The Lake
c 1930
GMA 3532

WHITEFORD, Kate
Symbol Stones: The Peacock
d 1983
GMA 3442

WHITEFORD, Kate
Symbol Stones: The Arc
d 1983
GMA 3443

WHITEFORD, Kate
Symbol Stones: The Snake
d 1983
GMA 3444

WHITEFORD, Kate
Red Spiral
1986
GMA 3459

WHONE, Herbert
Tramcar in Fog
d 1962
GMA 3353

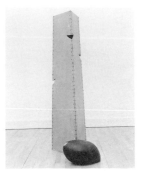

WILDING, Alison
Hand to Mouth
1986
GMA 3661

WILLIAMS, Andrew
Dordogne Landscape I
1988
GMA 3475

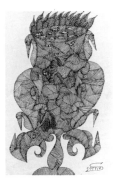

WILSON, Scottie
*Grotesque Design with Birds
and Fish*
c 1940
GMA 1676

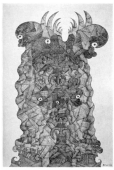

WILSON, Scottie
Untitled
c 1950
GMA 979

WILSON, Scottie
Design with Fish
c 1950s
GMA 895

WILSON, Scottie
A Whispering Paradise (or *Earth
and Heaven*)
1951
GMA 1997

WILSON, Scottie
Peaceful Village
1963
GMA 1677

WILSON, William
Toledo
1932
GMA 2281

WILSON, William
Girl with Guitar (or *The Guitar*)
c 1937
GMA 2271

WILSON, William
The Irish Jig
1948
GMA 3660

WILSON, William
*Design for a Stained Glass Window
for the North Aisle of Brechin
Cathedral (Three Lights: Abraham,
Adam and Isaac)*
c 1952
GMA 2527

WILSON, William
*Design for a Stained Glass Window
for the Clerestory of Brechin
Cathedral (St Mungo)*
1959
GMA 2537

WILSON, William
A Castle near Verona
d 1932
GMA 581

WISZNIEWSKI, Adrian
Bound to Love and Cherish
1984
GMA 3043

WISZNIEWSKI, Adrian
Kingfisher
d 1987
GMA 3042

WOLFE, Edward
The Model
1923
GMA 2918

WOOD, Christopher
Portrait of Jeanne Bourgoint
c 1925–26
GMA 1638

WOOD, Christopher
The Steps, Chelsea
1927
GMA 3523

WOOD, Christopher
Bridge over the Seine
1927
GMA 3524

WOOD, Christopher
Cumberland Landscape
1928
GMA 1637

WOOD, Christopher
Nude Boy in a Bedroom
1930
GMA 1712

WOOD, Christopher
Study of a Male Nude from Behind
GMA 1639

WOOD, Christopher
Standing Female Nude
GMA 3525

WOOD, Francis Derwent
Boy with Chanticleer
d 1925
GMA 1011

WOODROW, Bill
Clamp
1986
GMA 3007

WRAGG, John
Untitled
1964
GMA 3695

WRIGHT, John Buckland
Baigneuses Balinaises
d 1931
GMA 2838

WYNTER, Bryan
Still Life
c 1947
GMA 3526

WYNTER, Bryan
Cyclamen
d 1948
GMA 3527

WYNTER, Bryan
Hostile Tribe
1956
GMA 2479

WYNTER, Bryan
Sandspoor XI
d 1963
GMA 1687

YEATS, Jack Butler
Queen Maeve Walked upon this Strand
1950
GMA 1245

YULE, Ainslie
Proposition for a Floor Piece
1977
GMA 2070

ZADKINE, Ossip
La Danse [The Dance]
1927
GMA 769

ZADKINE, Ossip
Torse de femme [Torso of a Woman]
1943
GMA 2965

ZYW, Aleksander
Journey Woven in Imagination
1950
GMA 1518

ZYW, Aleksander
Movement
1953
GMA 1272

ILLUSTRATION ACKNOWLEDGEMENTS